Encyclopedia of
American Recessions
and Depressions

Encyclopedia of American Recessions and Depressions

Volume 2

Great Depression to Great Recession of 2008–2009

Daniel J. Leab, Editor

 ABC-CLIO

Santa Barbara, California   Denver, Colorado   Oxford, England

Library of Congress Cataloging-in-Publication Data

Encyclopedia of American recessions and depressions / Daniel J. Leab, editor.
    volumes cm
  Volume 1. Critical Period of 1783–1789 to Recession of 1920–1921 —
Volume 2. Great Depression to Great Recession of 2008–2009.
    ISBN 978-1-59884-945-5 (hardcover : alk. paper) — ISBN 978-1-59884-946-2 (ebook)
1. Recessions—United States—History. 2. Depressions—1929—United States.
3. Depressions—History. 4. Financial crises—United States—History. 5. United
States—Economic conditions. I. Leab, Daniel J.
   HB3743.E53 2014
   338.5'42—dc23   2013023216

ISBN: 978-1-59884-945-5
EISBN: 978-1-59884-946-2

18 17 16 15 14   1 2 3 4 5

This book is also available on the World Wide Web as an eBook.
Visit www.abc-clio.com for details.

ABC-CLIO, LLC
130 Cremona Drive, P.O. Box 1911
Santa Barbara, California 93116-1911

This book is printed on acid-free paper ∞
Manufactured in the United States of America

CONTENTS

Primary Documents

GREAT DEPRESSION, 1929–1933

Denise Lynn

To outside observers in early 1929 the stock market appeared to be booming. Those in the know, however, understood the boom could not continue: the bubble would either have to be artificially burst or a decline would come on its own, especially in light of the financing that fueled the boom. New York banks, borrowing from Federal Reserve Banks, used these funds to provide loans for stock purchases on margin. And in 1927 Federal Reserve funds became cheaper as the Federal Reserve Board decreased the already low interest rates from 4 percent to 3.5 percent.

Origins of the Crash

Speculators could use borrowed funds, termed a "call loan," to pay for stock buys, paying limited cash for the shares (sometimes as low as 10 percent of their total value, more often 40 percent to 50 percent); the speculator secured the remaining cost of the stock purchase (usually referred to as "the margin") with a loan using the shares as collateral and expected to repay the borrowed funds by selling the stock at a profit. If it's worth should decrease below its value as collateral, the bank could "call" for repayment. Even if cash had been paid for 50 percent of a stock's total price such payment involved risk since it often was *all* the ready money that a purchaser had available. Buyers of shares on margin depended on a rising market; they usually did not have the funds available to meet a "call."

While banks obtained the funds that were lent out for stock purchases from the Federal Reserve at a low interest, the "call loans" these banks wrote for those buying on margin had interest rates from 10 percent to 20 percent. As share prices for much of the 1920s seemed inexorably to rise, for many Americans, not just speculators, "call loans" seemed to be easy money, and a significant number of solid investors as well as speculators using such hired money made large profits during the 1920s.

Banks were not the only institutions involved. Corporations offered their own "call loans." And so, too, did investment trusts: their front men appeared to have expert knowledge of the market, therefore the public put its faith in them and bought their offerings using loans. To those in the know who closely watched the market, it became clear that if share prices for whatever reason did not continue to rise, a cataclysmic fall in the market would most certainly follow.

There have been many explanations for the fall that finally did take place, but who or what could have reined in the stock market has never been agreed on. President Calvin Coolidge (1872–1933) and Secretary of the Treasury Andrew Mellon (1855–1937) had a laissez-faire approach, as in the main did the only regulatory bodies with sufficient authority to control the market. These were the Board of the Federal Reserve, which oversaw American financial institutions, and its chief agent, the Federal Reserve Bank in New York City. The policies of laissez-faire cannot take all the blame.

In February 1929 some members of the Federal Reserve Board did become concerned about the finances of the boom. And the board attempted what some have called "moral suasion," instructing Federal Reserve Banks not to provide money to banks for margin loans. In the eyes of many involved with the stock market, not just speculators, the board's moral suasion had no teeth. In March 1929 Charles Mitchell (1877–1955), a director of the Federal Reserve Bank of New York as well as head of National City Bank (then the nation's largest), used Federal Reserve funds to back its loans in order to avert a crisis plaguing the market that month.

While Mitchell, who proved less respectable than he appeared at that time, drew criticism for this maneuver, many others resented *any* regulatory interference by the board, which itself feared intervening. In late 1929 the board did raise the rediscount rate 1 percent to 6 percent but failed to interfere any further, sensitive to past charges that the raising of its rates penalized small business owners, farmers, and others not involved in speculation.

Onset of the Depression

But the massive collapse of the stock market that would take place in October 1929 does not account for America's total economic decline in the following decade. When in December 1928 Calvin Coolidge presented his last State of the Union message to Congress he assured Americans that their economy was sound, and they could "regard the present with satisfaction and anticipate the future with optimism."

But not everyone in the United States could share those beliefs. Many farmers, for instance, did not. They had enjoyed prosperity while World War I raged. But after its end, American farmers found themselves with crop surpluses, large mortgages, and falling prices for their harvests. As the postwar decade wore on their debts mounted, their economic distress grew, and federal authorities were pressured to take some action.

Congress twice passed (1927, 1928) bills proposed by two Republicans, Oregon senator Charles McNary (1874–1974) and Iowa representative Gilbert Haugen (1859–1933) that included provisions allowing the federal government to purchase and dispose of surplus crops. Both times Coolidge vetoed the legislation. Meanwhile, more farmers continued to lose their land, becoming tenants or moving to urban areas. A hard-hit sector of the American economy, agriculture continued to decline during the 1920s.

Overrepresented in the numbers of rural poor were African Americans. Although many had moved to northern urban areas before and during World War I, the bulk of the black population still remained in the rural South working as tenant farmers or sharecroppers. Those African Americans who migrated north, although suffering de facto segregation, fared somewhat better than those who remained in the South where de jure Jim Crow rules governed. But all across the United States most blacks struggled against the greatest odds. Everywhere in the United States they faced poverty, unequal educational facilities, and denial of their rights.

While American popular culture in the 1920s celebrated the prosperity resulting from a new consumer-driven economy, there remained many deeply impoverished Americans who did not participate in the good times. In 1929 a significant number of Americans still lived without access to electricity or running water. In addition, the gap between rich and poor increasingly widened. By the beginning of 1929 the wealthiest 1 percent of Americans controlled 19 percent of American wealth. They had a strong ally in Secretary of the Treasury Mellon, who decreased their taxes.

Corporations also benefited during the 1920s from generous tax policies, as well as lax governmental controls. Many business mergers occurred during the 1920s and once these consolidations took place, the merged companies began to exercise control over wages, prices, and production; because of their concentrated power anything that disrupted these giant corporations had a ripple effect on the whole U.S. economy. In 1927 the privately held Ford Motor Company caused a brief economic downturn in the United States when, having determined to end production of its Model T, the company temporarily closed plants in order to refit them for production of the forthcoming new Model A automobile.

More problematic for the American economy was the lack in the United States of consistent, coherent centralized banking regulation. In 1929 over

52,000 U.S. banks faced over 50 regulatory systems that did not always mesh. Because of the lack of centralized control over the American banking system, bank failures were common. In the 1920s dozens of banks failed annually. The banking system as it existed when the Great Depression struck was unorganized, woefully inadequate, and unprepared to deal with a crisis such as the system faced in the early 1930s. Also, while bankers during a failure often took care of the interests of the well-connected, no such protection existed for the bulk of an institution's depositors.

Herbert Hoover

Yet despite the obvious existing weaknesses, the economy and the stock market appeared to be flourishing. In March 1929, Herbert Hoover (1874–1964), who as much as any public figure, represented the boom times, was inaugurated as president of the United States. Born in West Branch, Iowa, on August 10, 1874, to sober, serious Quakers who lived a simple life on the American frontier, Hoover was orphaned at age 11 and had a hardscrabble life during the next years, ultimately moving to Oregon to live with an uncle. He received a rudimentary education and worked hard in his uncle's many enterprises.

In 1891 Hoover entered Stanford University to study engineering. There he met his future wife, Lou Henry (1874–1944), who he married in 1899. Hoover had graduated in 1895. After unemployment and a series of poorly paid manual jobs, he obtained a job with an English firm that hired him to work in mining on the undeveloped Australian frontier; he proved successful there and subsequently in China. In 1908, Hoover went into business on his own as a consultant for struggling mining operations and did well as a "doctor of sick mines."

By 1913 the poor orphan had become a much in-demand engineer and had accumulated a small fortune of about $4,000,000. A fair if tough taskmaster, Hoover initially deplored government interference (especially as regarded workmen's compensation), increased hours and decreased wages as he saw fit, used a black list, and fired workers who complained. Of his personality, those who during these years came in contact with him thought that Hoover was determined, aloof, unemotional, and abrasive.

In 1909 he published *Principles of Mining*, whose text demonstrated a changing and more progressive attitude toward labor than he earlier had displayed in Australia and China. He advocated an eight-hour workday, mine safety, and higher wages. A generous Hoover, although still aloof and abrasive, anonymously supported financially strapped friends and family as well as donating substantial sums to Stanford University.

In Europe at the start of World War I (his offices were located in London), successfully he organized the evacuation of hundreds of Americans stranded there by the war. He was then asked to help with the relief of a Belgium devastated by war. He became chairman of the Commission for Belgian Relief, proved to be an able administrator, and used his abrasiveness to good purpose.

His outstanding success in aiding the Belgians landed him a role in the Wilson administration after the United States entered the war in 1917. Appointed food administrator, Hoover did an excellent job; his policies avoided the implementation of rationing. He counseled economy and conservation of the American food supply, organizing such events as "Meatless Fridays."

Before the war, Hoover—for all his renown in the mining field—was unknown to the public, but his success in Belgian relief and as food administrator literally made him a household name. He was so successful that Webster's dictionary included the word *Hooverize* (defined as economizing in the interest of the nation). Though his party affiliation was unclear, many Republicans and Democrats, including Wilson's assistant secretary of the navy, Franklin D. Roosevelt (1882–1945), clamored for him to run for president in 1920.

Hoover added to his reputation as a humanitarian when he led the effort to provide aid to the defeated Germans and organize relief to the stricken Bolshevik-controlled areas of Russia in 1921. To those who opposed his efforts on political grounds, Hoover's rejoinder won him more accolades: he asserted millions of people ". . . are starving. Whatever their politics, they shall be fed!"

Refusing to run for president, eventually Hoover allied himself with the Republican Party. After the 1920 Republican triumph he accepted in 1921 an appointment as secretary of commerce, a post that he held during both the Harding and Coolidge administrations. Once again he proved able, taking on extra tasks allotted him. During his well-regarded tenure he dramatically expanded the reach of his position and the Commerce Department's appropriations and authority, efforts that both earned him admirers and detractors. In 1927 Hoover gained further acclaim for his efficient relief work during the devastating Mississippi River flood.

In 1928 Hoover was seen as a Progressive Republican in the stripe of Theodore Roosevelt (1858–1919). He easily won the GOP nomination for president and overwhelmingly defeated Al Smith (1873–1944), the Democratic candidate. Upon Hoover's victory, his first-ever elected position, he became the first American born west of the Mississippi River to become president.

While many Americans, especially those who voted for him, were confident he could do no wrong, Hoover presciently warned that "If some unprecedented calamity should come upon the nation . . . I would be sacrificed to the unreasoning disappointment of a people who expected too much." And this, unfortunately for him, came to pass. Hoover's ambitious agenda as president

President Herbert Hoover signs the Agricultural Marketing Act in June 1929. (Library of Congress)

has been overshadowed by his difficulty in handling the social and economic problems raised by the Great Depression.

Days after his inauguration Hoover called a special session of Congress to deal with the ongoing agricultural crisis and with various tariff issues. Congress, after some delay, passed (August 1929) the Agricultural Marketing Act, whose provisions included the creation of a Farm Board to keep surplus crops from the markets in an effort to stabilize prices. The Marketing Act, however, would become a casualty of the general economic downturn that soon followed.

Congress also passed more controversial legislation. In 1930, after strenuous debate caused by much logrolling and lobbying, it voted for a strongly protectionist tariff proposed by two Republicans, Senator Reed Smoot (1862–1941) and Representative Willis Hawley (1864–1941). Despite the many outcries against it (in May 1930 over 1,000 economists signed a petition urging Hoover to veto the legislation) Hoover signed the bill.

The president did so because he believed that tariff increases would aid agriculture; they would lead to a price rise for American farm products. The proposed bill's critics feared its negative impact on trade. As enacted, Smoot-Hawley led to the largest rise of tariff duties in the history of the United States and created serious problems as other countries put prohibitive duties on American goods in retaliation. As the Depression hit home the stiff protectionism of Smoot-Hawley proved a major liability.

Despite Hoover's later reputation for being an inactive chief executive, the agricultural and tariff acts were only two of the several important measures implemented during his presidency. He implemented several of the reforms for which Progressives had agitated during the Harding and Coolidge administrations. He created the National Institute of Health, pushed vainly for reform of the banking system, and ordered the census to collect data on the number of unemployed. He also took up penal reform and created a Bureau of Prisons, supported the Women's and Children's Bureaus in the Department of Labor, and expanded the National Parks as well as barring oil exploration on public lands.

Prior to his election to the presidency Hoover reflected many of the racial ideas of his time (although on buying a house in Washington, D.C., he had refused to sign a restrictive covenant), and he had drawn strong criticism for ignoring reports about the brutal use by southern officials of African Americans as virtual slave labor during the 1927 Mississippi River flood. However, once in the White House, Hoover did positively address minority issues, even if only in a limited fashion.

As president he arranged for increased appropriations for Howard University and the Freedman's Hospital, both African American institutions in the nation's capital. He required a newly established Board of Parole to include African Americans, and with funds from a private foundation, set up a conference on the economic status of African Americans.

Hoover's actions with regard to Native Americans was much more dynamic. To head the Bureau of Indian Affairs, he appointed Charles J. Rhoads (1872–1956)—a Philadelphia Quaker and former president of the Indian Rights Association. The president, overruling the objections of his budget director, arranged for larger appropriations for the Indian Bureau. The allotment of these funds in effect endorsed the actions of Rhoads, which included ending segregation in Native American boarding schools and building hospitals on Indian territory to deal with the serious health issues plaguing Native Americans. These actions represented a giant step in redressing the nation's shabby record toward Native Americans.

The Crash

Nine months after Hoover became president, the bull market collapsed. In the months prior to the collapse those concerned about speculators and the continued use of "call loans," who had spoken out publicly about the dangers the market faced, had been roundly condemned by the media, brokers, and other self-professed experts. Those eager to benefit from the boom drowned out the voices of reason, claiming that stocks were not overvalued and that all was well in the market. They generally were believed; therefore, when the bubble finally burst the shock was enormous.

Black Thursday (October 24, 1929) and Black Tuesday (October 29, 1929) historically have been the markers for the final bust, when stock fell so precipitously that the tickers reporting share prices could not keep up. But economic experts have argued that really the booming market of the 1920s came to an end before the Crash, after reaching a peak on September 3, 1929: the downward spiral, it is argued, began there but not continuously or dramatically. Although the market sent signals that all was not well, that there was trouble ahead, the financial and business leaders with a vested interest in the upward spiral reassured investors. Speculation continued and brokers' loans increased.

During the summer of 1929 other problems had surfaced: the industrial index revealed sharp declines of production in heavy industries like steel, iron, and auto manufacturing. Production also began to outpace consumption, leading companies to cut back. Commodity prices began to decrease. Business was undergoing a slow, steady decline. But opinion makers and indeed Hoover himself assured the American public that a decline was a normal part of the business cycle, recovery would take place very soon, and that the economy of the United States was essentially sound.

Yet, throughout September and October 1929 the market was really anything but sound. The value of many shares began to fall, and nervous lenders put out calls for the shareowners to cover the margin on the loans for which stocks had acted as collateral. Desperate stockholders began to sell their shares to cover the cost of these loans. Still, bad days were followed by good days on which the market moved upward and made up for the "corrections" that had taken place.

Finally the bubble burst. On Black Thursday, the then remarkable number of 12,894,650 shares changed hands. Panic erupted that morning until around noon, when some of the country's leading financiers and bankers met, publicly established a multimillion dollar pool, and announced they would purchase shares—an announcement meant to reassure stockholders and the public.

The maneuver worked, and the day ended on a high note. On Monday the market however, went bad again; the same financiers and bankers who had met on Thursday met again, deciding not to intervene further. The next day, Black Tuesday, would be one of the worst in the history of the New York Stock Exchange, as shareowners dumped their holdings in a tidal wave of selling. Sales of over 16,410,030 shares were recorded, triple the volume of what exchange members till then had considered a big day, and a turnover not equaled for 39 years.

Although the markets took a catastrophic downturn, the United States was not yet in a depression. The stock market crash did wipe out various individual fortunes and destroy some businesses. And the most overwrought of those

A crowd gathers on the street in front of the New York Stock Exchange after a sharp drop in stock prices on October 24, 1929, now known as "Black Thursday." By the following Tuesday, the market had completely collapsed. The events of late October 1929 marked the beginning of the economic crisis known as the Great Depression. (Library of Congress)

affected did take their own lives, although the number that did so and the myth of massive suicides after the Crash have been largely overstated. The number-one casualty of the Crash was trust in the market and in the financial experts who had hyped it.

The Crash itself was not the beginning of the Depression nor was it the cause. It was a symptom. The Depression as it developed in the United States grew out of a confluence of systemic economic factors, including a widening gap between American rich and poor, falling consumer demand for key products of the American economy such as autos and construction, continuing serious problems in weak industries like coal and agriculture, a fragile corrupt banking system, and a foolhardy adherence to the international gold standard.

Indeed, only about an estimated 2.5 percent of Americans had invested in the stock market, hardly a substantial number. Some in the United States even viewed the Crash as a necessary purgative after the wild prosperity of the 1920s that would get the market back in order. Conventional economic wisdom held that such downturns are inevitable and that the government should not intervene, the less it did the better for the economy.

The President Responds

Hoover, however, swiftly responded to the Crash. He won a pledge from major business interests to maintain wage rates. His Farm Board was to help regulate prices for agricultural goods. He also struck a deal with building and maintenance interests and individual states to take up infrastructure projects with the support of $140 million in federal funds. In addition, Hoover cut taxes; for the average American the tax burden did not go down substantially; the tax cut only benefited those in the highest brackets, but they had been the high-spending consumers.

Hoover also held meetings with leading industrialists, heads of farm groups, union leaders, and other important business interests. He wanted to keep the government out of business but sought to project optimism that the downturn was temporary. Also wanting to avoid the negative connotations of the word *panic* used to describe previous American economic downturns, he instead used the word *depression*. By the winter of 1930 some, including Hoover himself, felt and predicted the worst was over.

But the economy continued its decline. The stock market began a downward slide that would continue until 1932. By the end of 1930 production in industries, including steel and automobile, was sharply reduced; the housing market was stagnant; over 26,000 businesses had failed; and the gross national product was down 12.6 percent from its 1929 levels. Unemployment reached nearly 9 percent.

Many Americans, however, at a time when the collection of economic data was primitive, inconsistent, and unreliable still believed it was just another temporary downturn, similar to the one in 1921 when unemployment briefly reached 11 percent. Some could even stretch their memories back to the 1893 panic that had taken an even heavier toll.

The Banking System Begins to Collapse

Hoover remained devoted to the idea that the voluntary measures like those he had persuaded businesses to take, such as regulating prices and maintaining wages, would help to turn the downward trend around. That optimism was still possible until the last weeks of 1930. In November 1930 banks began to fail, starting with the Louisville National Bank of Kentucky. A series of affiliated banks also started to collapse, prompting depositors to rush to their banks to withdraw funds. In an effort to save themselves banks called in loans and began to sell assets, putting more pressure on an already weakened economy.

The collapse of the rural banks, mainly in the southeastern part of the United States, became an epidemic, hitting larger banks in central urban areas of the nation as well. The largest collapse initially came in December 1930 with the closing of the Bank of the United States, a New York City bank serving mostly immigrant Jews. The bank, one of the largest in the United States, held some $286 million in savings for about 400,000 people, many of whom because of its name believed it was a federal institution whose deposits were guaranteed by the government.

After a run on the Bank of the United States began, prominent financiers as well as the Federal Reserve refused to aid the bank, which then closed. This situation panicked officers of many banking institutions, and confidence in the Federal Reserve collapsed. As news of the bank failure in New York City spread, there was a flurry of bank closings everywhere in the country. These closings slowed during early 1931 as once again people hoped the crisis had passed. The reality is that the American economy improved very slightly at the beginning of 1931. Hoover's efforts had kept wage rates steady even though cuts in hours worked had reduced take-home pay.

International Developments

Overall, however, the combined effects of a weakened market, industrial downturn, rising unemployment, a severely damaged agricultural sector, and the banking collapses made the United States vulnerable to the impact of European developments that compounded American problems in the coming months. To the end of his life Hoover insisted it was the collapse of the European banking system that transformed the domestic downturn of 1930–1931 into the Great Depression.

The 1919 Versailles Peace Treaty had been designed by the victors in World War I, including the United States, which never ratified it, not only to formally end the war with Germany but also to establish the League of Nations and to rework international relations. Hoover, critical of the treaty provisions that put an unrealistic reparations burden on Germany, maintained they were a major reason for the Great Depression.

To carry out the provisions of the Versailles Peace Treaty dealing with reparations, Germany borrowed money in the United States and used these funds to pay reparations to France and England. They in turn used the reparations paid by Germany to pay their war debts to the United States. The unreasonableness of the demands made on Germany had led to a series of conferences that reduced somewhat that debt but still left huge payments to be made. The

Great Depression helped end the cycle of payments and, with regard to Germany, it ultimately ceased paying reparations at all.

Hoover's Failed Effort

Now as each country involved in the payment cycle faced an economic downturn, the European countries discussed forgiving reparations if the United States would forgive war debts, a solution most Americans opposed. In addition, in spring 1931 German chancellor Heinrich Bruening (1885–1970)—attempting to lure domestic political support—suggested a customs union between his nearly bankrupt country and Austria. Fear of what financial pressure an angry, hostile France might apply prompted a series of Austrian bank failures (including that country's largest bank), whose effect spilled over Austria's borders into other countries. In June 1931, in a vain attempt to stop the banking crisis, Hoover proposed—and the countries involved accepted—a one-year moratorium on payment of reparations and debts.

For Hoover it was a desperate but domestically unpopular bid to stabilize international markets. The Smoot-Hawley tariff had ignited a nationalist fervor among other countries, damaging those markets. England had created the United Kingdom Preference system benefiting trade within the British Commonwealth. Germany would later adopt a national self-sufficiency program. These restrictions and others drastically reduced world trade.

Most European nations abandoned the gold standard (the United States did not) and began to withdraw gold and capital from American banks. A fresh U.S. panic was set off. Americans rushed to their banks in large numbers to withdraw funds. In the month that followed England's abandoning the gold standard in September 1931, 522 American banks failed. Many economists have argued that it was then that the United States officially entered a Great Depression.

Progressive contraction of credit took place in the United States as the Federal Reserve (following classic economic theory) further tightened the American money supply by raising the rediscount rate one point, a widely criticized maneuver some have credited with making the problem worse. No precedent existed for the kind of government spending many would later argue was the best tool to fight economic failure. Hoover, like many officeholders in his era sought a balanced budget (another maneuver criticized by contemporary economists), and with the Revenue Act of 1932 raised taxes in an attempt to increase government revenues. Hoover intervened in the economy more than any previous president had done, but his actions were far from enough; credit continued to tighten, a situation that plagued the economy.

The president continued his attempts to stall the escalating economic crisis without really increasing government interference. In January 1932 he had created the Reconstruction Finance Corporation (RFC); designed to use tax funds to provide emergency loans to banks, railroads, and building and loan societies, it amounted to direct federal aid to *private* business. The RFC did stall bank closings, which soon continued, but did not stimulate the economy (probably because only about 20 percent of its budget was spent on public works). Also in early 1932, Congress passed legislation sponsored by two Democrats, Virginia senator Carter Glass (1858–1946) and Representative Henry Steagall (1873–1943), that conforming to Hoover's beliefs, liberalized credit policies by widening the kind of assets that *commercial* banks could use to borrow from the Federal Reserve. The impact of the law proved minimal; credit remained tight, deflation continued.

The Depression's Impact on Americans

Meanwhile the average American dealt with the realities of unemployment, lost savings, and another year with no recovery in sight. Some of the first banks to fail, such as the Bank of the United States, were in ethnic ghettos. Mutual benefit associations, fraternal insurance societies, and religious groups in these communities could not keep up with the unprecedented demands for aid and collapsed. They and other charitable organizations, given the increasing number of people who needed assistance, outran their resources.

Unemployment grew rapidly and dramatically, spiking as high as 25 percent before Hoover left office in March 1933. In some areas unemployment was higher. At the beginning of 1933, for instance, 31 percent of Pittsburgh's white workers and 48 percent of the city's black labor force were jobless. By that time General Motors had laid off nearly half its workers. In much of the United States, those workers who managed to keep their jobs often were cut back to part-time employment or had their wages slashed as businesses reneged on earlier promises to Hoover. At least a third of the working population had hours reduced to part time and wages were slashed 35 percent. Many doctors and lawyers lost an estimated 50 percent of their annual incomes.

There was no federal unemployment insurance to help; state unemployment assistance, where available, was woefully inadequate. Some companies had established unemployment programs, but these were unable to cover even a small portion of those who lost work. In response to the growing crisis, Hoover created the President's Organization on Unemployment and the President's Emergency Committee for Employment. Both organizations counted on the voluntary capacity of employers and citizens to help; although raising huge sums of money from a willing public, these funds proved inadequate in view of the massive, increasing unemployment.

Breadlines and soup kitchens had emerged in the spring of 1930. Thousands would show up and hundreds would be turned away because of inadequate supplies. Teachers began to report that their students were listless and weak from hunger. In large cities, people scrounged in restaurant garbage cans for food. Miners in the mountains survived by eating wild greens and "bulldog gravy" (a combination of flour, water, and lard). Although Hoover claimed "nobody actually starved," hospitals reported deaths from malnutrition.

Americans from diverse backgrounds underwent tremendous suffering. Extended families, pooling their resources, moved in together. Happy couples put off having children; unhappy couples delayed divorce because of the cost. The marriage rate dropped to a new low as men and women chose to remain single so they could help support parents and siblings. People lost their homes, and some began to travel from town to town looking for work—as did thousands of teenagers facing an uncertain future who "took to the rails." Public shelters overflowed. New York City authorities housed homeless wanderers on a barge anchored at an East River pier.

That city's schools found 20,000 children suffering from malnutrition. In Detroit an estimated 4,000 children waited in daily breadlines. The growing number of jobless became a strain on municipalities. Hundreds of cities ran out of funds to aid the indigent. Typically, Raleigh, North Carolina, could afford only a nickel a day to support families. As city and state resources were stretched to their limits more people began to push for direct federal assistance to the needy. Despite the failure of the overwhelmed voluntary organizations to aid those in need Hoover continued to claim that voluntary efforts were keeping the crisis at bay.

Fearful of creating a generation of Americans dependent "on the dole," Hoover vetoed a relief bill to help create jobs and feed the hungry. As a compromise he agreed to the Emergency Relief and Construction Act, which allowed Congress to lend money to states for relief and public works projects. However, the money allotted was so stingily distributed that only 3 of 243 applications for funds were approved for public works projects.

Hoover, once associated with efficiency, economy, and effectiveness became an object of scorn and unkind jokes. The growing number of shantytowns built by the homeless from scraps were called Hoovervilles. Freight cars used by the jobless in their travels to find work were called Hoover Pullmans. The newspapers used by the homeless to keep warm in cold weather were nicknamed Hoover blankets. An empty pocket turned inside out became a Hoover flag. And jackrabbits caught and used for food were called Hoover hogs.

Hooverville outside of Portland, Oregon. When the failing economy did not respond to President Herbert Hoover's initiatives, the Great Depression worsened and Hoover was blamed for the collapse. Hooverville was the name given to shantytowns that were occupied by those most severely hurt by the economic calamity. (Library of Congress)

The Agricultural Depression

Environmental problems aggravated the agricultural crisis. Between 1929 and 1932 drought hit the South, Southwest, and the Great Plains. For years American farmers had stretched the topsoil to its limits attempting to grow large amounts of high-profit crops like wheat and cotton. Once drought struck the earth dried up, the topsoil became dust, thousands of tenant farmers and sharecroppers were forced to leave their homes in search of work elsewhere, and many farm owners defaulted on mortgage loans and found themselves in foreclosure.

The Farm Board's collapse had worsened the situation. It had been buying excess wheat, but falling prices left the board with huge surpluses. With no way to sell it, the board stopped buying, put the surplus on the market, and prices collapsed, exacerbating a bad situation for farmers. Hoover did nothing more substantial to sustain the agricultural sector. By the time he left office a quarter of American farmers had lost their farms, fields, stock, and homes.

Some farmers attempted to rectify the growing crisis by creating the National Farmer's Holiday Association in 1932. Its primary goal was to push for federal regulations that would match prices to production costs. It also hoped to drive up prices by encouraging farmers to take a "holiday" from shipping crops to market. Some activists forcefully stopped milk trucks on the way to market, dumping their loads. The association also lobbied for forgiveness of debts and reduced mortgages. Other farmers attended foreclosure auctions in large numbers and would intimidate possible buyers, auctioneers, sheriffs, and judges. Extremely low prices (sometimes as low as a penny) would be bid on the property and goods for sale in order to return them to the foreclosed owner.

Protests

The nation's gross national product plummeted, losing nearly 50 percent of its value between October 1929 and March 1933. Even more dramatic was the decline in the construction industry, which fell 82 percent. Industrial production also continued to decline. In 1932 factories produced less than they did in 1913. The output of the iron and steel industries was halved, and at one point the steel industry operated at 11 percent of capacity. The automobile industry substantially reduced its output.

In 1929, in a show of optimism, Henry Ford (1873–1947) had promised not to cut jobs and to increase wages. By 1932 his tune had changed dramatically (with outrageous comments about unemployment being beneficial), and Ford had laid off several thousand workers. On March 7, 1932, in what its organizers termed a "hunger march," thousands of unemployed marched to Ford's River Rouge plant in Dearborn, just outside the Detroit city limits, demanding work and company contribution to benefits for the jobless. Ford's private security force and Dearborn police confronted the marchers. A battle ensued; at the end of the melee four marchers were dead and dozens were wounded. Forty thousand attended the huge funeral held for the dead. The once revered Henry Ford now faced public condemnation.

In January 1932 a Pittsburgh priest, Father James Cox (1866–1951), with the support of much of the state establishment, brought thousands of Pennsylvanians to Washington, D.C., to petition Hoover for the creation of federal relief programs A delegation led by Cox met inconclusively with the president, and the marchers dispersed peacefully back to Pennsylvania.

That summer a group of about 20,000 World War I veterans descended on Washington, D.C., to demand immediate payment of a bonus promised to them for their war service, scheduled for payment in 1945. The veterans, many of them unemployed and in desperate need of the bonus, came to the nation's capital—quite a few with their families—to lobby Congress.

More than 10,000 American citizens march to the Capitol under the leadership of Father James R. Cox of Pittsburgh, January 7, 1932. (Library of Congress)

Dubbed the "Bonus Army," the veterans did not succeed in their demand for early payment of the bonus. The House voted to pay it; the Senate did not. After the congressional vote many of the Bonus Army left Washington, D.C., but some thousands stayed still hoping to pressure the administration.

On July 28, 1932, the U.S. Army, under the leadership of its chief of staff, General Douglas MacArthur (1880–1964), whose aides in this action included Dwight Eisenhower (1890–1969) and George Patton (1885–1945), dispersed the Bonus Army. Troops using tear gas with fixed bayonets and cavalry with drawn sabers, aided by six tanks, drove the Bonus Army out of the unoccupied government buildings that housed some of its units, burned the veteran's makeshift shacks and tents, and pushed the remaining veterans out of Washington, D.C.

The 1932 Presidential Election

Hoover's popularity had suffered before, but the news of the violent treatment of the veterans incensed Americans. Newspapers across the country pilloried Hoover. Although he later maintained his orders were clearly intended to limit

MacArthur's actions, after the event Hoover further damaged his image by defending the treatment of the veterans, claiming they were controlled by radicals, an obvious untruth. The Bonus Army disaster did benefit one man, and that was Franklin D. Roosevelt (1882–1945), who would be Hoover's opponent in the 1932 presidential elections.

Roosevelt had made a name for himself as governor of New York, advocating state-sponsored relief programs while Hoover continued to resist federal support of such programs. Hoover initially had felt secure about being reelected, although a growing number of people believed a second term was not possible or even desirable. During 1932 each day brought more bad economic news, and Hoover began to despair. His campaign left much to be desired. He gave speeches with no enthusiasm, cultivated a hatred for his opponent (so deep it would last well into Hoover's post-presidency years), and ignored clear indications the voting public did not favor him or his programs.

For Hoover the election was largely an ideological struggle; he could not envision a future that included direct federal aid because it was contrary to his views about America. Hoover failed to realize the election was a referendum on his presidency and its quixotic response to the Depression. He lost large, winning only the electoral votes of six states: Maine, Vermont, New Hampshire, Connecticut, Pennsylvania, and Delaware, and garnering less than 40 percent of the popular vote. The Republicans also suffered huge losses in Congress.

The Interregnum

The inauguration of the new president took place on March 4. In the four months between Hoover's defeat and Roosevelt's inauguration the United States faced total economic collapse. The winter of 1932–1933 was probably the most desperate time of the Great Depression for Americans.

During the interregnum unemployment reached a staggering 25 percent, even as the perilously inadequate relief structure almost totally broke down. Industrial production continued its precipitous decline (its index figure reaching an all-time low in March 1933), the markets remained in flux, farmers faced ever more trying situations, and the banking crisis intensified to the point that by March 4 the need for "bank holidays" (designed to stop bank runs) had spread all across the United States and the nation's banking system had almost completely closed down.

Hoover spent his last months in office trying vigorously and vainly to encourage the continuance of his failed policies by the president-elect. Hoover wanted Roosevelt to commit himself to adopting unmodified the administration's program, which the American public by its vote had just overwhelmingly rejected.

Roosevelt coyly but firmly refused. Hoover left the White House believing that the American people had made a terrible mistake and that Roosevelt was responsible for the collapse during the interregnum.

What Kind of President Was Hoover?

Some scholars have claimed that had the Great Depression not happened, Hoover would have remained a disappointment as president. His abrasive personality had caused several conflicts between himself and Congress, including members of his own party, who found it difficult to relate to the aloof president. Some congressmen quipped that Hoover was abducted and that the abductors threatened to return the president to the White House if the ransom was not paid. Typically, Hoover appointed as the Farm Board's head the president of International Harvester, a man who many farmers considered their enemy.

In the 1928 election Hoover had promised to maintain Prohibition. Even a commission appointed by him to investigate enforcement claimed that the constitutional amendment establishing it should be repealed, but paradoxically the commission also recommended continued enforcement. Hoover was accused of ignoring the findings of this commission and others, including one on child welfare that concluded ten million American children were in need. Hoover responded that the country's happy, healthy children far outnumbered those in need so the situation could not be too desperate.

It is clear that many factors outside Hoover's control caused the Great Depression. The two administrations preceding his had loosened the regulatory hold over the financial markets to the point where there was very little control by anyone. The extreme poverty of some Americans had been ignored for decades, while a few individuals continued to amass great wealth with the blessing of the government and the inaction of those who put disinterested politicians into government.

In addition, in the many economic downturns that preceded the 1930s, there was no precedent for aggressive executive action. Hoover took more action to try and stem the tide of the downturn and to reassure Americans than any other president ever had attempted. And no one, not even Hoover's severest critics, understood the extent of the collapse.

Nevertheless, as the crisis escalated Hoover remained committed to keeping government small, and some of his voluntary programs seem foolhardy in retrospect given the scope of the crisis. His refusal to provide direct aid to the hungry and homeless made him appear indifferent, which he was not. But for better or for worse, Hoover's name will forever be linked to the early years of the greatest and most far-reaching economic disaster in American history.

Further Reading

Baskin, Alex. "The Ford Hunger March—1932." *Labor History* 13 (1972): 331–60.

Galbraith, John K. *The Great Crash: 1929*. Boston: Houghton Mifflin, 1961.

Leuchtenburg, William E. *Herbert Hoover*. New York: Times Books/Henry Holt Company, 2009.

Perino, Michael. *The Hellhound of Wall Street: How Ferdinand Pecora's Investigation of the Great Crash Forever Changed America's Finance*. New York: Penguin, 2010.

Romasco, Albert U. *The Poverty of Abundance: Hoover, the Nation, the Depression*. New York: Oxford University Press, 1965.

Wilson, Edmund. *The American Earthquake: A Documentary of the Jazz Age, the Great Depression, and the New Deal*. Garden City, NY: Doubleday Anchor Books, 1958.

Great Depression, 1929–1933: Short Entries

Jason Roberts

Bank Holiday

Bank holiday is a euphemistic term coined in early 1933 during the darkest days of the Great Depression to describe the official closing by various state governments of American banks. Just exactly what was intended was not always clear (some states initially did not completely shut down all of a bank's operations). But the declaration of a bank holiday was intended, and generally did succeed, in halting the massive leakage of bank funds to both foreign and domestic depositors, who were restricted in their ability to withdraw their funds.

In the aftermath of the stock market crash in October 1929, a weakened economy exposed the serious flaws in the American banking system. During the generally economically prosperous 1920s (1921–1929), over 5,700 U.S. banks, large and small, shut down. From 1930 to 1932, almost as many, about 5,200, closed their doors. A full-scale bank panic took place in the interregnum between the electoral defeat of President Herbert Hoover (1874–1964) in early November 1932 and the inauguration of Franklin D. Roosevelt (1882–1945) scheduled for March 4, 1933.

During the last months of the Hoover administration the United States faced immanent financial disaster. Fearful Americans were estimated during 1932 to have hoarded a billion dollars in cash they had withdrawn from banks. Both Americans and concerned foreigners were draining gold from the banks at a rate estimated to be over a million dollars a day.

Between October 1931 and March 3, 1933, the day before President-elect Roosevelt was to be inaugurated, the governors of over 22 states (out of a total of 48) had found it necessary to declare bank holidays as government officials and bank officers tried to fix and make whole the shaky operations of both large and small American financial institutions. Where banks still operated they did so on a restricted basis, with shortened hours and drastic limitations on the amount of gold or cash that could be withdrawn (usually no more than 5 percent of a balance).

In October 1932 Nevada's governor ordered the first bank holiday, but lacking the legal authority to close the banks declared a "business holiday." He did so in a failed attempt to rescue the banking operations of George Wingfield (1875–1959), a prominent Nevada businessman and political figure. Ultimately Wingfield's banking operations were wiped out despite the holiday.

In early February 1933, at the behest of Louisiana senator Huey Long (1893–1935), who ran that state no matter the office he held, the State Hibernia Bank of New Orleans was rescued from collapse by an unusual bank holiday. On Friday February 3 bank officials informed Long that because funds from an emergency loan had not yet arrived, they could not open the next day, He ordered the governor to find a holiday to celebrate. Fortunately February 4 was the 16th anniversary of the severing by the United States of diplomatic relations with Germany prior to World War I and in its celebration the governor declared a holiday, and for the moment the Hibernia Bank was saved.

Some weeks later the American financial system simply began to give way. The situation of the banks in Michigan, a major industrial state, had become precarious; negotiations to rescue the banks foundered in part because of the recalcitrance of Henry Ford, one of the state's richest and most important manufacturers. On Valentine's Day 1933 Michigan's governor ordered an eight-day bank holiday, which subsequently was extended until the Roosevelt administration took office.

The collapse in Michigan led to a precipitous rise in bank closings. In state after state bank holidays were declared. After Baltimore banks had endured a frantic three-day run of withdrawals by panicky depositors, the governor of Maryland on February 24 ordered a bank holiday in that state. In the next week fear and panic were everywhere: a Wichita bank closed; in Little Rock the banks limited withdrawals; in Washington, D.C., one of the capital's leading banks closed its doors. Finally, early in the morning of March 4, New York City and Chicago, the nation's financial strongholds, could not hold out any longer, and the governors of their states declared a bank holiday.

The lame duck president Hoover failed in attempts to draw the president-elect into joint action to deal with the burgeoning financial crisis: Roosevelt refused to tie himself to any of the actions proposed by his predecessor. Although the two men were personally and ideologically at odds, some of their key staff, such as outgoing conservative secretary of the treasury Ogden Mills (1884–1937) and his most important aides, as well incoming secretary of the treasury William Woodin (1868–1934) and several Roosevelt advisors, were able despite their differences to work together.

Out of their discussions grew the dubious legal authority (i.e., the Trading with the Enemy Act of 1917) used by President Roosevelt on Sunday March fifth to contain the banking crisis. The new president declared a four-day national bank holiday, closing all the banks in the United States. A special session of Congress met on March 9 and in remarkable sessions the Senate and the House, in only a few hours, overwhelmingly passed the Emergency Banking Act, whose provisions confirmed President Roosevelt's action.

The legislation granted the president broad discretionary powers over American finance, called for stable banks to open under government supervision, and among other provisions extended the national bank holiday for four days. On Sunday March 12, the day before many banks were scheduled to be reopened, president Roosevelt broadcast his first "Fireside Chat" to an estimated 60,000,000 people.

In simple but convincing terms he explained to a vast radio audience what the federal government had "done in the last few days, why it was done, and what the next steps are going to be." And he laid out for his listeners how the banks were going to be bolstered and restructured: "we shall be engaged not merely in reopening sound banks but in the creation of banks through reorganization."

Roosevelt's words reinforced the impact of his administration's stopgap measures and helped restore confidence in the banking system. Those banks which reopened after the end of the national banking holiday, for instance, reported many more deposits then withdrawals. The New Deal would implement other necessary banking legislation, but the banking crisis faced by Roosevelt as he was inaugurated had ended.

The banking holidays on the state level, and more importantly on a national level, while symptomatic of the banking system's many weaknesses, had given American financial institutions and the federal government some breathing space, which the New Deal used well then and later when more ambitious regulatory legislation was passed.

Further Reading

Anderson, Patrick. *The President's Men.* Garden City, NY: Doubleday, 1968.

Awalt, Francis G. "Recollections of the Banking Crisis of 1933." *Business History Review* 63 (Autumn 1969): 347–71.

Badger, Anthony. *The New Deal: The Depression Years, 1933–1940.* Chicago: Ivan R. Dee, 1989.

Cohen, Adam. *Nothing to Fear: FDR's Inner Circle and the Hundred Days That Changed America.* New York: Thorndike Press, 2009.

Kennedy, David. *Freedom from Fear: The American People in Depression and War, 1929–1945.* Oxford: Oxford University Press, 1999.

McJimsey, George. *Harry Hopkins: Ally of the Poor and Defender of Democracy.* Cambridge, MA: Harvard University Press, 1987.

Sherwood, Robert. *Roosevelt and Hopkins: An Intimate History.* New York: Grosset & Dunlap, 1950.

Bonus Army (1932)

The Bonus Army was a group of unemployed and impecunious veterans suffering from the impact of the Great Depression, many with their families, who marched on Washington, D.C., from across the country in late May and early June 1932 seeking to lobby Congress to pay early their war bonuses due in 1945. The exact numbers who reached the nation's capital remains unclear but numbered at least 20,000. After the Senate voted to deny payment, the bulk of the Bonus Expeditionary Force (as they called themselves in reference to the American Expeditionary Force, the formal designation for the American troops sent to France to fight during World War I) left Washington, D.C., in late June and early July 1932.

The several thousand marchers who remained, often with wives and children, were camped in improvised or abandoned housing in downtown Washington, D.C., and at the edge of the city in the Anacostia Flats. They were violently dispersed on July 28, 1932, by saber-swinging U.S. Army cavalry and bayonet-wielding troops employing tear gas and tanks. The soldiers acted on the orders of General Douglas MacArthur (1880–1964), the army chief of staff, who believed the marchers' continued presence in Washington, D.C., represented a threat to national security. It is unclear if he acted as he did on the orders of President Herbert Hoover (1874–1964), but the army's actions for many Americans came to symbolize what was deemed the callous ineffectualness of the Hoover administration in dealing with the ravages of the economic downturn and guaranteed his defeat in the 1932 presidential election.

In keeping with the policy of payments and bounties for individuals who had fought for the United States in various wars, Congress was lobbied hard after 1918 by the newly formed American Legion, an organization of World War I veterans; as a result, during the early 1920s it attempted to pass legislation promising a bonus to Americans who had fought in World War I. The presidents opposed such legislation. In 1924 Congress passed over the veto of President Calvin Coolidge (1872–1933) the Adjusted Compensation Act,

Encampment built in 1932 in Washington, D.C., by veterans in the Bonus Expeditionary Force, a group of World War I veterans who demanded early payment of their war bonuses. (Library of Congress)

promising World War I veterans a maximum bonus of $500 in 1945. However, in the midst of the Great Depression hard-up, desperate veterans demanded the bonus be paid immediately. In 1932, approximately 20,000 veterans arrived in Washington, D.C.; the first to reach there toward the end of May 1932 were from the Pacific Northwest. Soon they were joined by marchers from all parts of the country to advocate early payment of the bonus.

They were not the first group to march on the nation's capital seeking redress from the impact of the economic downturn gripping the United States. In December 1932 a corporal's guard of Communists had undertaken a "hunger march" on Washington, D.C., to draw attention to their programs to fight the effects of the Great Depression; a few weeks later a Pittsburgh priest, James R. Cox (1886–1951), brought thousands of Pennsylvanians to the capital in the largest demonstration there to date as part of an effort to dramatize the need for federal relief expenditures. Unlike the Communists, who did not achieve much besides publicity, Father Cox did, with a delegation, manage to meet with President Hoover but got what proved only to be empty promises.

The Bonus Marchers came in the thousands to the nation's capital and by mid-June 1932 they, many with wives and children, were camped out all over the District of Columbia. They set up makeshift housing in abandoned government buildings, on various pieces of swampy land, and on acreage donated by sympathetic Washingtonians. The largest camp was in the Anacostia Flats at the edge of the city, where marchers with scraps of wood, cardboard, old signs, and anything that might offer protection from wind and rain built shacks typical of the "Hoovervilles" springing up across the country. The marchers were aided by the sympathetic chief of police, Pelham D. Glassford (1883–1959). The youngest general among the American forces in World War I, the recently appointed Glassford was anxious to avoid violence between the marchers and the forces of law and order. He arranged for donations of food, clothing, and materials to build shelters. He got the U.S. Army to lend the marchers cots and tents, and arranged for field kitchens to feed them.

Despite repeated requests, President Hoover refused to see representatives of the Bonus Army. He believed that immediate payment of the bonus would devastate the Treasury. On June 15, 1932, the House of Representatives passed a bill (209–176) proposed by liberal Texas Democratic representative Wright Patman (1893–1976) for payment of the bonus. Two days later the Senate rejected (82–18) the bill. The marchers took the rejection calmly. In early July Congress voted funds to pay transportation costs for those members of the Bonus Army still in Washington, D.C., who wished to return home. Thousands left, but a large number remained encamped in the nation's capital. A nervous Hoover determined to clear downtown Washington, D.C., of the marchers but wanted to use soldiers only if "absolutely necessary."

The police force and many of its officials were less sympathetic than their chief Glassford to the marchers. And on July 28 police clashed with marchers as they moved, at the behest of President Hoover, to clear government buildings downtown in which members of the Bonus Army had squatted. Glassford had managed that morning to talk marchers out of one of the buildings, but that afternoon police who panicked fired and killed two of the veterans who did not wish to leave another building. The president, anxious to avoid further unrest and under pressure from some of his advisors, called in the army.

President Hoover explicitly ordered General MacArthur not to clear out the Anacostia Flats camp of the Bonus Army. The general disobeyed his orders, sent the troops there to clear out the camps, and burned the makeshift homes of the veterans and their families. Army Chief of Staff Douglas MacArthur acted against Hoover's orders when he sent troops into the Bonus Army camp just outside of Washington, D.C., and drove them out. He falsely informed the press afterward that the Bonus Marchers were thugs, revolutionaries, and Communists.

MacArthur's actions reinforced the perception of a cruel and callous Hoover unmoved by the plight of the poor. The press reported numerous false stories that MacArthur's force had killed men, women, and children, myths that still are found in much of the literature about the action. Overall, the attacks on Hoover were unfair as he had not given MacArthur orders to attack the camp, although he stood by the general in the aftermath of the army's actions. Official intelligence had fed the president distorted and just plain wrong information about the dangers that the marchers represented. In any event the attacks on Hoover's handling of the Bonus Army resonated with voters, dropped his approval ratings precipitously, and were a major factor in his defeat in 1932.

Further Reading

Daniels, Roger. *The Bonus March: An Episode of the Great Depression.* Westport, CT: Greenwood, 1971.

Dickson, Paul, and Thomas B. Allen. *The Bonus Army: An American Epic.* New York: Walker & Company, 2004.

Cox, James Renshaw (1886–1951)

A Roman Catholic priest from Pittsburgh, James Cox was known as the "Pastor to the Poor" because of his active support of social justice to alleviate the desperate plight of the unemployed during the Great Depression and to provide them with sustenance and hope. In 1932 he led an unprecedented protest march, popularly known as "Cox's Army," to Washington, D.C., to advocate direct relief for the jobless. This march was the largest protest demonstration to have taken place in the nation's capital up to that time.

Cox was born on March 7, 1886, in the Lawrenceville District of Pittsburgh, a working-class area. His father was a Methodist mill worker; his mother was Catholic. The young Cox attended parochial school, Pittsburgh Catholic College of the Holy Ghost (now Duquesne University), and St. Vincent Seminary in Latrobe, Pennsylvania, before being ordained in 1911. He was raised in an environment that necessitated hard work and emphasized faith; before his ordination, Cox was employed as a newsboy, a steel mill worker, and a supervisor at a taxicab company.

After being ordained, he served six years as an assistant parish priest. During World War I, he served as a chaplain at a U.S. Army hospital in France. Subsequently, he earned a master's degree in economics at the University of Pittsburgh, and served as the chaplain at Mercy Hospital, Pittsburgh's only Catholic hospital. In 1924 Cox became pastor at Pittsburgh's Old St. Patrick's Church, which was a poor parish located in the Strip District among what have been described as "gritty factories and warehouses" rife with prostitutes and saloons. Cox, according to a press account, was "the youngest pastor in the oldest Catholic church in the city."

Although a colleague later maintained Cox had "inherited a dead parish," he also got a radio pulpit on WJAS, which had begun broadcasting in 1922 and served for some years thereafter as the CBS outlet in Pittsburgh. When Cox became pastor of Old St. Patrick, he began broadcasting Mass at noon daily. His homilies, which were provocative as well as attractive, not only gained him fame and the station an increasing audience but also helped to build up the church, whose membership rose dramatically. The congenial Cox broadcast until 1950. As another Pittsburgh priest later reported, Cox was "made for radio."

At the end of the 1920s as the economy worsened, Cox sought to help the Pittsburgh unemployed by providing them with food, clothing, and shelter. According to some accounts, the soup kitchen Cox organized supplied over two million free meals between 1929 and 1933. A shantytown sometimes housing over 300 people grew on the church grounds. Living in structures built from wooden packing crates, tar paper, burlap, and carpet remnants, the residents of the shantytown elected Cox honorary mayor in 1931. The priest also supplied families with coal and distributed medicine to sick children.

For months, Cox led demonstrations in Pittsburgh and in Harrisburg, the state capital, demanding improved unemployment relief. Finally, he decided to petition the federal government for aid. His determination to march to the nation's capital stemmed from the seeming indifference of the Hoover administration to the suffering of the unemployed and their families. Cox, like many other like-minded activists, also was alarmed at Communist efforts to organize the unemployed. Although supporting Communist rights to speak and to assemble without interference by the authorities, Cox was concerned about Communist subordination to Stalin's directives, and like many other religious people was dismayed by its commitment to atheism.

Cox was inspired by Coxey's Army and its 1894 march on Washington, but while Coxey enrolled only some few hundred, Cox brought thousands to Washington, D.C. To avoid any media suggestions of sexual impropriety along the way, only men were allowed to participate. On January 5, 1932, an estimated 6,000 set out from Pittsburgh, partly on foot, but mostly crammed into antiquated cars and trucks.

By January 7, when Cox's Army reached Washington, estimates of its numbers ranged as high as 25,000 and the parade of wheezy vehicles transporting them stretched out for an estimated eight miles. When Cox reached Harrisburg, Pennsylvania governor Gifford Pinchot (1865–1946), who planned to challenge Hoover for the 1932 Republican presidential nomination and who had initially brushed Cox off, issued a hearty welcome and arranged for food and shelter when he saw the numbers mobilized by the priest.

Thanks to Pennsylvania's savvy Republican senator James J. Davis (1873–1947), the demonstrators, who arrived in Washington during a torrential rain, ate at U.S. Army field kitchens. According to the AP, the men consumed 2,800 pounds of sauerkraut, 1,500 pounds of hot dogs, 11,000 apples, 650 gallons of soup, 450 loaves of bread, and 1,600 dozen doughnuts and rolls. Some demonstrators were housed at a local armory; others bedded down in their vehicles; Cox and some of his staff stayed at a cheap hotel.

On January 8, Cox's Army, with many of its members waving American flags, rallied in front of the Capitol; in addition to speeches, the band of the volunteer fire department of North Braddock, a Pittsburgh suburb, played patriotic songs that the crowd sang lustily. President Hoover finally agreed to meet with a delegation, including Senator Davis and Cox, who told the president that "the administration was acting like an ostrich with its head in the sand," assuming if troubles could not be seen they did not exist.

The priest presented a petition that called for massive federal spending on public works projects, on direct relief assistance to supplement exhausted state funds, and on aid to meet social problems, such as lack of medical care for children of indigent families. Hoover's response was politely sympathetic ("I greatly appreciate your coming here . . .") but noncommittal and included a short prepared statement that the Depression had run its course. Cox later recalled that out of respect for the presidency he refrained from commenting that Hoover's response seemed "inadequate."

That afternoon the orderly throng began its return to Pittsburgh. The overcrowded vehicles could not accommodate some 200 of Cox's Army. Veteran Republican congressman M. Clyde Kelly (1883–1935), who represented the Braddock area, negotiated discounted train fares for their travel home and obtained the necessary funds to pay the fares from Secretary of the Treasury Andrew Mellon (1855–1937). Dubbed by local newsmen as "the best known Pittsburgher in Washington," Mellon from his own pocket paid out $1,242 (equivalent to about $17,000 in 2012).

These funds seem not to have been Mellon's only contribution to the march. According to one history, Mellon had "quietly ordered his Gulf Oil service stations to dispense gasoline without charge" to Cox's Army. It is unclear why he might have done so, though Mellon seems to have become disenchanted with Hoover's handling of the economic downturn, and he and Hoover had never been close. Hoover seems to have learned of Mellon's actions after his aides investigated what many considered a Communist propaganda ploy or an attempt by the Vatican or the Democrats to embarrass the president.

Cox briefly entered politics in 1932 after returning to Pittsburgh. Buoyed by his success, the priest helped organize the Jobless Party, the platform of which called for federal unemployment relief, public works projects, old age pensions, and support for labor organizations. Cox accepted the party's nomination for president but threw his support to Democrat Franklin Roosevelt when the party's finances collapsed.

For the rest of Cox's life, he followed the social teachings of the Church and, as a later pastor of St. Patrick's put it, "fleshed them out, made them a reality," becoming well known for his charitable outreach. He staged Passion Plays, promoted devotions to Our Lady of Lourdes, and led pilgrimages there. Cox's well-delivered homilies and public stands extended beyond religious affairs. He fought all forms of prejudice, especially anti-Semitism. Cox eventually cooled on Roosevelt, but continued to vigorously advocate Progressive ideas, remaining a staunch supporter of labor unions. He died in Pittsburgh on March 20, 1951.

Further Reading

Heineman, Kenneth J. "Pilgrimage: Father James Cox and the Awakening of Catholic Social Activism." In *A Catholic New Deal: Religion and Reform in Depression Pittsburgh*. University Park: Penn State University Press, 1999, 11–33.

Mellon, Andrew William (1855–1937)

Andrew Mellon was a prominent financier who served as secretary of the treasury (1921–1932) under presidents Warren G. Harding (1865–1923), Calvin Coolidge (1872–1933), and Herbert Hoover (1874–1964). Mellon, during his tenure, presided over tax cuts, spending reductions, repayment of World War I loans by the Allies, economic expansion in the 1920s, and the onset of the Great Depression. Mellon was credited by many for the economic prosperity of the 1920s and at one point was called "the greatest Secretary of the Treasury since Alexander Hamilton," but when he left office in 1932 critics blamed his policies for the Great Depression. A noted discriminating art collector, in 1937 he donated his superb art collection to the United States, along with sufficient funds to build and maintain a National Gallery of Art in Washington, D.C.

He was born in Pittsburgh on March 24, 1855, into a prominent family. His father, a judge, successfully ventured into banking and real estate, and was close to industrialist Henry Clay Frick (1849–1919). Andrew Mellon was educated in the Pittsburgh public schools and attended the Western University of Pennsylvania (now the University of Pittsburgh) but left in 1872, three months shy of graduation. With money borrowed from his father at a standard rate of interest he founded a successful profitable lumber and construction business in the neighboring town of Mansfield (now Carnegie). Two years later Mellon "advantageously" sold the business and became an officer in his father's bank.

Wealthy industrialist and financier Andrew Mellon was secretary of the treasury during the Republican administrations of Warren Harding, Calvin Coolidge, and Herbert Hoover. (Library of Congress)

In 1880 Mellon accompanied Frick on a tour of Europe, during which he bought a painting, and supposedly began his love of collecting fine art. In 1882 his father made him president of the bank and turned over its ownership to him. He successfully expanded its investment ventures. Five years later his younger brother Richard became a partner in the bank and remained a lifelong close associate. In 1889 Andrew Mellon and Frick organized the Union Trust Company. In 1902 the family bank was incorporated as the Mellon National Bank, with the bulk of the capital stock held by Union Trust, which was dominated by Frick and Andrew and Richard Mellon (1858–1933).

Andrew Mellon's investments in various areas including construction, aluminum, oil, and real estate proved very profitable. He possessed a knack for loaning money to promising clients and realizing the potential of new industries. He created a number of new companies including the Aluminum Company of America (Alcoa) and the Gulf Oil Corporation. According to some estimates, the quiet, hardworking, fiercely ambitious Mellon by 1921 was worth approximately $100 million and had increased the family fortune to over $2 billion.

He had long been active in Republican Party circles in Pennsylvania, and provided financial support for many of its candidates, especially the state's two conservative GOP senators, Boise Penrose (1860–1921) and Philander Knox (1853–1921). In 1920, he donated money to the campaign of the victorious Republican presidential nominee Warren Harding, who at the suggestion of Knox selected Mellon to be his secretary of the treasury. The selection was a surprise as Mellon, despite his wealth, was relatively unknown outside Pittsburgh. As treasury secretary, Mellon would over the years deal with a variety of issues including the national debt, budget deficits, tax reforms, the tariff, and to a limited extent some international problems. During the 1920s, Mellon's economic policies were credited with the decade's prosperity.

As a conservative Republican businessman, Mellon supported high tariffs, believing they protected American businesses from foreign competition and were crucial to economic prosperity. During his time as treasury secretary, Congress—with his support—sharply raised tariff rates through the passage of the Fordney-McCumber Tariff in 1922 and the Smoot-Hawley Tariff in 1930, which imposed the highest duties ever in American history, hampering efforts by Europeans to sell their wares in the United States.

However, Mellon believed that Congress's first priority should be passage of tax relief and tax reform. During his tenure as treasury secretary he presided over a period of reduced national debt and budget surpluses. By 1927, federal spending had been reduced from $6.5 billion to $3.5 billion. By that same year, the national debt had been reduced by $6 billion, and the federal government was running a $636 million surplus.

Mellon during the 1920s crusaded against federal income taxes and succeeded in implementing tax reductions in 1921, 1924, and 1926. The 1926 Revenue Act eliminated the gift tax, dramatically reduced excise taxes, and exempted the first $4,000 in income. Various loopholes ensured that between 1924 and 1929 those who earned over $100,000 a year paid no income tax at all.

Unfortunately, Mellon seems never to have understood the illogic of combining high tariffs and attempts to increase trade. He was a driving force in 1924 behind the plan, named for banker Charles Dawes (1865–1951), that made it easier for Germany to pay the crushing reparations demanded by England and France. American loans went to Germany and were used by England and France to repay the sums borrowed by them from the United States during World War I. When the Great Depression hit the barriers to trade hindered Germany, and it was necessary in 1930 to work out another plan before reparations and repayment to the United States totally ceased (he was "unofficially present" at some of the negotiations that took place in drawing up the plan).

In 1928 Herbert Hoover had been elected president. Even though he disagreed with some of Mellon's policies and they were not close, the new president continued him as secretary of the treasury. Mellon's reputation as a financial genius was soon tarnished by the October 1929 stock market collapse and the economic problems stemming from the impact of the Great Depression. Budget deficits rose inexorably, reaching $1.4 billion by 1932 and the national debt increased by $1.5 billion.

Mellon, determined to avoid federal expenditures for relief, forcefully argued the federal government should let the business cycle take its natural course: "Liquidate labor, liquidate stocks, liquidate farmers, liquidate real estate." His message came across to Americans as cold and callous in the midst of the mushrooming unemployment and increased suffering. In February 1932, Mellon left the treasury to become ambassador to Great Britain, serving until May 1933.

On his return to Pittsburgh Mellon became a vehement critic of the New Deal's policies, such as unemployment relief and agricultural subsidies. He considered these efforts to be interventionist and unnecessary. Late in 1933 Mellon faced an investigation centered on his 1931 tax return. In 1934 a grand jury chose not to indict him on charges of tax evasion. The next year the Internal Revenue Service levied an assessment against him of over $3 million in taxes and penalties, but it was successfully appealed; the vindication came after his death but on technical grounds his estate paid a token settlement of over $450,000 plus interest.

While still living in Pittsburgh he had seriously collected art; after moving to Washington, D.C., in 1921 he became more ambitious and built a remarkable, unique collection. Using agents in New York, London, and Berlin he made numerous superb purchases. On one day in 1923 he paid $500,000 for four paintings. In the early 1930s he bought from the hard-up Soviets various masterpieces from the Hermitage Museum in St. Petersburg, spending about $10 million.

On December 22, 1936, Mellon, who had been mulling over a National Gallery of Art since 1927, wrote President Roosevelt offering the United States his art treasures and the funds necessary to build and maintain such a gallery. In early 1937 Congress in joint resolution accepted the offer, and that summer construction began. On August 25, 1937, Mellon died. He had hoped his collection would serve as a nucleus and so it did. In 1939, a philanthropist donated hundreds of Italian paintings and sculptures. On March 17, 1941, President Roosevelt formally opened the National Gallery of Art.

Further Reading

Cannadine, David. *Mellon: An American Life.* New York: Alfred A. Knopf, 2006.

Meyer, Eugene Isaac (1875–1959)

A marvelously gifted, multifaceted man, Eugene Isaac Meyer was successful as a financier, businessman, public servant, and newspaper publisher. He held a variety of government positions including head of the Federal Farm Board, a governor of the Federal Reserve system, and the first president of the World Bank. He was a remarkable man.

Born October 31, 1875, in Los Angeles, Meyer was the son of a French immigrant financier and grew up in San Francisco. After an indifferent year at the University of California, he attended Yale University, graduating (1895) with an AB degree, and he went on to study and work (1896–1897) in Europe. His father, a partner in the New York branch of Lazard Freres, obtained a job for him with that international banking firm.

Unhappy there, Meyer went (1901) on his own and quickly demonstrated a knack for making wise investments. At a relatively young age, he acquired a seat on the New York Stock Exchange. He made his fortune during various economic downturns by "running against the tide"; he found and purchased undervalued stocks being dumped by others, subsequently selling them a considerable profit. He also proved astute in his profitable investments in copper (helping to create Anaconda Copper).

By 1915 he was a powerful and respected figure on Wall Street, with a fortune estimated to be over $40 million. As a young man Meyer had planned to earn enough money by the time he was 50 so that he could afford to participate in public life. With U.S. entry into World War I in early 1917 Meyer entered government service as one of the dollar-a-year men who worked for the American war effort.

He advised the U.S. Army on the purchase of shoes and the Committee on Raw Materials (later the War Industries Board) on the purchase of nonferrous metals. In 1918 he was appointed head of the War Finance Corporation (WFC), and after the war's end Meyer continued with it to 1924 as the WFC was transformed into an agency one of whose major tasks was to assist farmers caught in the post-war economic downturn.

In 1920 Meyer working with the noted American chemist/businessman William Nichols (1852–1930) combined five smaller chemical companies to create what later became the Allied Chemical Corporation, which in time became part of Honeywell, a Fortune 100 conglomerate. This company at the time of its founding was designed to assist the fledgling American chemical industry to break free of the bounds of the German chemical giants who it was believed had hampered the United States during World War I.

A staunch advocate of expanding credit for struggling farmers, Meyer was appointed head of the Federal Farm Board in 1927 by President Calvin Coolidge (1872–1933), and in 1930 President Herbert Hoover (1874–1964) appointed him to head the Board of Governors of the Federal Reserve Board. After a series of acrimonious hearings he was confirmed by Congress and served from September 16, 1930, until May 10, 1933.

During his tenure the impact of the Great Depression on the American banking community meant he constantly dealt with various crises, especially the increasing number of bank failures. Meyer was an ardent proponent of expanding the credit supply and lowering interest rates in order to combat the Great Depression. He was instrumental in created the Reconstruction Finance Corporation (RFC), which lent money to struggling banks, businesses, and railroads, and was appointed its first director in January 1932. However, the energetic but fiscally conservative Meyer resigned after six months over policy differences with the president. Meyer, who disapproved of FDR's spending plans, resigned from the Federal Reserve Board in May 1933 shortly after the president's inauguration.

After leaving public life, Meyer entered the newspaper business when for $825,000 in June 1933 he purchased at a public auction the failing *Washington Post*. As its publisher Meyer over the next years sustained significant losses. The newspaper's losses often cost him over $1 million annually. But even though a very costly venture about which he had doubts from time to time, Meyer did not give up on the *Post*.

With the aid of hired journalism experts he made intelligent use of its assets (such as its Associate Press franchise), and cut out a great deal of dead wood, reorganized management and staff, hired first class talent, and encouraged fair, vigorous reporting, turning the *Washington Post*'s parochial, limited news sheet into a major American newspaper and one of the world's best newspapers.

While he editorially supported many of FDR's New Deal policies, he was not afraid to oppose the president. The most notable example was Meyer's outspoken opposition to FDR's Supreme Court packing plan. During World War II, Meyer loyally supported almost all aspects of the war effort. On the other hand, however, he criticized abuses of civil liberties such as the internment of Japanese Americans.

After World War II, Meyer in June 1946 was appointed the first president of the World Bank by President Harry Truman (1884–1972). He accepted the position reluctantly and because of his fiscal conservatism it was an unhappy experience for him. His son-in-law Philip Graham (1915–1963), the husband of his daughter Katharine, succeeded him as publisher at the *Post*.

Meyer, always a good administrator, as World Bank head hired a first-class staff, emphasized scientific research, and created a sound administrative structure. He resigned from the World Bank at the end of 1946, asserting that his mission of launching and stabilizing the World Bank was completed, and returned to the *Post* as chairman of the Board of the Washington Post Company; his son-in-law continued as publisher, working closely with Meyer.

In the next years the Post Company became involved with broadcasting, purchasing radio and TV stations. In 1954 it bought the *Times-Herald*, the competing morning newspaper and immediately jumped ahead in circulation of the then more prestigious afternoon paper, the *Evening Star*; in 1959 it passed the *Star* in advertising linage. On July 17, 1959, Meyer died.

Notwithstanding his conspicuous success in various business formats and his years of extensive public service, Meyer's legacy rests on his transformation of the *Post* from an ailing unimportant daily into an influential major newspaper of record, an accomplishment on which his successors have been able to build a voice on the American political scene to which attention must be paid.

Further Reading
Pusey, Merlo J. *Eugene Meyer.* New York: Alfred A. Knopf, 1974.

President's Organization for Unemployment Relief (POUR)

The President's Organization for Unemployment Relief (POUR) was a voluntary organization established in the late summer of 1931 to encourage states, localities, organized charities, and especially private individuals to contribute funds for the relief of the dramatically rising numbers of unemployed. President Herbert Hoover (1874–1964) strongly believed that the situation could be handled without the expenditure of federal funds, which if allocated would undercut the traditional American community spirit and would result in the establishment of a "dole" paid to the out of work.

In the face of nationwide suffering and deprivation caused by the inability of the traditional private and local agencies to deal with the effects of increasing unemployment, the Hoover administration referred to the so-called invisible relief of aid and assistance from friends and neighbors. It would be wrong to assert that the president was indifferent to the trauma; he seems to have strongly believed that local initiatives could handle the situation.

Prior to the organization of POUR, Hoover in October 1930 had set up the President's Emergency Committee for Employment. The naming of this committee seems to have been influenced by Edward Bernays (1881–1995), recently characterized as "the father of spin" and eulogized by many as "the father of public relations"; he suggested "for Employment" to accentuate the positive aspects of its mission, and "emergency" to underline the belief that the crisis would not last long.

The committee was headed initially by an old Hoover associate, Arthur Woods (1870–1942), an American educator, journalist, former New York City police commissioner, and colonel in the U.S. Army during World War I; he had headed such a committee during the downturn of the early 1920s, and this one proved equally ineffectual. Woods failed to grasp the gravity of the situation: unemployment had more than doubled to over an estimated 5 million since the Crash a year earlier and was continuing to rise. At the same time sufficient funds were not available for providers of relief, and the Hoover administration would not allow for federal expenditures; the committee did not have a penny to offer in aid.

Its mission in one historian's words was "to soothe the nation; not to alarm it." The committee churned out press releases urging that the unemployed be hired. Woods was unable to respond to requests from the media as well as various state and local officials as to the committee's plans to deal with unemployment since it had no plans. Moreover, Wood's makeshift operation made no attempt to collect reliable statistics about available local resources to assist the unemployed or about their mushrooming number. Woods, on the basis of anecdotal evidence, asserted that "the country had responded most heartily to the emergency."

And so it had, but quite insufficiently. Within a short time Woods had moved on and in August 1931 the defunct President's Committee was transformed into the President's Organization on Unemployment Relief. The functions of the President's Committee did not change; it was still designed per Herbert Hoover's words "to still the socialistic cries for the dole." The new somewhat reluctant director, the highly successful and energetic head of AT&T, Walter S. Gifford (1885–1966), had done a fine job as head of the Charity Organization Society of New York City; he had been instrumental in raising charitable giving by New Yorkers from $4.5 million in 1930 to $21 million in 1932.

POUR during the fall and winter of 1931–1932 raised an incredible amount of money for the private relief agencies in a remarkable fund-raising campaign. Making use of business and entertainment luminaries POUR used every type of publicity and venue: radio, newspapers, periodicals, and billboards; benefit dinners; collections by ushers in movie theaters and in legitimate theaters; gate receipts from games played by college football teams. Major magazines provided space gratis; ad agencies made important talents free of charge.

A typical ad sponsored by POUR displayed an unemployed worker saying, "They tell me there's five or six million of us—out of work. . . . We're not scared . . . the good old U.S.A. is in a bad way . . . temporarily." After some similar copy the tagline reads "I'll see it through if you will." How much such advertising buoyed the unemployed, who likely could not afford the periodical in which it appeared, is questionable, but such ads did raise a lot of money. The increased funds raised, however, were pathetically inadequate given the dramatic increase in the funds necessary to deal with the deteriorating conditions of the jobless.

Although the nearly $58 million collected in large part by POUR's fundraising was more than three times what had been donated for relief in 1930, it represented a 25 percent drop in the funds needed to be spent by the private and local relief agencies, which had to deal with the increasing numbers of jobless and found it ever more difficult to deal with the demands that placed on them. Gifford had worked hard but like many in the Hoover administration found it difficult to adjust his thought patterns in relation to what had become a dire emergency. Testifying before a Senate committee in 1932 he admitted that he did not have exact numbers about the number of jobless but asserted that it seemed to him that "the money spent" for relief in the United States was "the money needed." Queried by a senator about his attitude toward an improvement in economic conditions, he admitted to a lack of optimism but expressed hope, "I am always hopeful."

POUR was one more attempt by President Hoover to discourage the proponents of federal funding for local and private charities. Its organization reflected his strong views that the federal government should not be involved in directly providing relief for the unemployed. At the end of June 1932 Congress abolished POUR by denying it any appropriation.

If nothing else the committee's campaigns and its inability to raise the funds necessary to substantially alleviate the plight of the unemployed and their families proved the failure of the Hoover approach. One of the important lessons provided by POUR was that direct relief by the federal government was a crucial necessity if the unemployed were to be aided.

Further Reading

Kennedy, David. *Freedom from Fear: The American People in Depression and War, 1929–1945*. New York: Oxford University Press, 1999.

Leuchtenburg, William E. *Herbert Hoover*. New York: Times Books, 2009.

McElvaine, Robert S. *The Great Depression: America, 1929–1941*. New York: Times Books, 1984.

Reconstruction Finance Corporation (RFC)

Established by the Hoover administration in January 1932 to mitigate the downward spiral of the American economy, the Reconstruction Finance Corporation (RFC) did not realize the administration's goals. Subsequently, under the leadership (1933–1945) of Jesse Jones (1874–1956), a skillful Texas businessman, the RFC as a public development bank, mostly through loans, contributed millions to many New Deal projects and financially underwrote the bulk of America's economic warfare during World War II. Jones left the RFC in 1945 and subsequently it had a checkered history; a 1951 U.S. Senate investigation charged that under the Truman administration the RFC practiced corrupt loan polices and detailed instances of political favoritism and bribery. In 1953 Congress abolished the RFC's independent status, placing the agency under control of the Treasury Department, and by 1958 the RFC had ceased to exist.

The RFC was the first significant departure from the Hoover administration's dependence on voluntary associations and organized cooperation to deal with the doleful situations caused by the Depression. The concept of the RFC was suggested to the president by Eugene Meyer (1875–1959), head of the Federal Reserve. Drawing on his World War I experiences he proposed to President Hoover in early fall 1932 an agency patterned on the War Finance Corporation (WFC) that Meyer had directed, which had provided financial support to American industry and banks involved in the war effort. Such a corporation, argued Meyer, like its wartime model, could make loans to "banks, railroads, and insurance companies" facing bankruptcy; only through a "revival" of the WFC "could the emergency be met"; as Hoover later put it, the RFC would "make temporary advances . . . to established industries, railways, and financial institutions which cannot otherwise secure credit." Meyer assembled a small staff, drawn mostly from the Federal Reserve, to draft a bill to create an agency that could reactivate the WFC's wartime powers.

Historians have debated whether Hoover, an outspoken proponent of minimalist government, initially was reluctant to accept Meyer's arguments, but in early December 1932 the president in his annual State of the Union message advocated establishment of such an agency in the form of an Emergency Reconstruction Corporation (quickly changed to Reconstruction Finance Corporation). The Congress to which Hoover submitted the draft bill was torn by partisanship and acrimony in both the president's party and that of his Democratic opponents. The Republicans narrowly controlled the Senate, one of whose conservative members had recently damned that party's progressive legislators as "sons of the wild jackass." Democrats, who had gained control of the House, smelled victory in the 1932 elections given the country's economic slide, and acted accordingly. Both parties contained members dissatisfied with some of the draft bill's provisions, who also took contradictory stances on various major issues including the tariff, direct federal unemployed relief, tax increases, America's foreign policy, and Hoover's moratorium on war debts.

In charge of presenting the bill to Congress were two Republicans: Kansas representative James George Strong (1870–1938) and Connecticut senator Frederick C. Walcott (1869–1949); both were businessmen whose electoral career ended in the mid-1930s. The senator in a front-page *New York Times* article (January 17, 1932) detailed the anticipated workings of what the newspaper considered "one of the most important pieces of legislation . . . since the World War." Most legislators agreed; committee hearings were brief and despite bad feelings, some outspoken objections by key senators and representatives, and an adjournment for the holidays, the bill was adopted quickly by huge margins in the House and the Senate. Within days a conference report reconciled the different versions of the bill, and on January 22, 1932, some six week after first being proposed Congress passed the legislation establishing the

RFC. That night Hoover signed the bill into law one minute after it reached his White House desk.

The financially conservative Meyer, noted for his anxiousness about the failing American banking system, had been touted as RFC chair even before the passage of the legislation. In advance of being formally appointed he assembled former WFC staffers in Washington, D.C. Thanks to him, their talents and the experiences gained at the WFC were available to the newly established RFC, and it began to operate within ten days of coming into existence; soon nationwide over 40 field offices were in operation. Meyer, who remained head of the Federal Reserve, is credited by some historians as "almost single handedly" reviving WFC policies and putting them to use in a clone of that agency to deal with the credit of the country. Congress provided the agency with $500,000,000 in capital and authorized it to raise through debentures another $1.5 billion. In July 1932 an Emergency Relief and Construction Act boosted the RFC's resources by $2 billion and expanded its mandate to include among other functions loans for employment-producing, self-liquidating public works (e.g., toll roads).

On principle Hoover resisted using funds authorized by Congress for substantial relief of the unemployed even as he involved the federal government with the rescue of larger financial institutions, utilities, and railroads. The RFC was attacked as a "Beadline for Business" and a "Dole for Millionaires." The fiscally conservative president, concerned about balancing the budget and committed to austerity, strongly opposed using federal funds to aid the jobless (of the $300 million Congress allocated in mid-1932 to the RFC for work relief only about 10 percent was spent by the end of Hoover's term in March 1933). Despite the congressional appropriations for assistance to states who requested RFC funds to assist their needy citizens, the agency, under the influence of Hoover and Meyer, demanded states in effect take a paupers oath indicating all possible financial alternatives had been exhausted. Even then the RFC imposed limitations: the governor of hard-hit Pennsylvania requested funds equivalent for aid to the state's unemployed of 13 cents a day and received funds allowing three cents a day.

Hoover vociferously denied the RFC was "bailing out the rich," but though the first $61 million of RFC funds was disbursed widely to 255 banks, $41 million of that sum went to just three banks, and of the $264 million lent to railroads, $156 million went to three groups, one headed by J. P. Morgan Jr. (1867–1943). Most RFC loans did go to small institutions, but most of the money went to bigger ones. The RFC was well run; operating expenses represent about 1 percent of its total loans, and these loans did play an important role in averting total collapse of the American economy. But despite the RFC's achievements (e.g., bank runs diminished dramatically) it had a negative image, one exacerbated by incidents involving its officers, especially Charles Dawes

(1865–1971), the first RFC president, whose appointment in January 1932 met with general public approval.

Known as an outspoken administrator Dawes had built a Chicago bank into a major financial institution; among his other accomplishments he was first director of the Bureau of the Budget, authored the Dawes Plan to restore the German economy and establish more reasonable reparations payments (earning him in 1925 a Nobel Peace Prize), was 30th U.S. vice president (1925–1929), and served as an effective ambassador to Great Britain. On June 6, 1932, he abruptly resigned as RFC president, wanting to devote himself to saving his failing bank. Three weeks later the RFC loaned the Dawes bank $90,000,000 (ultimately fully repaid). Subsequently the RFC suffered further negative publicity when the public learned the RFC had lent $12 million to a Cleveland bank of which Dawes's successor, Atlee Pomerene (1863–1937), a former Democratic senator from Ohio, was a director.

The legislation establishing the RFC called for three of its seven officers to be Democrats. Pomerene was one; Jesse Jones was another. When FDR became president he named Jones RFC head, and under his leadership it became an effective, important tool of the Roosevelt administration in peace and war. FDR expanded RFC powers, and through their adroit use by Jones it funded many important New Deal projects and became a vital force in the American financial community; after 1939 the RFC under Jones's intelligent, forceful guidance disbursed over $20 billion funding the rearmament of the United States and financing the American war effort. The RFC faltered during the Hoover administration but proved its value in the following years. Ultimately, the RFC fizzled after Jones retired, ending in scandal during the 1950s.

Further Reading

Jones, Jesse H. *Fifty Billion Dollars: My Thirteen Years with the RFC, 1932–1945.* New York: Macmillan, 1951.

Nash, Gerald. "Herbert Hoover and the Origins of the Reconstruction Finance Corporation." *Mississippi Valley Historical Review* 46 (1959): 455–68.

Olson, James S. *Herbert Hoover and the Reconstruction Finance Corporation, 1931–1933.* Ames: Iowa State University Press, 1977.

Reno, Milo (1866–1936)

An activist leader of farmers, Milo Reno organized and participated in attempts by farmers during the last weeks of the Hoover administration to raise the already low crop prices, using direct action after they had dramatically collapsed in the latter part of 1932. Reno and his associates strongly advocated that farmers withhold their crops from the market in order to obtain higher prices for them. The actions of his National Farmers' Holiday Association failed, and in some Midwestern states the farmers' attempts to keep crops from the market led to violence. Reno's support among farmers eroded in 1934 as New Deal policies resulted in extensive if controversial government support for agriculture and higher prices for what farmers produced.

Reno was born January 5, 1866, on a farm near Agency, Iowa, a small town that had been an Indian trading post. He was the seventh son and the thirteenth child of a hardworking farm family. Better educated than most of his peers, he attended various rural county schools, a Quaker academy, and majored in theology at Oskaloosa College (an Iowa college then affiliated with the Disciples of Christ). Politically active from an early age, Reno was involved with parties and groups that advocated for higher farm prices and protection of the farmer, such as the Grange, the Union Labor Party, the Farmers' Alliance, and the Populists (on whose ticket he ran unsuccessfully for the Iowa legislature). Although never ordained, Reno, when campaigning for the causes he supported, was characterized as offering fiery sermons with evangelical zeal rather just giving speeches.

In 1918, after some two decades as a successful farmer, Reno joined the recently organized Iowa Farmers Union and by 1921 had been chosen its head, leading the organization until 1931 when replaced by his handpicked successor. During the 1920s Reno established several successful farmers' mutual insurance companies and livestock commission houses; his supporters proposed him for National Farmers Union president, but its conservatives denied him the office considering Reno too radical. The decade saw a long decline from the World War I highs in prices that farmers received for their efforts. Reno, a vocal advocate of farm relief, supported the McNary-Haugen proposed legislation calling for direct aid to farmers. In 1925 Reno helped form the Corn Belt Committee, a coalition of major midwest

Milo Reno, national leader of the Farm Holiday Movement, September 7, 1932. (Bettmann/Corbis)

farm groups; two years later it formally adopted Reno's argument that if relief through legislation could not be achieved for farmers they could refuse to deliver goods.

As agricultural prices tanked severely in 1932, Reno—who considered the major political parties corrupt and maintained that farmers could only achieve relief by "direct action"—presided over a mass meeting in Des Moines, Iowa, which under his leadership created the National Farmers' Holiday Association. There and elsewhere he energetically urged farmers to protest low farm prices by taking a "farmers' holiday"—in other words to go on strike against those offering such prices. He had deliberately chosen the word *holiday* to echo those in the United States who urged "bank holidays" to avoid runs on American financial institutions. Reno, as a friendly writer dubbed him, had become "a man of the barricades." By August 1932 Reno claimed to have over 175,000 pledges from angry farmers "to buy nothing, sell nothing, [and] stay at home" until they could at least achieve the cost of production and a small profit.

He called for peaceful actions, but desperate farmers were not willing to allow any agricultural commodities to reach markets. Within two weeks Iowa farmers had established picket lines around Sioux City, a major marketplace. At first the pickets tried informing drivers carrying goods to and from Sioux City about the farmers' doleful situation and with some success urged the drivers to turn back. But very soon drivers proved more obstinate, persuasion could not turn back blockade runners, and pickets turned to other means such as throwing logs in front of speeding trucks. The situation rapidly escalated: what had been envisioned as a peaceful picket line in support of a holiday became a battlefield that spread out over Iowa and the neighboring states. By the end of August 1932 the situation had garnered national media attention.

Recognizing that the association's tactics would not result in higher prices for commodities, Reno called a truce in early September. The governors of several midwestern states met in conference but were distracted by the coming elections and their own campaigns could not develop a coherent program. After the November elections more and more farmers faced dispossession through tax sales and mortgage foreclosures. During the four-month interregnum between Hoover's defeat and FDR's inauguration the situation of American agriculture precipitously declined, and Reno advised the Farmers' Holiday Association to block evictions. In numerous cases the association was able to peacefully arbitrate difficult situations, but often determined farmers refused to use peaceful methods. Desperate and assuming relief would not be forthcoming, they used intimidation and force to save farms for their threatened owners.

Foreclosure sales were broken up. A popular tactic was "penny sales," in which crowds saw to it that the only bidders allowed were friends who paid a few cents on the dollar for livestock, implements, or a house, which were then returned to the owner, with the debt settled. Mass marches by association members and supporters led to various farm state legislatures passing mortgage moratorium legislation. Reno led a series of strikes, some of which—as in Iowa and Wisconsin—led to violent confrontations as picket lines were attacked and breached; in Wisconsin a series of strikes (which were continued after Reno ended direct association involvement) were marked by bloody brawls that resulted in deaths, and in Iowa attempts to stop farm goods from coming to market led to the burning of railroad bridges. Such violence and other association activity that stretched from the fall of 1932 into the late spring of 1933 led governors—even those sympathetic to Reno's organization—to feel compelled to call out the National Guard to deal with civil disobedience.

After FDR's inaugural in March 1933, Reno and his organization, which initially had continued the bloody strike in Wisconsin, threatened to strike elsewhere unless Congress passed farm relief. The threatened strike was averted when in early May 1933 Congress passed the Agricultural Adjustment Act. It quickly and dramatically raised farm prices by limiting agricultural production. The legislation did not satisfy Reno, but he grudgingly supported it. However, he eventually became disillusioned with the president, and especially his secretary of agriculture, Henry A. Wallace (1888–1965), whom he dubbed "Lord Corn Wallace." Apart from policy differences (Reno continued to believe New Deal agriculture policies shortchanged farmers), he and Wallace, although fellow Iowans, personally did not like each other. As farmers were won over by the New Deal, Reno's power quickly subsided, especially given his criticism of the New Deal. Newspaper coverage of a speech he gave was headlined "Milo Reno in General Denunciation of Everything."

By 1935 he had become an ally of FDR's most outspoken opponents, such as Louisiana senator Huey Long (1893–1935) and Father Charles Coughlin (1891–1979), and supported organization of a third political party to challenge FDR. Reno died on May 5, 1936. A master public speaker who knew when and how to use evangelical invective, he benefited from the failures of the Hoover administration's agricultural policies. Those failures gave Reno, who throughout his life had supported the underdog, an opportunity to appear on the national scene. Desperate farmers appreciated his obvious zeal in support on their behalf. Reno had long campaigned, even during the ostensibly good times of the 1920s, to alleviate their plight. Circumstance allowed him to bring that plight and himself briefly to national attention at a key moment in U.S. history.

Further Reading

Dyson, Lowell K. "The Farm Holiday Movement." PhD dissertation, Columbia University, 1968.

White, Roland A. *Milo Reno, Farmers Union Pioneer.* New York: Arno Press, 1975.

Smoot-Hawley Tariff (1930)

Passed by Congress in June 1930, the Smoot-Hawley Tariff resulted in the imposition of very high tariff duties on imports to the United States. This legislation, popularly known by the names of its chief sponsors in the Senate and the House, raised duties in many instances to their highest rates in American history. Initially designed to aid American farmers who after World War I suffered economically, the Smoot-Hawley tariff legislation as finally enacted reflected the significant input of numerous lobbyists for special interests in manufacturing, and did much less for American agriculture than originally intended. The costly duties invoked by the Smoot-Hawley tariff legislation began to be felt just as the Great Depression impacted on nations around the world and led, for instance, to tit-for-tat trade policies affecting the United States as well as various other countries. Such policies had a deleterious effect on international trade and the global economy.

While much of American industry overcame the economic downturn that marred life in the United States after World War I, large parts of American agriculture continued to suffer as prices for most farm commodities continued to decline. During the mid-1920s congressional attempts to aid farmers failed; either the proposed legislation did not pass, or the president vetoed it. The Smoot-Hawley Tariff had its genesis in proposals to protect the American farmer. During the 1928 campaign for the presidency, Republican candidate Herbert Hoover (1874–1964) promised tariff aid to the suffering farmers. After he and the Republican Party won overwhelmingly, Hoover called for a special session of Congress (which began in April 1929) to provide farm relief in part by increasing tariff rates on agricultural goods imported into the United States and for a decrease in the rates on industrial imports, a reduction that was assumed should lead to lower prices for the goods farmers utilized. However, what began as a moderate downward revision of tariffs became an extremely protectionist effort.

Willis C. Hawley (1864–1941), a veteran Republican congressman (1907–1933) from Oregon and chair of the House Ways and Means Committee, supported what was known as "tariff equality" (i.e., reducing the duties on imported industrial goods and raising the rates charged on imported farm goods). After extensive hearings and long debates the House passed a bill in May 1929, which thanks to extensive lobbying by special interests tilted the proposed tariff revisions, according to one history of what took place, "nearly as much toward higher duties on manufactured goods as it increased duties on agricultural products."

The Senate sponsor of a tariff revision bill was another Republican veteran, Reed Smoot (1862–1941), then chair of the Senate Finance Committee, who

served as a Utah senator from 1903 to 1933. However, the Senate bill was ultimately shaped by Joseph Grundy (1863–1961), a textile manufacturer, banker,
head of the Pennsylvania Manufacturer's Association, and consummate lobbyist
who at the time was a Pennsylvania senator (1929–1930); he believed that anyone
who made a contribution to the party in return was entitled to higher tariff rates
protecting his interests. He put together a powerful coalition that rewrote the
Senate bill and in that version raised rates on many items between 50 and 100
percent of the already high previous tariff schedules. Roosevelt later charged the
Smoot-Hawley bill that was enacted should have been dubbed "the Grundy tariff."

Senate consideration of the House bill had lasted until March 1930; debate
was intense, and limited bipartisan support was achieved only after some
Democratic senators obtained protection for their constituents' interests (e.g.,
the textile industry). The Senate version, which resulted from a series of deals
brokered by Grundy between senators who spoke for various special interest
groups, contained more than 1,200 changes; generally these were an upward
revision of rates from the House bill, and in many instances raised rates to
record levels. The joint conference version of the bill in mid-June 1929 narrowly
passed the Senate and easily passed the House.

Once it seemed clear that the Senate and House in conference reconciling
their efforts would produce a tariff revision bill that dramatically raised rates
there was a hue and cry that demanded President Hoover not sign the proposed
legislation or exercise his veto. Among the critics was Henry Ford (1863–1947)
who went to the White House to convince Hoover to veto the bill, and J. P.
Morgan partner Thomas W. Lamont (1879–1948), who asserted the president
should not sign "the asinine Hawley-Smoot tariff." Hoover in May 1930 was
sent a petition to ignore the bill signed by over 1,000 economists, including
such eminent ones as Frank Taussig (1859–1941), credited with "creating the
foundations of modern trade theory," and Irving Fisher (1867–1947), who has
been called "the greatest economist the United States ever produced." One of
the organizers of the petition later recalled that while subsequently all these
economists diverged dramatically over issues of monetary policy and deficit
financing, they were "practically one in their belief that the Hawley-Smoot bill
was an iniquitous piece of legislation."

Hoover faced extraordinary pressure from both sides on the pending legislation. On the one hand, signing the legislation was consistent with Republican
orthodoxy, which insisted that a high tariff was necessary to protect American
businesses from foreign competition. On the other hand, Hoover had promised
the beleaguered farmers while running for president in 1928 that he would protect them from foreign imports by supporting a protective tariff on agricultural
goods. Despite whatever reservations about the final version that Hoover may
have had, on June 17, 1930, he signed the Smoot-Hawley bill into law, raising
tariff rates on over 20,000 imported goods.

While the Hawley-Smoot tariff legislation did not cause the Great Depression as many academics and politicians have charged over the years, it certainly made the situation worse, adding, as *The Economist* put it, "poison to the emptying well of global trade." Already during the prosperous 1920s the League of Nations had discussed a "tariff truce." When Smoot-Hawley was in the offing, 23 of the nations with whom the United States traded protested against the proposed higher rates. Smoot-Hawley erected significantly high tariff barriers, which even without the impact of the Great Depression stagnated global trade; imports to the United States were discouraged as by the beginning of 1932 the average American tariff on dutiable items was over 50 percent. Between 1929 and 1932 American imports fell precipitously; from Europe they fell from $1.3 billion to about $390 million. Those countries who during World War I had borrowed heavily from the United States bitterly complained they could not pay their war debts if unusually high tariffs restricted their sales in America.

As many economists and other critics of Smoot-Hawley had predicted, other countries retaliated by raising tariff rates on American goods. It became increasingly difficult for the United States to expand its markets abroad as these countries raised their rates on American goods. For instance, consider the impact of the tariff legislation on two neighbors of the United States. Canada, America's biggest trading partner when Hoover was elected president, warned that retaliation would follow the adoption of Smoot-Hawley, and the Canadian government imposed higher duties on American goods, lowered duties on British imports, and turned to that country for various goods that used to be bought from the United States. In the case of Cuba, Smoot-Hawley gave special protection to American sugar producers: the high rates imposed on Cuban sugar imports by their lobbying made it almost impossible to sell that product in the United States.

To many American policymakers—then and later—the Hawley-Smoot tariff rates, generally the highest in the 20th century, symbolized the dangers of the protectionist trade policies of the early 1930s and are seen as a folly and a terrible lesson. Beginning with Franklin Roosevelt, American presidents have repudiated the kind of protectionism offered by Smoot-Hawley and have increasingly supported free trade policies.

Further Reading

Irwin, Douglas. *Peddling Protectionism: Smoot-Hawley and the Great Depression.* Princeton, NJ: Princeton University Press, 2011.

"Protectionism: The Battle of Smoot-Hawley." *The Economist,* December 18, 2008. http://www.economist.com/node/12798595/print [accessed March 12, 2013].

Schattschneider, E. E. *Politics, Pressure, and the Tariff.* New York: Prentice-Hall, 1935.

Unemployed Councils

Created by the American Communist Party (CPUSA) in the early days of the Great Depression to mobilize the jobless and relief clients, the Unemployed Councils initially found considerable support, especially among the urban jobless, as the Communist-led groups fought evictions and organized demonstrations to increase the inadequate relief offered the out of work by municipal and state authorities as well as various private charitable agencies. But the CPUSA's sectarian stance was said to follow the iconoclastic policies dictated by the Comintern, the supposedly autonomous body in control of all Communist parties outside the Soviet Union. In reality it followed the guidelines laid out by that country's dictator, Joseph Stalin (1879–1953).

These guidelines enunciated in 1928 at the Comintern's Sixth World Congress proved prescient as they announced that a "third period" had arrived in the development of capitalism since the 1917 Bolshevik Revolution in Russia (the first period which ran from 1917 to 1924 had been marked by revolutionary offensives against capitalistic structures; the second period, 1924–1928, was defined as a period of partial, temporary stabilization of capitalism). The third period would mark the death agony of capitalism (that of course is what seems to have happened after 1929) and the radicalization of the masses. In leading them Communists could not cooperate with liberal or Left organizations for they were seen as "enemies of the working class."

In pursuit of that policy American Communists gave up their strategy of "boring from within" the U.S. labor movement and organized the Trade Union Unity League (TUUL), which embarked on a policy of "dual unionism." Among the TUUL's stated purposes was "organize the unemployed." Fortuitous circumstances allowed the TUUL to translate that announced goal into fact: the first TUUL convention took place August 31–September 1, 1929, and the collapse of the American economy began about the same time. The spirit of workers used to the prosperity of the 1920s had not yet become dulled as hard times dragged on, and the unemployed responded to Communist calls of "Fight—Don't Starve."

The CPUSA until the mid-1930s remained a small sectarian group, few in numbers, variously estimated at less than 15,000. Many more did join the party, but disillusioned by its Moscow-dictated policies many new members left quickly. The Unemployed Council proved no exception. Working initially through the TUUL, Communists organized the jobless into various local Pujo Committees. Communist organizers then and later sought out the jobless wherever the involuntarily idle gathered. During the early 1930s Communist Unemployed Council organizers could be found in parks, on breadlines, outside of soup kitchens, by flophouses, among the groups loitering at factory gates or waiting in crowded relief stations. Communists for a while successfully organized and expanded the Pujo Committee, and led marches, protests, and demonstrations, all demanding that something be done for the unemployed.

In urban areas, organization was often based on a neighborhood, a block, a large apartment house, or sometimes even along language lines (e.g., a Yiddish-speaking unit); in smaller towns or less populated areas organization was more difficult and attempted regionally. The councils' claimed numbers are unreliable; the turnout at demonstrations did not represent a stable membership but a hard core of Communists and ad hoc protesters; while the demands often were uniform they were rarely coordinated. An exception was the "International Day for Struggle against World-Wide Unemployment" which took place across the world on March 6, 1930, to protest "exploitation of the unemployed" and demanded "an end to hunger." It was organized by the Comintern, which encouraged Communist Parties everywhere to utilize their resources to make "the Day" memorable, and it was, especially in the United States.

There, because no provision for unemployment insurance existed, a key demand was "work or wages." Demonstrations took place all across the United States in almost every important industrial and commercial center, except in the South, where, as in Atlanta, Jim Crow laws were used to stop any marches or other demonstrations. Many were orderly uneventful affairs, even in Chicago where police violence was anticipated. In other areas there was significant violence, as in Washington, D.C., where police used tear gas to break up a protest in front of the White House. The most violent clash came in New York City, where police rioted, striking out indiscriminately at both thousands of demonstrators and hundreds of bystanders, many just sunning themselves in Union Square, the site of the protest.

The CPUSA made good use of the publicity that the events of March 6 produced. It cut through the media chatter of officials harping on a quick recovery. The violence in various U.S. cities added to the notoriety garnered by the more peaceful, less noteworthy events, all of which attested to the first large-scale attention to the relentless increase in unemployment and the inadequacies of jobless relief. At the end of March 1930 a Communist-organized "First Preliminary National Conference on Unemployment" met in New York City, supposedly bringing together 215 delegates from 19 industries in 13 states representing millions of unemployed. Speakers, mostly CPUSA members active in unemployed work, declared that the councils could stand independent of the TUUL and called for a meeting to establish them as a national organization.

Held in Chicago on July 4–5, 1930, it transformed the TUUL groups into the "Unemployed Council of the U.S.A.," whose main task was "immediate organization of the unemployed." The CPUSA leadership hoped the local councils under the umbrella of the national organization would serve as "transmission belts" to bring new members into the party. However, the day-to-day actions of the local councils did not serve as the anticipated "meaty bait." The national organization maintained its existence through various formats and names until 1936. It did conduct two "hunger marches" to Washington, D.C., in December 1931 and 1932 in support of its programs of aid to the unemployed. The brutal police treatment of the 1932 marchers was unconscionable. Neither march accomplished much besides gaining some not always favorable publicity. The turnouts for both, which claimed to represent thousands, were poor; the hundreds who marched for the Communists were dwarfed by the thousands who came to Washington, D.C., with the Bonus Army or with Father Cox.

The protests and demonstrations by the local councils did help the unemployed. Various local councils—for the most part in urban areas like Chicago and New York, and in manufacturing centers in the Midwest and the Pacific Northwest—did succeed in halting evictions of jobless tenants and home owners, in cutting through red tape at relief stations, in halting the turning off of water mains and gas lines, and in other ways aiding the out of work. But the councils could not sustain the support gained. The unemployed could not grasp why New York City Communist council leaders, under third period discipline, urged protest marches against soup kitchens organized by non-CPUSA agencies. Nor did the unemployed no matter how beholden to the councils want to march in "Defense of the Soviet Union." Ultimately the councils could not compete with other unemployed organizations that had less political ends.

With the advent of the New Deal the councils became irrelevant, having outlived their usefulness to the unemployed. As the federal government began to provide assistance to the jobless, protests at local relief stations proved unproductive. Moreover, most of the unemployed rejected radicalism and were not attracted by the Unemployed Councils. CPUSA membership did not much increase after their creation. They demonstrate both the potential and the limitations of radical activism. The Unemployed Councils did not realize the CPUSA's goals in terms of serving as "bait," but especially on the local level the councils did prove to be very helpful to the unemployed at a time when little was being done for them. It is interesting to note that even as the local councils faded into nonexistence, the national organization in its various guises existing solely on paper lobbied for national legislation in support of various Communist social goals.

Further Reading

Klehr, Harvey. *The Heyday of American Communism*. New York: Basic Books, 1985.

Leab, Daniel J. "United We Eat: The Creation of the Unemployed Councils." *Labor History* (Fall 1957): 300–316.

• 12 •

GREAT DEPRESSION, 1933–1939

Vanessa May

Franklin D. Roosevelt (1881–1945), on the day of his inauguration as president, faced the greatest economic calamity in American history. The economic downturn that began in 1929 had become a severe collapse by March 1933. A fragile banking system, hampered by a continuing unrealistic commitment to the international gold standard, had demonstrated conclusively that the nation's banks could not deal with the steep economic decline that wracked the United States.

This decline shocked the American public, for the Depression affected everyday life in the United States, resulting in tremendous suffering for Americans. President Hoover (1874–1964) had done what he assumed could and should be done to stem the crisis (more than any previous president had undertaken till then). And his elected successor, Roosevelt, despite some of his actions as governor of New York in attempting to provide aid for those affected by the downturn and a number of his campaign promises for reform and relief, did not seem all that different from contemporary politicians. He had won the election overwhelmingly because the alternative was Hoover and his failed policies.

The severe hard times continued through the 1930s. In contrast to Hoover's distant, somewhat cheerless, formal stiffness, Roosevelt's jaunty, pragmatic, seemingly ceaseless exuberance tended—even when during his second term a slowly reviving economy collapsed almost overnight—to distance the most dismal events from people's hopes for a better America. The unrelenting critics of both the Right and the Left failed to gain purchase with him.

When Franklin Delano Roosevelt (dubbed FDR by the media) entered office on Saturday, March 4, 1933, many Americans doubted the economy would ever rebound. They thought the U.S. economy could not create enough new jobs to support its people. Even FDR had doubts. It seemed "probable" to him, he said, that "our physical economic plant will not expand in the future at the same rate at which it . . . expanded in the past." To FDR and to what was probably the majority of the American people, the very future of capitalism in the United States seemed to be at stake.

In his inaugural address, Roosevelt attempted to reassure the struggling American people and raise their flagging spirits. He declared "the only thing we have to fear is fear itself," a statement that roused the crowd attending the event and the country at large. To meet the unprecedented crisis, to restore America, the new president promised "action and action now," pledging that "if the national emergency" continued "critical" he would ask Congress for "broad executive powers to wage a war against the emergency." And he did just that; right from his first days as president he pursued an unprecedented federal involvement in the economy.

Calling his agenda a "New Deal," FDR and his administration created a long list of federal agencies aimed at providing "relief, recovery, and reform." Historians, economists, and others have long argued about the character of the New Deal's agenda. Some argue that the New Deal was a radical departure from all previous efforts to assist the American poor and the under-classes, those who were in FDR's words "at the bottom of the pyramid."

Other scholars and many outside the academy argue that the New Deal represented a continuation of older Progressive reform traditions. Still others argue that New Deal policies served as a liberal compromise with capitalism and a turning away from more aggressive efforts to restructure the American class system. And there are those like Newt Gingrich, who maintain "business confidence is the key to economic expansion and that each step of the New Deal was a further blow to business confidence."

While there is no unanimity of opinion about just what the New Deal stood for, these commentators all agree, however, that the New Deal was a watershed moment in U.S. history, changing Americans' expectations both pro and con about government action in hard times and ushering in a new era focused on consumption and government spending as the twin engines of prosperity. The old shibboleths such as balancing the budget were not discarded, but they were ignored priorities.

However one views the New Deal policies formulated by FDR and his advisors, during the Depression years after 1933 these policies dictated the administration's response. And while these policies may—as some argue—have served to further the downturn, they did in the main contribute to the alleviation of the suffering of the jobless and their families whose very existence had outrun their personal resources and many of the private and public agencies geared to help them.

Stabilizing the Banking System

FDR first moved to stabilize the nation's banking system. Banking in America had always been a risky business. Soon after the stock market crashed in

1929, bank failures began to snowball. In 1930, 1,345 banks failed. Panicked depositors trying to withdraw their funds before they disappeared increasingly caused runs on financial institutions. As a result, more banks failed, over 2,000 collapsed in 1931, followed by nearly 1,500 in 1932.

America's entire financial system seemed to be imploding. In order to stop the runs taking place at financial institutions, state-imposed bank holidays spread across the United States. Responding to fears about the safety of banks, Americans reacted as they had traditionally and began to hoard gold; at the same time millions of dollars of gold were taken out of the United States by panicky foreign investors and shipped to Europe. The situation demanded immediate action.

During the last days of the interregnum between administrations, Hoover's secretary of the treasury, Ogden Mills (1884–1937), who in 1931 had replaced the long-serving Mellon, and his key staff had been working feverishly with a group of FDR's advisors, including Roosevelt's appointment to head the Treasury, William Woodin (1868–1934), a flexible business executive, to sort out possible options, to determine their legal underpinnings, and to draft the necessary legislation. Raymond Moley (1886–1975), a key FDR advisor, recalled that those working on the legislation "had forgotten to be Republicans or Democrats. . . . We were just a bunch of men trying to save the banking system."

On Sunday, March 5, the day after his inauguration, Roosevelt by executive order halted gold transactions and declared a four-day national banking holiday to go into effect on Monday, March 6. These actions, designed to staunch the bleeding of bank deposits, were a first step to restoring the nation's banking system. FDR also called Congress into special session to begin on Thursday, March 9. Its hundred days' session would be a period of frenzied policy making and a blizzard of legislation.

Among the first actions of that Congress was a vote on solutions worked on by the Mills-Woodin group, which resulted in the Emergency Banking Act. Because its final version became available only on the day of the special session's first meeting, the Government Printing Office did not have enough time to provide Congress copies of the proposed legislation, and the bill had to be read aloud in the House by the Alabama Democrat Henry Steagall (1873–1943), chair of its Banking and Currency Committee. Despite this remarkable procedure, representatives, anxious about what had become a shutdown of the nation's economy, shouted out "Vote, Vote" and the bill passed unanimously after only 38 minutes of debate.

The Senate took a few hours longer to pass the legislation because maverick senator Huey Long (1893–1935) attempted to amend the bill to assist what he called "the little banks at the forks of the creeks." Virginia senator Carter Glass (1858–1946), a staunch fiscal conservative Democrat proud to be seen as one of the fathers of the Federal Reserve system, and the crusty chair of the Senate

Banking Committee guiding this bill through that body, vociferously derided Long. These exchanges took time, but by 8:00 that night the bill passed with only seven opposing votes (Long voted for the measure; the naysayers were Progressives, supporters of nationalizing the banks who felt that the bill did not go far enough in establishing government control over the banking system that had failed the American people).

FDR signed the Emergency Banking Act into law at 8:30 PM that evening. The entire legislative process had taken only a little more than six hours, from the time that the bill had been presented to the House of Representatives to President Roosevelt signing the bill.

The act gave the president broad discretionary powers over gold and foreign currency exchanges, gave the Federal Reserve Board broader powers to issue currency to ensure there was enough paper money to go around, and gave the Reconstruction Finance Corporation (created by the Hoover administration) more power to buy stock in state and federal banks in order to make sure they had enough capital to continue functioning.

Finally, the act, confirming FDR's order to close the banks, gave Treasury officials the power to supervise their reopening. Later that night, making use of the newly enacted legislation, FDR extended the national bank holiday for a few days so that Treasury officials would have more time to differentiate between what FDR termed "sound banks" and those that were not.

Hoping to reassure Americans and to explain the complicated legislation, Roosevelt on Sunday, March 12, spoke to a radio audience of millions, discussing the nature of the banking crisis and the various actions that the government had taken. FDR had tossed aside a more complex draft prepared for him and spoke to his listeners in jargon-free plain language and in such familiar terms that Will Rogers said even bankers could now understand the system.

FDR, whose radio style displayed a warm firm voice and an informal friendly manner, had honed his radio skills while governor of New York when, because of the unbridled hostility of the upstate Republican press, he had to take to the airwaves. His talk about the banking legislation had been introduced by CBS announcer Robert Trout (1909–2000), who told listeners that the "President wants to come into your home . . . for a little fireside chat." The term lived on to describe the many such broadcasts FDR made during his presidency as he discussed his programs with a radio audience and worked to win over public opinion.

Millions had listened as he said "my friends, and I know you are all my friends, I want to talk with the people of the United States about banking." He explained the need for the national bank holiday, indicated that some banks would open the next day because they had been "found to be alright" and more would open in the days after that, and he assured "you, my friends, that it is safer to keep your money in a reopened bank than it is to keep it under the mattress."

His talk has been described as "a psychological masterpiece." As over the next days the banks reopened, Americans responding to Roosevelt's call to arms deposited more cash than they withdrew, and the banking system slowly found stable ground—notwithstanding its continued difficulties because of the Depression. Almost overnight most of the barter and self-help groups, organized by the jobless for mutual assistance during the interregnum, went away, as did the substitute currency, script, etc., that had been issued in order to deal with the collapse of banking facilities. The unemployed pressure groups that had been organized, mostly by radical groups such as the Communist Party, also began to lose their raison d'être as the federal government stepped in not only to regulate banking but to finance relief.

With the immediate banking crisis averted, Roosevelt and Congress set out to reform the way the nation's banks operated. The Banking Act of 1933 (commonly known as Glass-Steagall, for the senator and representative who were its congressional sponsors), a key piece of financial regulation, passed in mid-June over the vehement opposition of bankers; the legislation worked to correct the worst banking practices that had caused bank failures both before and after 1929. Glass-Steagall required banks to keep more money on hand and separated investment houses of their banking function.

President Franklin D. Roosevelt signs the Banking Bill into law, March 9, 1933. (AP Photo)

This division was made easier because of the well-publicized Senate hearings began during the last days of the Hoover administration, at which various eminent bankers and heads of investment houses testified. The relentless, intelligent probing by committee counsel Ferdinand Pecora (1881–1971), a former New York City assistant district attorney, exposed in detail the shady practices of such well-regarded bank heads as Charles Mitchell (1877–1955) of National City Bank, who when faced with financial difficulties obtained a substantial interest-free loan from his bank, and Albert Wiggin (1858–1951) of Chase National Bank, who sold short the shares of his own institution.

Testimony elicited by Pecora showed that the larger American banks, far from providing average depositors with prudent advice or sound financial instruments, pressured them into hasty, risky, ill-judged, speculative deals. Banks whose executives claimed to act with probity and maintained they acted in the welfare of customers relying on their advice proved to be sleazy operators who dumped overinflated bonds and stocks sold for the benefit of the banks' investment arms and who did not hesitate to rig prices. Pecora's interrogations also showed that bankers through questionable if legal practices avoided paying income tax and offered lucrative deals to insiders who purchased securities at prices well below those charged the public.

Glass-Steagall addressed some of the situations Pecora had brought to the public's attention. Besides requiring more transparency and the separation of commercial and investment banking, other provisions of Glass-Steagall allowed the Federal Reserve to set interest rates paid on savings accounts and to create the Federal Deposit Insurance Corporation (FDIC) to guarantee deposits in the nation's banks and assume control over a bank's closure if it failed. FDR had initially opposed this guarantee, believing it might be unworkable. The heads of various large banks opposed creation of the FDIC because they did not want to aid the nation's smaller, weaker banks.

Coverage to begin on January 1, 1934, was $2,599 per deposit, and raised to $5,000 six months later, to be paid the FDIC from funds assessed covered banks. The FDIC would also undertake inspections of these banks. The FDIC's impact has been described as "earth-shaking"; bank failures in the United States became a rarity. The new system reassured depositors and ended bank runs. In contrast to past decades, in 1934 only 61 banks failed.

Other financial regulations later strengthened these reforms. The Banking Act of 1935 centralized the power of the Federal Reserve, made its Board of Governors subject to Senate confirmation, and created an Open Market Committee (consisting of the governors and representatives of the Federal Reserve banks) to control the regulation of credit.

Glass-Steagall and the 1935 Banking Act highlight the difference between Hoover's outlook on regulation of the economy and Roosevelt's. Hoover believed government and business could and should work together to solve American economic problems. He sincerely believed in self-regulation and strongly opposed any legislation resulting in government intervention. Roosevelt and many in his administration, on the other hand, believed government was the only entity powerful enough to regulate the economy (and to alleviate the distress).

Despite the worries of business leaders and bankers about Roosevelt's commitment to economic interventionism, FDR proved to be a political moderate as well as a pragmatist. He did not try to nationalize the banks, nor would private industry be allowed to consolidate branch banks into a national banking monopoly. Instead, FDR attempted to preserve and improve the banking system already in place.

One manifestation of this attitude can be seen in his administration's response to the housing crisis caused by the Depression, which had resulted at one point in 10 percent of the nation's housing facing foreclosure and during the first half of 1933 led to 1,000 foreclosures a day. Through the Home Owners Loan Corporation (HOLC), established in June 1933, mortgage lending in the United States was dramatically transformed from short-term to long-term loans.

The HOLC took short-term mortgages, then typical of such instruments, off a bank's books if they were not performing well and replaced them with 15-year self-amortizing mortgages, investing over $3 billion in the American housing market; in effect by bailing out the banks, middle-class homeowners, especially those most directly affected by the economic downturn, had the opportunity to refinance through the HOLC. Between 1933 and 1935 the HOLC refinanced over one million mortgages. Not only did such refinancing provide a way for a borrower to achieve in time ownership free and clear, but in addition banks issuing mortgages benefited financially and attained renewed confidence.

Curbing Unethical Practices in the Stock Market

FDR's administration did not focus only on regulating banks; other reforms struck deep at the inner workings of the American economy. Before the 1929 stock market crash, there had been various ways to falsely inflate stock prices. Many companies did not publish any financial reports at all or issued reports doctored to improve a company's image. These practices made the stock market extremely volatile as well as inscrutable, if not dangerous, to honest investors.

To curb such practices, FDR instigated the 1934 creation of the Securities and Exchange Commission (SEC). The legislation establishing it (the Securities Exchange Act, passed June 6, 1934) was designed to prevent stock traders from misusing inside information and among other requirements compelled companies listed on public stock exchanges to disclose their financial information publicly and employ independent auditors to corroborate those financial statements. The SEC was created over the bitter objections of American business leaders, one of whom, Richard Whitney (1888–1974), the imperious head of the New York Stock Exchange—ignoring the 1929 crash—asserted that the New York Stock Exchange was a "perfect institution" (he later served a term in prison for his defalcations).

Joseph P. Kennedy (1888–1969), who had been a powerful successful player in the wild market manipulations of the 1920s, became the first SEC chairman. FDR chose him because by virtue of his experiences Kennedy knew the tricks of the trade, and his standing as a successful trader might lessen Wall Street's opposition to the agency. Despite liberal outcries against Kennedy's appointment, during his year-long tenure (1934–1935) he proved a very effective chairman, helping to achieve the business community's acceptance of the SEC and giving its administrative operations a sturdy, successful start.

Leaving the Gold Standard

Most spectacular of all was FDR's move in 1933 to take the United States off the gold standard, which required currencies to be convertible to gold. A country would maintain only so much money in circulation as its gold reserves warranted. Except for a brief hiatus during the Civil War, the United States since the mid-19th century had been on the gold standard; American paper money had been backed by gold held in the federal treasury. The system worked to curb inflation because the price of the U.S. dollar was fixed relative to a set amount of gold. As prices rose in the United States, foreign manufacturers, hoping to earn more for their goods, shipped them to American markets. These goods were paid for in gold-backed currency, thereby depleting the money supply and causing prices to fall.

In a normal economic cycle, the gold standard provided a useful check on inflation, but the Great Depression was no normal economic cycle. One of the hallmarks of the economic emergency caused by the Depression was deflation, or falling consumer and commodity prices. Roosevelt's strategy for the nation's economic recovery essentially rested on creating inflation. He approved massive government spending, which put more money into the economy and would, he hoped, raise prices. This effort was therefore wholly incompatible with the United States remaining on the gold standard.

In April 1933 FDR took the first steps to free the United States from its ties to gold. In his press conference on April 19, 1933, Roosevelt announced that the United States would leave the gold standard but promised that this measure was only temporary; he would work "to get the world as a whole back on some form of the gold standard." The leaders of other nations, particularly in Europe, saw stabilizing currency and exchange rates as a vital step toward global economic recovery and believed both of these aims were best achieved by a return to an international gold standard.

In July 1933 the United States sent delegates to a World Economic Conference held in London with the goal of achieving joint international action to deal with the global effects of the Depression. The world expected to hear them repeat Roosevelt's commitment about a return to the gold standard. Instead, Roosevelt sent a "bombshell" message to the conference, announcing that the United States would neither return to the gold standard nor participate in the conference's aim to set exchange rates between nations. By prioritizing the financial health of his own nation over international commitments, Roosevelt ended the London conference and halted any further talk of international cooperation to solve the economic emergency.

In line with the economic nationalism of his message, FDR continued his program of creating inflation to address the crisis and following the advice of Cornell University economist George F. Warren (1874–1938). The president became convinced that buying large quantities of gold would increase commodity and consumer prices, achieving economy-saving inflation. In October 1933 Roosevelt informed the nation that the RFC would purchase gold at a price fixed by the federal government. Even though the United States had abandoned the gold standard, FDR believed that buying gold could weaken the U.S. dollar by pouring more money into the economy, and would help the Depression's many debtors by enabling them to pay back their debts with inflated currency.

As the scheme unfolded, Roosevelt set the price of gold each morning and its price indeed increased substantially as American currency inflated. But the program did not increase American exports or raise domestic commodity prices. The program finally ended in January 1934 when FDR pegged the price of gold at $35 an ounce—where it remained for years. At the same time the Gold Reserve Act forbade possession of monetary gold (but not gold jewels, etc.) by American citizens, a policy that remained in effect until the 1970s. Manipulating the price of gold was just one way in which FDR enlarged the power of the federal government.

The National Recovery Administration

FDR was also committed to regulating industry, though he hoped it could self-regulate with the assistance of government. Among the raft of bills passed during FDR's first hundred days in office was that in June 1933 establishing the National Recovery Administration (NRA). Designed to revive stagnant

A woman hangs a National Recovery Administration (NRA) poster in a restaurant window to show support for the government program. The NRA was considered the cornerstone of the New Deal and was often controversial in its regulation of industrial codes of competition. (Franklin D. Roosevelt Presidential Library)

industrial production, to encourage business, and to reduce the vast army of unemployed, the NRA legislation allowed suspension of antitrust laws so that business leaders working under the supervision of NRA officials could create "codes of fair competition" that among other goals would end unfair business practices; stimulate the economy by allowing the artificial fixing of prices; and improve wages, hours, and working conditions.

The NRA demonstrated the Roosevelt administration's initial willingness to work with business and industry to rescue the economy. The NRA was hardly the radical reordering of capitalism that the Left advocated. The agency's creators and administrators imagined mistakenly there was a natural harmony between government and business, and allowed business leaders almost free rein in the drafting of codes. Initially popular, thanks to an enormous public relations campaign, the NRA eventually became mired in controversy as the codes proved unworkable and biased toward those who wrote them to their own advantage. The NRA fell far short of its goals and came to an unceremonious end in May 1935 when the Supreme Court declared it unconstitutional on the grounds that the federal government did not have the authority to regulate industry.

Section 7a of the legislation establishing the NRA granted workers the right to bargain collectively, and though it had not worked out as well as expected for labor, this aspect of the NRA was salvaged. Shortly before the Supreme Court struck down the NRA, New York senator Robert F. Wagner (1877–1953), a veteran Democratic supporter of workers and unions, introduced a bill into Congress governing collective bargaining. The National Labor Relations Act (known as the Wagner Act in honor of the man who for years had championed the rights of labor) gave workers the right to bargain collectively with their employers, set up a National Labor Relations Board (NLRB) whose mandate included ensuring management honored unions' right to exist, and barred a long list of "unfair labor practices" including firing workers for joining a union or refusing to bargain with union workers' selected representatives.

Although FDR initially was hesitant about the legislation, he belatedly supported it once the Senate in mid-May 1935 overwhelmingly passed Wagner's bill. The legislation introduced in the House by the long-serving Democratic Massachusetts Congressman William Connery Jr. (1888–1937) passed that body in mid-June. The president signed it into law over strong conservative opposition at the beginning of July 1935. Although the NRA had not survived, the Wagner Act ensured that the federal government would remain involved in the economy by regulating labor.

Recovery, Administrations, and Spending

Regulation, however, was not enough. The country needed recovery as well. The Banking Act of 1933 stabilized banking, but the act had not helped citizens who had no funds to deposit. Tens of thousands still struggled with economic want. Worse still was the psychic cost. Many unemployed considered themselves victims because there seemed to be no logical reason for their suffering. Keeping up appearances became increasingly difficult.

Most Americans believed that without meaningful work their lives were empty. The New Deal kept them from starving, but they felt guilt, shame, desperation, despair, fear, and insecurity. Direct federal spending had substantially improved local and state relief, but many of those who accepted such aid still suffered indignities from the system dispensing it. Blacks suffered disproportionately; in many parts of the United States unemployment for African Americans ran as high as 50 percent. Not uncommon were signs reading "No Jobs for Niggers Until Every White Man Has a Job."

Roosevelt's real innovation in pursuit of economic recovery was massive federal spending. Most early planning centered on the Public Works Administration (PWA) set up by the bill creating the NRA in 1933. The PWA's larger economic purpose was to pump federal dollars into the economy. Supervised by corruption-conscious secretary of the interior Harold Ickes (1874–1952), it spent carefully through state and local governments the vast sums allocated to the agency (initially PWA's budget was $3.3 billion; in 1933 that represented 16.5 percent of federal revenues and 5.9 percent of the nation's gross domestic product).

The PWA ultimately put many unemployed (e.g., engineers, architects, carpenters, plumbers, laborers) to work on a multitude of worthy construction projects such as dams, bridges, post offices, and schools, but Ickes's caution at first led to less "pump priming" than envisaged. Ickes (known as "Honest Harold") authorized projects only after all too thoroughly scrutinizing their legal basis, economic value, and practicality. The PWA, despite its massive budget, pumped less funds than expected into the depressed American economy. Ultimately, the PWA dispersed money throughout the country, commissioning projects in all but three of the nation's 3,071 counties. Still, the PWA made hardly a dent in U.S. unemployment. In 1935, under the supervision of former social worker Harry Hopkins (1890–1946), a close FDR associate, the Works Progress Administration (WPA) was created to supplement the PWA. Representing a much less cautious approach to spending and an even bigger federal investment in the economy (the WPA sucked up $4.88 billion, or about 6.7 percent of the 1935 gross domestic product), it quickly put many long-term unemployed to work. Together the payrolls of the PWA and the WPA were the largest in the nation, far outstripping those in private industry.

The WPA, created in April 1935, was committed to work relief. The jobless that the agency engaged had to pass a means test, and they were paid a thinly disguised dole (a "security wage"—a prevailing hourly rate for reduced hours of work). Geared to manual labor, a significant portion of its efforts were make-work, but

Works Progress Administration poster shows a blacksmith at work encouraging laborers to work for America. The WPA was the most comprehensive agency of Franklin D. Roosevelt's New Deal, providing jobs and income to the unemployed during the Great Depression. (Library of Congress)

during its existence the WPA also built highways and roads, constructed and repaired public buildings, and established and operated community and recreation centers. The WPA also hired writers, actors, artists, and musicians to apply their skills for the good of the nation.

The PWA and WPA represented a major intervention by the federal government in the economy, but they were hardly Roosevelt's only efforts on this front. The New Deal early on in a flurry of legislative and executive action created an "alphabet soup" of agencies and administrations, all with their own acronyms and all funded by the federal government in attempts to alleviate the ills of a sick economy.

On the advice of Hopkins, the president in November 1933 had initiated the Civil Works Administration (CWA). Its billion-dollar budget went toward employing upward of four million workers on projects, some make-work, others producing 400 airports and 200,000 miles of road. An emergency work-relief program, the CWA, designed to cushion the jobless during the winter of 1933–1934, was terminated in March 1934 by a nervous FDR, still hopeful that an upturn would substantially reduce unemployment and concerned that work relief would "become a habit" dulling the spirit of the country.

In May 1933 Congress passed the Agricultural Adjustment Act to help troubled farmers, who were among those hardest hit by the crisis. The legislation cited "the present acute emergency" but focused on an earlier prosperous World War I era as a basis for guaranteeing farmers a basic price for their products in return for a reduction in production to be paid for by a tax on processors of agricultural goods. The legislation left such details as the mechanics of benefit payments, reduction of acreage, limitation of animals, and amount of tax to be paid and by whom to an Agricultural Adjustment Agency (AAA), controlled by the president.

The act allowed FDR through the AAA to stabilize falling agricultural prices by using federal money to pay farmers to decrease the market supply of farm products. In a time of serious want this meant plowing under cotton, destroying wheat, and killing off piglets in order to avoid a glut and to stabilize prices (a paradoxical situation played up by the AAA's critics). Apart from the usual administrative drawbacks marking such federal centralization of authority, there were some unusual aspects to the AAA's mission: mules long trained to avoid stepping on cotton plants balked when used for plowing them up.

The AAA was one of several programs that in 1933 and afterward reached out to various groups of Americans in diverse ways; they all had in common their pursuit of relief and recovery through massive federal investment in the economy. FDR approved in May 1933 the Tennessee Valley Authority (TVA), a federally owned corporation that sponsored a costly plan of social engineering in some 80,000 square miles along the Tennessee River that included parts of

Alabama, Georgia, Kentucky, North Carolina, Mississippi, and Tennessee as part of the TVA's stated goals of achieving flood control as well as agricultural and industrial development.

In contrast to the TVA, which came under serious attack, the Civilian Conservation Corps (CCC) was one of the New Deal's most lauded (and successful) programs. Established in April 1933 and ended in 1942 as the country mobilized for war, it put young men, aged 17 to 24, whose families were on relief rolls, to work on projects to conserve the nation's natural resources. They lived in camps run by army officers and performed tasks that included building shelters for wildlife, planting trees, and fighting forest fires. The government paid them $30 a month, $22 of which was sent directly to the young workers' families. CCC programs gave the nation's youth dispirited by the Depression hope and useful work. FDR's "Tree Army" built an admirable record: for instance, of all the forest planting, public or private, undertaken in American history by 1942, more than half had been done by the CCC.

During the Roosevelt administration the federal government for the first time began to provide substantial direct aid to American jobless. In 1933, Congress at the prodding of FDR appropriated $500 million to fund the Federal Emergency Relief Administration (FERA), which through the RFC gave government grants to states to distribute relief to the unemployed (Hoover had been willing only to lend funds to the states). Hopkins served as Federal Emergency Relief Administrator.

In August 1935 Congress passed the Social Security Act, legislation that ensured retired workers a basic income and the jobless some kind of unemployment compensation. Social Security as enacted failed to set up a national system or national standards, as it did not reach all Americans. It left out farmworkers and domestic servants, and because workers had to contribute a percentage of their earnings (admittedly limited), it became a regressive tax burden for the poorer among them. Federal old-age benefits (even if not paid out until 1941) as well as federal grants to the states for such groups as the blind and dependent children were costly.

Taxes

With such programs increasing government spending, FDR also increased federal revenue. In August 1935 Congress passed a revenue act raising income taxes on the more well-to-do. FDR in the face of the continuing difficulties faced by the average American as the Depression dragged on called for steeper taxes to combat what he called "the unjust concentration of wealth and economic power." Sometimes referred to as the Wealth Tax Act, this legislation raised rates on incomes over $50,000 and added new brackets for taxes on incomes over $1 million, which went from 63 percent to as high as 79 percent. Estate, dividend, and corporate taxes also went up.

Such legislation answered calls for the government to use income redistribution to finance recovery. Contemporary critics of FDR charged he was pandering to Huey Long and Father Charles Coughlin (1891–1979), whose followings had increased as the hard times continued. In 1936, Congress at the behest of the administration enacted legislation taxing corporations that hoarded profits rather than distributing them as dividends or wages.

If imposition of these taxes was to raise revenues by an attempt to "Soak the Rich" it failed. Probably less than 100 millionaires were seriously affected, and contemporary estimates held that the new taxes would raise just about $250 million, a very small sum in the face of the massive public spending that FDR continued to hope would help America out of the Depression.

Cutting Spending and the "Roosevelt Recession"

FDR's spending, however, was not without controversy. Economic and political orthodoxy had always held that a balanced federal budget was the key to a healthy economy. Hoover's allegiance to this belief had stopped him from enacting more robust public spending programs in the Depression's first years. Even FDR was uncomfortable with a federal budget deficit for any long period of time.

In the first 100 days of his administration, even while encouraging inflation and enacting expensive government programs, FDR cut the budget by some $500 million, closing government agencies, lowering the pay of civil servants and other government workers, even cutting pension payouts to veterans. As FDR spent what to most Depression-era Americans must have seemed staggering sums, he was careful to note that the funding came out of an "emergency budget" created specifically to deal with the economic crisis. FDR insisted he was committed to keeping the "regular" federal budget balanced.

During 1935 and the run-up to the 1936 presidential election the economy seemed to improve. FDR had good reason to hope his cautious strategy was bearing positive results. The gross national product soared to $88 billion in 1935 compared to just $73 billion in 1933. Positive signs continued to appear into 1936. Unemployment, although still massive, shrank as millions of workers found private or government employment. In 1936 the gross national product reached nearly $100 billion.

In the first months of 1937, after Roosevelt had overwhelmingly won reelection, the economy seemed to gain further strength. Although the unemployment rate remained high, hovering around 12 percent, all signs seemed to point to economic recovery. By mid-1937 the Federal Reserve's index of industrial production exceeded that of 1929. National income during the first eight months of 1937 ran at an annualized rate that if it continued would double that of 1929. Tax revenues were up. Prices were rising, having increased by more than a third since FDR took office.

Many economic historians, however they view the New Deal, agree its effectiveness was limited because FDR did not spend enough federal money. New Deal spending amounted to less than 6 percent of the gross national product between 1933 and 1936. And while FDR did spend money, many states trimmed their budgets, thereby undermining the Roosevelt administration's drive toward economic expansion. Yet Roosevelt looking at the economy in early 1937 could assume the emergency seemed to have passed.

The president and many of his advisors such as Secretary of the Treasury Henry Morgenthau (1891–1967) believed that it was time to move the federal budget into the black. Moreover, a bipartisan conservative coalition had begun to form in Congress. Outraged by what they saw as Roosevelt's squandering of public monies, they pressured the president to cut the budget. It was time, as Morgenthau put it, to "strip off the bandages, throw away the crutches" and let the economy "stand on its own two feet." FDR and his allies in Congress began to strip the federal budget. In 1937 government spending dipped to $9.6 billion from $10.3 billion a year earlier. The budgets for the PWA and the WPA shriveled.

These cuts, combined with the regressive Social Security tax that went into effect in January 1937 as well as high interest rates, spelled disaster for the economy and the American people. In August 1937 the steepest drop in American industrial production ever recorded took place. In October the stock market crashed once again, eventually losing 80 percent of its value. The fallout in the wider economy was swift and brutal. Relief rolls in industrial

As President Franklin D. Roosevelt's secretary of the treasury from 1934 to 1945, Henry Morgenthau worked to stabilize the value of the dollar during the Great Depression and oversaw the raising of the capital necessary to win World War II. (Library of Congress)

cities like Detroit expanded fourfold; corporate profits fell by nearly 80 percent. By early 1938 unemployment had crept up toward 20 percent.

This severe downturn, the first since Roosevelt's inauguration, was eagerly labeled by his critics "the Roosevelt Recession." Many of FDR's advisors were despondent about the turn of events. Marriner Eccles (1894–1977), chairman of the Federal Reserve, worried that "the New Deal and all it stands for is in danger of being discredited." Early New Dealer A. A. Berle (1895–1971) concluded, "the economic situation begins to look like a major recession." Maury Maverick (1895–1954), a voluble Democratic supporter of FDR and the New Deal in the House lamented, "We have pulled all the rabbits out of the hat, and there are no more rabbits. . . . We are a confused, bewildered group of people."

Some in the administration, led by Morgenthau, believed that the recession had been caused by the deficit itself. This group argued that deficit spending had undermined business confidence. If the administration wanted to encourage businesses to increase production and payrolls, it should cut the budget further. Other New Dealers, especially Eccles, Hopkins, and Ickes, influenced by the theories of British economist John Maynard Keynes (1883–1940), called for more spending to stimulate consumption. They argued—as had Keynes—that deficits were an important government tool to put money into the hands of consumers, who when flush with cash, would purchase goods, thereby lifting the economy.

On the one hand, Roosevelt was suspicious of Keynesianism and generally in favor of balanced budgets. On the other hand, FDR knew his policies lent themselves to deficit spending, and he recognized something had to be done about the downturn. As FDR considered his options for dealing with the recession, months ticked by. Finally, in April 1938 Roosevelt asked Congress to appropriate a $3.75 billion stimulus package. Through 1939, FDR remained committed to running deficits in order to boost consumer buying power.

FDR had become the first American president to embrace, however hesitantly, the principles of Keynesianism. Deficits slowly crept up. By 1939 the deficit had reached $3.8 billion. In truth, however, the 1938 stimulus package was small compared to the kinds of deficits Keynesians advocated. The stimulus package represented a mere 3 percent of the total economy's value, a small sum in light of the huge numbers of unemployed.

FDR may have been the first American president to embrace Keynesian ideas, but he did not embrace them wholeheartedly. Not until after World War II would Keynesianism truly become the heart of American economic policy.

After 1937

It was not just Roosevelt's reluctance that limited reform after 1937. After four years, the nation—as it did during the Progressive era—lost much of its taste for reform. The bipartisan conservative coalition was gaining power in Congress, and reform on the state level was drying up. Meanwhile, Roosevelt had lost political capital with his failed schemes to pack the Supreme Court with judges sympathetic to his policies, or to purge the Democratic Party of conservative political opponents.

When the Supreme Court declared the NRA unconstitutional in 1935, the nation's workers had been left without the security of wage and hour legislation. In 1938, the Roosevelt administration changed that, successfully pushing through after an arduous bitter battle the Fair Labor Standards Act, which prohibited child labor and guaranteed many of America's workers a minimum wage and overtime pay for every hour over a forty-hour work week. Unlike the NRA, this legislation did not depend on cooperation from industry; rather, it required acquiescence to terms set by the government.

But, to circumvent constitutional limitations to federal regulation of labor, the act only applied to industries involved in interstate commerce, which the federal government had an established right to regulate. And to overcome conservative resistance the act explicitly excluded domestic and agricultural workers and disproportionately left out of coverage African American and women workers (as amended over time, however, the legislation eventually covered most workers in the United States). This act would be the last major piece of New Deal legislation.

Roosevelt's later 1930s spending packages had a relatively tepid effect on the American economy. There was some recovery, but America's economic output would not rebound to pre-recession levels until the federal government began gearing up for World War II and spent money to equip the American war machine, proving that Keynesianism worked. Government spending during the war reached a third of the nation's gross national product. America's $57 billion wartime deficit made the $4 billion deficit Roosevelt so hesitantly approved in 1938 look puny.

Where Roosevelt's reluctant spending had failed, the enormous government wartime investment in the economy succeeded. Unemployment fell as 17 million Americans found work in war industries and in the military. The gross national product doubled. After war's end, workers spent their newfound cash on a plethora of consumer goods, buoying the economy into the 1960s.

FDR and the New Deal: Aftermath

The New Deal did not end the Great Depression, but New Deal policies did ameliorate the massive suffering caused by the severe economic downturn. For those who wished for a radical solution to the problem of economic inequality in America, the New Deal did not offer much. The Roosevelt administration did not redistribute income or radically alter the structure of American capitalism. Nor, despite the almost hysterical outcry about the New Deal's attack on traditional American values, did it during the Roosevelt administration's heyday substantially recast them. Indeed, the New Deal halted the spread in the United States of rival radical ideologies.

The New Deal, moreover, did not offer Americans a coherent plan to combat severe economic downturns like the Great Depression. Roosevelt and his advisors pursued an ad hoc set of solutions that were sometimes contradictory. For instance, Roosevelt's faith in balanced budgets seems out of character considering his creation of expensive public programs. The late 1930s trust-busting also seems out of place in a policy agenda that included the NRA, designed to allow industry to set prices and exempted some companies from antimonopoly legislation.

And yet, whatever its internal contradictions, the New Deal was a transformative moment. Roosevelt's policies successfully fostered a sense of economic stability when the Depression environment evoked worrying fluidity. Regulatory agencies like the SEC created ground rules for a destabilized, demoralized, and dethroned Wall Street, while the Banking Acts regulated both big banks and small, striving to ensure in so far as possible that all the players used the same rule book.

Veteran Socialist Norman Thomas (1884–1968), in assessing the vicissitudes of Depression life in the United States, noted "the American people were extraordinarily patient." In the Great Depression, by providing subsistence to millions of Americans the New Deal offered hope to the patient as well as the much smaller number of vocal restless. The New Deal changed American expectations of the federal government, as citizens now looked to it, whether headed by Keynesians or not, to protect the nation's economic health and to provide for their social welfare.

During the Great Depression, not for the first time in American history, people looked to their leaders to protect the nation's economic health and to provide for their social welfare. Unlike what happened in previous severe economic downturns, they were not disappointed, as FDR committed the federal government to the handling of the social and economic problems facing the American people in the 1930s. The United States was not free of unrest during the New Deal era, but the industrial violence, for instance, resulting from efforts by the working class to gain the rights promised by legislation such as the Wagner Act, was not directed at tearing down the State. Unlike the aftermath of previous American downturns, which produced few permanent changes, when "Dr. New Deal" gave way to "Dr. Win the War," as World War II engulfed the United States, FDR's actions in dealing with the Great Depression had a lasting impact.

Further Reading

Aaron, Daniel, and Robert Bendiner, eds. *The Strenuous Decade: A Social and Intellectual Record of the Nineteen-Thirties.* Garden City, NY: Anchor Books, 1970.

Black, Conrad. *Franklin Delano Roosevelt: Champion of Freedom.* London: Weidenfeld & Nicolson, 2003.

Hiltzik, Michael. *The New Deal: A Modern History.* New York: Free Press, 2011.

Leuchtenburg, William E. *Franklin D. Roosevelt and the New Deal.* Reprint ed. New York: HarperPerennial, 2009.

Schlesinger, Arthur M., Jr. *The Coming of the New Deal, 1933–1935.* Boston: Houghton Mifflin, 1958.

Schlesinger, Arthur M., Jr. *The Politics of Upheaval, 1935–1936.* Boston: Houghton Mifflin, 1950.

Shlaes, Anity. *The Forgotten Man: A New History of the Great Depression.* New York: HarperCollins, 2007.

Taylor, Nick. *American-Made: The Enduring Legacy of the WPA—When FDR Put the Nation to Work.* New York: Bantam Books, 2008.

Great Depression, 1933–1939:
Short Entries

Alphabet Agencies

Jason Roberts

Alphabet agencies was a term used by the media and the public to refer to the plethora of new federal government agencies established by the New Deal after the inauguration of Franklin D. Roosevelt (1882–1945) as president on March 4, 1933. They came to be known by their initials. This use of acronyms extended to the president's name. He was increasingly referred to in the press as FDR rather than his full name.

The earliest and among the most notable "alphabet agencies" were created during the special session of the 73rd Congress called by FDR to deal with the most immediate financial and social problems facing the United States as a result of the impact of the Great Depression. This session, which lasted from March 9 to June 16, 1933, has been called "the Hundred Days."

During this term major legislation was initiated, for instance, dealing with the desperate situation of American banking. The New Deal also through legislation and executive order created a whole slew of agencies whose task was to combat the effects of the economic downturn plaguing the people of the United States. These agencies, designed to pump increasing amounts of money into the economy were soon referred to by their initials by journalists and the public and quickly became known as the "alphabet agencies."

They were depicted and popularized in cartoons and other media by their initials, and sometimes they were not lauded. In the summer of 1933 an agency such as the Agricultural Adjustment Administration (AAA) aroused a great deal of critical controversy because of the policies (plowing under crops; killing baby hogs) it followed in raising the prices farmers would receive for their efforts. These individuals in turn were on the whole very satisfied with the cash AAA provided them.

The New Deal dealt with domestic issues from 1933 to 1939 (when the outbreak of World War II resulted in foreign affairs taking precedence over domestic policy in the federal government). It created a massive number of

National Recovery Administration (NRA) poster displayed by businesses to show support for the government program. The NRA was considered the cornerstone of the New Deal and was often controversial in its regulation of industrial codes of competition. (National Archives)

new agencies, never more so than during the Hundred Days. In that short span of time were enacted not only some of the most important New Deal legislation, such as the Federal Emergency Relief Act, which put the government into the relief business, and the Emergency Banking Act, which gave the government unprecedented oversight of the nation's financial system, but also created were some of the New Deal's most recognizable and important alphabet agencies.

These included the CCC—the Civilian Conservation Corps, the TVA—the Tennessee Valley Authority, the HOLC—the Home Owners Loan Corporation, the NRA—the National Recovery Administration, and the PWA—the Public Works Administration. All were mainly geared to recovery. Many of the agencies subsequently created were geared not so much to recovery as to reform; these included the SEC—the Securities and Exchange Commission, the FHA—the Federal Housing Administration, the REA—the Rural Electrification Administration, the NYA—the National Youth Administration, the USHA—the United States Housing Authority, and the TNEC—the Temporary National Economic Committee.

FDR, a masterful, extremely pragmatic politician, often governed by indirection, not infrequently creating competing agencies—as with the Public Works Administration (PWA) and the Works Progress Administration (WPA)—in order to avoid decisions that might cause him to lose support or might result in hard feelings among those administering the agencies. FDR's actions often did not avoid the latter and sometimes did result in administrative confusion. Congress all too often did not provide oversight of these agencies or their administration since much of this "alphabet soup" did not depend on the legislators for funding; the agencies at times were a part of larger unrelated programs.

However one judges FDR's administrative techniques, by raising federal involvement in everyday life to hitherto unprecedented levels the alphabet agencies did help the American people to deal with the Great Depression. Thus the CCC put thousands of young Americans to work outdoors on conservation projects and the pay these boys and young men, mostly between the ages of 18 and 23, earned went to their families who were on relief; the REA provided electricity to rural areas that had been neglected by the power companies; the PWA built large public works such as dams, airports, and tunnels; the WPA employed millions of Americas on small public works project such as constructing roads and building schools as well as just raking leaves.

Not all the alphabet agencies proved successful: some such as the AAA were found to be based on unconstitutional legislation. The NRA was greeted with acclaim initially, but its attempts at a managed economy were found wanting in the long run and proved ultimately to be very unpopular. The TVA, in addition to its other missions, successfully practiced a kind of social engineering at the time, but its policies later proved to be problematic. While the alphabet agencies did not, as was hoped and often expressly intended, end the Great Depression, they were instrumental in alleviating for many Americans the fears and difficult times that it had brought into their lives.

Estimates reckon that the number of alphabet agencies created between 1933 and 1939 at over 50, and even though resulting from attempts to deal with the Great Depression, many still continue to function to this day. Without a doubt these alphabet agencies changed the economic, political, and social landscape of the United States.

Further Reading

Leuchtenburg, William E. *Franklin D. Roosevelt and the New Deal: 1932–1940*. New York: HarperPerennial, 2009.

Ray, P. Orman. "Alphabetical Agencies." In James Truslow Adams, ed., *Dictionary of American History*. Vol. 1. New York: Charles Scribner's Sons, 1940.

Schlesinger, Arthur M., Jr. *The Age of Roosevelt: The Coming of the New Deal*. Boston: Houghton Mifflin, 1958.

Civilian Conservation Corps (CCC)

Jason Roberts

Probably the most popular New Deal program, the Civilian Conservation Corps (CCC) for almost a decade starting in 1933 enrolled millions and spent billions sprucing up the public domain and providing employment to young

Young Civilian Conservation Corps recruits transplant beavers from a ranch location where they were damaging crops to a forest watershed where they will help to conserve the water supply, Salmon National Forest, Camp F-167, Idaho. (Franklin D. Roosevelt Presidential Library)

men who could not find a job and whose families were on relief. The CCC, although enrolling only young men, helped U.S. families to overcome some of the miseries they faced, increased American awareness of the nation's outdoors, and developed much of its neglected natural resources. The CCC's impressive legacy includes reforesting thousands of acres; building hundreds of bridges, dams, and fire stations; marking innumerable trails; digging ponds; and improving hundreds of parks and beaches. The CCC also fought forest fires and aided victims of natural disasters. It improved the physical and mental condition of enrollees, providing them with adequate meals as well as educational and vocational opportunities. The CCC brought together American youths who might never have met: many of the enrollees, from urban areas and from rural communities hard-hit by the Depression, were sent to CCC camps far from home.

The CCC's genesis lay with President Roosevelt (1882–1945), who for decades before he became president in 1933 had ardently lobbied for conservation legislation and been active in reforesting his Hyde Park estate. As New York governor in the early 1930s, he put 10,000 jobless to work on state conservation projects. On March 14, 1933, he told an advisor of plans to put unemployed youth to work rejuvenating America's forests; on March 21, he sent Congress a draft bill, his first legislative proposal for a federal agency to combat massive unemployment among American youth, transmitted with a message urging immediate passage, asserting, "I propose to create a civilian conservation corps to be used in simple work . . . confining itself to forestry, prevention of soil erosion, flood control . . . and similar projects." He envisioned enrolling 250,000 young men who would be provided a stipend, meals, housing, uniforms, and other essentials. Congress fast-tracked the bill; there was only cursory debate, limited hearings, and voice votes. The Emergency Conservation Work Act had passed both Houses of Congress by March 31, 1933. A few days later FDR signed (April 5) an executive order establishing the CCC. He, the media, and the public from the CCC's inception referred to it as the Civilian Conservation Corps, but it did not come into formal existence until 1937 when it became an independent agency.

Various critics denounced the CCC during its gestation. William Green (1873–1952), American Federation of Labor (AFL) head, who represented a constituency important to the president and the Democrats, told a congressional committee the AFL opposed establishment of the CCC because it smacked "of Fascism, of Hitlerism, of a form of Sovietism." Roosevelt's personal lobbying mellowed Green's opposition as did the appointment of an AFL union official as CCC director. Robert Fechner (1876–1939), a vice president of the International Association of Machinists (IAM), who during World War I negotiated with then assistant secretary of the navy Roosevelt settling labor disputes and, in 1932, had played a key role in the IAM's endorsement of Roosevelt for president. Fechner ran the CCC until his death; he was replaced by close friend, fellow IAM leader, and CCC associate director James McEntee (1884–1957); he oversaw the CCC until it suspended operations in 1942.

FDR retained a serious personal interest in the CCC until international events began to preoccupy him; he visited the camps, dealt directly with Fechner, and at the end of the 1930s although overburdened found time to help design a spiffy green uniform for CCC enrollees to replace the drab clothes issued them till then. Fechner ably oversaw the complicated administration of the CCC, which included representatives from various cabinet departments involved with the agency: Interior and Agriculture through agencies like the Forest Service and the National Park Service organized and supervised work projects; Labor handled recruitment; War handled the logistics, U.S. Army officers were in charge of the CCC camps and handling transportation to them. The first, Camp Roosevelt, located in the George Washington National Forest near Luray, in northwest Virginia, opened on April 17, 1933. The first enrollees had signed up a week earlier in New York City. The Roosevelt administration's initial plans called for an enrollment of 250, and it was reached by July 15, 1933. Enrollees signed up for six months, but could extend their participation for six-month periods up to two years. As the slump continued the New Deal expanded the CCC program; enrollment peaked in mid-1935 at 505,000 in 2,900 camps coast-to-coast as well as Alaska and Hawaii.

Enrollees initially had to be between ages 18 and 25 (later 17–28), a member of a family on relief (a requirement eliminated in 1937), single, unemployed, and a U.S. citizen (later veterans of the Spanish-American War and World War I were admitted). Enrollees earned $30 a month, of which $22 was sent to their families (those few in each camp helping with administration could earn up to $45 a month); in addition each camp employed vocational trainers, "educational advisors," and "local experienced managers" (LEMs). The latter advised CCC youths about their camp's unfamiliar environment and trained the unskilled enrollees on how to do their work. Ultimately, the CCC employed over 25,000 LEMs, usually drawn from a camp's vicinity and paid prevailing wages. The LEMs provided necessary advice to the enrollees, and their hiring also tended to blunt any hostile local public opinion.

Housing quickly improved; drafty tents gave way to improvised barracks often later replaced by more substantial buildings. Camps generally had a complement of 200 enrollees, broken up into sections of 25. Some camps remained bleak, but in time each—whatever its surroundings—usually had a mess hall, an infirmary, workshops, and a building serving as a recreation center and also containing classrooms and a primitive library. Each camp was administered by Regular Army officers; as the CCC grew they were joined by Reserve officers willing to be called back because of the economic hard times. Unlike similar camps in Nazi Germany the enrollees in the CCC were not under duress, did not drill or salute, and were not subject to military discipline. Fears about army control proved groundless. Officers in charge, per the secretary of war, governed "by leadership, explanation, and diplomacy." Except for criminal actions involving local authorities, the harshest penalty meted out was discharge from the CCC, severe given the contemporary economic situation.

The camps provided substantial meals for youth who before their enrollment often went hungry. Said Fechner, the fare was "wholesome, palatable, and the kind that sticks to the ribs." Workdays began at 6 AM, breakfast was a half hour later, then after a policing of the living spaces, work began at 8 AM, with a break at noon for lunch, ending at 4 PM. Dinner was at 6 PM. After dinner came free time until 10 PM and "lights out." During this time voluntary training in vocational skills (e.g., typing, truck driving) or education in academic subjects (illiterates could learn to read and write; others earned high school degree equivalents) were available; many took advantage of these opportunities; others played sports or tried to woo local girls.

As the United States geared up defense efforts in the late 1930s the economy improved, enrollments in the CCC declined, and federal funding was diverted from relief. The need for the CCC and interest in it grew less, even though it remained very popular. In 1939, reorganization of relief agencies led to the CCC losing its independence and becoming part of a newly established Federal Security Agency. Its numbers declined to less than 200,000. In 1942 the

CCC was suspended. Congress never voted to terminate the program, but after long, acrimonious debates refused to fund it. Since its organization in 1933 the CCC, in fulfilling FDR's plans, enrolled over 3,000,000 youth, contributed over $2 billion to relief, and left behind a remarkable and beneficial legacy of intelligently developing the nation's natural and human resources. In its heyday during the mid-1930s, the CCC was certainly among the New Deal's most effective agencies.

Further Reading

Maher, Neil M. *Nature's New Deal: The Civilian Conservation Corps and the Roots of the American Environmental Movement.* New York: Oxford University Press, 2009.
Salmond, John. *The Civilian Conservation Corps, 1933–1942: A New Deal Case Study.* Durham, NC: Duke University Press, 1967.

Eccles, Marriner Stoddard (1890–1977)

Jason Roberts

A prominent successful banker and businessman as well as a dedicated effective public servant, Marriner Eccles served as a governor and chair of the Federal Reserve (1934–1951) and was instrumental in its restructuring by the New Deal. He played a key role in the drafting and passage of the Banking Act of 1935 and in dealing with the impact of the dramatic economic downturn in 1937. During his long tenure as head of the Federal Reserve it significantly increased its involvement in the American economy and became a more independent institution.

Eccles was born on September 19, 1890, in Logan, Utah, into a well-to-do Mormon family. He attended the high school part of Brigham Young College and graduated in 1919. Subsequently, he served as a missionary for the Church of Jesus Christ of Latter Day Saints in Scotland. After the sudden death in 1912 of his father, Eccles—as the oldest of the family's males—took on management of some of his father's enterprises, including various banks. The companies he controlled thrived, while those managed by other member of the family did not. An energetic, forceful, and thoughtful businessman, he was a millionaire by his early twenties.

In 1925 Eccles, assisted by his brother George, joined with the Browning family of Ogden, Utah, to form Eccles-Browning Affiliated Banks. By 1928 the brothers and their partners operated 17 banks as well as a building and loan company in three states (Utah, Idaho, and Wyoming), and organized the First Security

Corporation, purportedly the first multibank holding company in the United States, to manage their financial endeavors. The corporation and its constituent parts did not fall prey to the various problems that plagued American banking in the early days of the Great Depression and withstood runs in several of its banks.

A telling clue to the Eccles management style can be found in his response to these runs: when they began he instructed the tellers to count out individual withdrawals very slowly, sometimes twice, in order to stall, but once the banks had in hand the necessary funds to pay off depositors, Eccles, in order to avoid lines at the bank, speeded up the withdrawal process and ordered depositors be paid off as expeditiously as possible.

As a leading and successful banker in the western United States his speeches on the banking situation caught the attention of various New Dealers, and Eccles was invited to Washington, D.C. He became involved with the drafting of the Emergency Banking Act (March 1933), which took radical steps to rescue the American financial system, and the creation of the Federal Deposit Insurance Corporation (June 1933), which by insuring depositors against bank failures brought a till then unheard of stability to banking arrangements in the United States.

Eccles, initially a conservative Republican, changed his political views as a result of the impact of the Great Depression. He became very sympathetic to the ideas of extensive government spending and increased regulation in order to improve the economy, and he always claimed his espousal of such ideas predated the "pump priming" theories of noted British economist John Maynard Keynes (1883–1946). Eccles also insisted that he had independently reached his ideas about the need for federal deficit spending.

In 1934 Eccles spent a short stint at the U.S. Treasury Department as assistant secretary for monetary and credit affairs. Later that year a position on the Federal Reserve Board opened up, and the president appointed him. He became chair late in 1934 (the Senate confirmed him in February 1935). Eccles wrote the bulk of the 1935 Banking Act, which dramatically restructured the Federal Reserve system. It passed despite the determined opposition of Virginia Democratic senator Carter Glass (1858–1946), who viewing himself as the Reserve's "Father" tenaciously opposed any changes that would lead to increasing the input of the federal government in the system and its centralization in Washington, D.C.

The 1935 legislation did just that: the Federal Reserve Board became the Board of Governors of the Federal Reserve system, and no longer were the comptroller of the currency or the secretary of the treasury members ex officio. The board's number was increased from six to seven with the president able to select members who would serve 14-year terms. One governor was to be elected chair and would serve for four years. The new board would have more control over the regional Federal Reserve banks since their chief officers could be chosen only with its approval. The governors now had greater authority over the rediscount rates and the reserve requirements set by member banks. Control over regulation of credit had been vested in a committee whose members were drawn from various Reserve banks but was now to be concentrated in a Federal Open Market Committee comprised of a majority of board members.

Through the fiscal policies Eccles implemented, he made many contributions to the revival of the American economy from the Depression's ravages, but never more so than during the dramatic economic downturn that took place in 1937. The president had heeded the advice of those in the administration such as Secretary of the Treasury Henry Morganthau (1891–1967), who as advocates of "sound money" and a balanced budget convinced Roosevelt to cut back on government spending. Eccles found fault with those arguments, made his opinions known, and played a leading role in persuading the president to increase government spending on programs of public works and social welfare. Eccles declared that the government "must be the compensatory agent in this economy; it must unbalance its budget."

In 1936 Eccles had been chosen chair of the Board of Governors of the restructured Federal Reserve system, and he was renominated in 1940 and 1944. During his tenure, the Federal Reserve aggressively used interest rates and monetary policy to influence the American economy. Eccles was a consistent advocate of government spending. Eccles is credited with turning the Federal Reserve Board into a more independent institution. A gifted and enthusiastic speaker, to sell his monetary policies he addressed business groups, appeared on radio talk shows, and wooed successfully a variety of journalists.

During World War II, Eccles, a chief advisor to President Roosevelt on various economic plans, supported increased military appropriations, and participated in various conferences both during the war and after that led to the creation of the World Bank and the International Monetary Fund. He was not as close to President Harry Truman (1994–1972) as he had been to FDR but was a strong advocate for a multibillion dollar loan to the UK and for the Marshall Plan. After the war Eccles argued forcefully but without much success for anti-inflation fiscal and monetary policies. Truman did not reappoint him as chair in 1948, and in 1951 Eccles retired from the Federal Reserve Board of Governors.

Upon leaving public life, he ran with considerable success various family businesses, which over the years scored substantial profits. Eccles established various foundations that benefited life in Utah and the states around it. He continued to speak out vigorously on various public issues of concern to him, such as overpopulation, American failure to recognize Communist China, and U.S. involvement in Vietnam. He died on December 18, 1977, in Salt Lake City.

Further Reading

Eccles, Marriner. *Beckoning Frontiers: Public and Personal Recollections*. New York: Alfred A. Knopf, 1951.

Hyman, Sidney. *Marriner S. Eccles: Private Entrepreneur and Public Servant.* Chicago: University of Chicago Press, 1977.

Hopkins, Harry Lloyd (1890–1946)

Jason Roberts

One of President Franklin D. Roosevelt's closest advisers, Harry Hopkins held various positions dealing with domestic policies and foreign affairs. During the New Deal's heyday in the 1930s he oversaw many of its relief efforts, including service as head (1933–1935) of the Federal Emergency Relief Administration (FERA) and as director (1935–1938) of the Works Progress Administration (WPA). In these roles he changed American attitudes toward relief. Subsequently he served as secretary of commerce (1938–1940), and he also served President Roosevelt (1882–1945) and briefly his successor Harry Truman (1884–1972) as an effective foreign affairs troubleshooter.

Born in Sioux City, Iowa, on August 17, 1890, he moved with family around the Midwest, settling in Grinnell, Iowa, in 1901. Raised in modest circumstances Hopkins attended Grinnell College, graduating cum laude in 1912. At Grinnell College, Hopkins showed a great interest in politics; he was elected president of the class of 1912 and was instrumental in bringing then New Jersey governor Woodrow Wilson to the Grinnell campus in 1911 during his quest for the presidency.

After graduation Hopkins moved to New York City and began a successful social work career with various agencies. During World War I he worked in the South with the American Red Cross. Back in New York City the imaginative, energetic Hopkins soon attained executive positions with various social work agencies. At the end of 1929, as the economy collapsed and unemployment grew, he headed a Red Cross–sponsored work relief program; in 1931 Roosevelt, then New York State governor, appointed Hopkins to manage the state Temporary Emergency Relief Administration. Hopkins aggressively spent money to hire the unemployed, emphasizing jobs rather than simply doling out cash, and helped New Yorkers to survive some of the Depression's grimmest years.

In May 1933 the newly inaugurated president Roosevelt appointed Hopkins head of the Federal Emergency Relief Administration (FERA). It did not put the federal government directly into the relief business but provided millions of dollars in grants to states for programs they continued to administer, but Hopkins felt that more was necessary and convinced the president to establish in November 1933 the Civil Works Administration (CWA) to provide work

Harry Hopkins was the principal architect of immediate relief programs during the New Deal and a major foreign policy adviser to President Franklin D. Roosevelt during World War II. (Library of Congress)

relief for primarily unskilled and the semiskilled unemployed in order that they would have the funds necessary to survive the winter.

Hopkins, who managed to spend $5 million during his first two hours in office, admittedly was careless in his desire to put the jobless to work and clashed repeatedly with the cautious Harold Ickes (1874–1952), who directed the Public Works Administration (PWA), which had a $3 billion appropriation in hand almost none of which had been spent by the end of 1933 because of his policy of not "wasting" government funds on what he considered "insubstantial projects."

Ultimately the PWA, expected to be a primary weapon against the impact of the Depression, utilized many otherwise employable skilled workers on its projects. It achieved magnificent results, and many of its large-scale projects remain important and useful to this day. However, the PWA never achieved the hoped-for goals of providing a massive number of jobs, and the multitudes of unemployed were not touched by it.

During its brief life (November 1933–March 30, 1934) the CWA spent about a billion dollars on work relief as Hopkins sought to quickly assist the unemployed; at its peak the CWA employed about 4.2 million people on about 400,000 limited projects. In the worst winter weather in years CWA workers refurbished all of New York City's parks and improved thousands of the nation's public buildings such as schools, libraries, courthouses, and jails. Thanks to CWA funding hundreds of airports were improved, 12 million feet of sewer pipe were laid, and hundreds of unrehabitable buildings across the United States were torn down. Hopkins and his aides also found work in their professions for almost 200,000 unemployed such as teachers, artists, librarians, bookbinders, and others who the CWA classified as "professional and non-manual."

When the CWA expired about half the agency's laid-off workers were taken on by the FERA, which Hopkins had continued to head. He steadfastly lobbied the president for a jobs program and in fall 1934 was made part of a troika that included Ickes to develop a work relief plan. He and Ickes continued to clash, especially after Roosevelt—although not denying the PWA support—accepted Hopkins's plans for work relief. In early April 1935 Congress passed the Emergency Relief Appropriations Act, which FDR in a "'fireside chat" (April 28, 1935), referring to "this work relief program," characterized as part of a "national crusade to destroy enforced idleness . . . an enemy of the human spirit." While some funds were allocated to the PWA, the vast bulk went to what became known as the Works Progress Administration (WPA), with Hopkins as its head.

The WPA during its existence employed jobless persons to build schools, hospitals, roads, and bridges. Hopkins not only wanted WPA workers to earn the means for subsistence but also to feel useful: they participated in school hot lunch programs, worked as specialized staff at museums, assisted in anthropological digs, built the San Antonio River Walk, conducted Americanism classes for immigrants, trained mechanics, and helped clean up New England after the devastating September 1938 hurricane. The WPA also hired artists to paint murals, historians to conduct oral history interviews, and actors to perform in plays.

In the main WPA handled lesser projects, but the clashes between Hopkins and Ickes continued as their agencies often competed for funds notwithstanding their diverse approaches. Hopkins emphasized putting people to work and quickly; Ickes stressed cost-effective projects and delayed approving proposals until they were thoroughly vetted. While critics often regarded Hopkins as a symbol of overzealous centralized government and—with some justification—charged various WPA operations were wasteful boondoggles, he never lost the confidence of President Roosevelt, who admired the speed and effectiveness with which Hopkins succored millions of jobless Americans and put them to work.

The WPA's rolls peaked at over 3 million in late 1936 and were cut drastically during 1937 as a conservative bloc began to dominate Congress after FDR's failed attempt to "pack" the Supreme Court. In August 1937 the American economy began to collapse as what was termed "the Roosevelt recession" set in; Hopkins with limited success fought against the cuts to WPA appropriations but was sidetracked by personal problems. His wife died (October 1937) after a long battle with cancer, and Hopkins, plagued by ill health, underwent surgery for serious stomach ailments.

In December 1938 he resigned his federal relief positions (including WPA director) to become secretary of commerce, serving until September 1940. At the time of his appointment many believed Hopkins was being groomed for the presidency since Roosevelt had not yet committed to breaking tradition and running for a third term. Hopkins' record as commerce secretary was undistinguished as he spent much of his tenure in the hospital recovering from illness, but he did manage the Democratic convention that renominated Roosevelt.

Throughout World War II, despite his fragile health, Hopkins served as an influential trusted adviser to Roosevelt. The president sent Hopkins on trips to meet with major Allied leaders including British prime minister Winston Churchill (1874–1965) and Soviet premier Josef Stalin (1879–1953). Hopkins was a major participant in many of the wartime conferences with Allies including the first meeting between Roosevelt and Churchill off the coast of Newfoundland (1941), Cairo (1943), Casablanca (1943), and Yalta (1945). Hopkins was also involved in many other wartime efforts including Lend Lease, and his actions overall won the confidence of U.S. Army chief of staff General George C. Marshall (1880–1959) and other military leaders.

After Roosevelt's death in April 1945, Hopkins formally left federal government service because of ill health. But for new president Harry Truman he traveled to Moscow to gain Stalin's support for the United Nations. This trip temporarily alleviated the growing tensions between the United States and the Soviet Union. Hopkins retired to New York City in July 1945 to serve as an impartial chairman of the Women's Cloak and Suit Industry. He died January 29, 1946, from stomach cancer that had plagued him for years.

Further Reading

McJimsey, George. *Harry Hopkins: Ally of the Poor and Defender of Democracy.* Cambridge, MA: Harvard University Press, 1987.

Roll, David. *The Hopkins Touch: Harry Hopkins and the Forging of the Alliance to Defeat Hitler.* New York: Oxford University Press, 2013.

Sherwood, Robert. *Roosevelt and Hopkins: An Intimate History.* New York: Harper Brothers, 1953 (1948).

Ickes, Harold Le Claire (1874–1952)

Jason Roberts

A self-styled "curmudgeon," Harold Ickes was known for his fierce temper and intemperate clashes with colleagues. A man of incorruptible honesty and unflinching liberalism, he served as secretary of the interior for twelve years (1933–1945) in the administration of President Franklin D. Roosevelt (1882–1945) and briefly (1945–1946) in that of FDR's successor Harry Truman (1884–1972). Ickes throughout his tenure in the cabinet would threaten to resign. Ickes also during its life (1933–1943) directed the Public Works Administration (PWA), a New Deal alphabet agency that constructed large-scale public works projects.

Born on March 15, 1874, in Hollidaysburg, part of the metropolitan district of Altoona, Pennsylvania, he moved to Englewood, a suburb of Chicago, at the age of sixteen when his mother died. After graduating (1892) as valedictorian of his high school class, Ickes attended the University of Chicago, working his way through with a variety of jobs including teaching English in night school to immigrants; he earned a bachelor's degree in 1896, went to work as a newspaper reporter, and became involved in Chicago politics.

Between stints managing the unsuccessful campaigns of municipal reformers he earned (1907) a law degree from the University of Chicago and subsequently became active in Chicago legal and political circles. While running a successful legal practice, he became a strong supporter of the Progressive Party, and later of the Progressive wing of the Republican Party. In 1924 he supported the failed bid of Progressive senator Hiram Johnson (1866–1945) for the Republican presidential nomination, and in 1928, 1930, and 1932 directed his wealthy Progressive first wife's successful campaigns for the Illinois Assembly. Early in 1932 Ickes agreed to head a "Western Independent Republican Committee for Franklin Roosevelt" in support of his presidential candidacy.

They met for the first time in February 1933, and FDR offered Ickes the Interior Department secretaryship, hoping to appeal to Progressive Republicans by selecting him. The middle-aged Ickes was a relatively unknown figure outside of Chicago political circles when he was appointed. FDR's choice has been characterized by one of Roosevelt's chief aides as "one of the most casual appointments to a cabinet position in American history," and it proved to be one of the most successful.

Ickes proved to be a fiercely loyal secretary of the interior, who over time handled a variety of tasks. He revamped the notoriously corrupt and incompetent Bureau of Indian Affairs, appointing as commissioner John Collier (1884–1968)—an outspoken advocate for Native Americans. Ickes was a staunch advocate of conserving natural resources and worked successfully to reduce erosion on public lands. During his tenure Ickes added 12 million acres to lands already protected by the Interior Department. Among the territory he added to National Park lands were the Smoky Mountains, the Everglades, and the Shenandoah Valley.

President Roosevelt admired Ickes's honesty, loyalty, and administrative abilities; FDR also tolerated the thin-skinned Ickes's feuds (often initiated by him) with other members of the administration as well as his frequent outbursts at cabinet meetings and his frequent threats to resign. Roosevelt seemed more amused than upset by these outbursts and threats, many caused by Ickes's rivalry with Harry Hopkins (1890–1945) for the favor of the president and their fight over who should control the spending of federal funds on work relief as well as what type of projects should prevail.

Ickes had begun administering the Public Works Administration in 1933. The PWA was designed to invest in and construct large-scale public works projects to aid the unemployed. Thanks to Ickes the results of the program initially were mixed. In the short term, the PWA did not spend quickly the funds allocated by Congress. The frugal and cautious Ickes insisted on reviewing every proposed project to make sure that taxpayer money was not being wasted. In addition, because of his successful resistance to any possible hint of corruption, it took considerable time to plan projects, receive approval from local communities, and make certain that no graft was involved. As a result, the slow-moving Ickes initially only spent $110 million out of more than $3 billion appropriated by the legislation establishing the PWA.

By comparison, the Federal Emergency Relief Administration (FERA) directed by Hopkins quickly provided direct relief to the unemployed. In addition, the Civil Works Administration (CWA), also run by Hopkins, was created by executive order to help American society deal with the effects of the Depression; during the CWA's short existence (November 1933–March 1934) it employed more than four million individuals, boosting their morale and enabling them to withstand the rigors of the 1933–1934 winter.

Whereas Ickes focused on waste and efficiency, Hopkins stressed quickly providing direct relief and creating jobs, often on make-work local projects. The rivalry of Hopkins and Ickes for the favor of FDR and their fight over who should control the spending of federal funds and what types of projects should prevail would only intensify after the creation of the Works Progress Administration (WPA) in mid-1935 and continued until Dr. New Deal gave way to Dr. Win the War, as the United States faced World War II.

Despite misgivings by Ickes about Hopkins and his operations, the projects of the PWA, which ultimately spent over $6 billion, were often more successful in the long term. The PWA succeeded in rebuilding much of the nation's infrastructure. Examples of PWA accomplishments include involvement in the construction of the Lincoln Tunnel and La Guardia Airport in New York City, the overseas highway linking Florida and Key West, and the aircraft carriers *Yorktown* and *Enterprise*. Over the years the PWA was involved in about 19,000 projects including over 500 municipal water systems, some 600 sewage systems, and at least 500 schools and 260 hospitals as well as innumerable highway projects and many of the facilities of the Tennessee Valley Authority. Whatever the public reaction to the federal government's involvement, its opponents could never find any impropriety in what the PWA did under the direction of "Honest Harold."

Ickes stood out during Franklin Roosevelt's administration as a strong supporter of civil rights. He was the first cabinet officer to employ an advisor on "Negro affairs," hired African Americans for more than menial positions, ordered all Department of Interior facilities integrated (including its cafeteria), and in the U.S. Virgin Islands (under the Interior Department's control) appointed the first black federal judge. When the Daughters of the American

Revolution in 1939, following local custom, would not allow black singer Marion Anderson to perform in that organization's segregated hall, he helped organize the celebrated African American contralto's very successful concert in front of the Lincoln Memorial (which the Interior Department controlled) to an audience of about 75,000 while millions more heard the broadcast.

After FDR's death in April 1945, Ickes continued as secretary of the interior but never established a close relationship with President Truman. When in February 1946 Truman nominated Democratic Party fundraiser and oilman Edwin Pauley (1903–1981) to be undersecretary of the navy an outraged Ickes threatened to resign. Unlike FDR, President Truman accepted Ickes's resignation. Thereafter, he remained a combative supporter of a variety of liberal causes, making his opinions known in articles in newspapers and magazines, most notably the *New Republic*. He died February 3, 1952.

A Progressive Republican who became an outspoken Democrat, Ickes never wholly adopted the New Deal's welfare program. He had a distrust of big government, an attitude exemplified by the way he administered the PWA. Definitely not a man who got along by going along, he was one of the first public opponents of Senator Joseph McCarthy (1908–1958). Ickes was a difficult man, given his outspoken likes and dislikes as well as his lack of patience with his colleagues. But unlike many of his peers, in government and out, Ickes believed in a positive vision of the United States even though his personality all too often clouded that vision.

Further Reading

Clarke, Jeanne N. *Roosevelt's Warrior: Harold L. Ickes and the New Deal*. Baltimore: Johns Hopkins University Press, 1996.

Ickes, Harold. *The Inside Struggle, 1936–1939*. New York: Simon & Schuster, 1954.

Ickes, Harold. *The Lowering Clouds, 1939–1941*. New York: Simon & Schuster, 1954.

Ickes, Harold. *The Secret Diary of Harold L. Ickes: The First Thousand Days, 1933–1936*. New York: Simon & Schuster, 1954.

Watkins, T. H. *Righteous Pilgrim: The Life and Times of Harold L. Ickes, 1874–1952*. New York: Henry Holt Company, 1992.

Johnson, Hugh S. (1882–1942)

Jason Roberts

A versatile, talented, erratic, and charismatic individual given to self-described periods of "demonic activity," Hugh Johnson served as the first head of the

National Recovery Administration (NRA), a key New Deal alphabet agency in the fight against the impact of the Great Depression by the newly inaugurated Franklin D. Roosevelt (1882–1945). However, the NRA after initially eliciting an enthusiastic response became very unpopular. The agency turned out to be very complicated to administer, did not achieve its goals, and Johnson's actions added to the controversy that led to his forced resignation in early fall 1934.

Born on August 5, 1881, in Fort Scott, Kansas, Johnson grew up in a family that in an attempt to improve its circumstances moved repeatedly before winding up in Alva, a town located on Oklahoma's Cherokee Strip. He entered West Point in 1899 and was commissioned in 1903. During the next decade he had a variegated army career: Johnson served with the cavalry along the Texas border with Mexico; as an acting quartermaster oversaw army relief in a San Francisco suffering from the aftereffects of the 1906 earthquake; served a tour of duty (1907–1909) in the Philippines; during 1910–1912 was stationed in America's national parks including Yosemite; and in 1912 was appointed superintendent of Sequoia National Park.

While serving then and later Johnson began a successful remunerative career as an author; he wrote two juveniles (*Williams of West Point* in 1908 and *Williams on Service* in 1910) as well as over 25 adventure stories published in such popular magazines as *Collier's* and *Everybody's*. In 1914, selected by the army for legal training, he undertook a cram course at the University of California Law School. Graduating in 1916 he immediately joined the punitive expedition sent to Mexico to deal with Pancho Villa (1878–1923), earning high marks from its commander general John J. Pershing (1860–1948). Later that year he became a law officer in the Bureau of Insular Affairs, in charge of civil litigation.

After the United States entered World War I in April 1917, Johnson—because of his key roles in the nation's mobilization—became nationally prominent, rising to the rank of brigadier general. He successfully wrote key sections of the Selective Service Act of 1917, and for his successful contributions to the administration of the draft was awarded the Distinguished Service Medal. Johnson also served on the War Industries Board (WIB), gaining a reputation of being a master organizer and administrator; his achievements in co-coordinating military procurement with the board's operations impressed financier Bernard Baruch (1870–1965), WIB's chairman. During fall of 1918 Johnson was appointed commander of an army division scheduled to go overseas, but the war ended before the troops could embark, and in February 1919 a disappointed Johnson resigned from the army to enter the business world. In September 1919 he became an executive with the Moline Plow Company, headed by former WIB associate George Peek (1873–1943).

The continuing post–World War I agricultural slump led Johnson and Peek to develop an "Equality for Agriculture" plan calling for intervention of the federal government to rid the market of price-reducing crop surpluses and lobbied for such legislation. Between 1924 and 1928 Oregon senator Charles McNary (1874–1944) and Iowa representative Gilbert Haugen (1859–1933), both Republicans, presented bills in Congress designed to raise farm incomes; the proposed legislation in essence called for the government to buy up crop surpluses and sell them overseas, a process that would maintain "a fair price" domestically. The McNary-Haugen bills, after failing at first, passed Congress in 1927 and 1928, but they were struck down by vigorous presidential vetoes. In 1927 a disappointed Johnson went to work for Baruch as an assistant and "idea man."

During Roosevelt's successful 1932 campaign for the presidency, Johnson joined the "Brain Trust" as a "Baruch man" and contributed ideas and speeches. Subsequently, in early 1933 he helped draft the National Industrial Recovery Act, adopted by Congress in June 1933, establishing the NRA. This agency was expected to stimulate the depressed economy by ending the "destructive business competition," which many believed impeded recovery, by establishing a new cooperative system based on "codes of fair competition." Adherence to these codes drawn up with the aid of government was ostensibly "voluntary," but Johnson with the evangelical intensity with which he promoted the NRA, asserted that those ignoring the codes were "chiselers" who would get "a sock right on the nose." The NRA, it was anticipated, would among other activities regulate business practices, maintain price stability, and foster positive relations between management and labor. Over 500 codes were drawn up, in major industries such as auto and steel as well as many minor ones such as dog food and burlesque. Johnson on becoming NRA head had warned that "it will be red fire at first and dead cats afterward."

Johnson went to enormous lengths to make the nation NRA-conscious and the agency an effective operation, but ultimately he and it failed. The concept of national planning, which underlay the creation of the NRA, was being discredited. He had seemed to be the right choice to run the agency with his business experience and proven track record as a skilled administrator and organizer. But Baruch, who had not recommended him to run the NRA, proved prescient in observing that Johnson was "a good number three man, maybe a number two man . . . but he's not a number one man." The NRA codes had quickly come under fire from most of the groups they were intended to serve. Small businesses complained that they favored big business. Labor unions criticized the codes for their voluntary nature (the benefits destined to improve working conditions were not mandatory). The public found many code provisions baffling and complicated. A cross section of critics demanded extensive revision of the codes.

Despite Johnson's considerable abilities, he no longer inspired confidence. All too often he was temperamental, unwilling to compromise, tended to be impulsive in his public remarks (at one point Johnson denounced NRA's critics as "perfumed guys" in whose veins "there must flow something more than a trace of rodent blood"), and charged with substituting bluster and invective for coherent policies. In addition, his public displays of alcoholism and openly discussed extramarital affair with his attractive secretary proved extremely embarrassing. The president found Johnson to be a liability, and by October 1934 Johnson had been replaced as head of what had become an unpopular and controversial agency—months before the Supreme Court unanimously ruled (May 27, 1935) the NRA's activities and the legislation establishing it were unconstitutional.

After a short stint in 1936 as WPA administrator in New York City, Johnson, specializing in political topics, became a syndicated newspaper columnist and a radio commentator. Politically he moved away from Roosevelt. He did support the president's reelection bid in 1936 but became a bitter critic of his policies, endorsing in 1940 Republican presidential candidate Wendell Willkie (1892–1942), and also becoming an outspoken promoter of isolationism, actively participating with the America First Committee. Johnson died in Washington, D.C., on April 15, 1942.

Further Reading

Johnson, Hugh. *The Blue Eagle from Egg to Earth.* Reprint ed. New York: Greenwood Press, 1968.

Ohl, John Kennedy. *Hugh S. Johnson and the New Deal.* DeKalb: Northern Illinois Press, 1985.

Kennedy, Joseph Patrick (1888–1969)

A. E. L. Martin

A remarkable man whose life encompassed successful careers in various fields ranging from banking to public service, Joseph Kennedy was ruthless in pursuit of his ambitions for himself and his family. He was a very self-contradictory figure; publicly a devout Catholic and family man, he was also a known womanizer and a masterly often unethical stock market manipulator in the 1920s. Some years later as the first and one of the most effective chairs of the Securities Exchange Commission (SEC), he oversaw an end to many of the techniques he had utilized and brought government regulation to the nation's stock markets. Kennedy's money and influence paved the way to the presidency for his son; but for him to be elected, the father—whose

Joseph Kennedy, American businessman, politician, and ambassador. (Library of Congress)

post–World War II reputation was less than attractive—had to drop out of public life and until he died in 1969 kept a low profile.

Joseph Kennedy was born in Boston on September 6, 1888; his father was a prosperous saloon keeper, respected businessman, and important local Democratic politician. The son attended the prestigious Boston Latin School and graduated (1912) from Harvard with an undistinguished record and a BA. In October 1914 he wed Rose Fitzgerald (1890–1995), oldest daughter of John F. "Honey Fitz" Fitzgerald (1863–1950), a former Boston mayor, onetime congressman, and among the state's more powerful Irish Catholic politicians. Rose and Joseph Kennedy had nine children, including President John F. Kennedy (1917–1963) and Senators Robert F. Kennedy (1925–1968) and Edward "Ted" Kennedy (1932–2009).

Appointed an assistant state bank examiner, Kennedy within a year became head of a tiny bank, the Columbia Trust Company, founded by his father. During Joseph Kennedy's two-year tenure, even though Columbia Trust remained a tiny player in Massachusetts banking, he significantly built up its assets. It served as a useful vehicle in later years—on the side he began to speculate in real estate. After American entry into World War I in 1917 Kennedy moved on to become assistant general manager of Bethlehem Steel's Fore River Shipyards (about 10 miles from downtown Boston); commissioned to build 45 destroyers, the company hired Kennedy not as a shipbuilder but as a man who knew how to get things done. By all accounts he did a splendid job before resigning on June 30, 1919.

Kennedy then joined the brokerage firm of Hayden, Stone, a respected minor player in a Boston financial world governed by WASP elites. Hired as a manager of the firm's brokerage department, he helped it weather the 1920–1921 economic downturn. Subsequently, as the markets ticked upward Kennedy and accounts he controlled for the firm's clients benefited. At the end of 1922 his mentor Galen Stone (1862–1926), the firm's cofounder, decided to retire; Kennedy left soon afterward to deal for himself. Using insider information, juggling accounts, borrowing money from Columbia Trust without proper collateral, taking financial risks, Kennedy soon became a millionaire.

Various sources have charged that during Prohibition the funds he used came from bootlegging. Other biographers, refuting such charges, argue no evidence of any kind exists to support them and point out Kennedy earned huge sums from diverse activities, especially the movie industry, which the Boston financial elite scorned. By 1927 the Irish Catholic Kennedy had moved to New York, because notwithstanding his economic success he found Boston "a bigoted place" denying his family social opportunities.

He plunged into the movie business, his chief interest from 1926 to 1930. As a biographer put it: Kennedy "entered the industry a rich man, but . . . departed a multi-millionaire." Earlier he had organized a syndicate that controlled film distribution and exhibition in much of New England. Subsequently, he vigorously and economically ran FBO, a minor studio. At one point Kennedy controlled three studios and was paid enormous weekly salaries. He proved a very efficient cost slasher but was unable to improve the quality of the films produced.

He made substantial personal profits by swapping stock or selling short, all actions based on inside information—at best unethical even if then not illegal. His last venture in Hollywood was typical of his dealings there; he made a killing on a merger that resulted in Pathe becoming part of RKO, in whose formation he also played a part. Kennedy profited from the Pathe deal, but most stockholders did not.

A fascinating aspect of his involvement with the movies was his notorious relationship with film star Gloria Swanson (1899–1984). Throughout his life Kennedy was an unabashed womanizer; his liaison with Swanson was unusual because of its intensity and length—and for becoming an open secret. A bitter Swanson later discussing the finances behind their relationship claimed that "creative book-keeping . . . had left him rich and her poor."

Their relationship ended in March 1930, six months after the Crash with the Depression in full swing. Kennedy had been remarkably prescient in pulling out of the stock market early; he did not trust it, knowing from the inside that share prices did not always reflect the true worth of a company. Kennedy emerged unscathed from the market's collapse.

In the early 1930s, while continuing to build up his fortune, Kennedy turned to politics. He helped Franklin Roosevelt (1882–1945) gain the Democratic presidential nomination in 1932 and contributed financially to his candidacy. After FDR's triumph he ignored Kennedy; the president's advisors were leery of a man identified with the worst of Wall Street's practices, and that attitude was bolstered by Senate hearings about pool operations in liquor stocks (Kennedy was involved) during the summer of 1933 as the termination of Prohibition was under way.

New Deal legislation to eliminate unethical and illegal stock market practices and to regulate others that had contributed to the 1929 Crash aroused strong hostile reactions in the American financial and business communities. To dampen that hostility FDR chose Kennedy, who had wide-ranging ties within those communities and was admired if not always respected for his money-making abilities, to head a new regulatory body, the Securities and Exchange Commission. When some of the president's colleagues protested the choice, Roosevelt is supposed to have asserted "it takes a thief to catch a thief."

Kennedy served as SEC chairman from July 2, 1934, to September 23, 1935. He worked diligently to establish the SEC's authority, intelligently and forcefully used its policing powers, thoroughly deflated his critics, and blending the reform spirit with marketplace realism earned the regulatory body and himself numerous accolades. On his retirement *Time* dubbed the SEC "the most able New Deal agency in Washington." Kennedy supported Roosevelt's reelection in 1936, contributing thousands to the campaign and paying for production of a book, *I'm for Roosevelt*, which enthusiastically supported FDR as the man who had rescued American capitalism.

In March 1937 Kennedy became chair of the U.S. Maritime Commission. His strenuous efforts to reinvigorate a stagnant American merchant marine ran afoul of the uncooperative mossbacked ship owners and the newly militant seamen's unions. His disappointing ten months' tenure ended when the president in December 1937 appointed him ambassador to Great Britain. The president apparently considered appointing the Irish Catholic Kennedy to represent the United States at the Court of St. James "a grand joke."

Kennedy took up his post in March 1938. Initially a great social success, Kennedy had begun to lose popularity in the UK before the outbreak of World War II in September 1939 because of his support of the appeasers. Moreover, his clear reluctance to confront the antidemocratic forces in Europe, defeatist isolationism, and fear of a German victory led him to veer from the Roosevelt administration's foreign policies. Kennedy returned to the United States just before the 1940 presidential election and despite misgivings made a radio address supporting FDR's reelection (useful for Roosevelt because of Kennedy's importance as a prominent Catholic).

By 1941 Kennedy's comments on the war and a qualified opposition to American involvement had led to his involuntary retirement from public life. He continued to build his fortune, earned nearly $100 million during the war, invested heavily in New York City real estate (he was accused of being a "rent gouger"), and in 1945 bought control of Chicago's Merchandise Mart, the world's largest commercial building. In 1960 his fortune was estimated to be at least $200 million.

After World War II he supported various conservative causes: for instance, aiding Wisconsin's rabidly anti-Communist Republican senator Joseph Mc-Carthy (1908–1957). Kennedy used his money and wide range of contacts to further the political career of his son John F. Kennedy (1917–1963). Shortly after election of his son to the presidency in 1961, the father suffered a stroke, and his health progressively deteriorated until he died on November 18, 1968. For all his political and financial success, probably his most important role was as founding patriarch of a still-evolving political dynasty.

Further Reading

Nasaw, David. *The Patriarch: The Remarkable Life and Turbulent Times of Joseph P. Kennedy.* New York: Penguin, 2012.

Lewis, John L. (1880–1969)

Jason Roberts

Dictatorial, mercurial, ruthless, theatrical: these are some of the words used to describe John Llewellen Lewis during his long tenure (1920–1960) as head of the United Mine Workers (UMW), whose members benefited from his leadership. So, too, during the 1930s did American industrial workers as Lewis, a man of imposing countenance and remarkable oratorical skills, led the fight to unionize workers laboring in mass production industries. The American Federation of Labor (AFL) was recognized as "the voice of American labor," but its constituent unions, with few exceptions (e.g., miners, garment workers), ignored U.S. industrial workers. AFL membership in the main consisted of skilled workers, the so-called "princes of the working class." The Depression hurt most of the working class but increased the misery in industrial workers' lives; they suffered intensely. Lewis for reasons not wholly altruistic began unionizing American industrial workers. Aided by the Roosevelt administration, which saw political gain in his activities, Lewis helped found the Congress of Industrial Organizations (CIO), which rivaled the AFL. For much of the 1930s he was the most powerful labor leader in the United States.

Lewis was born to Welsh immigrants on February 12, 1880, in an Iowa hamlet (Cleveland) near Lucas, a small town in the state's southcentral region. The family moved repeatedly to different Iowa towns as the father sought work. In the early 1890s it moved to Des Moines. There, Lewis attended high school but did not graduate as the family moved back to Lucas, and Lewis went to work in the local coal mines, joining the UMW. Although by 1901 he been elected secretary of the UMW local, the ambitious Lewis left Lucas and for the next years worked at mining and construction jobs in various western states. In 1905 he returned to Lucas, became involved in various fraternal organizations, failed to gain election (1907) as mayor, and opened a grain and feed business wiped out during the Panic of 1907. The next year, Lewis, his new bride, and most of his family moved to Panama, Illinois (a recently established town in the state's southcentral area, built around rich coal veins), where he briefly worked as a miner.

In 1909 Lewis was elected head of the Panama UMW local, one of the state's largest unions. Not long after he became UMW legislative agent in Springfield, the Illinois state capital. In 1911 he joined the AFL as an organizer and served as a troubleshooter for AFL head Samuel Gompers (1850–1924). The UMW in 1917 appointed him statistician, a key figure in its collective bargaining efforts. Later that year he was appointed UMW vice president and in 1920 was easily elected president. The previous year he had proved to be a canny strike leader, winning a compromise settlement despite public hostility to the strike

John L. Lewis, president of the United Mine Workers from 1920 to 1960, speaks at a United Mine Workers Convention in 1938. (Library of Congress)

and opposition from federal agencies. In 1921, by a large vote margin, he lost a challenge to Gompers for the AFL presidency. Over the next years his support of successful Republican presidential candidates did not benefit the UMW, the sick coal industry, or Lewis. He did manage to consolidate his hold on the UMW and defeated (1926) a serious challenge to him by John Brophy (1883-1963), candidate of a coalition of insurgents, reformers, and Leftists including the Communists, but only by use of thugs, Red-baiting, and ballot box stuffing. Given the UMW's state at the beginning of the 1930s Lewis was seen as just another ineffective leader of a dwindling union in a sick industry.

During the 1920s, that industry suffered from overproduction, falling prices, and dramatically increased competition from heating oil. As pit closures increased and mechanization increased UMW numbers fell precipitously: by 1933 the dues-paying membership had declined over 75 percent from 1920 to less than 100,000. The union's clout faded as its numbers fell; coal operators in key states such as Illinois and Kentucky successfully attacked the UMW, legally and extralegally. Pittsburgh Coal, the largest in the United States, despite a contract with the UMW, closed down, and then reopened with nonunion workers; a strike to force the company to honor the contract ended in violence and failed. Operator after operator emulated such tactics. A long strike toward the end of the decade further weakened the union. With the 1933 advent of the pro-labor New Deal, Lewis determined to resurrect the union. Using the UMW's dwindling resources and exploiting FDR's great popularity and Section 7a of the National Industrial Recovery Act guaranteeing workers the right to organize, Lewis sent organizers into the coal fields asserting "the President wants you to join the union" without clarifying which president was meant. The massive all-out drive was enormously successful; by the end of 1933 UMW membership stood at over 350,000, and the union had even penetrated previously antiunion coal fields.

Convinced the UMW's future depended on organizing the thousands employed by the "captive" mines owned by the avowedly "open shop" steel industry, Lewis strenuously urged AFL organization of industrial workers. After 1933 many such workers organized independently, sought admission to the AFL, and were discontented about its insistence that mass production workers be organized along craft lines (e.g., an automobile plant's carpenters belonged in the carpenter's union, and so on). The AFL leaders were not receptive as was Lewis to the creation of all-inclusive units (whatever the division of labor in a plant all auto workers belonged in a union of automobile workers). At Lewis's behest the 1934 AFL convention (he had become a member of the AFL's executive council), voted to commission a report on the situation. The 1935 convention, controlled by traditionalists, after a bitter debate rejected the report, favoring changes in policy. Lewis provoked a leader of those opposed to industrial unionism, "Big Bill" Hutcheson (1874–1953)—head of the Carpenter's Union—into calling him a "bastard," whereupon an ostensibly outraged Lewis punched Hutcheson, bloodying him. The punch was a dramatic symbolic gesture. On November 9, 1935, the day after the convention concluded, Lewis along with allies in various other unions established *within* the AFL a Committee on Industrial Organization (CIO).

The next years represented the peak of Lewis's power, and he dominated the American labor scene. In 1936 Lewis and the CIO (which became the Congress of Industrial Organization in November 1938) were expelled from the AFL. Augmented by Leftists like Brophy (earlier harried out of the UMW) as well as Communists he had previously excoriated, Lewis eloquently and with great skill guided workers seeking to organize in industries such as steel, auto, rubber, longshoring, and electrical appliances. The CIO initially flourished, aided by provisions of the 1935 Labor Relations Act (the Wagner Act), its interpretation by a sympathetic National Labor Relations Board that accepted worker militancy such as "sit down" strikes, and the friendly Roosevelt administration. Lewis used the revived UMW's treasury to funnel vast sums into building the CIO (estimates assume the UMW provided 70 percent of the new organization's initial funding, about $7 million). Among the CIO's most noteworthy early accomplishments was obtaining a contract with U.S. Steel; notorious for its fervent antiunion stance, the corporation signed in February 1937 with a CIO affiliate, the Steel Workers Organizing Committee (SWOC).

The CIO and Lewis began to suffer setbacks. Management defeated a SWOC strike against the "Little Steel" companies begun in late May 1937. The severe economic downturn that began in mid-1937 (the Roosevelt Recession) hampered CIO membership drives. A rejuvenated AFL proved surprisingly nimble in contests for members with the CIO. Internal disputes broke out in some of the new CIO unions, curbing their effectiveness. Lewis became increasingly antagonistic to FDR. In 1936, Lewis had created Labor's Non-Partisan League, which contributed $500,000 to FDR's reelection campaign. By 1940, Lewis had become disenchanted with the president. He was outraged that FDR in 1937 did not support the "sit down" strikes or condemn the violence Little Steel inflicted on SWOC. Perhaps personal ambition played a role in his belief that no president should serve more than two terms: Lewis had been mentioned as a possible candidate. Moreover, like many Americans Lewis feared FDR would embroil the United States in a European war. In fall 1940 Lewis supported FDR's Republican opponent, pledging to resign as CIO head if the president won. FDR did; Lewis resigned on November 18, 1940.

During World War II, Lewis infuriated the public by calling a strike: over 500,000 miners walked out in 1943. Lewis was undaunted by charges his actions were treasonous during wartime. His influence and power diminished after World War II. In 1946 Lewis led the UMW back into the AFL, but when the next year its leaders would not join him in noncompliance with the Taft-Hartley Act (redressing some of the Wagner Act's pro-labor provisions), he led the miners out. In 1948 Lewis led an unsuccessful strike in defiance of a federal court order and was forced to pay a heavy fine. In 1950 Lewis determined to follow less aggressive policies and during the decade collaborated with operators in the sick coal industry. Even though both the industry and the UMW were in decline he remained a force, gaining miners through compromise instead of bitter confrontation, and establishing welfare and pension benefits as well as improved hours, wages, and working conditions. He resigned as UMW head in January 1960, continuing to chair the UMW Welfare and Retirement Fund until he died on June 11, 1969.

Further Reading

Alinsky, Saul. *John L. Lewis: An Unauthorized Biography.* Reprint ed. Urbana: University of Illinois Press, 1986.

Dubofsky, Melvyn, and Warren Van Tine. *John L. Lewis: A Biography.* New York: Quadrangle Books, 1977.

Olson, Floyd (1891–1936)

Jason Roberts

Floyd Olson was a charismatic, inspiring leader as well as a savvy, clever politician, three-time elected governor of Minnesota (1930, 1932, 1934), and was well on his way to the U.S. Senate when pancreatic cancer cut short his career. Olson, running on the Farmer-Labor ticket, made excellent use of his skills as a dynamic orator with a pleasing radio voice as well as an intuitive grasp of how Minnesota's electoral politics were changing to break the Republican stranglehold on the office of the state's chief executive (prior to Olson 18 Republicans had served as governor for over 63 years; 4 Democrats had been elected for less than 10 years; Olson was the first Farmer-Labor candidate to be elected governor). His election represented a distinct turn in Minnesota politics as he mobilized state resources and New Deal agencies to combat the terrible toll exacted on the state by the Depression. While Olson worked well with FDR and his administration, the governor represented a challenge to the New Deal from the Left. Nationally his outspoken, articulate commitment to social justice as governor made him the darling of left-wing intellectuals and politicians, many of whom believed he could be a third party non-Communist Left alternative to the traditional candidates.

Olson was born on November 13, 1891, to impoverished Scandinavian immigrant parents and brought up in a slum area of north Minneapolis, a predominantly Jewish section of a city then characterized as "the most anti-Semitic" in the U.S." During his early years he was a "shabbos goy," earning small sums performing actions for Orthodox Jews on the Sabbath such as turning on electricity forbidden them by their religion to undertake on that day. Subsequently, Olson won the votes of Yiddish-speaking voters with his command of the language he had gained, and his early ties with the Minneapolis Jewish community later stood him in good stead as did his fluency in Scandinavian languages, which gained him support from other minority groups. Olson had a limited formal education. He graduated (1909) from high school, attended (1910) the University of Minnesota for a year, and then labored at a series of odd jobs in Alaska and Canada before working as a stevedore in Seattle, where he joined the IWW. In 1913 Olson returned to Minneapolis, found employment as a law clerk, and at night attended Northwestern Law College (later merged into the William Mitchell College of Law), earning a degree in 1915.

For the next years Olson was in private practice. In 1919 he was appointed assistant to the county attorney for Hennepin County (with Minneapolis as county seat it was the state's most populous by far). The next year, after the Hennepin County attorney was accused of taking bribes, Olson succeeded him. He held that position for ten years, being elected in 1922 and reelected in 1926, both times with large majorities. In this position he gained a reputation as a crusading official who confronted the Ku Klux Klan as well as prosecuted corrupt politicians and scheming businessmen, one group of which hired a thug to blow up a union leader. In 1924 Olson won a hard-fought primary and ran for governor as a candidate for Minnesota's newly reorganized Farmer-Labor Party (a tenuous coalition of Progressives, farmers, and workers interested in social and economic reforms, it proved for over two decades to be the most effective third party in American political history). Olson lost to the Republican candidate but made a good showing, running way ahead of the Democratic candidate. In 1930 he again ran for governor on the Farmer-Labor ticket and won with 57 percent of the vote, carrying 82 of the state's 87 counties; the popular Olson was easily reelected in 1932 and 1934. At that time the Minnesota legislature was ostensibly nonpartisan, and each house was organized into liberal and conservative caucuses. During Olson's first term both houses were controlled by the conservatives. Thereafter he dealt with a divided legislature; a liberal caucus gained control of the lower house, but the upper house remained conservative. Olson's electoral triumphs ended nearly a century of Republican dominance in the state.

As governor, Olson talked radically and acted pragmatically in dealing with a state hard-hit by the Depression: one in four Minnesotans was unemployed, farmers—about a third of the state's workforce—suffered from falling crop prices and rising debts, an increasing number of "red ink counties" had run out of funds for welfare relief, and many school districts had exhausted their capacity to pay bills. Olson asserted, "I am not a liberal. I am . . . a radical" and preached "a gospel of government . . . ownership of the means of production and distribution." Before New Deal financial aid kicked in, he achieved many of his objectives, including the creation of state unemployment benefits, the cessation of farm foreclosures, funding for the construction of highways, and implementation of a more progressive tax system. Olson, faced with the collapse of the state's banking system, implemented a bank holiday days before FDR did so nationally; indeed, over the years many of Olson's initiatives were echoed by New Deal legislation.

Olson enacted much of his program through a series of executive orders, but he also had considerable legislative and public support, which he wooed with his first-rate oratorical and political skills. He cajoled, pleaded, and intimidated the conservative upper house and generally won his way with it. Until his premature death, Olson retained his enormous appeal to rural voters, the urban poor, and Minnesota's growing working class. During his tenure, Olson supported the rights of labor unions to engage in collective bargaining and persuaded the state legislature to prohibit injunctions in labor disputes. His personal intervention in bitter strikes taking place in Austin (1933) and Minneapolis (1934) dismayed management, which expected the state's chief executive unstintingly to support employers.

Headed into the 1936 election season, Olson, who had become a national figure, was viewed by many as a possible radical third party alternative for U.S. president, but the governor preferred the U.S. Senate, was campaigning hard despite illness, and was assumed to be way ahead in the race for that seat. Olson, who had carefully cultivated the state's ties to the New Deal, unhesitatingly in 1936 supported the president's reelection. Olson and his administration did come under attack from seasoned journalist Walter Liggett (1885–1935), who in his independent limited circulation weekly repeatedly charged there were links between organized crime in Minnesota and individuals close to Olson. Liggett was beaten, prosecuted unsuccessfully on a nonexistent sodomy charge, and on December 9, 1935, shot down in an alley besides his house in front of his daughter and wife. She and some neighbors identified the killer as Kid Cann (1900–1981), the non de plume of Isadore Blumenfeld, a notorious, powerful Jewish organized crime figure in Minneapolis. As with other prosecutions he had faced till then, Kid Cann to the shock of many was acquitted in 90 minutes by a jury that doubted the credibility of Mrs. Liggett and the neighbors who witnessed the shooting. An ill Olson, who was in and out of the Mayo Clinic, promised to do all that was possible to find the killer, but not too long after, on August 22, 1936, died of cancer.

Olson was an appealing figure to an American public that had seen too many politicians in a time of desperation attempt to finesse their positions. Although he stood publicly as an unabashed radical his actions in the main were not. He died young, and how he would have matured is not clear. As the state's chief executive his program was designed to win over as many voters as possible. Olson did greatly expand the powers of the state's government in the interests of social justice and introduced many social and economic changes in Minnesota. Agree with them or not, he stands out because of his actions and skills in promoting them. Attesting to his popularity is the fact that about 150,000 people attended his funeral.

Further Reading

Mayer, George H. *The Political Career of Floyd B. Olson.* With a new introduction by Russell W. Fridley. St. Paul: Minnesota Historical Society, 1987.

McGrath, John S., and James J. Delmont, eds. *Floyd Bjornsterne Olson: Minnesota's Greatest Liberal Governor, A Memorial Volume in Honor of the Memory of the Late Governor of the State of Minnesota, 1930–1936.* St. Paul: McGrath & Delmont, 1937.

World Economic Conference (1933)

Jason Roberts

Also known as the London Monetary and Economic Conference, the World Economic Conference was an early 1930s economic summit. The nations of the world, suffering from the impact of the Great Depression, agreed to send representatives to London for an international conference to discuss ongoing diplomatic and economic issues, most notably the best methods of dealing with the damaging economic downturn.

There had been in the decade preceding this meeting over 20 conferences dealing with different aspects of international relations such as security, debts, reparations (i.e., the financial burden that the European victors in World War I had saddled on the defeated Germans), and currency fluctuation. Despite America's generally isolationist foreign policy the United States participated in many of these conferences such as the ones dealing with reparations because of the large debts these victors owed to them, that were being paid by the UK

WORLD ECONOMIC CONFERENCE (1933)   577

and France from the reparations due them from the Germans who in turn were able to pay because of loans from American financial institutions.

An international conference had been discussed widely since 1931. President Herbert Hoover (1874–1964), a strong believer in the efficacy of international cooperation and eager to settle the financial issues plaguing the world economy, urged (June 1931) a twelve-month moratorium on both inter-allied debts and war reparations. Hoover also wanted discussions on such issues as disarmament and world peace. The British and the French, eager to discuss a renegotiation of their World War I war debts owed to the United States, also wanted to see stability in exchange rates and a reduction in the trade barriers caused by high tariff duties (the Smoot-Hawley legislation enacted in 1930 by the U.S. Congress had resulted in compensatory implementation of high duties by other countries).

Based on communications with the Hoover administration, European leaders believed that a series of agreements could be reached at a conference. Under the aegis of the League of Nations, an organization committee, composed of representatives from six major countries including the United States, met in Geneva during 1932 and hammered out a conference agenda; the topics included restoration of the gold standard, stabilization of commodity prices, and increasing world trade (which had decreased by nearly 25 percent since 1929). However, the Americans sent by Hoover to Geneva disagreed with their European counterparts about how and when the war debts should be paid (not surprising, since for fiscal 1931 payment of the interest represented nearly six percent of the U.S. Treasury's income).

By March 1933 the United States had a new President, Franklin D. Roosevelt (1882–1945), and various world leaders trooped to Washington, D.C., to sound him out on what should and could be done. Visitors included the finance ministers of such countries as Canada, China, Italy, and Mexico, as well as British prime minister Ramsay MacDonald (1866–1937), Reichsbank head Hjalmar Schacht (1877–1970), and the prominent and very active French politician Edouard Herriot (1872–1957).

For Hoover, one of the main causes of the Depression in the United States had been international fiscal mismanagement; Roosevelt had a different outlook. In contrast to Hoover, FDR did not believe that the Depression tormenting the United States could be dealt with internationally; he saw it as being domestic in origin. For him raising prices was more important and a pressing issue. Roosevelt felt no obligation to follow the policies of his predecessor but did not broadcast his views; the men who conferred with FDR seem to have been reassured by their discussions with him. But the president had tipped his hand when in the weeks after his inauguration the United States in effect abandoned the gold standard, severing the ties between the metal and the dollar.

The conference organizing committee had invited delegates from every corner of the globe. Of the 67 entities invited 66 responded positively; only Panama declined, asserting it could not afford to send delegates. Among the hundreds of official delegates, many of whom came with technical experts, were the president of Switzerland, eight prime ministers, and 20 foreign ministers. The American delegation, which represented diverse views and lacked harmony, was headed by Secretary of State Cordell Hull (1871–1955); his deputy was Ohio politician, newspaper publisher, and defeated 1920 presidential candidate James M. Cox (1870–1957), whose running mate had been Roosevelt. Other American delegates included veteran key congressional Democrats Key Pittman (1872–1940) and Samuel McReynolds (1872–1939), chairs respectively of the Senate Foreign Relations Committee and the House Committee on Foreign Affairs.

The conference, held at London's Geological Museum, was opened on June 12, 1933, by King George V; many of the sessions were presided over by Prime Minister MacDonald. Much of the conference's work was done in committee and being very technical was negotiated by experts who accompanied the delegations, such as the American banker James Paul Warburg (1896–1969). President Roosevelt, who had not explicitly spelled out his beliefs to the American delegates, went on vacation sailing off the coast of New England. On June 20 he was briefly joined by his then close associate Raymond Moley (1886–1975); a former Columbia University professor and trusted speech writer, he was an organizer of the "Brain Trust," a group of advisors many of whom joined FDR's administration. Moley had made a well-publicized mad dash from Washington, D.C., to meet the president. After their short discussion on economic policy Moley sailed for England with the media relentlessly discussing what message he carried from FDR.

Arriving in London at midnight on June 27, Moley in the next days negotiated a statement of policy that the irresolute president ultimately spurned. Leaks about Moley's agreement for currency stabilization (i.e., fixed exchange rates) led to an unwanted strengthening of the dollar and weakening of the New York stock market. A vacillating Roosevelt for weeks had sent mixed signals to the American delegation; on July 1 he cabled Moley rejecting his efforts. Two days later in a message to the conference he repudiated any agreements into which Moley had entered, asserted that the United States would not agree to exchange rate stabilization, did not plan to return to the gold standard in the foreseeable future, and condemned "old fetishes of so-called international bankers."

Roosevelt considered the gold standard too constricting and believed inflating the money supply without reference to fixed exchange rates was crucial to ending the economic downturn in the United States The president, in what then and later has been described as a "bombshell message," scuttled the conference. Thanks in large part to Hull's strenuous efforts the conference did not issue a formal statement criticizing Roosevelt. His economic nationalism made American cooperation unlikely, and without it nothing substantial could be achieved. The conference lingered on for a while, adjourning on July 27.

Roosevelt's actions elicited strong criticism from most Europeans, reinforcing their hostile views of the United States. Already angry about Smoot-Hawley, they were bitterly resentful; typical was the statement that the president's message was "for all times a classic example of conceit [and] hectoring." A notable exception was economist John Maynard Keynes (1883–1946), who declared the president had been "magnificently right." Also positively responding to the president were the leaders of Nazi Germany, who following a policy of economic nationalism had determined their country could not pay reparations, and would not.

Roosevelt understood that implementation of the New Deal program demanded inflation, and the legislation he sponsored was based on that assumption. The bulk of the delegates to the World Economic Conference with their emphasis on stable exchange rates (as well as an alleviation of war debts and reparations) had different goals.

Further Reading

Badger, Anthony. *The New Deal: The Depression Years, 1933–1940.* Chicago: Ivan R. Dee, 1989.

Burns, James McGregor. *Roosevelt: The Lion and the Fox.* New York: Harcourt, Brace & World, Inc., 1956.

Davis, Kenneth S. *FDR: The New Deal Years, 1933–1937.* New York: Random House, 1979.

Kennedy, David. *Freedom from Fear: The American People in Depression and War, 1929–1945.* Oxford: Oxford University Press, 1999.

Moore, James. "A History of the World Economic Conference, London, 1933." Unpublished PhD diss., SUNY Stony Brook, 1971.

Nichols, Jeannette P. "Roosevelt's Monetary Diplomacy in 1933." *American Historical Review* 56 (1951): 307–21.

Schlesinger, Arthur M., Jr. *The Age of Roosevelt: The Coming of the New Deal.* Boston: Houghton Mifflin Company, 1958.

ECONOMIC DOWNTURNS, 1974–1984

Jason Roberts

The period from 1974 to 1984 was a time in American history. During this decade, although the economy was not always in the doldrums, it confronted an often serious array of problems, most notably "stagflation." As the American economy oscillated between severe bouts of recession and runaway inflation, Presidents Richard Nixon (1913–1994), Gerald Ford (1919–2006), "Jimmy" Carter (b. 1924), and Ronald Reagan (1911–2004) and their advisers responded to the diverse economic crises in various ways, not all being successful, and some proving harmful; the average American suffered and lost confidence in the government and the people in charge of the economy.

Root Causes

America's economic problems had a number of causes. These included presidential reluctance to raise taxes despite substantial boosts in federal spending on both domestic social programs and the Vietnam War, generous pay raises awarded to corporate executives and to labor unions, and the harassing actions of the Organization of Petroleum Exporting Countries (OPEC) using oil as a weapon. Other economic problems included an ongoing decline in large-scale manufacturing jobs, massive government spending at the state and local level (leaving once prosperous cities like New York on the verge of bankruptcy), and increased competition from German and Japanese car companies that began not only to produce a superior product but whose management realized that in a decade of rising gas prices American consumers were likely, at least temporarily, to turn to the smaller fuel-efficient cars these companies produced.

A major economic trend in the 1970s was the decline of the traditional American manufacturing centers in the Northeast and the Midwest (or "Rustbelt" as these areas were informally dubbed) and the remarkable economic resurgence of the South and Southwest (or "Sunbelt" as these regions came to be called). Rustbelt states like Ohio, Pennsylvania, and Michigan, experienced job loss and high unemployment as their industrial base declined. On the other hand, the Sunbelt boomed as it created jobs at a faster rate in the 1970s than did any part of the Rustbelt. The population of the South increased over 30 percent during the decade, due to a considerable extent from migration by Americans from other parts of the United States looking for work.

Factors in the Sunbelt's economic success include less business regulation, right to work laws (limiting organized labor), and generous state and local incentives. Commentators have also pointed out that the Sunbelt boom was aided by the region's long-serving congressmen who were able to funnel federal funds to the aerospace and defense industries increasingly centered in this region. The Sunbelt states received more in federal government benefits than they paid out in taxes.

Faltering during Nixon's Presidency

Economic faltering, which ultimately in one form or another affected most of the country, can be traced back to the final months of Richard Nixon's presidency. He was the first president in modern times to face simultaneously the serious problems of high inflation and high unemployment, and he did so only months after taking office in January 1969. He and his advisers hoped to guide the American economy to what was called a "soft landing" through policies of financial restraint that would keep inflation under control without unduly raising unemployment.

By late 1970 unemployment had reached 6 percent (a figure then considered really worrisome), and by 1971 had increased to 6.2 percent and was moving upward. At the same time inflation, which the Nixon administration seemed unable to control, was also steadily increasing. At this time some economists and media pundits referred to an *inflationary recession*, a term of which Nixon strongly disproved, soon replaced by the catchy phrase *stagflation*.

Gearing up for the 1972 presidential election, Nixon decided that inflation and unemployment were threats to his reelection and must be dealt with. In 1960, as he recalled in one of his memoirs, the administration (1953–1961) of Dwight Eisenhower (1890–1969) had emphasized fighting inflation rather than unemployment. Nixon believed that this choice had validity, but that the 1960 monetary tightening policies of the Federal Reserve with a subsequent rise in unemployment had contributed significantly to his razor-thin loss in that year's presidential election.

Nixon wanted nothing to hamper his reelection bid in 1972 and undertook a number of measures to deal with the economy, joblessness, and inflation, in a manner that would as he recalled enhance his chances as well as the welfare of the American people. These measures taken in August 1971 included a 90-day wage and price freeze (later extended with regular controls), cutting taxes, imposing a 10 percent surcharge on duties paid by imported goods, and perhaps most importantly closing "the gold window."

With this action Nixon ended the American government's international obligation to redeem the U.S. dollar for gold, thus doing in terms of the world market what President Franklin D. Roosevelt (1882–1945) had done domestically in 1933, when to stop the run on the nation's gold reserves he ended the opportunity for U.S. residents or American citizens to exchange their paper currency for gold. By shutting the gold window Nixon ended the post–World War II system of fixed exchange rates between world currencies and devalued the U.S. dollar in an attempt to make American goods cheaper and more competitive in the world marketplace.

The economy began recovering in late 1971, and America began to experience an economic boom. Federal Reserve chairman Arthur Burns (1904–1987) played a significant role in boosting the economic recovery by lowering interest rates in 1971 and 1972. Burns, a Columbia University professor whose service to the Eisenhower administration included a stint as chairman of the President's Council of Economic Advisors, had joined the Nixon administration as a counselor to the president responsible for domestic and economic affairs, and he became chairman of the Federal Reserve Board of Governors in 1970, promising to restore price stability without dampening the economy.

During his tenure as chairman (February 1970–January 1978), Burns seemed less concerned with price stability, and consumer price inflation rose about 9 percent annually. Burns since then has been sharply criticized for his lack of independence via the presidents he served (most notably Nixon and his successor Gerald Ford) and for his expansive monetary policy, which resulted in easy access to credit. Burns later maintained that the country and most politicians would not have accepted the high rates of unemployment necessary in his opinion to quell inflation. Moreover, although deeply concerned about inflation, he argued, as a reflective *Economics Quarterly* article put it, that "the Federal Reserve should not be expected to cope with inflation single-handedly."

The boom that began in late 1971 continued through 1972, and as might be expected, greatly assisted Nixon's reelection bid. In the 1972 presidential election, he routed his hapless Democratic opponent, South Dakota senator George McGovern (1922–2012), receiving over 60 percent of the popular vote and winning the electoral votes of 49 of the 50 states. All the contemporary pundits and subsequent chroniclers of the era agree that the improved economy was a major factor in Nixon's reelection triumph.

Cars line up on December 23, 1973, at a gas station in New York City at the height of the energy crisis of 1973. Motorists waited in long lines and paid high prices for gas when the Organization of Petroleum Exporting Countries (OPEC) declared an oil embargo on the United States in October 1973. (AP Photo)

However, the economy took a significant turn for the worse in Nixon's second term. The annual rate of inflation increased dramatically. A major reason for the inflation was an oil embargo imposed in October 1973 by the Organization of Petroleum Exporting Countries (OPEC) on the United States in retaliation for the Nixon administration's support of Israel during the Yom Kippur War. Overseas oil quickly went from less than $2 a barrel to over what then seemed an unfathomable $10 a barrel. Even the shah of Iran (1919–1980), ostensibly an ally of the United States, raised the price of his country's oil several times in a few months. The price of heating oil and gas rose rapidly. And suddenly as Americans fueled their autos there were long lines at gas stations all over the United States.

By the time Nixon left office in August 1974 (he resigned due to the repercussions of the Watergate scandal) both inflation and unemployment had increased, and his economic policies were attacked by both conservatives and liberals. Conservatives condemned Nixon for closing the gold window and imposing wage and price controls. They also recoiled at Nixon's statement that to deal with the problems plaguing the economy he was now a Keynesian. On the other hand, liberals chafed at Nixon's impounding of domestic appropriations and his vetoes in the name of financial responsibility of bills directed at alleviating the distress of the jobless and those hard-hit by the inflation.

Ford's Efforts and Failures

After Nixon resigned, Vice President Gerald Ford succeeded him as president, taking the oath of office on August 9, 1974. Ford, chosen as vice president in October 1973 by Nixon after then vice president Spiro Agnew (1918–1996) resigned amidst charges of bribery and income tax evasion, had been overwhelmingly confirmed by votes in both Houses of Congress. After earning a law degree from Yale University and military service during World War II, Ford had returned to Grand Rapids, Michigan, to practice law. Elected to Congress in 1948 he had served since then, easily winning reelection. Very popular among his peers, he had been chosen in 1965 by his fellow Republican legislators to serve as minority leader in the House of Representatives.

Despite his conservative beliefs (especially on fiscal issues), the engaging Ford was an amiable person who was able to forge close relationships across political lines. However, like Nixon, the new president would be fiercely challenged by the economic problems of the 1970s. Nixon's legacy included uncontrolled federal spending, huge budget deficits, sagging productivity, declining American competitiveness in the world marketplace, growing inflation, accelerating unemployment, rising inflation, and job stagnation except in the less-well-paid service sectors (an AFL-CIO official charged that the United States was becoming "a nation of citizens busily buying and selling cheese burgers and root beer floats").

Ford and his advisers were aware of the problems the United States faced. In choosing how to deal with the deteriorating economy the president decided to focus on inflation as the graver threat that had to be dealt with. Ford assumed that if his administration could stop the ongoing rise in prices and lower them that the joblessness and at least some of the other problems would be cured. But Ford proved to have little luck with his endeavors to improve the economy.

A downturn that began in mid-1973 seriously accelerated during 1974. Increases in productivity, which averaged 3 percent or better annually between 1947 and 1965, continued to fall after 1973 (ultimately reaching a disappointing 1.2 percent in 1979). At the end of Ford's first five months in office the rate of inflation climbed to 12 percent (the highest to that date in modern American history). During 1974 retail prices increased by an estimated 11 percent, wholesale prices by an estimated 18 percent, and unemployment rose significantly. The real gross national product fell by 2 percent.

The next year was not much better. In October 1975 the index of the leading economic indicators reported the largest monthly drop in 23 years. By the end of 1975 the Dow Jones Industrial Average had fallen nearly 37 percent. Unemployment in April 1975 reached 8.7 percent, the highest to that date since 1941; in June unemployment peaked at 9.2 percent, the highest point in the Ford years. The gross national product again fell in 1975, this time by nearly 3 percent.

President Ford responded to the country's economic problems in many ways, not all well-received. In the fall of 1974 he held relatively ineffective "domestic summits" (which included union, business, and government leaders) to discuss possible solutions to the worsening economy. Critics ridiculed his campaign to "Whip Inflation Now" (WIN), as a cynical propaganda stunt; Ford had urged Americans to wear WIN buttons, to save money, to cut consumption, and to conserve energy. Ford's refusal to bail out a financially stricken New York City was seen as cold and heartless, and led to a New York City's *Daily News* banner headline "Ford to New York City: Drop Dead." He had rejected a $90 billion federal loan to the city. However, in fairness to Ford, he was rightly skeptical about the financial reliability of a city that had recklessly spent itself $14 billion into debt; by 1975 the city's spending exceeded revenue by at least 7 percent. (After the state approved a city tax increase Ford eventually did sign legislation providing New York City with $2.3 billion in aid.)

Furthermore, the president seemed inconsistent in his treatment of the country's economic problems. His policies veered from proposing tax increases to suggesting reductions in taxes to attempting to impose spending cuts. Initially he asked Congress for a 5 percent tax increase on corporations and high-income earners. When this proposal proved to have no purchase he suggested tax cuts to stimulate the economy and deal with the growing deficits. Ultimately, Congress did pass a $22.8 billion tax cut but without any real reduction in spending. Ford strongly denounced the cost of the tax cut, but nonetheless reluctantly signed the bill into law, feeling he had no other choice.

Very concerned about the nation's obvious increasing dependence on foreign oil, Ford over and over again urged Americans to conserve energy, and he proposed energy legislation to Congress. In December 1975, after months of debate, Congress finally passed legislation, whose provisions included a mandate for a phased decontrol (over 40 months) of domestic oil prices on the assumption that the higher prices resulting from decontrol would result in conservation because of costs and would also lead to further exploration of oil sources in the United States because of potential profits. Ford, who had vigorously argued for immediate decontrol, did sign the legislation into law.

Ford's relationship with Congress was combative; he vetoed 66 pieces of congressional legislation during his 875 days in office, many of his vetoes arguing that the proposed legislation would result in deficit increases. Congress overrode his vetoes 17 times. Despite the constant wrangling between him and Congress he finally at the end of 1975 signed a tax bill similar to legislation he had earlier vetoed; it did include substantial tax cuts but only vague congressional promises to reduce spending. During his stay in office Ford, in attempting to deal to with the nation's economic problems, constantly sought to cut discretionary spending, especially on social services; he had relatively little success.

By the end of 1975 the economy began to improve and continued to do so during the first half of 1976. Although unemployment remained high, an estimated 4 million more people had gained employment in early 1976. Inflation leveled off; it was less than 4 percent in April 1976, the best in four years. And during the first quarter of 1976 the gross national product grew by over 7 percent. Whether the natural business cycle or Ford's efforts were responsible for the upturn remains unclear. Many Americans, however, even among Republicans, were unhappy about Ford's performance in dealing with the economy. In the spring of 1976 his reelection bid faced a serious challenge from the affable Ronald Reagan, a former movie actor and formidable campaigner who since his election as governor of California in 1966 had become the darling of the party's conservatives.

Reagan strongly attacked Ford's economic stewardship. He was especially critical of the growing multi-billion-dollar national budget deficit. Reagan strenuously blamed Ford for not doing enough to control government spending. Ford defended himself by noting he repeatedly vetoed spending bills, but he found it difficult to blunt the Reagan challenge. Thanks to Ford's use of presidential patronage he won the nomination, but Reagan contested him (with some success in the primaries) all the way to the convention, and was only narrowly defeated on the first ballot (Ford won 1,187 to 1,070).

Jimmy Carter

In the 1976 election, Democratic presidential nominee Jimmy Carter made the economy a major issue in the campaign. James Earl Carter Jr. (who preferred to be called Jimmy) was born and raised in the tiny rural community of Plains, Georgia. A bright, driven, ambitious man, Carter seemed to excel at whatever he undertook. He attended the Naval Academy, graduated 59th out of 850 classmates, and served with distinction in the navy's prestigious nuclear submarine program for a number of years. His father's death forced him to return to Georgia, where he successfully ran the family's peanut business.

Carter became active in politics after his return home, served two terms as a Georgia state senator (1963–1966), ran (1966) a losing campaign for governor, and in 1970 was elected the state's chief executive. Carter gained a reputation in office as a principled, honest man who understood the details of governing. On the other hand, critics noted Carter could be unnecessarily stubborn and was often aloof from other politicians with whom he needed to cooperate. Carter—a fiscal conservative—made state government more efficient by eliminating various redundant public agencies. In winning the Democratic nomination for president in 1976, Carter—initially dismissed as a "long shot"—stressed

CHAPTER 13

his honesty, morality (he was a "born-again Christian"), and outsider status. He subsequently stressed these traits to American voters.

In his campaign for the presidency, Carter used the term *misery index* to describe the combined inflation and unemployment rate under Gerald Ford. He noted that the misery index, a term coined by economist Arthur Okun (1928–1980), was over 13 percent under Ford in 1976, despite the improved economic conditions. The unsettled American economic situation (as well as continued public anger over Ford's 1974 pardon of President Richard Nixon and a Ford flub during a presidential debate where he mistakenly claimed that the Soviet Union did not dominate Eastern Europe) played a major role in the presidential election campaign. Ford lost narrowly to Carter, who at one point had a 20 percent lead in the polls. The Democrat squeaked out a razor-thin victory, receiving 50.1 percent of the popular vote (40,830,000) to 48 percent for Ford (39,148,000), with the electoral vote split 291 for Carter to 241 for Ford.

Carter's Efforts

Carter and his advisers made strenuous but unsuccessful efforts to deal with the economic problems continuing to plague the United States like a bad cold that would not go away. Carter at first tried stimulating the economy and reducing unemployment by the use of traditional Keynesian "pump priming" techniques. Congress, responding to presidential initiatives, passed legislation in 1977 authorizing the spending of billions of dollars for public works and public service jobs. The minimum wage was raised and mandated to rise again in each of the next four years. These and other efforts did reduce unemployment somewhat, but during Carter's presidency the rates of joblessness stayed between 5 percent and 7 percent.

In dealing with unemployment (and inflation) Carter faced the same conundrum that had hampered his predecessors. Government stimulus to ease unemployment led to a rise in prices; alternatively focusing on inflation forced prices downward and unemployment worsened. Carter initially tried to deal with both issues, and this led to his flip-flopping on a $50 rebate for taxpayers that was part of a stimulus bill. The measure, which also included substantial tax cuts and with the $50 rebate included, passed the House of Representatives. However, alarmed by the increasing size of the deficit (and fearing that the legislation would be too inflationary), Carter opposed the rebate, which was dropped from the final measure. Liberal supporters felt betrayed at his reversal.

He toyed with the idea of bailing out "sick" industries in the manufacturing sector but worried about the costs. Carter concentrated on deregulation, believing it would stimulate competition, lower prices, and aid consumers.

President Jimmy Carter holds a White House press conference to announce that he is scrapping his plan to give $50 tax rebates because the economy is improving without the stimulus, April 14, 1977. (AP Photo)

The Carter administration began deregulation of the airline, railroad, trucking, and natural gas industries, but it also drove firms out of business, increased unemployment, and in the absence of government controls perpetrated abuses. Like his predecessor, Carter grappled with a series of diverse economic problems that impacted on the American economy and on life in the United States, but none was more pressing than inflation.

Double-digit inflation undermined the real per capita income of American workers. Their buying power had diminished thanks to the runaway inflation that had zoomed to 10 percent during Carter's first year in office and was 13 percent in 1980. During Carter's presidency it became clear that the American family needed more than one breadwinner. The decline in real earnings meant that many American families were becoming two-income households, dependent on what wives earned. The "shrinking dollar" necessitated that married women, especially in blue-collar families, had to work for wages to sustain their family's standard of living. During the Ford and Carter presidencies the proportion of women in the workforce aged 25 to 54 increased by over 25 percent, and their number would continue to grow. Not all of this increase represented wives; many more single women also found employment.

Paul Volcker

To deal with inflation Carter appointed Paul Volcker (b. 1927) to head the Federal Reserve in August 1979. Controversial because of his views on tightening the money supply to fight inflation, Volcker had been a financial economist, bank executive, and treasury official; when appointed Volcker headed the Federal Reserve Bank of New York. He is credited with ending "stagflation," but critics charge that in doing so Volcker inflicted economic pain on many

Americans. His tough-minded stance on the money supply led to significant rises in unemployment (nearly 8 percent in Carter's last year as president) and the prime rate (i.e., the rate of interest that banks charged their best most desirable customers), which rose to nearly 20 percent, a then unheard-of level.

Volcker served as chair of the Federal Reserve for eight years (under both Carter and his successor Ronald Reagan), and his controversial polices in the long run generally have been credited with being beneficial for the American economy—though the high interest rates he elicited drew great waves of protest, especially from a construction industry dependent on loans to finance new projects and from indebted farmers, many of whom in protest blockaded the Federal Reserve building in Washington, D.C., with their mortgaged heavy machinery. His policies did end stagflation but also resulted in a full-scale recession, in which America's energy policies played a significant role.

In the early 1970s (just exactly when remains unclear) domestic oil production proved insufficient for the needs of the United States. The 1973 OPEC policies underlined the impact of that shortfall and increasing dependence on foreign oil. Nixon and Ford tried to develop a workable energy policy as America's budget deficits increased sharply. In part to pay for foreign oil, Carter almost immediately on taking office concluded that America's economic problems resulted in large part from the nation's increasing costly need for foreign oil and in April 1977 laid out a comprehensive energy plan that he called "the moral equivalent of war." Those words became an unfortunate acronym ("MEOW") for his plan, which lacked stringency; Congress rejected the plan and MEOW quickly faded from view, but the deficits did not.

As Carter's term began in January 1977 a worldwide recession had cut the demand for petroleum products; there was an oil glut. For the United States, deficits were an increasingly severe problem; supply was not. The difficulties caused by OPEC a few years earlier were bad memories. While the price of gas remained higher than it once had been, for the moment the price situation at the pump seemed under control. However, at the beginning of 1979 Mohammed Reza Pahlevi, the imperious shah of Iran, was ousted from power. Iran under his rule had been a key American ally in the Middle East and was a major oil supplier to the United States. Anti-American Islamists seized control of Iran and during the ensuing unrest oil exports to the United States almost ceased.

OPEC, using the Iranian revolution as an excuse, jumped oil prices four times in five months, the most notable rise coming in June 1979 when the price of oil skyrocketed to the then unfathomable price of almost $40 a barrel. These jumps led to dramatically higher gas prices, and that late spring and summer, due to the more limited supply of oil, there were often long lines at gas stations as Americans sought to keep their automobile gas tanks as full as possible despite increasingly higher prices. Many of these stations found it necessary to limit customers to purchases on certain days of the week, and others found it expedient to close on some days because of shortages resulting from the limited supply.

Carter's actions in dealing with the energy crisis, some symbolic (such as installing a wood-burning stove in the White House living quarters) and some effective (such as the phased deregulation of domestic oil prices that led to a rise in domestic oil output), had less impact on the public's perceived economic woes than he intended. For Carter the critical situations caused by the spike in oil prices and the shortfall in supply were among the most significant and challenging that he faced as president.

Moreover, even before the oil crisis of the summer of 1979, Carter, despite his best efforts, was unable to reduce the budget deficit; $68 billion when he entered office, it continued to rise (by his final year as president the deficit had reached $73 billion). In fairness to Carter, however, it must be noted that as a fiscal conservative the president frequently clashed with the many liberal Democrats in Congress who felt that he did not spend enough on domestic programs and allocated funds for them.

Carter's tenuous relations with his own party were both strategic and personal. He seems sincerely to have believed his own rhetoric about being an outsider. Speaker of the House Thomas Phillip "Tip" O'Neill (1912–1994) believed Carter never understood "how Washington worked." The liberal O'Neill loyally supported Carter but was distressed by the president's emphasis on fiscal conservatism and budget cuts. O'Neill and other Democratic congressional leaders also complained that Carter overwhelmed them with the sheer number of proposals sent to Congress, maintaining the president should have sent a smaller number of proposals and prioritized them.

Members of Congress also complained about their relations with Carter and his staff. One representative later said that he only saw Carter twice: once when Carter came into office and then when he left. To many on Capitol Hill, Carter seemed to disdain social encounters with them, and his staff did not prove helpful in dealing with the country's economic problems. Many congressmen found the immediate staff (mostly composed of individuals that the president had brought with him from Georgia) arrogant, immature, ignorant of America's economic problems, and parochial in their proposed solutions.

The Malaise Speech and the Hostage Crisis

A crucial moment for Carter domestically was his "malaise" speech on July 15, 1979 (though Carter never used the word in his address), crafted after ten days of intense consultation with dozens of the nation's business, government, and educational leaders at Camp David, the president's mountain hideaway. In the

A gas station manager watches President Jimmy Carter deliver his "malaise" speech on July 15, 1979, in Los Angeles as one of his employees fills a customer's gas tank in the background. (AP Photo)

speech, officially titled "Energy and National Goals," Carter, addressing the nation over radio and television, focused attention on America's dependence on foreign oil, detailed plans to achieve "an energy secure nation," called for immediately reducing dependence on oil imports ("this Nation will never use more foreign oil than we did in 1977"), and emphasized alternative energy sources such as solar energy as well as conservation.

What struck listeners most about this speech broadcast nationally was Carter's emphasis on a "crisis of confidence" in America. He strongly argued that the United States was going through a spiritual and psychological crisis, chided Americans for being too materialistic, and called for a "restoration of American values." Initially, the speech was popular with the American people. Carter was viewed as a forceful, straight-talking leader who laid out viable solutions. However, Carter ruined the impact of the speech by ineptly calling for the resignation of his entire cabinet and accepting five of them, in effect firing these individuals, including well-regarded energy secretary James Schlesinger (b. 1929) and HEW head Joseph Califano (b. 1931), who was close to liberals inside and outside Congress.

A further detraction came when the media and eventually the public focused on that section, of what in reality was a complex, multifaceted speech, dealing with materialism and Americans' quest for consumer goods. It seemed as if Carter was blaming the American people for the nation's economic problems; as one newspaper editorial put it, Carter was "scolding his fellow citizens" like "a pastor with a profligate flock." Americans increasingly came to view the speech as unnecessarily gloomy and pessimistic.

The speech may have hampered Carter in achieving his goals, but his ultimate undoing came a few months later. On November 4, 1979, mobs in Teheran, Iran, stormed the American embassy and seized its occupants, later releasing some but retaining 52 as hostages, while the revolutionary government demanded that the shah who had come to the United States for cancer treatments be returned to Iran, that the United States apologize for its support of his regime, and that it turn over his financial assets to the new Iranian government. Carter refused and froze Iranian assets in American banks. For the next 14 months the hostage crisis almost paralyzed Carter's presidency, as the media dwelt on the hostages (ABC-TV, for instance, ran a highly rated nightly broadcast, "America Held Hostage"). The economy remained a problem but seemed to fade from public consciousness in the face of the media attention paid to the hostages.

A military rescue attempt failed embarrassingly in April 1980; the shah died in July, removing one obstacle to negotiations on the fate of the hostages. In September Iran and its neighbor Iraq went to war, and Iranian leaders searching for funds to sustain their military began negotiations about the hostages through the good offices of the Algerian government. At the end of 1980 representatives of the Iranian and American governments began direct negotiations. Although the United States refused Iran's demands to apologize for supporting the shah's regime it agreed to issue a statement of policy to refrain from interference in Iranian affairs and to unfreeze billions of dollars of Iranian assets in the United States and turn them over to the revolutionary government. Final agreement was reached the last day of Carter's term in office, but the Iranians waited until his successor had been sworn in before releasing the hostages on January 20, 1981.

As Carter in 1980 turned to his campaign for reelection, he faced a challenge within his own party from Massachusetts senator Edward ("Ted") Kennedy (1932–2009), youngest brother of late president John F. Kennedy (1917–1963). The senator represented the Democratic Party's left wing, which was offended by Carter's fiscal conservatism. Senator Kennedy, who advocated increased spending on jobs programs, welfare, and health care, also attacked Carter for not doing enough to rehabilitate the inner cities of the United States. In a bruising fight Carter ultimately won the nomination, helped by Kennedy's personal problems (i.e., his well-publicized relentless womanizing as well as the Chappaquiddick incident, which resulted in the death of a woman who the senator may have let drown) as well as the senator's inability to explain the rationale for his candidacy in a widely seen TV interview.

Ronald Reagan

In the 1980 presidential election Ronald Reagan was the Republican presidential nominee. Born in Illinois, he attended Eureka College there and after graduating worked for a number of years as a sports announcer in Iowa. Reagan moved to Hollywood in the late 1930s, became a Warner Brothers contract player, and was a lead in B-movies and a supporting actor in A-productions. After leaving Warner he worked for various studios until his career on-screen petered out in the mid-1950s. During his years in Hollywood, Reagan was head (1947–1952, 1959–1960) of the Screen Actors Guild and negotiated a series of difficult contracts for the union.

Initially an ardent Democrat who supported Franklin Roosevelt (1882–1945) and Harry Truman (1884–1972), he became by the end of the 1940s an active anti-Communist liberal and during the 1950s moved right politically; in 1962 Reagan formally changed his political registration to Republican. After the mid-1950s his career was mostly in television. From 1954 until 1962 he served as a genial host and sometimes actor on a TV series sponsored by General Electric. He also became a very effective part of the corporation's public relations operation, touring the country speaking at GE facilities and meetings.

In 1964 Reagan came to political prominence delivering a well-received and effective televised campaign speech for Republican presidential candidate Barry Goldwater. Two years later, Reagan was elected governor of California, and in 1972 he was easily reelected. Despite his conservative rhetoric, Reagan was a politically astute pragmatist who knew when and how to compromise; he worked across party lines to raise taxes to meet budget shortfalls and to have significant welfare reform legislation adopted, including a liberal abortion bill. After the governorship (California law limited an individual to two consecutive terms), Reagan ran unsuccessfully (1976) against Gerald Ford for the Republican presidential nomination. Ford's electoral defeat put Reagan in a good position four years later.

Reagan in the 1980 presidential election relentlessly pointed out that Carter's misery index exceeded 20 percent, benefited from the fact that Keynesian economics had failed to solve America's problems, and vigorously rejected Carter's talk of an age of limitations. For Reagan there was no crisis of confidence. Drawing on the 17th-century words of John Winthrop (1588–1649), the Puritan governor of the Massachusetts Bay Colony, Reagan described the United States (as since 1630 had many Americans echoing Winthrop) as "'a city upon a hill,' whose best days were yet to come." Reagan saw the United States as "a place in the divine scheme of things that was set aside as a promised land."

Reagan's proposed solutions called for an unusual combination of increased funding for defense, tax cuts, reduced regulation, and elimination or reorganization of various government programs. Reagan, a skilled communicator and salesman of his ideas, argued he could simultaneously implement these policies and balance the budget. He vigorously criticized Carter's economic performance, claiming that recovery would arrive only when the president lost his job.

The election appeared close in most polls until the first (and only) debate between the two candidates, during which Reagan, who handled himself much better than Carter, asked: are you better off than you were four years ago? Voters overwhelmingly answered no on election day. Reagan got almost 51 percent of the popular vote and 489 electoral votes; Carter received 41 percent of the popular vote and 49 electoral votes. Reagan's win was all the more impressive in light of a strong third party challenge from veteran socially moderate, fiscally conservative Illinois congressman John Anderson (b. 1922), who received over 7 percent of the popular vote. Carter was the first incumbent president to lose his office since Herbert Hoover (1874–1964) in 1932.

Supply-Side Economics

Reagan, claiming a popular mandate for his policies, was initially influenced by the theory of "supply-side economics": the idea that reductions in top tax rates would lead to dramatic economic productivity and growth. Cutting tax rates would result in American high-earning individuals, profitable corporations, and successful investors retaining more income after taxes, and having more income would give them the incentive to earn even more. Supply-siders believed their policies would generate so much tax revenue there would be an economic surplus. There was no need to pay for tax cuts; they would pay for themselves.

Noted proponents of this theory included former star quarterback and New York congressman Jack Kemp (1935–2000); economist Arthur Laffer (b. 1940); and *Wall Street Journal* editorial writer Jude Wanniski (1936–2005), credited with coining the phrase "supply-side economics." In the late 1970s Republicans Kemp and Delaware senator William Roth (1921–2003) proposed bills, as well as amendments to pending legislation, calling for significant income tax reduction; they did not succeed in Congress, but their proposals gained increasing popularity and support in political circles for supply-side economics.

Reagan sincerely believed high tax rates made individuals less productive because working more resulted only in paying more of one's earnings in taxes.

While governor of California he sought unsuccessfully to convince the state's voters to pass measures limiting the amount of taxes that could be imposed. When Reagan in January 1981 became president he immediately sought to make supply-side ideas a reality, energetically pushing a combination of tax and spending cuts.

At first, it appeared he would have difficulty implementing his views. While the Senate was narrowly controlled by the Republicans, the House of Representatives was controlled by Democrats, and Speaker of the House Tip O'Neill (a staunch liberal Democrat) predicted it would not pass Reagan's economic agenda. Despite Reagan's image as a lazy, disengaged president, he actively pursued votes in Congress. Members saw more of Reagan during his first months as president than they had of Carter in four years. Reagan strenuously lobbied members of Congress; he invited them to the White House, worked the phones, and visited Capitol Hill. At one point, he called members of Congress who were on a trip to New Zealand with O'Neill and asked them for their support.

He was helped by a failed assassination attempt upon him in late March 1981 in Washington, D.C., by a disturbed young man who thought he could impress the actress Jodie Foster (b. 1962) by assassinating the president. Voters were impressed by Reagan's courage, resiliency, and humor in the face of death. His approval rating increased dramatically, and a speech after he recovered before a joint session of Congress was well-received. Key to passage of Reagan's economic agenda were conservative southern Democrats (or "boll weevils") who overwhelmingly supported his proposed tax and spending cuts.

Reaganomics

Despite his benign public image, Reagan was a tough negotiator, proved to be a flexible pragmatist, and managed to get about 90 percent of his program enacted during the two-year (1981–1982) congressional session of his first term. This Congress enacted more tax changes than any previous Congress, starting in August 1981 with the Economic Recovery Tax Act, which embodied many of the principles earlier laid out by Kemp-Roth. This act called for nearly $140 billion to be slashed over a three-year period from funding for federal programs. At Reagan's behest this Congress also voted 25 percent across the board income tax cuts to be implemented over three years, reduced taxes on capital gains taxes by 40 percent and on investment income by 28 percent, raised exemptions on inheritance and gift taxes, and reduced the windfall profits tax on oil producers.

Supporters and critics alike would later talk about "Reaganomics" and the "Reagan Revolution." Yet the Reagan economic program was not as revolutionary as either supporters or critics believed. George H. W. Bush (b. 1924), in his short-lived challenge to Reagan for the presidential nomination in 1980, dubbed supply-side theories "voodoo economics." But as realized "Reaganomics" differed from its theoretical base. While rhetorically Reagan promised through tax cutting to balance the budget, he was unwilling to cut entitlement spending (aside from a failed attempt to reduce Social Security benefits for early retirees) and felt it necessary to significantly increase defense spending to challenge the Soviet Union in the Cold War. Many of Reagan's heralded tax cuts were actually reductions of increases in future spending. Contrary to Reagan's critics, he did not destroy the welfare state. Reagan's budget director David Stockman (b. 1946) found that Reagan was more of a politician than an ideologue when it came to the budget.

Against powerful odds, Reagan succeeded in enacting his economic agenda. The supply-siders who supported Reagan's tax cuts theorized that these reductions would lead to increases in government revenues, a jump in productivity, lower interest rates, and a decline in inflation. Thanks as much to Volcker's policies as the legislation, inflation decreased from 12 percent when Reagan took office to 3.9 percent in the latter part of 1982, the lowest rate of inflation since 1972. Interest rates also dropped dramatically, going in one year from over 20 percent to 11.5 percent. However, the rate drops were accompanied by a sharp decline in the economy; the recession that began during Carter's last days in office sharply intensified toward the end of 1981, in considerable part due to tight money policies undertaken by Volker, who was still convinced inflation was the primary economic challenge.

The economy went into a tailspin. During 1981–1982 the country suffered what has been called "a full dress recession." Construction and manufacturing declined sharply. The gross national product in 1982 was recorded as growing at negative 2 percent. In 1981 nearly 16,000 businesses collapsed, and the following year over 24,000 failed. Between 1980 and 1983 both the consumer price and producer prices indices fell dramatically before stabilizing. During those years loan rates on new cars reached an astonishing 18 percent, and as a result the number of factory sales of passenger cars dropped by 1,000,000. Industries like steel ran at 25 percent of capacity.

Unemployment was at times well over 10 percent of the workforce, and at one point during 1982 over 11 million people were estimated to be jobless—the largest number of unemployed in the United States since the Great Depression. Between 1980 and 1983 the index figures for "the average duration of unemployment" nearly doubled. By November 1982 it was reckoned that one in seven Americans, about 32 million, were living below the poverty line. Suicide rates shot up.

Critics ridiculed "Reaganomics," condemned Reagan's economic policies, and contended that the Reagan tax cuts caused the recession. Reagan's approval

President Ronald Reagan points to a chart during a televised speech from the Oval Office on
July 27, 1981, promoting tax reduction legislation pending before Congress. The Republican
plan called for a reduction of income tax rates, the addition of deductions to encourage investment and savings, and adjusting tax rates for inflation. (Ronald Reagan Library)

rating dropped to a low of 35 percent. However, supporters of Reagan noted
that the tax cuts were not implemented until the fall of 1981 after the recession
had begun and that the biggest chunk of the tax cuts would not take effect until
1983. Despite vociferous demands that Reagan exert pressure on Volcker to
change his policies, Reagan stood by the Fed chairman's tight money policies:
the president also believed inflation was the greatest threat to the economy.
Reagan urged the public to "stay the course."

Many economists and scholars since then consider the Federal Reserve's
assault on inflation (with Reagan's strong support) to be the greatest economic
achievement of the Reagan administration. While causing short-term economic distress, the actions taken by Volcker broke the vicious cycle of inflation. During the 1982 midterm election, Republicans paid the price for staying
the course, losing 26 seats in the House; the Democrats also made substantial
gains in the Senate (though Republicans narrowly retained control).

Reagan Regroups

Already a year earlier many members of Congress had expressed concern about
the impact of the recession and the probable shortfall in federal revenues. In

November 1981 California Democrat Fortney Hilman "Pete" Stark (b. 1931), an outspoken former banker turned liberal congressman, sponsored legislation that modified many of the reforms passed just a few months earlier. It took months of difficult, stormy negotiations between the Democratic House, the Republican Senate, and President Reagan (and his staff) before a final version of this legislation was agreed on and passed by Congress.

In September 1982 Reagan signed into law the Tax Equity and Fiscal Responsibility Act. It modified various provisions of the previous legislation and to the outspoken dismay of supply-siders raised taxes. Reagan, having overstated the revenues that would come to the federal government, reluctantly agreed to $98 billion in tax increases. The measure ended some tax breaks for businesses as well as imposed excise taxes on tobacco, airports, and communications. Reagan succeeded in preserving many of his 1981 tax cuts but reluctantly accepted the hikes as necessary.

Reagan, although a committed conservative, was not an ideological supply-sider. Despite his reputation as a tax cutter, he supported tax increases throughout his political career when necessary; as governor of California he had done so repeatedly and now as president did so when economic growth stalled government revenues necessary to support defense spending. Reagan also agreed to a rise in payroll taxes in 1983 as part of a bipartisan effort to reform Social Security, and he raised taxes again in 1984 as part of the Deficit Reduction Act designed to raise $50 billion over a three-year period to cover shortfalls.

Fortunately for Reagan, the economy began to recover after 1982. The economy grew at an average rate of 8 percent from 1983 to 1984, and for the rest of Reagan's time as president there was an economic boom. Inflation was reduced; unemployment fell; interest rates declined. Reagan reaped the political credit for this economic prosperity. Running for reelection in 1984, he argued that it was "Morning in America," and the country's voters agreed, reelecting him in a landslide: Reagan received 59 percent of the popular vote and lost only the electoral votes of Minnesota and the District of Columbia). His opponent, Minnesota senator Walter Mondale (b. 1928), Jimmy Carter's vice president, received just about 40 percent of the popular vote.

Aftermath

By the end of Reagan's presidency in 1991, the inflation that scarred America from 1974 to 1984 was down to less than 4.4 percent, and unemployment had leveled off at about 5.4 percent, a rate once deemed high but now acceptable. Of the 18 million jobs created in the 1980s, most were not in manufacturing. Critics claimed, not without reason, that too many of the jobs created were low-wage service jobs. Many Americans considered their standard of living to have improved even though maintaining that standard often demanded a family have two-incomes. Reagan supporters credited his economic policies for the nation's prosperity during the years after 1983. Yet as with job creation, critics pointed to a variety of problems with the Reagan economy.

There was an increasing gap between America's well-to-do and the rest of the population; the country's trade deficit soared as the United States for the first time in generations again became a debtor nation; the federal budget remained out of balance by billions; America's national debt advanced into the trillions (between the fiscal years 1980 and 1989, the U.S. national debt increased from $914 billion to $2.7 trillion). These trends during the Reagan years were partly a consequence of his actions but also were due to a bipartisan unwillingness by Congress to contain entitlement spending. In the years to come these trends would be exacerbated by both Republican and Democratic administrations to the detriment of the American people as they tried to deal with renewed economic doldrums.

Between 1974 and 1983 the United States had suffered among other economic ills an unheralded stagflation, high unemployment, and a sharp recession. By 1984 many of the challenges that had faced Presidents Nixon, Ford, Carter, and Reagan had faded away. In October 1987 panic gripped the New York Stock Exchange as share prices collapsed. But 1987 was not a replay of 1929; the market quickly bounced back. No depression or recession followed, despite the gloomy prognostications of those supposedly "in the know."

Their failure and Reagan's downplaying of such soothsayers speaks volumes about his popularity (he described professional economists as "the sort of people who see something in practice and wonder if it will work in theory). For the United States, the years after 1983, except for the brief 1987 stock market hiccup, were years of economic prosperity and the beginning of a long period of economic growth, one of the best in American history. Whether due to Reagan's policies and actions or to the natural turn of the business cycle is still being debated by scholars.

Further Reading

Berkowitz, Edward. *Something Happened: A Political and Cultural Overview of the Seventies.* New York: Columbia University Press, 2006.

Diggins, John Patrick. *Ronald Reagan: Fate, Freedom, and the Making of History.* New York: Norton, 2007.

Greene, John Robert. *The Presidency of Gerald R. Ford.* Lawrence: University Press of Kansas, 1995.

Kaufman, Burton I. *The Presidency of James Earl Carter Jr.* Lawrence: University Press of Kansas, 1995.

Morgan, Iwan. *The Age of Deficits: Presidents and Unbalanced Budgets from Jimmy Carter to George W. Bush.* Lawrence: University Press of Kansas, 2009.

Patterson, James. *Restless Giant: The United States from Watergate to* Bush v. Gore. New York: Oxford University Press, 2005.

Wilentz, Sean. *The Age of Reagan: A History, 1974–2008.* New York: HarperCollins, 2008.

Economic Downturns, 1974–1984:
Short Entries

Jason Roberts

Apple Computers

On April Fools' Day 1976, Steve Jobs (1955–2011), Steven Wozniak (b. 1950), and Robert Wayne (b. 1934) began a company in Cupertino, California, to sell the Apple I, a kit put together by Wozniak that today would be considered a personal computer. It went on sale in July 1976, and the company was incorporated in January 1977 without Wayne, who was bought out by Jobs and Wozniak for $800. With the financial aid and business expertise of venture capitalist Armas "Mike" Markkula (b. 1942), who later served as CEO (1981–1983) and chairman of the board of directors (1985–1997), they introduced the Apple II in April 1977.

More than any other company, and it had considerable competition in its early days, Apple was responsible for the growing demand for personal computers in the 1980s. Apple ultimately was commercially very successful, but it did not go from strength to strength without some hiccups. The company had its share of commercial failures. The Apple III introduced in 1980 was an ill-fated attempt to compete with IBM and Microsoft in the business computing marketplace.

Nonetheless, when Apple went public in 1980 it captured so much public interest that it generated more capital than any IPO since the Ford automobile company went public in 1956. Apple's next years saw in-fighting among its executives as they fought over what they considered the proper direction that the company should take. John Sculley (b. 1939), a very successful soft drink marketing executive hired to head the company in 1983, clashed repeatedly with the brilliant, hardworking, but difficult, uncompromising Jobs, who attempted

On April 24, 1984, Apple president John Sculley, flanked by Apple co-founders Steve Jobs (left) and Steve Wozniak (right), unveil the new Apple IIc to more than 3,000 dealers and software sector representatives in San Francisco, California. (Bettmann/Corbis)

a putsch against him, lost, and resigned from Apple in mid-1985 to start his own company (NeXT). After he left, Apple flourished for some years as it moved away from expensive-to-produce hardware to the less costly Macintosh platform.

However, over time the company lost ground to Microsoft, which gained substantial market share with its concentration on software for inexpensively produced personal computers. After a series of product flops Sculley was replaced in 1993 by Michael Spindler (b. 1942), who after joining Apple in 1980 had risen through the ranks to become head of the company's European operations. He had some success but also presided over the introduction of various failed operating systems as well as inconclusive takeover talks with various companies. Apple replaced him in 1996 with Gil Amelio (b. 1943), a technology executive successful at Fairchild Semiconductor and National Semiconductor; he took over a company that had a shortage of cash, lacked a viable strategy, and was burdened with low-quality products. He had almost no positive results during his 500 days as the head of Apple, and described the company as a "ship loaded with treasures," but with "a hole in the ship" and his job as trying "to get everyone to row in the same direction."

In February 1997, after some months of negotiations, Amelio bought NeXT, the company started by Jobs after he left Apple, and brought him back to Apple as a part-time advisor. That was not in his nature, especially as Apple was doing poorly, and Jobs orchestrated a boardroom coup that led to the ouster of almost all of the board of directors and his becoming the interim CEO. Jobs subsequently formally took on the job after it became clear that no candidate would be willing to accept it while Jobs was involved with the company.

When he took over as head of the company it was suffering crippling financial losses. Michael Dell (b. 1965), then a more successful competitor, when asked what Jobs should do on taking over Apple, replied, "I'd shut it down and give the money back to the shareholders." Jobs, a ruthless administrator with a passion for perfection and a consummate salesman with a splendid gift for marketing, over the next years—through intelligent purchases, striking in-house developments, and highly effective advertising and PR campaigns—oversaw the extremely profitable introduction of a wide range of smartly designed Apple products such as the iPod, the iPhone, and the iPad as well as subsequent upgrades to them. Apple did not abandon computers, but the introduction of such products shifted the company's focus toward consumer electronics. In recognition of that shift Apple in 2007 dropped the word *computer* from its corporate name and became Apple, Inc.

Jobs and his company became icons of a new environment. The continuing successful development of Apple as an attractive and admired brand remains significant because it marked the dramatic change in the nature of the computer industry and of the relationship of the individual to technology. Before Apple, computers in the main were large mainframes or hardware tied to businesses. Apple alone did not change the personal computing environment: neither Bill Gates (b. 1955) nor Microsoft or other lesser competitors should be ignored. But Jobs and Apple, and the tremendous brand loyalty that both engendered, led millions of Americans to buy and use personal computers and the subsequent technologic innovations that have further miniaturized instruments of communication.

For many in the world, and not just in the United States, the death of Jobs from pancreatic cancer in 2011 was a personal blow (he had stepped down as head of the company earlier that year; previously he had taken a six-month leave of absence in 2009). Apple (the company) and Jobs (the man) may more than any other influences be responsible for the technological revolution that transformed life and business in the United States during the last part of the 20th century and the first years of the 21st century, and they continue to do so.

Apple in 2012 was a multinational corporation that designs, produces, and sells diverse consumer electronics; a wide range of computer software; and personal computers, both online and in over 350 retail stores in ten countries. At the end of 2011, Apple had over 60,000 employees worldwide and was the world's most important technology company in both revenues and profit, with overall sales of over $100 billion. In terms of market capitalization Apple is among the largest publicly traded companies in the world.

Apple has also been the subject of criticism for its environmental practices from nonprofit organizations such as Greenpeace and Climate Counts. Much of Apple's production takes place offshore, especially in China, and working conditions there have been described as those of "dangerous suicide sweatshops" despite the company's attempts to improve the situation.

Further Reading

Isaacson, Walter. *Steve Jobs.* New York: Simon & Schuster, 2011.

Lashinsky. Adam. *Inside Apple: How America's Most Admired—and Secretive—Company Really Works.* London: John Murray, 2012.

Wozniak, Steve, and Gina Smith. *iWon: From Company Geek to Cult Icon—How I Invented the Personal Computer, Co-Founded Apple, Had Fun Doing It.* New York: Norton, 2006.

Employee Retirement Income Security Act (ERISA)

The Employee Retirement Income Security Act (ERISA) was passed by Congress and signed into law by President Gerald Ford (1913–2006) in September 1974. The legislation's chief and most vigorous sponsor was New York senator Jacob Javits (1904–1986), a veteran member of Congress and one of a small group of liberal Republicans. ERISA is a law that mandates minimum standards for the various pension plans offered within private industry.

The origins of ERISA can be traced back to the administration of John F. Kennedy (1917–1963). He had established a Committee on Corporate Pension Plans to study pension reform, a major impetus being that in 1958 the Studebaker-Packard corporation had for lack of assets terminated the retirement plan of employees of the former Packard Motor Car Company. The issue of pension default gained more prominence in December 1963 when on the closing of the Studebaker automobile manufacturing facilities in South Bend, Indiana, it became clear that the company's pension obligations significantly outran the assets available to pay them, some employees would get as little as 15 percent of what they had been promised, and many workers would get nothing.

In the early 1960s staff of the United Automobile Workers (UAW) under the leadership of their head, Walter Reuther (1907–1970), worked out a detailed plan for "pension reinsurance," a precursor of one of ERISA's chief provisions. And in 1964 Indiana senator Vance Hartke (1919–2003), a Democrat, as a result of the agitation aroused by the Studebaker situation and alluding to the work of the President's Committee on Corporate Pension Reform introduced a bill calling for "Federal Reinsurance of Private Pensions," which included some of the provisions of the UAW plan. Hartke's effort, despite engendering considerable support, did not succeed, although the Studebaker shortfall remained a strong rallying cry for those within and outside government pushing for pension reform.

In 1972, as part of a campaign orchestrated by Senator Javits, who intended to sponsor what became ERISA, NBC-TV broadcast a program titled *Pensions: The Broken Promises,* which focused on the Studebaker shortfall as well as on various other poorly funded pension plans, arguing that they were a national epidemic and an ongoing disgrace. In the aftermath of the television broadcast and the stir aroused by the program, Congress held hearings on corporate pension plans. To support his proposed legislation Javits made use of an array of actuarial experts but also was aided by the bipartisan support he received from Democratic congressional allies such as New Jersey senator Harrison Williams (1919–2001). The supporters of what became ERISA mobilized the media to publicize such horrors as what had happened at Studebaker to many of its workers.

When President Ford signed into law the ERISA legislation he asserted that with its enactment that "the men and women of our labor force will have much more clearly defined rights to pension funds and greater assurances that retirement dollars will be there when they are needed." Since 1974 the law has been amended a number of times but in one form or another continues to provide improved protection for the hard-earned benefits of workers.

In regulating the various private pension programs available to workers ERISA continues to establish fiduciary standards of conduct, minimum vesting standards, and a federal government-run insurance program as the agencies overseeing enforcement of ERISA seek to ensure that no employer can default on its pension promises. ERISA does not mandate that a company must establish a pension plan for its workers, but the original legislation and its amendments do regulate such a plan once it is created, requiring that complete and comprehensible information on the plans be provided to workers over the course of their employment.

Further Reading

Wooten, James A. *The Employment Retirement Income Security Act of 1974: A Political History.* Berkeley: University of California Press, 2004.

Franklin National Bank

In October 1974 the Franklin National Bank collapsed and subsequently came under the supervision of the Federal Deposit Insurance Corporation (FDIC). Once the 20th largest bank in the United States with assets of about $3.6 billion, the Franklin National Bank had become a victim of the downturn in the economy and of poor, probably criminal mismanagement, which centered on dubious foreign exchange transactions. The closing of the "gold window" and the end of fixed foreign exchange rates had led to dramatic changes in the international financial markets that directly affected the bank and its operations.

Founded in 1926 in suburban Long Island as the Franklin Square National Bank, it grew under aggressive, dynamic, and innovative leadership, merging over the years with other local Long Island financial institutions, and in 1947 dropped "Square" from its name. By 1965 the Franklin National Bank, describing itself as "A Country Bank in New York City," had opened branch offices in New York City and in 1970 the ambitious, hard-driving, knowledgeable Laurence Tisch (1923–2003) had added Franklin National Bank to his diverse portfolio of investments.

In 1972 Tisch, who had become vice chairman, sold his shares (about 22 percent of the outstanding stock) to Michele Sidona (1920–1986), an Italian banker with close ties to the Vatican and to the Mafia. Sidona, known in Italian banking circles as "The Shark," controlled various banks in that country and very quickly assumed control of Franklin. Tisch, whose many investments included hotels in Italy, was later criticized by the U.S. controller of the currency as an "unqualified director" because of various conflicts of interest in making it possible for Sidona to take over Franklin. Tisch later was sued by the FDIC for "breach of fiduciary duty" in selling his shares to Sidona.

Over the next few years, Sidona and his American associates, many of whom were later convicted or pleaded guilty to fraud and falsifying financial records, used the bank for laundering drug money and for a variety of illegal operations. The severe downturn in the American economy as well as general mismanagement, large losses in foreign currency speculation, and poor loan policies led to the Franklin National Bank's profits in 1974 falling by over 95 percent compared to the previous year. Depositors rushed to withdraw vast sums, and the Federal Reserve Bank of New York lent Franklin about $1.5 billion as part of an attempt to keep it afloat and avoid a bank failure.

Ultimately, however, the Franklin Bank failed. After Franklin was declared insolvent the FDIC supervised a policy of "purchase and assumption," which led to many of the remaining assets of the closed institution being sold to the European-American Bank, a New York-chartered bank, much smaller than Franklin but a subsidiary of several very large European banks (and in time part of Citigroup). The failure of the Franklin National Bank contributed to the problems then gnawing at the international banking system that led to attempts in the United States and in Europe to set up standards that would help prevent future financial crises.

The financial empire that Sidona, once hailed as the "saviour of the lira," had created and which allowed him to gain control of Franklin, unraveled after its collapse and as his less than savory Mafia ties became known. In 1979 he staged a bogus kidnapping to conceal an 11-week trip to Sicily to influence his past often politically influential Italian associates in an effort to rescue his banks there and the Mafia's money. On his "release" he surrendered to the FBI, and after a lengthy trial in 1980 was convicted on 65 counts—including fraud, perjury, and misappropriation of bank funds. Four years later, while serving a long term in an American prison, he was extradited to Italy, tried, and found guilty for ordering the murder of the Italian lawyer liquidating Sidona's holdings. Sentenced to prison for 25 years, he died in his cell in March 1986, poisoned by cyanide in his coffee. It remains unclear if he was murdered or committed suicide. His death marked the end of the story of the slow rise and rapid fall of the Franklin National Bank, whose collapse well symbolized the tangled banking economics of the early and mid-1970s.

Further Reading

Spero, Joan Edelman. *The Failure of the Franklin National Bank: Challenge to the International Banking System*. Washington, D.C.: Beard Books, 1999.
Tosches, Nick. *Power on Earth*. New York: Arbor House, 1986.

Laffer, Arthur B. (1940–)

An influential economist, best known for "the Laffer Curve," which he argued illustrates a theory that between a zero tax rate on income and a 100 percent rate there is a point at which maximum tax revenues will be earned by government. His illustration was used to explain the benefits of tax reduction by its proponents; Laffer strongly believed that tax reductions would lead to increased revenues and influenced many Republican politicians, including Ronald Reagan (1911–2004). To many critics of Laffer's arguments his curve illustrates the bankruptcy of President Ronald Reagan's economic policies. Supporters of the ideas represented by the Laffer Curve maintain that the overall prosperity of the Reagan years vindicate the economist's arguments.

Arthur Laffer, born in 1940, raised in the fancy Shaker Heights section of Cleveland, received (1962) a BA in economics from Yale University, and from Stanford University an MBA (1971) and a PhD in economics (1971). Tenured at the University of Chicago Business School, Laffer impressed Dean George Shultz (b. 1920) who took him to Washington, D.C., when appointed director of the Office of Management and Budget. After a two-year stint with the government, Laffer returned to Chicago and in 1976 joined the faculty at the

Arthur B. Laffer, a conservative economist and a leading theoretician of supply-side economics. His theory that lowering tax rates would result in economic expansion and higher revenues was a major influence in the economic program and policy of President Ronald Reagan. (AP Photo)

John Marshall School of Business at the University of Southern California. He played an important role in the writing of Proposition 13, the state of California's property tax cap initiative that dramatically reduced property taxes and inspired such tax caps in other states.

He is the prime proponent of an economic theory that has been dated back to the 14th century. This theory maintains that raising tax rates beyond a certain point is counterproductive. What has been described as the "Laffer Curve" is a theoretical point at which raising taxes will not increase revenues. It is not necessarily a fixed point, but it is one between zero, which raises no taxes, and 100 percent, which results in actions that destroy incentives to work or in avoidance of tax payments. That point is not fixed but is an intermediate one between these extremes and therefore raises a maximum amount of tax revenue; even the strongest proponents of the Laffer Curve have disagreed substantially on what is the intermediate point at which tax revenue is maximized.

The term *Laffer Curve* is said to have been coined by *Wall Street Journal* editor Jude Wanniski (1936–2005). According to an account that may be apocryphal but has the ring of validity, Wanniski was present at a 1974 meeting at which Laffer criticized President Gerald Ford's economic policies with his then advisors Dick Cheney (b. 1941) and Donald Rumsfeld (b.1932). Attempting to win them over to his point of view, Laffer sketched the curve on a tablecloth to illustrate the concept. Laffer later asserted he had no recollection of this meeting but maintained that he used "the so-called Laffer Curve all the time in my classes" and urged the concept on "anyone . . . who would listen to me."

Laffer argued that a reduction in tax rates can increase government revenues; he also admitted that even though a 100 percent tax rate could result in no government revenues because there would be no incentive to earn income, there were exceptions—such as a country being at war. For Laffer the curve was not an absolute, and in 2007 he said that adherence to the concept of the curve should not be the only basis for the raising or lowering of tax rates. He also seems to have understood on the basis of his comments that public finance cannot be sustained by a single tax rate, given the complexities of the streams of government revenues.

It has proved difficult to quantify the Laffer Curve. During the last quarter of the 20th century, at a time when Laffer's arguments proved popular, various economic models suggested different maximum tax rates for the United States and for other industrialized countries, ranging from 65 percent to 32 percent. Just what should be the proper tax rate for maximizing revenue has remained a subject for debate. For example, a 2007 study commissioned by the American Enterprise Institute, a conservative think tank, *Revenue Maximizing Corporate Income Taxes: The Laffer Curve in OECD Countries*, found that the optimum rate was about 26 percent, compared to about 34 percent in the 1980s.

Both Laffer and Wanniski were active proponents of supply-side economics, a school of thought active in American political circles that argued that the well-being of society is achieved by lessening the barriers to the production of goods and services (i.e., the "supply side" of an economy) and that this could be accomplished by lowering taxes, downsizing government, and easing regulatory burdens it imposed. Obviously the implementation of at least some of these policies transcended taxation, but advocates of supply-side economics such as Wanniski maintained that lower taxes would result in the benefits it promised.

Adhering to the theory of the Laffer Curve, supply-side economists and their supporters argued that attaining beneficial goals with regard to goods and services could be achieved by lowering taxes: a tax cut would result in more goods and services as well as raising tax revenues. A belief in the Laffer Curve and the arguments set forth by supply-side proponents initially inspired Reaganomics and such legislation as proposed in various Kemp-Roth proposals. The advocates of cutting tax rates forcefully argued that lower rates would result in increased tax revenue, and during Reagan's presidency the top tax rate fell by almost 40 percent—from 70 percent to about 31 percent—while revenues increased.

That situation did not continue. In the aftermath of the Reagan tax cuts the budget deficit and the national debt exploded. Laffer may have been right about the positive economic impact of the tax cuts (an estimated 20,000,000 jobs were created, and both unemployment and inflation were dramatically reduced). But he clearly misjudged the impact of the tax cuts on the budget and economic future of the United States. Moreover, John Kenneth Galbraith (1908–2006) criticized the use of the Laffer Curve for allowing Reagan to "lower taxes on the affluent," and he as well as other economists expressed concern about the increasing social gap among Americans.

The height of Laffer's influence was during the early 1980s, and during those years and the decades that followed he worked with a variety of research and consulting firms (some of which he organized) that advised pension operations, financial institutions, corporations, and hedge funds. A prolific writer, he published in scholarly journals and more popular publications such as the *Wall Street Journal*. He taught at Pepperdine University and in 2008 was named Distinguished University Professor of Economics by Mercer University. Over the years the conservative Laffer has proved to be independent-minded politically. In 1992 and again in 1996, for example, he supported for president the Democratic candidate Bill Clinton (b. 1946), citing his fiscal economic policies.

Probably Laffer's major significance was providing the intellectual justification for dramatic tax reduction. While the results of these reductions since the 1980s have been mixed, both the Democratic and Republican parties have in the main moved right on the issue of taxes since the Laffer Curve promoted supply-side economics in the 1970s. However one views his theories, there is no gainsaying their impact on a continuing major issue of vital importance to the American people.

Further Reading

Trabandt, Mathias, and Harold Uhlig. "The Laffer Curve Revisited." *NBER Working Paper*, #15343, September 2009. http://www.nber.org/papers/w15343 [accessed March 12, 2013].

Wanniski, Jude. "Sketching the Laffer Curve." *The Yorktown Patriot*, June 14, 2005. http:www.yorktownpatriot.com/printer_78.shtml [accessed March 12, 2013].

Professional Air Traffic Controllers Organization (PATCO)

In the early 1980s the Professional Air Traffic Controllers Organization (PATCO) staged an ill-conceived, poorly organized, and futile strike against its employer, the Federal Aviation Administration (FAA), the American government agency that controlled air traffic in the skies over the United States. The strike was launched against a national backdrop of double digit unemployment, excessively high interest rates, and a general economic downturn. Given the FAA's labor policies, and its fractious relationships with the air controllers, PATCO's leaders felt they had reasonable cause for the strike, but the militants who pushed for it should have realized that economic conditions in the United States at that time did not favor such action.

PATCO's members faced enormous often unnecessary stress and fatigue in monitoring air traffic because of outmoded or inefficient equipment, were poorly trained, suffered from indifferent administration and unreasonable work rules, and generally were not paid commensurate with their responsibilities. And the FAA had an unenviable record of broken promises to improve technology and working conditions so as to make commercial aviation safer. PATCO's members—like most government workers—had all taken an oath not to strike. Nonetheless, between 1962 and 1981 over 35 illegal work stoppages had taken place (e.g., of Library of Congress employees and of postal workers) without any significant federal government legal action against the strikers or their organizations.

Prior to PATCO there had been predecessor air controller organizations; although interested in improving their members' working conditions they were equally committed to professionalization of air control. PATCO, when it was established in January 1968 with the assistance and counsel of noted attorney F. Lee Bailey (b. 1933) and such aviation enthusiasts as TV personality Arthur Godfrey (1903–1983), had been organized with such aims. But as membership grew PATCO became a trade union, and by 1970 was officially designated as such. Persons like Bailey dropped out. There was considerable infighting as many new members were militants, determined to control PATCO, committed to improve their economic lot, and unwilling to accept the FAA's style of dictatorial management.

To counter it without breaking the law, and to gain some improvements, PATCO members during the 1970s delayed flights by "working to rule" and "sick-outs." The PATCO membership by the time of the strike in 1981 was overwhelmingly male, white, and ex-military (the bulk had learned their specialized skills in the armed forces). Often of working-class origin and lacking a college education, they had moved to middle-class status because of their work as air traffic controllers. PATCO leaders and their members were not concerned with the needs of the few minority or women controllers. Both groups faced a kind of institutional prejudice from the leaders of the organization and its members.

Contract negotiations between the FAA and PATCO stalled during the first months of 1981. PATCO, one of the few American unions (along with the pilots and the teamsters) to support the campaign of Ronald Reagan (1911–2004) for president, expected him to reciprocate, and his administration did offer PATCO what to many outside observers was a generous package (e.g., a 11 percent pay increase). However, after months of negotiations PATCO's leadership continued to seek a better contract. While the president sympathized with the union's grievances with the FAA, he felt that PATCO asked too much in difficult economic times: PATCO's final demands included reduction of a five-day, 40-hour work week to one of four days and 32 hours, as well as a $10,000 across-the-board wage increase for all controllers (whose wages in 1980 ranged from about $20,000 annually to nearly $50,000) and benefits allowing full paid retirement after 20 years.

PATCO threatened to strike if its demands were not met. Roughly 95 percent of PATCO's 15,000-plus members rejected the government's improved counteroffers, and a strike began on August 3, 1981 (during the height of the airlines' summer surge of business, which the carriers had hoped would offset revenue lost during the economic downturn). Under provisions of the Taft-Hartley Act governing American labor relations President Reagan ordered the strikers back to work for a "cooling off period"; only about 1,300 determined to do so. An angry president warned PATCO that a walkout violated federal law banning U.S. government workers from striking, threatened to fire any striking controller, and in an unprecedented move gave the strikers 48 hours to return to work.

On August 5, 1981, true to his word the president fired the approximately 11,000 controllers remaining on strike. They had seriously misjudged the president's resolve and the government's capacity to deal with the situation. Rallying behind the cry "They Can't Fire All Of Us," they had believed they could seriously hamper if not halt all U.S. commercial aviation. They were wrong. To the surprise of the strikers as well as nearly everybody else the Reagan administration won the battle with PATCO.

Contingency plans minimized the strike's impact. Hundreds of supervisors and other staff personnel, joining approximately 2,000 non-striking controllers, and aided by about 1,000 individuals from the military, all working often 60-hour weeks, manned an admittedly reduced system. Air traffic was successfully monitored with less workers; there were a number of "near-misses," but no accidents. Major airports temporarily scheduled less flights in peak periods; smaller regional fields shut down for a while; the FAA's training school for air controllers dramatically increased its enrollment and shortened its course of study (given the economic hard times, within four months of the strike's onset over 45,000 people had applied to the FAA for controller jobs). Air freight generally remained unaffected by the strike; soon an estimated 80 percent of passenger flights operated as scheduled.

PATCO gained little support from the public or from organized labor. A public that had suffered from the delays and cancellations caused by PATCO's sick-outs and working-to-rule had little sympathy for what was viewed as the efforts of a relatively privileged group of workers to achieve excessive demands at the expense of taxpayers while the economy was slack. PATCO's strike was bereft of almost any public support. Moreover, there was genuine admiration for President Reagan's resoluteness and his refusal to accept the advice of some in Congress and his administration to compromise; his willingness to stick to his guns was admired.

Organized labor offered PATCO little more than lip service. Remarks by AFL-CIO head Lane Kirkland (1922–1999) in support of the strikers lacked bite, and the organization took no significant action to back PATCO (it did not discourage members from crossing PATCO's picket lines). Individual unions such as those of the machinists or the pilots who could have substantially aided the controllers acted inconclusively and offered little even in terms of moral support; the officers of such unions seem to have been in the main concerned about the illegality of PATCO's actions.

For PATCO and its members the strike was a disaster. They lost their jobs, were in effect blacklisted (banned from federal service), and because of a fear of reprisals by the American government were not able to find air traffic control jobs outside the United States. Many strikers were reduced to poverty levels. PATCO was decertified in October 1981, went bankrupt, and subsequently was dissolved. Attempts to formally ameliorate the ban failed until August 1993 when President Clinton (b. 1946) ended the prohibition on hiring any PATCO strikers; thereafter some 800 were rehired.

There were a number of other consequences to the strike. First, it reinforced Ronald Reagan's image in 1981, both at home and abroad, as a strong leader. Former Federal Reserve head Alan Greenspan (b. 1926) feels the president's response to the strike was his "most important . . . domestic initiative." He successfully carried out his threat to fire the striking PATCO workers, and his administration had managed to keep American air traffic flowing smoothly and safely. The president had also successfully invoked the law that striking government employees forfeit their jobs; until then no president had upheld the law, and it was cynically believed none ever would.

Second, the PATCO strike demonstrated the increasing weakness of American labor unions. A historian in his study of the strike in 2011 concluded that "more than any other labor dispute of the past three decades Reagan's confrontation . . . [with] PATCO undermined the bargaining power of American workers and their unions." The outcome of the PATCO strike empowered management in various areas to challenge unions, and it has continued to do so in the economically stagnant times following the "Great Recession" that began in 2008.

Further Reading
McCartin, Joseph A. *Collision Course: Ronald Reagan, the Air Traffic Controllers, and the Strike That Changed America*. New York: Oxford University Press, 2011.

Proposition 13 (People's Initiative to Limit Property Taxation, California) (1978)

On June 6, 1978, the people of California overwhelmingly voted (by about a two-thirds margin) for the "People's Initiative to Limit Property Taxation," and it became law, reducing property tax rates on homes by about 57 percent. Proposition 13 (so-called because of its number on the ballot) was a product of the state's constitution, which provided that a proposed law or state constitutional amendment could be offered to voters if its advocates collected a sufficient number of signatures on a petition.

The initiative, along with recall and referendum, had become part of California's legislative process in 1911 as part of a Populist program for direct democracy by the newly installed governor Hiram Johnson (1866–1945). He also pushed through a variety of other electoral reforms, including direct election of U.S. senators (in advance of the 17th Amendment to the U.S. Constitution) and vigorously lobbied for women's suffrage. A strong supporter of Theodore Roosevelt's (1858–1919) failed 1912 presidential campaign as a Progressive, Johnson in 1917 would jump from the governorship to the U.S. Senate where he served as a Republican and strong proponent of isolationism for 28 years until his death in 1945.

Proposition 13 was rooted in the resentment of many Californians about rising property taxes while state and local governments continued their unchecked growth (between 1973 and 1977 expenditure on these governments per $1,000 of personal income was 8.2 percent higher than the national norm; for a quarter century from the late 1950s to the mid-1970s employment in the California public sector grew faster than it did in the private sector; by 1978 14.7 percent of California's workforce were employed by the government, about double the number of two decades earlier).

At the same time, as a result of the national economic downturn and inflation of the 1970s state property taxes increased incrementally (they had doubled since 1975); many older residents, who had bought their property years ago and lived on fixed incomes, found it difficult to meet constantly increasing tax bills. More affluent taxpayers, because of state court rulings on equitable distribution of tax revenues for education, had come to realize that much of their property tax payments would no longer benefit their local schools as they had in the past.

State legislative inaction roiled the voters. When in the fall of 1977 the California legislature adjourned without curbing government spending or without passing any significant property tax relief, even though 22 reform plans had been proposed, voters quickly gravitated toward the initiative that had been promoted by Howard Jarvis (1903–1986) and Paul Gann (1912–1989), who convincingly argued that it was a measure not only for property tax relief but also a necessary constraint on the size of government.

Jarvis, born in Utah, had come to California in 1930. A Los Angeles businessman, unsuccessful Republican politician, and fervent antitax activist, he had organized the Howard Taxpayers Association and in 1978 was employed as a lobbyist by the Los Angeles Apartment Owners Association. Paul Gann, Arkansas-born, had moved to California in 1935. A conservative political activist, the Sacramento-based Gann has been described as an "on-again off-again political ally" of Jarvis.

The Los Angeles lobbyist led the drive to gather the tens of thousands of signatures necessary to place the Jarvis-Gann proposal on the ballot and gained national attention as he spearheaded the drive to get the tax-cutting initiative passed. At first it did not seem likely to pass. A succession of tax-cutting initiatives had failed during the past decade. Jarvis led a ragtag collection of supporters; opponents to Proposition 13 included big business, organized labor, and leading figures in both major political parties. Critics predicted that if adopted it would lead to economic disaster for California, claiming that it would cost the state 450,000 jobs and that 150,000 state employees would be fired. A month before the election a poll found the electorate almost evenly divided on Proposition 13.

During the last weeks of the debate on the proposition events began to favor its passage: a direct mail firm sent property owners a card telling them what their taxes were and how much "Yes on 13" would save them, the Los Angeles County assessor sent out notices showing the area's property taxes were about to be raised dramatically, and the press revealed that the state had a massive budget surplus. In the June 1978 election voters responded to these details: over 65 percent of those voting (nearly 70 percent of the state's registered voters) approved Proposition 13.

It promised property tax relief for Californians—over $7 billion in its first year of operation. To achieve that goal sweeping changes were initiated in the property tax system. No longer could a property be reassessed because of market value by 50 percent with owner tax bills increased accordingly. Tax rates were capped "with limited exceptions . . . at 1 percent of full cash value at the time of acquisition." The proposition called for an assessment roll back for tax purposes to 1976 values and replaced annually reassessing property at market value with "a system based on cost at acquisition." Property would now be reassessed for tax purposes only when it changed owners; as long as a property was not sold increases in assessed value were limited to "an annual inflation factor" of no more than 2 percent.

In an attempt to hold back the growth of government spending Proposition 13 required that any measure for increasing state revenues be approved by a two-thirds vote of each branch of the legislature (a requirement that continues to be attacked). A two-thirds vote of approval by voters was also made necessary for any measure to raise taxes by local governments for special projects.

There has continued to be debate about the efficacy of Proposition 13. Supporters have noted that its legality was upheld by the Supreme Court (8-1) in *Nordlinger v. Hahn*. Critics point out that Proposition 13 has limited the ability of California to raise taxes and revenue for necessary expenditures and that states such as Louisiana, Massachusetts. Nevada, and South Carolina, states that followed California's lead in alleviating the anger of American voters over taxes, also faced problems with raising revenues.

The California initiative vote may have presaged a taxpayer revolt that contributed to the election of Ronald Reagan (1917–2004) as president. *The New York Times*, which closely followed the debate over Proposition 13, deplored the outcome of the vote and asserted editorially that it was "a Primal Scream against Big Government"; more than one chronicler has agreed, expressing concern about aroused "conservative activism"; yet one should note that at the local level in the presidential election year of 1980 only 13 of 30 antitax measures up for a vote passed. Nonetheless, Proposition 13 did provide momentum to those at the national level who advocated cutting taxes to stimulate the American economy and did foreshadow passage of significant federal tax reduction legislation in the 1980s.

Further Reading

O'Sullivan, Arthur, Terri A. Sexton, and Steven Sheffrin. *Property Taxes and Tax Revolts: The Legacy of Proposition 13*. Cambridge: Cambridge University Press, 1995.

Smith, D. A. "Howard Jarvis, Populist Entrepreneur: Re-evaluating the Causes of Proposition 13." *Social Science History* 23, no. 2 (1999): 173–219.

Regents of the University of California v. Bakke (1978)

A landmark Supreme Court decision, the Bakke case was argued in October 1977 and the ruling (438 U.S. 265) was handed down June 28, 1978. Very narrowly decided, this case was among the first major constitutional tests in education of "affirmative action," a complex principle developed during the 1960s as a result of civil rights legislation, executive orders, and court rulings— all of which, simply put, were designed as a "color-blind" principle to compensate "protected groups" such as African Americans, Latinos, and Native Americans for past discrimination caused by unequal practices.

This policy was extended to women in the early 1970s and later, if somewhat ineffectually, to age discrimination. As a scholar dealing with the Bakke case has argued, affirmative action resulted in "an intractable conundrum" between an individual's claim to equal treatment and government's attempts to foster equality among all its citizens. As directed at "employment discrimination," the policy impacted significantly on the American economy in good times and bad. Though challenged repeatedly in the courts during the 1960s and early 1970s affirmative action had been enforced and generally accepted but also become increasingly controversial, especially in education, where to many it seemed special efforts were made to accommodate minorities and that reverse discrimination had taken place.

Allan Bakke (b. 1940), a white former National Merit Scholar, graduated from the University of Minnesota with a 3.51 GPA. He met his ROTC obligation by serving with distinction in the Marines, including a tour of duty in Vietnam. Discharged in 1967 as a captain, he found employment as an engineer with NASA but had become interested in medicine. Bakke, who earned a GPA of 3.46 while taking science courses at night to qualify for medical school, scored in the top 3 percent on the Medical College Admissions Test (MCAT). But because of his age (he was considered above "the stated limit"), all the medical schools to which he applied in 1972 and 1973 rejected him, including the University of California, Davis (UC Davis) Medical School. One of its faculty members believed Bakke was handicapped by "the unavoidable fact . . . he is now 33 years of age."

After being rejected again by the UC Davis Medical School in 1974, he sued to compel admission. His suit argued that "special applicants" were admitted with significantly lower test scores and grades than he had earned; that the school reserved 16 places in each entering class of 100 for "economically/and or educationally disadvantaged" as well as for "qualified" minorities as part of the university's affirmative action program to redress their past unfair exclusion; that although many disadvantaged Caucasians had applied none had been accepted; and that in 1974 the committee overseeing the admission of special applicants had determined to consider only those from the explicitly enumerated minority groups. Bakke claimed that he was a victim of "reverse discrimination."

Although directly concerned with procedures in the field of education, the almost contradictory rulings in the Bakke case on both the local and federal

Allan Bakke is trailed by news and television reporters after attending his first day at the Medical School of the University of California at Davis on September 25, 1978; Bakke sued the university for reverse discrimination after his application was rejected in 1973 and 1974. (AP Photo)

level highlighted the contentious issues involved in affirmative action. The decisions of the California courts presaged the complexity of the Supreme Court's ruling. A trial court rejected the claims of UC Davis and maintained that Bakke's rights had been violated. The state appellate court agreed with this verdict but also ordered his admission to the medical school. Appeals were made to the U.S. Supreme Court.

Unlike its response to other such cases questioning the use of race in admissions, the court agreed to review the Bakke case. And it ruled (5-4) in favor of Bakke (the majority maintaining his rights were violated under the equal protection clause of the 14th Amendment) but did so with what has been characterized as "a resounding lack of consensus" and a plethora of concurring opinions and dissents. While four justices agreed that Bakke suffered reverse discrimination, four justices argued that the UC Davis medical school's affirmative action plan properly applied the provisions of the 1964 Civil Rights Act. The "swing man," Justice Lewis Powell (1907–1998), a conservative who cast the decisive vote and wrote the court's ruling, in an unusual opinion sided with both viewpoints but opted for Bakke's admission to the medical school.

The Supreme Court's rulings in the Bakke case, because they were open to positive interpretation by both the proponents and opponents of affirmative action, for a while quieted some of the controversy over the policy. Bakke graduated in 1982, became a resident at the Mayo Clinic in Minnesota, and went on to a successful medical career.

Affirmative action was introduced as a term by President John Kennedy (1917–1963) in his 1961 executive order designed to ensure that federal funds were not used in any endeavor that treated African Americans unequally. Subsequent executive orders by President Lyndon Johnson elaborated on the need for such an approach to ensure equal opportunity. Generally acceptable as a policy after its introduction in the 1960s, affirmative action had become increasingly controversial during the following years (one evidence being the Bakke case).

As stagflation dramatically increased and as Paul Volcker (b. 1927) implemented his draconic solutions, involving extraordinarily high interest rates and massive unemployment, the groups most affected by the twists and turns of the economy were also those most impacted by affirmative action. Public support for the policy significantly eroded.

The Reagan administration during the 1980s tried to stop the spread of affirmative action, which had become the subject of much bitter contention. The Supreme Court, following its decision in the Bakke case, pursued what has been described as a "zigzag course" with regard to enforcement of the policy during the numerous affirmative action cases brought before the justices. Overall, they and the judiciary in general—like the legislative and executive branches of government—have during prosperous times and economic downturns reaffirmed the American commitment to affirmative action.

Further Reading

Ball, Howard. *The* Bakke Case: *Race, Education, and Affirmative Action*. Lawrence: University Press of Kansas, 2000.

Belz, Herman. "Affirmative Action." In Kermit L. Hall, et al., eds., *The Oxford Companion to the Supreme Court of the United States*. New York: Oxford University Press, 1992, 18–22.

Shultz, George P. (1920–)

A prominent public official who served in the administrations of Richard Nixon (1913–1994) and Ronald Reagan (1917–2004), Shultz was considered by both presidents as a trusted adviser. Born December 13, 1920, in New York City, he grew up in New Jersey; graduated (1942) from Princeton with honors; and after service with the Marine Corps during World War II, earned (1949) a

PhD in industrial economics from the Massachusetts Institute of Technology. He taught (1948–1957) at MIT both in its economics department and in its Sloan School of Management, taking a leave of absence in 1955 to serve a stint as a senior staff economist on President Eisenhower's Council of Economic Advisors.

In 1957 he became a professor of industrial relations at the University of Chicago Graduate School of Business, becoming dean in 1962. While Shultz was at the University of Chicago his belief in the free market economy was reinforced by faculty such as economists Milton Friedman (1912–2006) and George Stigler (1911–1991). In 1969 President Richard Nixon appointed Shultz secretary of labor. He avoided the use of injunctions to delay strikes, preferring to allow the parties to work out an arrangement. But he was the first federal executive officer to impose racial quotas, which he did when Pennsylvania construction unions refused to accept African Americans as members.

Nixon was impressed with Shultz's steady temperament, tough negotiating skills, and willingness to be a team player, and in July 1970 Shultz became director of the newly reorganized Office of Management and Budget (OMB), serving until June 1972. OMB's predecessor was first created in 1921 by President Harding (1865–1923) and in its various permutations helped the president to prepare the federal budget and oversaw its administration. Shultz handled these tasks skillfully and impressed Nixon with his management capability.

In June 1972 Shultz was appointed secretary of the treasury by Nixon. Although not always in accord with Nixon's economic policies, he did his best to carry them out and oversaw the lifting and reimplementation of price controls. He also dealt with the problems created by Nixon's closing of the "gold window." Shultz dealt with the aftermath of what is sometimes referred to as the "Nixon Shock" and the resulting float of diverse currencies.

In May 1974 he became an executive with the Bechtel Group, a large, powerful, privately held, family corporation with diversified interests; it has both a distinguished record for its many construction and other ambitious projects and a controversial history of involvement with dubious operations. Shultz resigned in July 1982 on becoming President Reagan's secretary of state, rejoining Bechtel on leaving government service in January 1989 and serving as a director and senior counselor until 2006.

As secretary of state, Shultz improved relations with China, despite an initial hiccup over Taiwan; strenuously opposed negotiations with the radical Nicaraguan government headed by Daniel Ortega (b. 1945); improved relations with various Western European governments; and did his best to institute relations between Israel and its chief protagonists. With regard to the Soviet Union, a tough stance marked his dealings with Soviet counterparts, but Shultz also advocated personal contact and continued negotiations. He encouraged

President Reagan's meetings with Soviet leader Mikhail Gorbachev (b. 1931), one result of which was the 1987 Intermediate Nuclear Forces Treaty that pledged to eliminate most of such Soviet and American missiles from Europe by 1992.

During Shultz's tenure as secretary of state, President Reagan, like President Nixon, was impressed by his steady temperament and team player approach. After Shultz left office he returned to Bechtel, became a professor of international economics at Stanford University, and was appointed Distinguished Fellow at the Hoover Institution. The recipient of many awards, including the Medal of Freedom, Shultz continued to be consulted by many prominent Republicans.

Further Reading

Shultz, George P. *Triumph and Tragedy: My Years as Secretary of State*. New York: Scribner's, 1993.

Three Mile Island (1979)

Three Mile Island was the location of a nuclear power plant near Middletown, Dauphin County, Pennsylvania, not far from Harrisburg, the state capitol. Three Mile Island was also the site of a frightening meltdown at the end of March 1979, only some 13 months after this very expensive reactor had gone into operation. What happened at the Three Mile Island power plant surprised many federal and state officials as well as both proponents and opponents of nuclear energy, raising—both then and now—a variety of serious concerns and questions about the safety of such power plants and their owners' ability to operate them properly.

The incident began early in the morning of March 28, 1979, when a partial nuclear meltdown occurred at Unit 2 of the Three Mile Island nuclear facility (TMI2) in a pressurized water reactor (running at 97 percent of full power). The reactor's fuel core became uncovered, and about one-third of the fuel melted. Supposedly automatic safety measures did not come fully into play, in part because of mechanical failure. Human factors (later described as "operator error") then compounded the situation as plant staff, due to inadequate instrumentation and faulty training, failed to grasp the consequences of such factors as a stuck valve.

About two hours into the malfunctioning of TMI2's safety systems the top of the reactor core was exposed, radiation alarms went off, a supervisor announced a general emergency, and government officials were notified. The situation, especially with regard to radiation leakage, initially was unclear. TMI2's managers and owners downplayed the severity of the accident; a commissioner of the Nuclear Regulatory Commission (NRC) responsible for the oversight of nuclear power plants later recalled that the NRC did not learn "for years . . . that by the time the plant operator . . . called, roughly half of the uranium fuel had already melted."

At first, in part because it was believed that the situation was under control, a mass of contradictory, ambiguous, and confusing public statements were issued to the media by TMI2 public relations people and nuclear industry representatives as well as various Pennsylvania state agencies. Throughout the crisis much of the media mismanaged the news and contributed to the confusion, the difficulty of understanding just exactly what was taking place, and the rising public mistrust.

As March 28 wore on, concerns among TMI2's staff and the NRC's on-site officials were eased because the nuclear core had cooled and the reactor seemed stable. However, these concerns were quickly renewed when it was revealed that radiation had leaked out into the surrounding atmosphere and that there was uncertainty about the quantity of that leakage and the condition of the plant. Thanks to often garbled communications between those dealing with the accident as well as unnecessarily scary media reports, an atmosphere of growing uncertainty that impacted on an increasingly fearful public was created.

The public's fears were further exacerbated when Pennsylvania's governor decided on March 29 after consulting with NRC commissioners that it would be prudent to evacuate families with pregnant women and preschool age children (those assumed to be the most at risk) within a five-mile radius of "the Three Mile Island facility." The next day, March 30, that zone of evacuation was extended to a 20-mile radius. Within a short time over 125,000 individuals had left the area; in about three weeks about 98 percent had returned to their homes.

By April 1 the situation at TMI2 was stabilized—if far from resolved. Badly damaged and irreparably contaminated, the ruined reactor would never function again. Permanently closed, it was gradually deactivated. Initially efforts concentrated on decontamination of the site (the building at first was too contaminated to walk through). Not until December 1993 was the cleanup (whose cost has been estimated at a billion dollars) officially concluded.

Considerable research has been done over the years by a wide variety of government and independent agencies as to the impact of the accident on the health of people in the area surrounding TMI2. Almost no radiation contamination of the environment was found by these studies, and many of them agreed that the average radiation dose for individuals living within a radius of 10 miles of TMI2 was just about equal to a chest X-ray, no more than the annual average level of radiation to which Americans are exposed normally. Nor did these studies find any evidence of unusual adverse health patterns among individuals exposed to fallout from TMI2; it was claimed that the accident did not increase radioactivity enough to cause additional cases of cancer or leukemia.

Two weeks after the accident happened President Carter (b. 1924) appointed a 12-person commission headed by John Kemeny (1926–1992), the innovative president of Dartmouth College, a respected computer specialist and prize-winning mathematician, to report on "The Accident at Three Mile Island." The commission's final report based on extensive hearings and intense document collection was issued in October 1979. The report was highly critical of the Three Mile Island corporate management, found its actions "inappropriate," and recommended the implementation of numerous changes to ensure the safety of nuclear plants. The report also concluded that because "in this case the radiation doses were so low . . . the overall health effects will be minimal."

Since issuance of the Kemeny Commission's report antinuclear power groups and the "alternative" media, while agreeing with many of its conclusions, have argued TMI2 radiation emissions have been responsible for various ailments (such as cancer, leukemia, birth defects, and respiratory problems) suffered by the population surrounding the power plant at the time of the accident. A 1997 study by University of North Carolina researchers found increases in lung cancer and leukemia among individuals living near the Three Island plant during the meltdown and suggested that a much greater amount of radiation had been released than had been believed.

Although a class action lawsuit filed by 2,400 Pennsylvania families failed, at least $15 million has been paid in out-of-court settlements, and $71 million has been paid out for "loss of business revenue, evacuation expenses, and health claims" under provisions of the Price-Anderson Nuclear Industries Indemnity Act. Sponsored by Illinois representative Charles M. Price (1905–1988) and New Mexico senator Clinton Anderson (1895–1975), both Democrats, this 1957 legislation, now extended to 2026, is according to the NRC "designed . . . to satisfy liability claims . . . of the public for personal . . . and property damage in . . . nuclear accidents involving a commercial nuclear power plant." The last of the litigation resulting from the Three Mile Island meltdown was settled in 2003.

The Three Mile Island accident raised concerns about the dangers of nuclear power. The surge toward nuclear power had been slowed by the soft economy of the 1970s. After Three Mile Island many Americans lost faith in the use of nuclear power. Kemeny, very much concerned by both the industry's and the NRC's failure to ensure adequate safety provisions, in a separate note to his commission's report "very much regretted" there had not been a temporary halt to the issuance of construction permits for new nuclear power plants. However, in the aftermath of Three Mile Island, federal operating requirements became much more stringent, and opposition by local residents became much more strident and at times could not be overcome.

Further Reading

Report of the President's Commission on the Accident at Three Mile Island. http://www .pddoc.com/tmi2/kemeny/ [accessed March 12, 2013].

Walker, J. Samuel. *Three Mile Island: A Nuclear Crisis in Historical Perspective.* Berkeley: University of California Press, 2004.

Volcker, Paul (1927–)

His reputation for moral probity, unbiased unerring financial analysis, and a steely determination to do what he considered right for the U.S. economy has buttressed both Republican and Democratic administrations since the 1970s. The grandson of German immigrants, Volcker was born in Cape May, New Jersey; raised in Teaneck, New Jersey, where his father served as its first municipal manager; graduated (1949) summa cum laude from Princeton University; and earned (1951) an MA in political economy at the Harvard University Graduate School of Public Administration, after which, as a Rotary Foundation Fellow, he attended (1951–1952) the London School of Economics.

He began his career with the government during the summers of 1949 and 1950 working as a research assistant at the Federal Reserve Bank of New York, which hired him as a staff economist in 1952. He moved in 1957 to the Chase Manhattan Bank, which took him on as a financial economist, and in 1962 he was hired by the Treasury Department as director of its Office of Financial Analysis. A year later he became deputy undersecretary for monetary affairs; in 1965 he rejoined Chase Manhattan as a vice president and director of forward planning.

Between 1969 and 1974 he served as undersecretary of the treasury for international monetary affairs and played a moderating but important role in the closing (1971) of the "gold window" and the end of fixed currency exchange rates. Volcker advocated international solutions to monetary problems. He served a stint (the academic year 1974–1975) as Senior Fellow at Princeton's Woodrow Wilson School of Public and International Affairs before becoming (1975) head of the Federal Reserve Bank of New York. He functioned well in that position, and in 1979 President Jimmy Carter (b. 1924) appointed him to chair the Board of Governors of the Federal Reserve system; President Ronald Reagan (1917–2004) reappointed him in 1983.

Under Chairman Paul Volcker's direction, the Federal Reserve, by curbing the growth of the money supply and establishing high interest rates, helped end a period of unprecedented inflation in the United States in the 1970s and 1980s. (UN Photo/Sophia Paris)

As chairman of the Federal Reserve, Volcker instituted monetary policies that were credited with ending the stagflation that had been a persistent problem since the early 1970s. He ruthlessly and unrelentingly advocated and implemented policies that aroused intense opposition. In response to the twin threat of unemployment and inflation, he believed that the key to improving the economy was tackling inflation. Volcker, unlike his immediate predecessor, strenuously tightened the money supply in 1979, 1980, and 1981, raising the federal funds rate, which was 11.2 percent when he took office, and peaked at 20 percent; in mid-1981 the prime rate rose to 21.5 percent.

The extremely high interest rates Volcker imposed hurt the construction industry as well as many farmers, and without any doubt contributed to increased unemployment, which at one point stood at over 10 percent. But Volcker's policies, while very controversial and arousing angry political attacks—perhaps the most widespread and intense in the Fed's history—did end the vicious corrosive cycle of stagflation. Inflation that stood at over 13 percent in 1981 had been reduced to less than 4 percent by 1983, and by the end of that year both interest rates and unemployment had been substantially reduced.

In the short term, Volcker's tight money policy led to recession as well as some social unrest. However, in the long run his policies had been proved correct as they broke the back of the stagflation that had so bedeviled the United States. Notwithstanding the vicious and vitriolic criticism leveled at Volcker, President Reagan had consistently supported Volcker's tight money policy and in 1983 reappointed him Federal Reserve chairman. But the president and some of his associates found Volcker too independent-minded in his opposition to the administration's plans to deregulate the American banking system, and he was not reappointed to a third term as chairman.

Volcker remained active in many spheres after his retirement from the Federal Reserve but in the words of a *New Yorker* correspondent was "widely regarded as an out-of-touch fuddy-duddy." For a while he served as chair of a prominent New York investment firm. In 1996 he served effectively as head of a commission investigating dormant Swiss bank accounts of Holocaust victims, helping achieve a settlement. He oversaw an inquiry into controversial activities of the son of the UN's secretary-general. Active in the Trilateral Commission and the Bilderberg Group, he remained in demand as a speaker at distinguished gatherings. Service as an economic advisor to Barack Obama (b. 1961) during his successful electoral run in 2008 led to appointment in 2009 as head of the President's Economic Recovery Advisory Board (PERAB), part of President Obama's campaign to deal with the aftermath of the 2008 financial crash.

Already prior to his appointment a deeply concerned Volcker had actively advocated financial reform. Legislation sponsored by two Democrats, Connecticut senator Chris Dodd (b. 1944) and Massachusetts representative Barney Frank (b. 1940), to implement some financial reforms included Volcker's recommendation for restoration of the divide between commercial and investment banking. In January 2010, at a White House press conference with the 6'7" Volcker towering over him, President Obama urged Congress to enact financial reform legislation, including what he called "the Volcker rule." In July 2010 the president signed into law the "Dodd-Frank Wall Street Reform and Consumer Protection Act . . . to promote the financial stability of the United States [and] . . . to protect consumers from abusive financial services practices."

Despite aggressive lobbying against the Volcker rule by the financial services industry Dodd-Frank included a modified version. To go into effect in July 2012, it banned banks from using their own money to undertake risky trades or to invest in hedge funds. Despite the president's endorsement Volcker had "rocky relations" with him and his top economics staff; in 2011 the president decided to reconstitute the PERAB without Volcker's input or further participation. One insider asserted the Obama administration used Volcker's known independence and integrity "to look tough on regulation, and now . . . they're saying good bye."

Whatever the impact of the Volcker rule, which at the time of this writing the financial services industry still contested, his most lasting legacy is his successful yeoman fight against inflation throughout the later 1970s and early 1980s. Inflation had been a problem that had baffled public officials, consumers, businessmen, and just about anyone attempting to tackle it. Volcker successfully dealt with it, and since then inflation has not been a significant problem for the American economy.

Further Reading

Cassidy, John. "The Volcker Rule." *The New Yorker*, July 26, 2010. http://www.new yorker/reporting/2010/07/26/100726fa_fact_cas [accessed July 29, 2013].

Onaran, Yalman, and Hans Nichols. "Volcker Sidelined as Obama Reshapes Advisory Panel," January 6, 2011, Bloomberg News On-linhttp://www.bloomberg.com/news/print/2011-01-06/volcker-sideline... [accessed July 29, 2013].

Treaster, Joseph B. *Paul Volcker: The Making of a Financial Legend.* Hoboken, NJ: Wiley, 2004.

• 14 •

GREAT RECESSION OF 2008–2009

Victoria Phillips

Between the last part of 2008 and the end of the first quarter of 2009, the United States suffered a financial collapse marked by the largest underperformance of equities in relation to government-issued treasury securities since 1896, when the Dow Jones Industrial Average opened. By the end of 2009, a recession was in full swing, and unemployment had more than doubled, with an estimated real rate of over 16 percent—including those who had ceased looking for work. For African American youths, the unemployed number in some regions stood at over 40 percent.

What came to be called "the Great Recession" by many in the media did not just fade away. After months of continued downturns in disparate parts of the American economy the situation improved, but at the time of this writing, significant aspects of that economy remain soft, and it still remains a long way from being generally healthy. Unemployment remained high, especially as many Americans had determined to stop seeking jobs that could not be found. Government aid at all levels mitigated the recession's severest effects: unlike the early 1930s no one starved, and it is doubtful if many were totally deprived of social services. Yet there was abroad in the land a bitter divide between those who benefited from the economy and those who did not.

The financial implosion of 2008–2009 resulted from a variety of causes, not least from the attempts to maintain a core America tenet, that home ownership for every family defines citizenship and is a desirable good. Although home ownership is personal, the goal had become political. No one could or should dispute that home ownership is good for the average person, for the economy, and for the country. Deregulated banks joined the government alongside insurance companies and corporations to realize that dream for "everyman." By the start of the 21st century, that myth had turned mantra and had sealed the bonds among Republicans, Democrats, competing financial institutions, the business community, and American citizens in support of the concept of universal home ownership.

Officially, recovery from the recession began toward the end of 2009, but that recovery was constantly hampered by such factors as rising oil prices, natural disasters (such as the tsunami that hit Japan in 2011), and a continuing economic downturn in much of Europe caused by an ongoing debt crisis. The property market in much of the United States remained in collapse; lenders continued to prove reluctant; consumers, on whose spending much of the American economy depended, hung back; state and local governments, because of declining tax revenues, faced fiscal crises and moved to scale back the nanny state; and a series of stimuli offered by the federal government kept the economy from deteriorating more but proved unable, at least initially, to significantly improve the economy.

Even though at the time of this writing in early 2013 the stock market had recovered, interest income remained very low because of Federal Reserve attempts to stem inflation, official unemployment rates hovered above 7 percent, the gross domestic product (GDP) saw growth limited to about 2 percent (it averaged only 1.7 percent in 2011 in the United States), and many loans and mortgages continued to fall into default. Americans and their economy were continuing to pay the price for having lived beyond their means for years.

There long had been discussions about such "bubbles" in the economic literature. In 1841 Scottish journalist Claude Mackay (1814–1889) noted in his *Extraordinary Popular Delusions and the Madness of Crowds* that his book was merely, "A chapter in the great and awful book of human folly which yet remains to be written." Describing among other economic bubbles the Dutch Tulip Mania (1636–1637), the French Mississippi Schemes (1718–1720), and the English South Sea Bubble (1720), MacKay documented how these popular delusions started with "seasons of recklessness" that turned into "moral epidemics."

Numerous bubbles began, it has been noted, with financial ties between government and institutions meant to ensure greater liquidity and promote an idealized product that people could have and hold. Decades after MacKay wrote, Edwin Lefèvre (1871–1943) noted in his semi-fictional *Reminiscences of a Stock Operator* (1923) that on Wall Street "speculation is as old as the hills," adding: "Whatever happens in the stock market to-day has happened before and will happen again." At the onset of the 21st century, circumstances once again brought together both the bonding of usually vying institutions and the fetishization of an object (i.e., home ownership). Wall Street fueled the mania, as its denizens sought to profit from the situation.

Indeed, the 2008 mortgage crisis did not originate in unadulterated greed. The demand for housing increased the need for bank loans enabling these purchases, and government securitization of the loans stemmed from a desire to create a secure society. To attribute the crash of 2008 merely to the greed of bankers or the investing public defies logic, although both bankers and the public at large have admittedly been notoriously greedy throughout the ages. As in early stages of most bubbles, the recent "season of recklessness" led to a mortgage bubble, reckless speculation, and moral disintegration only because a confluence of fronts that already existed in the American system brought about the perfect storm and economic disaster.

Nationalism and Home Ownership

The collapse of 2008 began with the national tenet of homeownership built on the ideals articulated by such Founding Fathers as Thomas Jefferson (1743–1826). He, like many of his peers in the early days of the republic, was suspicious of government banking; indeed, while both the First and Second Banks of the United States failed to gain public backing, Americans continued to favor government support of homeownership (e.g., the Homestead Act of 1862) and the power of the homeowner remained a foundational American belief.

In the early 20th century, bankers and financiers led government intervention into private securities markets, but only when this practice suited their agenda. New legislation then and later protected consumers of housing loans by prompting national banks to enter the market as reliable lenders, to displace the local companies dominating the home-lending market, who solicited deposits door-to-door and made loans through the real estate brokers who sold the properties. Both Republicans and Democrats supported legislation to disenfranchise local financial institutions, which had profited by collecting interest payments that gouged the public and by artificially inflating home prices. This legislation required domination of the market by professional bankers. This reformed system, in turn, encouraged lending because the banking-government relationship had made it stable. Herbert Hoover (1874–1964), while still a cabinet officer in the 1920s, called the United States the "land of homes," and claimed that "to possess one's own home is the hope and ambition of almost every individual in our country." After the 1929 Wall Street bust, home prices in the already hard-hit farm belt tumbled, credit tightened, and banks imploded. In response, President Hoover's administration created the Home Loan Bank in 1932 to provide liquidity to the market. As the American financial system weakened, the new administration of Franklin D. Roosevelt (1881–1945) enacted sweeping reforms. His 1934 Housing Act was far more decisive than Hoover's Home Loan Bank, yet the two administrations' belief in the American homeowner followed each other in lockstep. Hoover linked homeownership to spirituality, morality, and the American ethos. For Roosevelt, allowing foreclosures indicated "a loss of spiritual values—the loss of that sense of security for the present and the future so necessary to the peace and contentment of the individual and of his family."

However effective during the 1930s, Roosevelt's solutions created the underpinnings of the 21st-century's problems. Roosevelt's Federal Housing Administration (FHA) provided capital and insurance to lending institutions, relying on a national pool of mortgagees. In 1938 his administration created the Federal National Mortgage Association, or Fannie Mae, to provide local banks with federal money for financing home mortgages, offering fixed interest payments with low down payments to home buyers. Backed by the government, Fannie Mae could sell investment-grade bonds to fund its own liquidity. Due to the assumed safety of these bonds as well as new requirements requiring insurance companies to own investment-grade securities, the demand for these Fannie Mae bonds increased exponentially.

After World War II, FHA programs expanded to include such operations as mobile home parks. At the same time, loans to veterans under the GI Bill fueled the demand for homes. Government and financiers became bonded with the "forgotten man," who became the homeowner they could not afford to forget. Relationships became both circular and self-reinforcing. The government-backed process of pooling loans to create liquidity, and thus increasing demand for home purchases with easy credit, began as a solution that would echo past problems. Stock market excesses in the 1920s had been enabled by self-serving and unregulated financial institutions that both issued securities and lent funds for their purchase against the rising prices of securities, with no cap on debt. Price declines thus forced sales of securities held as collateral. As banks called in loans, the cycle pushed the system into free fall. Roosevelt understood that government oversight was essential to create public trust in the financial system.

The Glass-Steagall Act (passed in 1933 during the first 100 days of the Roosevelt administration), separated investment banks, which made financial products, from depositary and loan institutions; regulated interest rates offered by banks to savings accounts; insured these accounts; and mandated the percentage of the total value of a stock that had to be put down to borrow against it. These rules did not apply to home loans. The Securities and Exchange Commission (SEC) was established in 1934 to protect the investor. Although the SEC worked well, it provided loopholes in the system that readied it for 2008. Fannie Mae, for instance, remained exempt from SEC reporting standards.

Also international financial relations established during World War II allowed the global breadth of the 2008 collapse. A 1944 conference held at Bretton Woods, New Hampshire, created the International Monetary Fund (IMF) to coordinate central bank practices among major industrial nations and established the U.S. dollar as a reserve currency backed by gold reserves. Because the United States held vast reserves and pumped dollars into the

European economy, the dollar became the currency of international exchange. The hegemony of the U.S. dollar expanded exponentially over time.

In 1949, as U.S.-dollar-denominated investments took on global appeal for wealthy investors, the first "hedge fund" opened; these funds offshore were limited to "sophisticated investors" and were exempt from SEC control as long as they had fewer than 499 participants. International players also invested in dollar-denominated American home mortgages to achieve greater profits. The Cold War, pitting the United States against the Soviet Union, led to global ideological battles, heightened the ideology that home ownership defined Americans and helped define the home as a symbol of "freedom." The 1959 American National Exhibit in Moscow showcased a home advertised as affordable to all in the United States, although in reality it was beyond the reach of many. This model home, site of the "Kitchen Debate" between Vice President Richard Nixon (1913–1994) and Soviet premier Nikita Khrushchev (1894–1971), became a potent symbol for many Americans and reinforced domestic home-ownership ideology in the United States.

President Lyndon B. Johnson (1908–1973), as part of his "War on Poverty," pushed the ideal of home ownership even further. In 1968 the Johnson administration privatized Fannie Mae, which removed it from the national budget and generated profits for its stockholders, who enjoyed both the benefits of exemption from oversight and government securitization. In the same year, the Government National Mortgage Association (Ginnie Mae), made affordable housing loans available to families. In 1970 the Federal Home Loan Mortgage Corporation (Freddie Mac) was established to expand the U.S. secondary market for mortgages and, like Fannie Mae, became a publicly traded stock. With the U.S. government at its back, Fannie Mae's securities received triple-A ratings from agencies such as Moody's and Standard & Poor's. Circumventing oversight from accounting disclosure, this highly rated but flawed family of securities enabled the 2008 housing debacle to unfold.

The Sweet Point: Trading in Heaven

The 1970s brought changes solidifying the U.S. dollar's hegemony while creating new opportunities for banks when assets became undeliverable. President Nixon pulled out of the Bretton Woods agreement thus cancelling conversion of the U.S. dollar into gold. Surprisingly, the "Nixon Shock" reinforced the hegemony of the U.S. dollar, and commodities continued to be traded, exchanged, and valued in dollars; global investors purchased dollar-denominated debt. Another 1970s event that helped create the mania of 2008 occurred when the U.S. Treasury and the Federal Reserve granted permission to exchanges to trade derivatives on currencies. Futures derivatives were not new; they were sanctioned by the English in the 18th century to facilitate liquidity for commodity markets. A contract stipulated the delivery of a particular amount of a commodity on a specific future date at an exact price, although delivery was rarely exercised for oil, orange juice, pork bellies, or the like. These contracts were supposed to assist companies that imported or exported these products. By 1975 futures traded on the markets included government bonds. In 1976 the U.S. government approved interest rate futures contracts. As a new market, these engineered products did not command mandatory margin requirements.

Such developments during these years created a toxic financial turning point; financial securities became firmly decoupled from underlying assets. Dollars could not be delivered for gold, and interest rates could not be delivered at all. Wall Street "financial engineers" stripped debt securities and parceled them into separate pools of interest and principal payments. Mortgage loans supported by a national ideology of homeownership became a perfect repackageable candidate. In theory, investors could bank on income flows from monthly payments, or onetime income surges with repayment of principal. Rating agencies made the assumption that despite questionable practices, the "pooling effect" for these private loans—though not government insured—would spread risk and thus guarantee steady payments. These bundled securities were given triple-A ratings.

In turn, pooling allowed federally insured and regulated banks and insurance companies to purchase the new securities. Foreign companies and governments joined in. Traders gave stripped and bundled consumer loans names that corresponded to a deliverable object that seemed to be backed by real people: Fannie Mae, Freddie Mac, Ginnie Mae. Bundled securities became nouns, such as CARS for automobile industry receivables. The assets in "asset-backed" securities became increasingly unidentifiable. Although called "essentially industrial raw materials," they were only identifiable as goods because they were traded on exchanges. Wall Street pundits began to call them "toxic waste." Indeed, financiers traded only in promises that could not be met when they came due, except with other promises. Ronald Reagan (1917–2004), who took office in 1981 in the wake of the disastrous presidency of President Jimmy Carter, promoted a patriotism that included dedication to American home ownership. For Reagan, "a love of home is one of the finest ideals of our people"; home ownership "supplies stability and rootedness." Supported by economists and financial lobbyists, his administration started a 30-year period of financial deregulation to unlock and expand the economy. Ties between financiers, insiders, and government firmly moved the spiral upward. In 1981 Reagan chose Donald Regan (1918–2003), CEO of the investment firm Merrill Lynch, as secretary of the treasury.

Depositors line up in the parking lot of Old Court Savings & Loan waiting to withdraw their savings, Randalstown, Maryland, May 1985. (Marty Katz/Time Life Pictures/Getty Images)

The Reagan team rekindled fundamental American tenets that redirected and refueled the energy for the 21st-century boom. Reagan expressed a distrust of federal banking control, an antipathy that dated back to the Banks of the United States. The administration oversaw deregulation of savings and loans institutions, allowing them to make risky investments with depositors' money. This led to a speculative boom in which insiders shared agendas with regulators. In 1985, when they investigated S&L chieftain Charles Keating (b. 1923) for manipulation and fraud, he hired economist Alan Greenspan (b. 1926) as part of his defense team. Keating later went to prison, followed by executives of other financial institutions. Yet, in 1987, President Reagan appointed Greenspan chair of the Federal Reserve. By the end of the 1980s, hundreds of savings-and-loan companies had failed, many individuals had lost their life savings, and the crisis cost taxpayers $124 billion. The excesses of individuals such as Keating caused them to become known as the faces of greed.

The crumbling of the Soviet Union in 1991 crowned the United States as the triumphant safe harbor for money. American confidence spurred financial creativity, and the number of hedge funds mushroomed. Investment professionals had always used leverage, or borrowing, to engage in "hedging techniques." Purchases of securities were offset by stocks sold short, or shares increased in value when other investments declined. The number of funds increased exponentially as profits skyrocketed; fund managers switched from being viewed as rogue traders to being seen as leaders on Wall Street. With offshore funds, they could skirt SEC control and invest for increasing numbers of wealthy American and international investors.

Just as unexpected alliances had regulated depressed financial markets in the Depression, they reformed to deregulate when prosperity reigned. Under President Bill Clinton (b. 1946), Democrats acted like Republicans. Tracing his ideology from Jefferson and Hoover to Johnson and Bush, Clinton stated, "More Americans should own their own homes, for reasons that are economic and tangible, and reasons that are emotional and intangible, but go to the heart of what it means to harbor, to nourish, to expand the American Dream." In support of such ideas Clinton appointed treasury secretaries from the financial industry: first Robert Rubin (b. 1938), former CEO of Goldman Sachs, then Lawrence Summers (b. 1954), a Harvard economics professor who subsequently acted as a hedge fund advisor and earned millions. In 1996 Clinton reappointed Greenspan.

In 1998 deregulation spurred consolidation in the financial sector as FDR's regulations were dismantled. With a strong economy at its back, the Clinton administration expanded upon Reagan's theories. Citicorp (a commercial bank holding company) and Traveler's Group (an insurance company) merged to form Citigroup, the largest financial services company in the world. The merger violated the Glass-Steagall Act, prohibiting banks with consumer deposits from engaging in investment banking activities. Greenspan remained silent, and the Federal Reserve granted the companies an exemption for a year. Under Clinton, Congress overturned Glass-Steagall with the Financial Services Modernization Act of 1999, sponsored by three Republicans: Texas senator Phil Gramm (b. 1942), Iowa representative Jim Leach (b. 1942), and Virginia representative Thomas Bliley Jr. (b. 1932).

The consolidation of investment and commercial banks recoupled the financier with the lender. Deregulation paired with earlier innovative products and new advances in technology led to an explosion of complex financial products and derivatives. Home mortgages became targeted by "rainmakers"; the financial community reveled in the promise of government-insured products that ensured profits. By the late 1990s, derivatives had become a $50 trillion market. With banks making, selling, and loaning money to purchasers—despite promises of "Chinese Walls" between the divisions of financial institutions—conflicts of interest became inevitable. Numbed to risk because savings accounts were insured under Roosevelt's legislation, the public began to put savings into uninsured money market accounts that offered higher returns.

Both the unknowing public and more sophisticated professionals reaped the benefits of higher rates offered by derivatives. In May 1998 the Commodity

Futures Trading Commission issued a proposal to regulate derivatives. Bankers subsequently met with Secretary of the Treasury Robert Rubin and argued that regulation would limit profits. Greenspan and SEC chairman Arthur Levitt (b. 1931) agreed. Senator Phil Gramm supported their arguments. Regulation seemed to be in direct conflict with the American way.

The Culmination

As the global markets entered the 21st century with the dollar firmly fixed as the global reserve currency, triple-A mortgages became increasingly attractive to international investors who wanted seemingly riskless higher returns, even though markets supposedly only paid "increased dividends" to those who assume greater risk. In addition, the promise of homeownership gained international traction; even foreign banks loaned money globally to realize this dream for their own nationals.

In the first year of the 21st century, the Dow Jones Industrial Average was beset by uneven and jagged moves created by the hotly contested presidential election between George W. Bush (b. 1946) and Al Gore (b. 1948), increasing worries about the stability of the economy, and the popping sounds of an Internet stock bubble. The Dow Jones Average reached a high of 11,722 in January 2000 followed by declines. Although professionals expressed concerns about soft or hard economic landings, the economy moved forward. Inflation remained in abeyance, productivity continued strong, and the jobless rate matched a three-year low.

Yet optimism remained limited throughout the year. The 2000 sell-offs fueled speculation that the bull market in stocks had ended. In late December 2000 Congress passed legislation *banning* regulation of derivatives; the market for these securities exploded—particularly for those capitalizing on real estate—as people invested in homes.

The tragic events of September 11, 2001, brought national shock and mourning. Coupled with a California energy crisis and steep declines on Wall Street, they made distressing economic news. Unemployment rose. The Federal Reserve slashed interest rates 11 times, thus lowering rates available for loans. The financial sector consolidated in response to market turmoil and became more powerful. Financial conglomerates Citigroup and J. P. Morgan wielded increasing power. Goldman Sachs, Morgan Stanley, Lehman Brothers, Merrill Lynch, and Bear Stearns dominated investment banking. Insurance companies grew, particularly American International Group (AIG).

The ratings agencies, including Moody's and Standard & Poor's, which were paid fees by the investment banks to rate their bonds, gave triple-A status to derivatives. This created new profit opportunities in the wake of a weakening and unpredictable stock market. Home prices rose, as mortgage standards weakened, a result of the lack of proper regulatory supervision. In essence, margin requirements for consumer stock purchases did not apply to investments in American homes. In the face of domestic tragedy, the home became a more desirable investment, and one that was increasingly accessible.

Government Takes Action to Preserve the Confidence of Its People

In 2001 and 2002 President George W. Bush advanced home ownership as both the realization of the "American Dream" as well as a means to fight the American enemy. In June 2002 he celebrated a newly created "Home ownership Month," stating, "I believe owning a home is an essential part of economic security." Home ownership also took on a global potency that Bush linked to military might when he insisted, "Let me first talk about how to make sure

President G. W. Bush makes remarks on home ownership at the Department of Housing and Urban Development in Washington, D.C., June 18, 2002. Bush called for a boost in home ownership among minorities, saying he wanted the number of black and Latino homeowners to increase by the end of the decade. (AP Photo/Ron Edmonds)

America is secure from a group of killers, people who hate—you know what they hate? They hate the idea that somebody can go buy a home." Although Bush has been blamed for the 21st century U.S. economic crisis, he supplied no new ideological input into the American system either through rhetoric or financial practices.

By the time Bush took office, subprime loans had already begun to explode in volume, and all the trends set by his predecessors surged forward. A subprime loan was defined by the borrower's financial position; many of these prospective homeowners had limited incomes or credit scores between 500 and 600 on a scale from 300 to 850. With no regulations on the amount of leverage borrowers could assume, transactions increased in size and volume. As housing prices trended upward, homeowners took second and third mortgages. Creative loans made borrowing easier and came with initial low payments to be reset in the future. The more risky the borrower, the more banks charged for a loan. The more the bank charged for a loan, the greater the return to the investor. Since returns were assumed to be insured or guaranteed, investors were not paid to take risk. They were paid for buying securities.

The Promise of the Home Binds the "Everyman" to the Markets

Americans at large "drove while looking in the rearview mirror." While ratings agencies continued to assert the safety of mortgage investments due to their historical performance when pooled, mortgage lenders demanded less and less of home buyers. As prices of homes increased alongside the availability of loans, borrowers borrowed. The higher and higher rates borrowers paid promised greater returns for investors in debt securities. Mortgage lenders sold the loans to banks and thus increased fees. The banks grew to prefer subprime loans: higher volume brought increased fees to the rating agencies. The cycle was firmly set.

Greed infused the American way as the cycle included Roosevelt's "everyman" alongside the banker. Despite the twists and turns of the Dow Jones Average as well as FBI warnings as early as 2004 of an epidemic of mortgage fraud, returns on the derivatives seemed assured, creating profits for banks, mortgage lenders, and ratings companies. People sold or refinanced homes and purchased new goods (e.g., cars and washing machines), also on credit. This activity created jobs and new borrowers. The number of mortgage loans nearly quadrupled. Fannie Mae and Freddie Mac largely controlled the nation's secondary mortgage market, and lack of oversight led to abuses. Indeed, Fannie Mae overstated earnings by more than $10 *billion* dollars between 1998 and 2003. CEO Franklin Raine (b. 1949), once President Clinton's budget director, received over \$52 million in bonuses. Subprime lending increased from \$30 billion to over \$600 billion a year at its peak.

Thanks to the Home Ownership and Equity Protection Act passed by Congress in 1994 and Regulation Z of the Federal Reserve Board, the government possessed broad powers to regulate mortgage industry practices, such as predatory lending, but regulators remained passive. The SEC lost investigators to the profit-making firms and cut positions due to reductions in budget. Individuals who remained with such regulatory agencies often became overworked or complacent. Lobbyists successfully derailed regulation of derivatives and consumer debt because regulation seemed to work against the realization of the American dream. SEC chairman Christopher Cox (b. 1952) remarked, "The free and efficient movement of capital is helping to create the greatest prosperity in human history."

"Greed Is Good"?: The Face of Fraud

In 2005 the financial greed that had infiltrated the system became apparent to some, but not many. Despite a 2005 report filed with the SEC entitled "The World's Largest Hedge Fund is a Fraud," the investment company of Bernard Madoff (b. 1938) remained, for the most part, unaudited. His techniques, which promised investors between 12 percent and 15 percent in annual returns, seemed advanced enough to beat the odds. He took money from knowledgeable investors, including those who headed charities and foundations, and banked on a booming housing market to cover his manipulations. Although his funds had been limited to the "sophisticated," even small investors pooled assets to get the above average returns Madoff seemed to deliver, and individuals took first, second, and even third mortgages to get from Madoff above average cash returns.

Madoff's operation had two arms: a legitimate business—a National Association of Securities Dealers (NASD) trading firm, and the investment fund— which provided fictitious returns to private investors. Because of his legitimate trading firm activities, Madoff became chairman of NASD's board of directors, sat on the Quality of Markets Committee (which brings industry leaders together with regulators), and drafted and signed letters regarding trading rules and policy to top regulators at the SEC. Industry insiders noted that Madoff's firm often hired SEC lawyers who could have caught an important hitch in his investment company's scheme. Every Wall Street firm is given a clearing number, and each trade is matched with the trade on the other side at the close of each market day. No regulators ever checked Madoff's number; had they done so, they would have seen that he had cleared no trades.

The Promise of Borrowed Money

As the 21st century moved forward, government deregulation and lax supervision fueled both speculation and fraud. Investment banks became leveraged up to the level of 35-1, but the promise of insurance justified risks. AIG, the world's largest insurance company, sold credit default swaps to investors owning Collateralized Debt Obligations (CDO). If one defaulted, AIG promised to cover losses. Investors paid a fee for this insurance. Unlike traditional insurance taken out against tangible events such as floods or fires, these policies could be sold short, or traded so as to profit from the decline in CDOs that no one owned. Unlike a home, which is insurable only once against damage, these assets allowed nonexistent homes to be insured many times over, depending on demand from financial markets for the insurance-backed product. Insurance companies like AIG did not keep adequate reserves against potential losses. In 2007 AIG's auditors expressed warnings that went unheeded.

Both the public and the elite in government and business benefited from the upward spiral. Individuals profited from increasing home sales; they offered greater cash flow with which to purchase consumer goods. Between 2001 and 2007 Americans went on a borrowing binge; household debt nearly doubled. Although banking and financial executives became increasingly detached from the mechanics of their business, bonuses swelled their inflated incomes. New hot markets included private jets bought with debt and bodies reshaped by plastic surgery. The close links of bankers to regulators continued as a revolving door operated between government and private employment. For instance, Henry Paulson (b. 1946), chief executive of the investment firm Goldman Sachs and once the highest paid Wall Street executive, became treasury secretary in 2006.

The New Century Unfolds

On March 9, 2007, the second largest subprime mortgage lender in the United States, aptly named New Century Financial Corp., disclosed it had not met its lenders' minimum financial requirements, was the subject of a federal criminal investigation, and could not pay creditors demanding their money. The markets reacted quickly; some government agencies less so. New Century had sold the subprime mortgages it originated to institutions that repackaged them, keeping some in their "warehouse" for income and profits. In February 2007 a share of New Century's stock sold at over $30; with the news of March 9 it dropped to $22 and then fell further quickly to $6. On March 12 the New York Stock Exchange halted trading in the company's shares at 72 cents and delisted the corporation the next day. About that time, the SEC requested a meeting with the company to discuss the restatement of New Century's financial statements. On March 14, 2007, Fannie Mae terminated a mortgage selling and servicing contract with the firm.

Home price growth had slowed nationally but had not yet reversed; still, subprime lenders began to collapse as the fundamental problem of lending money to poor borrowers, even in a good market, surfaced. A slide began in real estate prices, particularly in some areas of the United States. An economic downturn had begun despite assurances to the contrary by government officials. Even as housing prices ticked downward in October 2007, the Dow Jones Industrial Average hit a high of just over 14,000.

As months passed, home prices continued to slide. By February 2008 home prices in Detroit were below their 2000 level. In other areas, home prices fell by up to 20 percent-plus from their 2007 highs. Profits from subprime mortgages (seemingly the most promising securities with the greatest returns) not only dried up but turned into losses. Bear Stearns, a global investment bank and securities trader, became the first major casualty. In late November 2007 it had $13.4 trillion in derivative financial instruments and carried $28 billion in subprime assets, all versus an equity position of $11.1 billion (a leverage ratio of

Federal Reserve chairman Ben Bernanke testifies on Capitol Hill before the Senate Banking Committee hearing on the government bailout of Bear Stearns, April 3, 2008. From left are, Bernanke, Securities and Exchange Commission (SEC) Chairman Christopher Cox, Treasury Undersecretary for Domestic Finance Robert Steel, and Federal Reserve Bank of New York President Timothy Geithner. (AP Photos/Susan Walsh)

35.5 to 1). Although government regulations required individuals to maintain margin reserves in brokerage accounts, the same rules had been waived by legislation for firms in the name of "modernization." As defaults began, confidence in Bear Stearns decreased, and its stock price tumbled, becoming a sign of the firm's acute distress. The acceleration of the firm's downward spiral was compounded due to redemptions by unregulated, highly leveraged hedge funds that cleared trades and kept accounts with Bear Stearns. In addition, short-sellers of the firm's stock smelled increased profits. A run on Bear Stearns began that ended with its collapse. At the end of 2007 ratings companies had deemed Bear Stearns bonds AA; in March 2008 the company ran out of cash. In January 2007 Bear Stearns shares reached a stock-price high of $171; in March 2008 the firm was bought for $10 a share by JPMorgan Chase, and the Federal Reserve backed the deal with $30 billion in guarantees.

As the Dow Jones Industrial Average dipped below 11,000, other investment banks scrambled to merge, be acquired, and raise cash to reassure investors, clients, and the public. With hindsight, the burst of the speculative bubble seems clear, but hope remained as the Dow Jones Average went back to over 12,000. However, as housing prices continued to slide, Fannie and Freddie's stock tumbled. On September 7, 2008, Treasury Secretary Paulson announced their takeover by the federal government, which impacted the private sector, although Lehman Brothers collapsed because of its own mismanagement. Like Bear Stearns, Lehman Brothers had an AA credit rating, but two days after the Fannie/Freddie takeover, it announced losses of $3.2 billion, and by Friday, September 12, this venerable firm had also run out of cash in the face of redemptions. The sustainability of all large American financial institutions came under scrutiny. A meltdown of epic proportions seemed probable.

With Lehman all but gone save a government bailout, the sustainability of Merrill Lynch seemed dubious. Any of the others left standing could be next. International markets felt the undertow. Over the weekend following September 12, Paulson and Timothy Geithner—president of the New York Federal Reserve Bank—at a meeting of major bank CEOs, called for a rescue of Lehman and a shoring up of other firms, most notably Merrill Lynch. The only suitor willing to consider Lehman was Barclays, a British firm, and it demanded financial guarantees from the Fed like those offered JPMorgan Chase when it took over Bear Stearns. Paulson refused, Lehman failed, and Bank of America bought Merrill. With it shored up, the conferees believed confidence in the financial system would return on Monday. Clumsy as these interventions may seem in retrospect, without them, a meltdown would surely have occurred since the globe had become debt denominated.

Despite the weekend's seemingly triumphant work, the Lehman failure did reverberate globally, causing the collapse of the commercial paper market.

Many companies depended on this market for funds to pay immediate operating expenses. Money market funds now became vulnerable as the public began to pull out funds having realized that account balances were not insured. Lehman assets that cleared through London, including the funds of many offshore hedge funds, became frozen due to British bankruptcy laws. AIG owed $13 billion in credit default swaps, which is "insurance," but had insufficient reserves to pay the claims as they came due.

The entire system began to freeze. On September 17, 2008, the U.S. government took over AIG and subsequently funded a $150 billion bailout. The next day Paulson and Federal Reserve chairman Ben Bernanke (b. 1953) advised President Bush to ask Congress for $700 billion to bail out all the banks. This controversial approach was signed into law on October 4. Could the capitalist U.S. government become a private lender? With the meltdown and patchwork solutions that seemed to fly in the face of traditional American tenets, remarkably, the power of belief in the U.S. dollar trumped rationality as during the 2008 crash international investors took a "flight to safety" toward the United States, where the collapse had begun.

U.S. corporations, which had participated in the American boom by lending money to consumers for cars and home appliances, had also begun to suffer economic distress. General Motors and Chrysler faced bankruptcy; General Electric began to crumble—evidence of long-term systemic problems. In 1896 GE became one of the first 12 companies included in the Dow Jones Industrial Average; in 1917 V. I. Lenin (1870–1924) called GE's financial statement "jugglery," viewing it as representative of the capitalist greed that he assumed would eventually fell the system. In the late 20th century General Electric's Credit Corporation invested in derivative securities for increased profits. GE's systemic problems became clear as the Dow Jones Industrial Average spiraled downward to just above 8,000. The federal government then insured $139 billion in GE debt, proving Lenin at least partially correct. Yet the capitalist economic system remained standing because the United States government became its largest investor.

The stripped debt products created by "financial engineers" had severed concrete ties between borrowers and lenders, and not just domestically. The resulting debacle also had international impact. For example, because deregulation promised profits, four Norwegian towns purchased stripped subprime American home loan derivatives. As U.S. homeowners defaulted, the securities ceased paying and the Norwegian municipalities were unable to pay employees. Although the default link was immediate and personal, recoverability was not possible. Even if the Norwegian towns had tried to get their money back by seizing an American home, the lending bank would have been unable to provide them with an address.

In December 2008 the most extreme moral lapse of the bubble market unfolded when Bernard Madoff confessed to the largest Ponzi scheme in history. Although Madoff remains a symbol of excess, he was not an outlier. Certainly he was not alone, as is demonstrated by subsequent prosecutions and convictions, but he clearly demonstrated the interlocking gears of finance and government. Madoff used to brag he spent 30 percent of his time in Washington, D.C. Although the SEC head that should have regulated the firm could not remember how to pronounce Madoff's name on television, the defrauder referred to him as a "dear friend" in a jailhouse interview. Various professionals have acted illegally when defrauding the public, but Madoff perfected his scheme the "old-fashioned way," by becoming a government insider.

Wrapping up the Bubble

The election of Barack Obama (b. 1961) as president in 2008 seemed to promise renewal. Although hard-hit, the markets recovered powerfully. On December 4, 2009, Bank of America successfully sold the largest equity offering in global financial history. Issuing 1.3 billion shares of stock, the company raised over $19 billion to deploy funds in both domestic and international markets. It could once again sell bonds, shares of stock, and loans to corporations while supplying credit cards, mortgages, and advice to customers. The stock rallied upward in trading that day. Furthermore, bailed-out GE's stock participated in one of the largest rebounds in the history of the Dow Jones Industrial Average— from its lows in 2009 to over 13,000 in March 2012. Few such epic rebounds have ever taken place, except after market panics and collapses.

The 2008 Economic Stimulus Act appropriated $152 billion for business and banking programs. Despite a call for Roosevelt-era projects to put people to work, the legislation targeted individuals only through banking relationships and limited home mortgage relief. Home loan defaults did not abate. According to one estimate, in the five years after 2006 American homeowners saw the value of their homes drop a total of $7 trillion. Nor did the situation of individuals improve in 2009 when Congress passed an $800 billion American Recovery and Investment Act to promote investment and consumer spending. The stimulus program was "back-loaded," and only a third of the money was spent in the first year. Passage of this legislation reflected the political dysfunction of the United States, which hampered recovery—in a divided Congress no House Republicans and only three Senate Republicans voted in favor of the bill.

Unemployment at high levels persisted. Between 2000 and 2010, reported unemployment spiked from 4.2 percent to a high of 10.1 percent, and was still over 8 percent at the beginning of 2012. Dealing with the out of work had proved almost intractable. Even though unemployment was down from its peak, it was estimated at the end of 2011 that over 40 percent of the unemployed had been out of work for more than half a year, and many had not been employed for more than a year. There seemed to be a reluctance on the part of employers to hire the long-term unemployed, and the creation of new jobs was proving ephemeral.

It was estimated that the United States saw an 8.9 percent loss in GDP (or about $420 billion in output) during the 18 months between the 2008 collapse and the "official" end of the recession in 2009. During that year estimates are recorded that the American economy shrank over 3 percent. Entering 2010, President Obama felt it necessary to propose a new round of stimulus spending. Midway into his presidency, Obama became the first president since the start of World War II to see a net loss in jobs. Government debt spiraled upward. Notwithstanding official claims of recovery, the U.S. economy limped along. Even though American productivity increased, dreary economic news continued; for instance, Nevada's construction industry, which boomed during the years prior to the recession, had virtually disappeared by the beginning of 2010 and remained in limbo. The continuing U.S. downturn affected the economically weakened Eurozone, suffering from long-term unemployment, an aging population, and a continuing debt crisis.

The elements that allowed for the 21st-century American "Season of Recklessness" are built into the system: an ongoing belief in home ownership, financial ingenuity in overcoming regulation, a distrust of government regulation, a dependence on its guarantees, and the promise of modernization. When housing prices spiraled upward, men and women engaged in the financial system became blinded by the promise of unbridled profits. This "moral epidemic" infected politicians, financiers, and the people. Home-owning mania became the perfect bubble, and one that Mackay would have relished. Although President Obama continually promised "change," when his administration enacted financial reforms in critical areas, such as monitoring rating agencies, the influence of lobbying, and monitoring conflicts of interest in revolving door government agencies, nothing significant was proposed or enacted.

While unemployment did not diminish significantly, housing prices ticked up briefly only to dip down again and again. Exceptions like the high-end New York City apartment market generally ignored the economic downturn and remained reasonably strong, fueled by continued, if shaved executive Wall Street bonuses. When the CEO of Merrill Lynch left the firm, he took $151 million with him as executive compensation. The following year, his successor earned $87 million. With the government stuck in gridlock at the start of 2012, a *New York* magazine cover summed up the situation: "The Post-Crash: Wall Street Won."

The ongoing necessary intervention of the federal government, not only through its financial support of the banks but also of the unemployed by a continuation of jobless benefits, masks the weakness of the U.S. economy and even its usually dependable service sector. The only service sectors thriving as of this writing are those serving the government through demands created by war. The National Bureau of Economic Research has collected data on every U.S. economic downturn since the 1850s. In the area of job creation, President Obama's record is worse than that of any U.S. president since the 1890s, excepting that of Herbert Hoover (1874–1964), whose term in office coincided with the first years of the Great Depression.

Referring to the 1929 stock market bubble, legendary trader and speculator Jessie Livermore (1877–1940) noted, "It is not so much greed made blind by eagerness, as it is hope bandaged by the unwillingness to do any thinking." Indeed, at the end of the first decade of the 21st century, the rules and regulations that Madoff helped push through the SEC for trading stock on the NASDAQ (the largest U.S. electronic equity securities market) remain on the books while Madoff sits in jail. Few significant regulatory changes have been enacted. Banks and investment houses stay bonded. At this writing, the beginning of 2013, the economic future looks less than rosy for a United States that continues to be dependent on foreign investors, especially China. Despite a remarkable, unfounded, dramatic rise in stock prices (by mid-2013 the Dow Jones average had risen to its highest point ever), the country teeters on a financial precipice. The impact of the financial collapse of 2008–2009 on most branches of the economy continued.

Coda: A New Revolution

Thomas Jefferson (1743–1826), who first articulated the ideals of American homeownership, wrote: "Every generation needs a new revolution." With the collapse of the promises Jefferson had articulated as a founding tenet of the nation, a new generation began the "Occupy Wall Street" movement in downtown New York City. From September 12 through November 20, 2011, people from all walks of life gathered and lived in Zuccotti Park, a 33,000-square-foot publically accessible private park near the financial district. Just as Wall Street and homeowners had used debt to perpetuate a false bull market, the protestors looked out over a large sculpture of a bull meant to symbolize a surging American stock market. Indeed, some posed with the statue. While rumors abounded that infamous financial trader George Soros (b. 1930), among other Wall Streeters, financed some of their activities, the peaceful protestors received food and support from local and elite restaurants and shopkeepers.

Occupy Wall Street protestors march through the financial district the day after successfully resisting a potential eviction from their camp in Zuccotti Park in New York, October 15, 2011. As many as 1,000 protesters marched to a Chase bank branch in the financial district, banging drums, blowing horns, and carrying signs decrying corporate greed. (AP Photo)

Unlike protests of the 1960s, "sex, drugs, and rock and roll" were not much in evidence.

The media success of the New York movement led to Occupation movements in other cities, communities, and college campuses to highlight the argument that 99 percent of the American population suffered economically after the 2008 debacle, while the other 1 percent emerged relatively unscathed after reaping untold profits. Despite the intelligently mobilized operations, and an egalitarian belief that the movement should have no leaders, the "occupy" efforts began to crumble as internal rules of order were challenged, joiners began to abuse the privileges available, violence among protestors took place, and unsavory sanitary conditions took their toll. For much of fall of 2011 media savvy Occupy movements demanded that the stalemated federal government act, but Congress and the executive continued to fail to reach compromises for an active approach and concrete solutions to job creation, greater controls over lending and credit card activities, or effective banking legislation. The "occupiers" did not fulfill their initial promise in a time of crisis. Ultimately, the authorities in New York City and elsewhere forcefully evacuated the protestors, and they did not reconvene in a significant way. Only a few individuals continued to camp out in various city sites and universities.

It looked like business as usual: government leaders returned to campaign fundraising for the next election, the unemployed took marginalized jobs or slept in the streets, Wall Street layoffs for support staffs continued. Perhaps the moment for change had been lost. Had "Hope been bandaged" by the everyday? Yet protests on university campuses took a new twist. For the banks, the Ivy League schools had been a fertile hunting ground for replacing laid-off and expensive senior professionals; for decades the banks recruited young blood during the spring of each year. Presentations extolled the opportunities on Wall Street, followed by cocktail receptions during which eager, occasionally ruthless students pushed past classmates, vying for a casual interchange with a senior partner over white wine and a canapés.

One group of protesters made use of these receptions. At Princeton, some 30 students masquerading as job applicants entered two Wall Street informational sessions and asked, "How do I get a job lobbying the U.S. government to protect Wall Street interests?" and then posted the event on You Tube. A Bloomberg News report on what happened at Princeton quoted a leader of the "leaderless" movement: "My goal is to change the dominant campus culture . . . that assumes that going to work for Goldman Sachs and JPMorgan is the most prestigious thing you can do. We're very privileged to be here . . . getting an incredible education. All just for us to be sending 30 percent, 40 percent of our graduates to the finance sector?" Author Michael Lewis (b. 1960) noted, "The students at Ivy League schools are our most devastating ammunition in this looming cultural war." A battle at the Ivy Leagues could unbandage hope and bring another battle for reform.

In any event, the Occupy Movement made widely known what it considered the inequity caused by the continuing American economic downturn. The seemingly spontaneous movement had intelligently mobilized its supporters, and had, to the consternation of local law enforcement, initially uncertain of how to deal with the movement, successfully occupied diverse public and private spaces in the United States and elsewhere (as in London) in a remarkable effort to highlight its arguments.

Further Reading

Acharya, Viral V., et al. *Guaranteed to Fail: Fannie Mae, Freddie Mac, and the Debacle of Mortgage Finance*. Princeton, NJ: Princeton University Press, 2011.

The Financial Inquiry Report: Final Report of the National Commission on the Causes of the Financial and Economic Crisis in the United States. New York: Public Affairs Press, 2011.

Henriques, Diana B. *The Wizard of Lies: Bernie Madoff and the Death of Trust*. New York: Times Books, 2011.

Lewis, Michael. *The Big Short: Inside the Doomsday Machine*. New York: Norton, 2010.

Lewis, Michael. "To: The Upper Ones, From: The Strategy Committee, Re: The Alarming Behavior of College Students." *Bloomberg,* December, 29, 2011.

Lowenstein, Roger. *The End of Wall Street.* New York: Penguin, 2010.

Mackay, Charles. *Extraordinary Popular Delusions and the Madness of Crowds, Financial Panics and Manias.* Reprint ed. New Castle, DE: Oak Knoll, 2009.

Mallaby, Sebastian. *More Money than God: Hedge Funds and the Making of a New Elite.* New York: Penguin, 2011.

Morgenson, Gretchen, and Rosner, Joshua. *Reckles$ Endangerment: How Outsized Ambition, Greed, and Corruption Led to Economic Armageddon.* New York: Henry Holt, 2011.

Sorkin, Andrew Ross. *Too Big to Fail: The Inside Story of How Wall Street and Washington Fought to Save the Financial System—and Themselves.* New York: Penguin, 2009.

Taibbi, Matt. *Griftopia: A Story of Bankers, Politicians, and the Most Audacious Power Grab in American History.* Revised and expanded paper edition. New York: Spiegel & Grau, 2011 (2010).

Great Recession of 2008–2009: Short Entries

Kate Doyle Griffiths-Dingani

Auto Industry Bailout (2008–2009)

Considerable controversy exists about the federal government funds made available to industry and financial institutions after the economic crisis that began in fall 2008. The United Auto Workers (UAW), one of the major American industrial unions, has received both criticism and commendation for its role in the "bailout" of the U.S. auto industry.

Government aid, deemed necessary for the industry's survival, came after its near collapse following the financial crisis of 2008–2009. Already before then, and certainly since, the nonunion workers, mostly those employed in producing foreign marques, operating in U.S. "right to work" states, did not earn the high wages paid unionized workers nor their comprehensive benefits.

Such employer obligations, which also extended to retired auto workers, were estimated to result in an hourly wage differential of $50.00 between unionized and nonunion auto workers. In 2009 one study maintained that GM over "the past 15 years" paid out about $100 billion and thereby added about $2,000 to the cost of each new car GM produced. These excessive costs go hand in hand with the industry's management failures. Both understandably have been blamed for the American auto industry's lack of competitiveness.

Given management's incompetence, major concessions by the union were insufficient to stave off a crisis in the American auto industry. As crude oil markets drove up fuel prices, auto sales weakened, particularly with respect to sport utility vehicles (SUV) and pick-up trucks, which tend to burn relatively high amounts of fuel. The profits on production of such vehicles were particularly important to the sales of GM, Ford, and Chrysler.

As bankruptcy loomed for these companies, they requested emergency loans from the United States Treasury to cover immediate costs. Bankruptcies, it was argued, would result in major job losses and destabilize America's manufacturing sector. Financial markets would also suffer as pension funds would most likely have to be liquidated.

Fear of such possibilities resulted in the U.S. government—along with that of Canada—providing an unprecedented $85 billion subsidy to the auto industry, allowing GM and Chrysler to separately file for Chapter 11 bankruptcy. Following the bankruptcy GM was transformed into an entity owned primarily by the U.S. Treasury, and the UAW along with Fiat (a giant Italian automaker) owned Chrysler. While not unscathed, Ford—thanks to a large credit line—avoided bankruptcy.

The bailout deal included major concessions by the UAW and its members. Many of these concessions were imposed by negotiators for the federal government in exchange for the bailout. These major concessions amended the already concessionary 2007 contract between the UAW and the auto companies, and included the suspension of programs such as the 25-year-old "jobs bank" under which laid-off union members received 95 percent of their regular pay and benefits while waiting to be rehired.

In addition, the UAW and GM signed a contract establishing a two-tier wage system: the pay of younger workers was brought much closer in line with the low-wage industry standard, while benefits for senior workers were slashed, including pensions that represented for many a lifetime of deferred wages. The union also agreed to a ban on future strikes.

Ironically, the deal took place near the 75th anniversary of the founding of the UAW, whose organization resulted from militant action, such as the "sit down strikes" of 1937. The sit downs, carried out by low-wage, Depression-era autoworkers who occupied car plants for days, mobilized entire communities. Such strikes and other militant action by the UAW, aided by local, state, and federal governments that generally declined to intervene on behalf of management, had forced automakers by 1941 to recognize the UAW as the legitimate representative of the auto industry workforce.

In the current period, given the lack of jobs in a diminished industry, it is possible to understand the UAW's willingness to make concessions to replace high-wage, permanent positions that include retirement benefits and health care, with low-wage "flexible" work and limited benefits. High unemployment has workers waiting in long lines at auto plants for $14 an hour entry-level positions.

As he sought reelection in 2012 President Obama (b. 1961) took credit for the auto industry bailout and the positive subsequent developments caused by it. However, the bailout and the UAW concessions resulting from it were initiated under the lame duck Bush administration, although continuing under President Obama once he was inaugurated in January 2009.

Congressional hearings on the auto bailout began on November 19, 2008. The next day GM share prices reached their lowest price since the Great Depression. Democrats Nancy Pelosi (b. 1940), congresswoman from California and Speaker of the House, as well as Nevada senator Harry Reid (b. 1939), the Senate Majority Leader, requested that the CEOs of Chrysler, Ford, and GM present Congress with a restructuring plan by December 2, and outlined various conditions whose inclusion would ultimately shape the final agreement. The presentation by the auto industry executives included such details as restricted CEO pay.

By December 10 the House Financial Services Committee proposed a bailout package, but it was rejected by the Senate on December 11. On December 19 President Bush (b. 1946) approved a plan to use funds appropriated to TARP (Troubled Asset Relief Program), arguing that letting the auto industry fail would be irresponsible. Some argued that the president overstepped his bounds, as TARP funding was limited to "financial institutions" and could not be applied to manufacturing. President Bush used executive authority to end the debate, declaring that TARP funds could be used to bailout the auto industry.

Subsequently President Obama in February 2009 established a Presidential Task Force to deal with the bailout. Ultimately, key Obama administration economics advisors Lawrence Summers (b. 1954), head of the National Economic Council, and Secretary of the Treasury Timothy Geithner (b. 1961) handled a second round of lending to the auto companies. The Obama administration linked this support to further job cuts as well as development of environmentally friendly technologies by the industry.

The UAW concessions and support for the bailouts may have saved some jobs for union members, but industry management continued to be fallible. In April 2009 Chrysler declared bankruptcy, closing one quarter of its dealerships. GM followed on June 1; its restructuring with nine plant closures resulted in 20,000 workers losing their jobs. Ford at one point eliminated dividends to shareholders, to the detriment of many members of the Ford family who keenly felt the absence of income.

As of the summer of 2012, GM, Ford, and Chrysler had recovered to some extent but still faced significant problems. Questions continue about the quality of the cars they produce. The companies, barely maintaining their share of the American market, depend heavily on international sales, which face an uncertain future. In China, for instance, domestic production challenged GM, threatening necessary profits stemming from sales there, and GM's German subsidiary nearly tanked.

The less than brilliant management of GM, Ford, and Chrysler could no longer count on political aid from a much reduced and weakened UAW, which had become less of a major player in national politics and had few concessions left to give. The government had rescued the industry, but critics continued to ask if this bailout was effective.

Further Reading

Flanders, Laura. "The Deal That Saved Detroit . . . ," *The Nation*, February 2, 2012. http://www.thenation.com/blog/166031/deal-saved-detroit-and-bann . . . [accessed July 29, 2013].

Slaughter, Jane. "Low Expectations Are Met in GM-UAW Deal." *Labor Notes*, September 19, 2011. http:///labornotes.org/blogs/jane?page=1 [accessed March 12, 2013].

Geithner, Timothy F. (1961–)

An intelligent, talented, hardworking, ambitious economist and government bureaucrat, Timothy Geithner became secretary of the treasury in January 2009. Respected and admired for his handling of complex, high-visibility financial issues, he had been short-listed for that cabinet post both by President Obama (b. 1961) and defeated Republican candidate John McCain (b. 1936).

Born in Brooklyn on August 18, 1961, he has an interesting pedigree: his father had emigrated with his parents from Germany and after an air force career ran the Ford Foundation's Asia programs during the 1980s and 1990s; his mother was a Mayflower descendent whose father had overseen public relations for the Ford Motor Company in the 1950s and early 1960s before retiring to Cape Cod and becoming first selectman of a community there.

Geithner attended various Asian secondary schools, studied (1981–1982) Mandarin at Chinese universities, graduated (1983) from Dartmouth College, and earned (1985) an MA from the Johns Hopkins University School of Advanced International Studies. He held a number of jobs in the private sector and in the government associated with international economics before in 1998 becoming undersecretary of the Treasury for International Affairs. During the 1990s he helped manage financial crises in Asia and Latin America. Various sources have called him a protégé of Secretaries of the Treasury Robert Rubin (b. 1938) and Larry Summers (b. 1954), both before and during their official tenure.

After a stint as a fellow of the Council on Foreign Relations he joined the International Monetary Fund as a director of its Policy Development and

Treasury Secretary Timothy Geithner announces an overhaul of the Troubled Asset Relief Program (TARP) at the Treasury Department in Washington, D.C., on February 10, 2009. (Shawn Thew/epa/Corbis)

Review Department. In this position as in all his previous appointments he performed exceptionally well and in October 2003 became head of the Federal Reserve Bank of New York, the most important and powerful in the system.

His performance there has been seen in several ways. Critics charge that his assistance to treasury secretary Henry Paulson (b. 1936), a former Goldman Sachs managing partner, in arranging the bailout of AIG just days after their failure to support a collapsing Lehman Brothers firm contributed to the worsening of the financial crisis. Geithner won praise for his handling of the rescue and sale of Bear Stearns, one of the first institutions to fail as a result of insufficient capital and toxic debt. Given his position later as secretary of the treasury, there is irony to his consistent advocacy while head of the New York Federal Reserve bank of less regulation of financial institutions and the reduction of capital needed to operate them.

During the Senate confirmation hearings for treasury secretary it came out that Geithner owed thousands of dollars in self-employment taxes for the years he worked for the IMF (as an international agency it did not deduct FICA taxes but left that to employees who were liable). The Senate hearings also revealed that Geithner had over-deducted child care expenses, failed to pay the penalty for early withdrawal from a retirement plan, took ineligible charitable contributions, and illegally wrote off utility costs that went for personal rather than business use.

Geithner paid the money due with interest and apologized for his "careless" errors. Many of his critics were skeptical of his exculpatory comments. But on January 26, 2009, despite the minor controversy, the Senate confirmed his appointment by a 60-34 vote, and he was sworn in as secretary of the treasury, some of whose duties he had assumed. Immediately after Geithner became the presumptive nominee as treasury secretary of the incoming administration he began to work closely with the lame duck Bush administration to secure political support for a bailout of the financial industry. Geithner played a central role in its development.

As secretary of the treasury, Geithner was given decision-making power with respect to the second half of the $700 billion bailout fund approved by Congress in October 2008. Before doling out these funds Geithner proposed isolating toxic assets in government-owned "banks" developed with both private and public funds. Additionally, he called for further infusions of capital into shaky banks and a trillion dollars in loans to help prevent a collapse of the secondary market for consumer credit.

In return financial institutions would agree to cut salaries, bonuses, and other perks for top managers. Tim Geithner and his plan were undermined in the public eye by the demands of AIG (Associated International Group). After being saved from bankruptcy by a $170 billion government bailout, it nevertheless paid hefty bonuses to top executives. Geithner, as head of the New York Federal Reserve Bank, protested but accepted the argument that because of contractual obligations payment could not be "legally blocked."

Geithner's contacts with AIG continued to land him in hot water. While head of the New York Federal Reserve Bank, he laid the groundwork for a deal that became notorious for its appearance of influence peddling and corruption. In 2009, with Geithner now heading the Treasury, a report by the inspector general responsible for oversight of bailout funds criticized a scheme whereby some of these funds were used to purchase worthless derivatives held by major banks insured by AIG; these financial instruments cost taxpayers over $62 billion because the government paid the banks the presumed value of the contracts before the 2008 crash rather than current market value.

When e-mails between AIG and the New York Federal Reserve Bank emerged, they suggested a conspiracy to withhold the true nature of the arrangement from the taxpaying public. The matter was then investigated by Congress, with an inquiry by the House Oversight and Government Reform Committee. In a January 27, 2010, hearing, Geithner and his predecessor stoutly denied any involvement in withholding information, but he quickly became a political target for Populist congressmen from both parties.

The hearings also probed the connections between former Goldman Sachs employees, such as Geithner's mentor Robert Rubin, at the New York Federal Reserve Bank, the Treasury Department, and major beneficiaries of the bank bailout such as AIG. It was noted that Mr. Geithner's phone records showed more telephone calls to Dan Jester, a Treasury adviser and former Goldman Sachs employee, in the fall of 2008 while the bailout was being hammered out than to any person save Henry Paulson, then treasury secretary (and also previously a top manager at Goldman).

Geithner's concern with deficits is widely viewed as a symbol of the close ties of the Obama administration to Wall Street and a conservative approach to economic recovery. But Geithner has opposed extension of the Bush tax cuts and opposed new stimulus spending. Political opponents, policy makers, and commentators, both from the Left and the Right, have frequently called for his resignation or removal as a signal the president would choose "Main Street" over Wall Street. Liberal critics like economist and *New York Times* writer Paul Krugman (b. 1953) and former World Bank president Joseph Stiglitz (b. 1943) have argued that such a move could pave the way for a more Keynesian bailout strategy in which government funds went directly into public spending on infrastructure and associated new jobs.

Geithner publically stated that should Barack Obama win a second term, he would move on. As of mid-2012, he was the only remaining member of President Obama's original economic team. Controversy continued to plague Geithner (e.g., the scandal arising from the manipulation of the London Interbank Offered Rate [Libor] by British bankers). In January 1213, right after President Obama began his second term, Geithner resigned.

Further Reading

Prial, Dunstan. "Geithner Cut Wide Swath in Tumultuous Four Years." January 25, 2013. http:///www.foxbusiness.com/government/2013/01/15/geithner-cu-wi . . . [accessed July 29, 2013].

"Timothy Geithner Suggested Hillary Clinton Be His Successor: Report." *Huffington Post*. June 15, 2012. http://www.huffingtonpost.com/2012/06/14/timothy-geithner -hillary-clinton_n_1598233.html [accessed March 12, 2013].

Walsh, Mary Williams. "Drawing Fire, Geithner Backs Rescue of AIG." January 28, 2010. http://www.nytimes.com/2010/01/28/business/28aig.html [accessed March 12, 2013].

Goldman Sachs

An innovative Wall Street firm, Goldman is notable or notorious depending on your point of view. The personnel of the firm, its "alumni," and its actions during the financial crisis that began in 2008 and in the run-up to it have been very controversial. Goldman Sachs has had to defend itself against well-publicized—sometimes unproven—charges that it and many of its employees behaved illegally, immorally, and unethically.

The firm's history dates to the Civil War era. Marcus Goldman (1821–1904), who emigrated from Germany in 1848, 21 years later set up business in New York City as a broker of commercial paper. In 1882 31-year-old Samuel Sachs (1851–1935) married Goldman's youngest daughter and joined his father-in-law's firm, which had begun to underwrite securities offerings. It prospered and grew.

Goldman retired in 1894; a decade later—after his death—the firm, which had diversified its business activities, became Goldman Sachs. In 1896 the firm, which continued to do well even during the hard times of the 1890s, was invited to join the New York Stock Exchange. During the 1920s boom Goldman Sachs made some serious investment errors and the firm was almost wiped out. Sidney Weinberg (1891–1969), later known as "Mr. Wall Street," became head of the firm in 1930 and saved it from bankruptcy, and during the 1930s, World War II, and afterward he transformed Goldman Sachs from a floundering mid-tier firm to one of the world's premier investment banks.

His successor Gus Levy (1910–1976), who had developed new trading strategies such as block trading, became the firm's senior partner in 1969. Levy, whose motto was "Don't Tell Me What I Can't Do, Tell Me What I Can Do," propelled Goldman Sachs to even greater growth, but the firm's reputation was tarnished by controversies presaging criticism of its actions prior to the 2008 financial crisis and later.

In the 1970s, in the aftermath of the Penn Central bankruptcy, Goldman Sachs barely survived. The firm had sold over $80 million of the railroad's commercial paper and continued to market it even though learning Penn Central's finances were rapidly deteriorating. The firm then demanded that Penn Central buy back from it the railroad company's paper at 100 cents on the dollar, even though it was worth far less. The firm did not inform its clients that Penn Central paper was far from creditworthy.

When the reality of the situation became known Goldman Sachs faced an SEC investigation (settled quickly) and numerous lawsuits (most settled for pennies on the dollar). Those that came to trial exposed the firm's less than fair treatment of its clients and cost Goldman Sachs millions in litigation fees and legal settlements. And there were other controversies involving the firm or its present or former employees.

Despite its sometimes checkered record the firm had by 1999 gone from being an upstart Jewish company headed by immigrant owners to being an important, if not central, player in the U.S. and global markets. In 1999 Henry Paulson became senior partner, and about 12 percent of the firm was made available in a public offering. Since then there have been further stock offerings, but a significant part of the firm was still held by the partnership pool. At the end of 2009 it was estimated that two-thirds of the stock was owned by institutions such as pension funds and other banks. After the firm went partially public the energetic Paulson became its chief operating officer, leaving in 2006 to become treasury secretary.

In the run up to the 2008 economic crisis, Goldman Sachs, it has been charged, played a significant role. First, the firm led the way in developing novel financial instruments that helped to inflate the subprime real estate market. At the peak of the housing boom in 2006, Goldman Sachs produced nearly $80 billion in mortgage-backed securities, selling them with AAA ratings to investors, despite knowing many of these mortgages were subprime and likely to default. A Goldman Trust known as GSAMP represented nearly $500 million worth of mortgages, many dubious subprime deals involving little or no equity, and often with little documentation as to the name or whereabouts of the mortgage holder. GSAMP began to collapse just 18 months after issuing half a billion dollars in securities, and according to many commentators helping to trigger the subprime mortgage crisis.

Second, as the market collapsed the firm developed a strategy for profiting from the crisis, exacerbating the downward spiral. Two Goldman Sachs traders, gambling that the subprime market would collapse, used "short-selling" to generate a profit: they borrowed a subprime-backed mortgage security and sold it with the intention of returning an identical asset to the lender when the price of the asset dropped, profiting from the difference as the asset price declined. The two traders garnered $4 billion for the firm: the *New York Times* said that Goldman Sachs was peerless in the world of investment banking; others accused the firm of hypocrisy or securities fraud, for simultaneously selling toxic assets to unsuspecting investors and at the same time betting the value of these assets would decline drastically in the near future.

Finally, the firm's close connections with public policy makers meant Goldman Sachs influenced and benefited from government attempts to halt the crisis. As the housing bubble ran its course, Goldman Sachs began to look to the commodities market to sustain its profits; lobbied for exemption from regulations limiting speculation in commodities; and began to invest in oil futures, helping to drive prices dramatically upward. When that bubble, too, collapsed in the summer of 2008 Goldman Sachs seems to have been able to negotiate a government bailout of finance that would be particularly beneficial to the firm.

Even as treasury secretary Henry Paulson (b. 1946) was negotiating the bankruptcy of Lehman Brothers, a major competitor to Goldman Sachs in the investment banking sector, he was simultaneously orchestrating the bailout of insurance giant AIG, which was then able to repay 13 billion in debt owed to

Goldman Sachs. Unlike many holders of subprime mortgages, Goldman Sachs received 100 percent for its toxic assets. It was also a major recipient of government funds ($10 billion) from the Troubled Asset Relief Program (TARP), a program managed by a former Goldman Sachs banker. The firm used part of the funds to pay employees at least $900 million in bonuses, although top managers forewent bonuses, because as firm CEO Lloyd Blankfein (b. 1954) put it "we are part of an industry that's directly associated with the ongoing economic distress."

Meanwhile, the firm opted to change from an investment bank to a holding company to qualify for TARP funds and other less publically scrutinized government subsidies and guarantees. In June 2009 the firm repaid the Treasury $10 billion, with interest, but accepted other government aid, borrowing over $780 billion during 2008–2009. Critics have argued Goldman's special regulatory status results from "insider" status with the Federal Reserve, the Treasury, and other regulators, all staffed at high levels by ex-Goldman Sachs employees. Critics also charged that the notoriously high pay and bonuses offered by Goldman Sachs were funded with taxpayer money.

Some commentators see a "repeat of history" in the firm's central role in market bubbles and financial crises from 1929 to the present day. Since the financial crisis began in 2008 Goldman Sachs has come under heavy criticism. Certainly, some of it has been justified, especially given the SEC response to many of the firm's actions as well as various court decisions. But the constant harping by critics may be overstating the case. Goldman Sachs may have rigged the playing field, but its team knows how to play.

Further Reading

Cohan, William. *Money and Power: How Goldman Sachs Came to Rule the World.* New York: Doubleday, 2011.

Ellis, Charles. *The Partnership: The Making of Goldman Sachs.* New York: Penguin, 2008.

Taibbi, Matt. "The People vs. Goldman Sachs." *Rolling Stone.* May 11, 2011. http://www .rollingstone.com/politics/news/the people-vs-goldman-sachs [accessed July 29, 2013].

Hedge Funds

Hedge funds are a category of investment that have fewer legal trading and investment regulations because they are restricted to certain categories of investors, including high net worth individuals and institutions. By choice these funds are not open to the usual public or retail investors. Managers of hedge funds typically invest their own money in the operations they oversee, and in theory therefore are aligning their interests with those of their investors. They got their name because many of these funds in "hedging" against a market downturn take both what have been called long and short positions ("going long" means holding onto shares of companies expected to increase in value; "shorting" in the final analysis means disposing of shares by various means in companies likely to decrease in value). A more traditional mutual fund cannot bet on a market's decline.

Hedge funds typically employ a broad range of sophisticated people who develop complex investment strategies. The much admired Renaissance Technologies operation, for instance, was founded in 1982 by James Simons (b. 1938), a prize-winning mathematician who employed in the main theoretical physicists, philosophers, statisticians, and mathematicians like himself. They reviewed any statistical anomaly that could serve to predict moves in a company's shares in the stock market, and with these individuals Simons built a group of funds including the enormously successful Medallion fund, which for over two decades had spectacular returns and thereafter continued profitable, although less so than in the past.

The funds make maximum use of various strategies, generally considered high risk, including short-selling and the holding of highly leveraged investments. Short-selling consists of borrowing a given asset, like a mortgage-backed security owned by another company, then selling it with the intention of purchasing and returning an identical asset to the lender when the price of the asset drops, thus netting the difference as the price of the asset declines. A highly leveraged investment such as shares in a company are bought with borrowed funds, the intent being to make a profit on the sale of such stock that exceeds the interest rates of the loan.

Generally, hedge funds allow investors to withdraw or invest funds in regular cycles. Annual management fees, based on the size of a fund's assets, usually range from 1 percent to 4 percent. Designed to cover a fund's operating costs, higher management fees have increasingly come under strong criticism as being excessive, especially when a fund's profits are nil or negligible. The managers of a fund also charge a performance fee, supposed to reflect their ability to generate profits; such fees can range between 10 percent and 40 percent annually.

After the technology bubble burst in 2000 hedge funds boomed. Even though they did not fare well during the early days of the global financial crisis that began in 2008, they subsequently grew as investors sought out vehicles they assumed would protect their capital. Billions poured into the funds as investors rejected traditional buy-and-hold techniques for one that supposedly would protect them from downward market volatility.

By the beginning of 2012 the total capital invested in hedge funds exceeded $2 trillion. Even after some declines because of stock market responses to financial blips, this figure represents an exponential expansion since 1990 when hedge funds represented just $40 billion in assets or the equivalent of some individual funds in 2012. Bridgewater Associates, headquartered in Westport, Connecticut, and reputed to be the largest U.S. manager of hedge funds, handled assets estimated to be over $122 billion.

Compared to publicly traded securities, hedge funds are subject to many fewer regulations, although attempts have been made to supervise them. Following the passage (2010) of the Dodd-Frank Wall Street Reform Act, sponsored by two Democrats, Connecticut senator Chris Dodd (b. 1944) and Massachusetts representative Barney Frank (b. 1940), fund managers with at least $100 million in assets are required to file quarterly reports and register with the SEC. If a fund owns more than 5 percent of the class of any registered equity security this must be disclosed; previously fund share holdings were registered only on a volunteer basis. Hedge funds also became subject to specific antifraud regulation.

In 2008, at the onset of the global financial crisis, managers of the five largest U.S. hedge funds were called to testify before Congress, but the role of such funds in the crisis went largely unexplored in the main because their profitability set them apart from the then-failing banks and auto giants. By 2010 public anger at such firms, their executives, and policy makers with close ties to them ultimately pressured the Security and Exchange Commission (SEC) to formally file fraud charges against Goldman Sachs, alleging that what it had described as "short-selling" was in fact a "bet" against the market requiring the firm's managers to simultaneously represent some assets as sound and then act on their true understanding that the assets were unsound.

All those involved denied any wrongdoing. Nonetheless, the SEC case highlighted the dubious role of some hedge funds. The timeline established by the investigation suggested that Goldman Sachs and other firms managing funds helped to inflate the housing market while at the same time recognizing its unsustainability and betting on its failure. According to a report by *ProPublica*, Goldman and Magnetar Capital made the most questionable deals, putting products on the market made up solely of toxic subprime mortgages; traditional Wall Street firms like Citigroup and Merrill Lynch were also implicated in these transactions, which resulted in a court case against J.P. Morgan.

The dubious roles played by various hedge funds during the economic downturn that marked the decade after the 2008 financial crisis is far from unprecedented. Hedge funds existed in one form or another before they became increasingly popular from the 1960s onward. But none then and for years afterward had the clout they achieved during the 1990s. Indeed, during the 1970s a number of funds collapsed under the weight of nondiversified trading strategies.

The potential of hedge funds to spark and profit off a crisis was demonstrated in the 1980s by those individuals who took advantage of the high-flying stock market. Notwithstanding various high-profile investigations, a series of fraud cases, and some convictions, the stage had been set for the hyper-leveraged quick-moving funds of the later 1990s and beyond. It remains to be seen whether the ongoing investigations and charges that continue to be brought against fund managers by the SEC in the United States as well as regulatory officials in Europe will result in successful prosecutions or increased regulation of the hedge fund industry.

Further Reading

Gandel, Stephen. "How the Goldman Case Sheds Light on Hedge Funds." *Time Business.* http://www.time.com/time/business/article/0,8599,1982950,00.html#ixzz209lUi KCO [accessed March 12, 2013].

Turner, Giles. "The Darkest Dates from Hedge Fund History." *Financial News*, October 2011.

Lehman Brothers, Collapse of (2008)

A veteran Wall Street firm, Lehman Brothers' filing for bankruptcy in September 2008 both symbolizes the global financial crisis that followed and the reckless striving for profit by investment institutions that caused it. Lehman's bankruptcy, the largest in American history to that date, has resulted in a welter of political accusations, self-justifying explanations, unresolved economic problems, and continuing litigation.

Lehman Brothers had its roots in a cotton brokerage firm developed by three German Jewish immigrant brothers in pre–Civil War New Orleans. In 1858 Mayer Lehman (1820–1897) opened a New York office (which a decade later became the firm's headquarters); in 1870 he was one of more than 100 cotton merchants who formed the New York Cotton Exchange. Between then and the 1930s the firm was transformed from a family business into a major investment institution whose profitable innovations included lending money to newly developing consumer goods companies and guiding them as they went public. The firm's first underwriting was in 1906 for Sears, Roebuck preferred

Media and pedestrians gather in front of the Lehman Brothers headquarters in New York on September 15, 2008, the day the 158-year-old financial firm filed for bankruptcy. (AP Photo/ Louis Lanzano)

shares. By 1925 the firm, sometimes in conjunction with Goldman Sachs, had helped list shares of some 30 companies on the New York Stock Exchange, including department stores such as R.H. Macy as well as more traditional companies such as Continental Can.

After World War I, investment banking became the firm's primary business. In 1922 Lehman Brothers set up a separate bond department. Flexibility as well as averseness to risk helped it to weather the 1930s Depression, as did its tapping of insurance company funds; Lehman Brothers was the first to do so, and playing a role in this effort was the imaginative Robert Lehman (1891–1969), who became a partner in 1921 and in 1936 head of the firm.

He had helped push the firm into areas neglected by other investment banks, including the financing of movie companies and the airline industry. Under his aegis Lehman Brothers flourished; he had a knack for bringing people and companies together in various ways beneficial to them and to Lehman Brothers (1891–1969), which earned substantial fees. His Investment Advisory Service, geared to investors with $500,000 or more, soon had Lehman Brothers controlling over $2 billion.

Shortly before Robert Lehman's death in 1969, Lehman Brothers was listed as one of the four top American investment banks. However, by 1977 the firm, partly because of the country's economic difficulties, faced hard times, and there were serious tensions between Lehman's investment bankers and its aggressive traders. Lehman Brothers undertook a series of mergers with various companies including American Express, whose investment arm it became.

After a series of gyrations about Lehman's role and how it should function it was spun off by American Express, went public, and survived some poor management decisions that nearly led to its demise. After 9/11, which resulted in one employee's death and the destruction of the firm's headquarters in the financial district, Lehman head Richard Fuld (b. 1946) managed to ease the tensions between traders and investment bankers.

In 2003 Lehman was one of ten Wall Street firms that settled with the SEC and other regulatory agencies about undue influence by research departments' positive reports about risky investments being sold to the public. While Lehman remained a prestigious firm, during the mid-2000s many of its personnel—like many in the global financial world—became obsessed with annual bonuses and developed shaky ethics as they increasingly focused on ventures such as risky commercial real estate and subprime securitization.

In retrospect, Lehman's filing for bankruptcy on September 15, 2008, was not the beginning of a worldwide financial crisis; it had been preceded by a bursting real estate bubble and a wave of failures of smaller banks and financial firms. It was, however, a signal moment in the process; when Lehman went bust, it was clear to all intelligent observers that the crisis would be severe.

Moreover, the bankruptcy made clear the need for government intervention to bail out an economic system teetering on the edge of irreversible disaster. Like the 1929 stock market crash, Lehman's bankruptcy marked the moment when the reality of economic chaos became undeniable to financiers, politicians, journalists, and the public. This major bankruptcy was triggered by the collapse of an overheated real estate market, in which Lehman had significant holdings, and by Lehman's strategy of "leveraging," borrowing large amounts to facilitate its investments. Unlike depository banks, which are federally insured, investment banks like Lehman were not subject to the same regulations limiting risky investment and borrowing. Security for these loans on Lehman's books proved insignificant and chimerical.

Lehman's collapse began more than a year before the bankruptcy with the closure of BNC Mortgage, the firm's subprime arm. Like other lenders in this category it helped create a real estate bubble by issuing questionable mortgages to individuals unlikely to be able to pay. BNC used novel products such as adjustable rate mortgages (ARMs) in which interest rates fluctuated over time, often leaving borrowers unable to pay the higher rates or stuck with substantial balloon payments.

Homeowners using such instruments usually fell into default several years into the mortgage. Yet, many of these mortgages required little proof of income or assets. Despite the obvious problems sure to arise, granting these mortgages was profitable to companies like BNC because rather than hold the dubious debt, they repackaged them into mortgage-backed securities sold to investors. Through this flimflammery the obligations now seemed a safe bet for individuals and banks like Lehman. Its assets also included a large number of complex derivatives, the true value of which was difficult to calculate once the issuer came under scrutiny, but obviously less than its face value.

The collapse of the real estate market and the revelation that Lehman was holding billions in worthless mortgage-backed securities resulted in steep price declines in Lehman stock. The firm's CEO Dick Fuld initially reacted with a plan to separate the company's toxic assets into a separate business, but investors responded unfavorably and the crash in stock prices continued unabated, with a decline of 75 percent during a single week. In a second attempt to avoid bankruptcy, Lehman pursued acquisition deals.

Bankruptcy loomed for Lehman and came at a time when a government bailout would have met strong resistance. It has been charged that Henry Paulson (b. 1946), then treasury secretary, denied Lehman the support of government funds and left the firm to its fate because as former head of Goldman Sachs he wished to eliminate a rival. Whatever his feelings, Paulson attempted to organize the heads of competing banks into a private bailout that would divide Lehman's worthless assets among more sound financial institutions, stating no government bailout would be forthcoming. During the long weekend of negotiations it became clear to all involved that the opening of the Japanese stock market on Monday was the deadline for a buyout, bailout, or bankruptcy.

Ultimately, attempts at acquisition or bailout were unsuccessful because Lehman's competitors, burdened with their own toxic assets and already on shaky ground, were not sound enough to absorb the troubled company without government guarantees. Hours before the Monday morning deadline, when Fuld learned that plans for acquisition of Lehman had failed, it filed for bankruptcy.

The collapse had major ramifications. Thousands directly employed by Lehman lost their jobs, but even more significantly, the collapse of the company threatened to unravel the complicated financial web of derivatives that linked investment companies, insurance firms, and major manufactures. Companies (such as insurance giant AIG) held credit default swaps on Lehman debt, essentially a bet on the risk of a default by Lehman. Its collapse immediately rendered these "assets" worthless, shaking the already rickety structures of other financial institutions.

Despite widespread public anger at the high-paid executives (Fuld earned $450 million in pay and bonuses) who engineered the toxic assets and financial relationships at the heart of the global economic crisis, Lehman's collapse paved the way for future bailouts of failing mega-corporations (such as AIG and GM) because its bankruptcy demonstrated the domino effect of such a failure being likely to spread to manufacturing, small business, and government.

Further Reading

"The Case against Lehman Bros." *60 Minutes*. April 22, 2012. http://www.cbsnews.com/8301-18560_162-57417397/the-case-against-lehman-brothers/?pageNum=3&tag=contentMain;contentBody [accessed March 12, 2013].

McDonald, Lawrence G. *A Colossal Failure of Common Sense: The Inside Story of the Collapse of Lehman Brothers*. New York: Crown Business, 2009.

Tibman, Joseph. *The Murder of Lehman Brothers: An Insider's Look at the Global Meltdown*. New York: Brick Tower Press, 2009.

Madoff, Bernard L. (1938–)

"Bernie" Madoff, as he was known to friends, associates, his many victims, and the public, is famous as the perpetrator of what is thought to be the largest Ponzi scheme ever, and certainly the largest investment fraud in American history.

Born in Queens, New York City, April 29, 1938, the grandson of Jewish immigrant grandparents, Madoff grew up in modest circumstances. Graduating (1960) from Hofstra University, he briefly attended Brooklyn Law School. In 1960, with the financial and organizational support of his father-in-law, he founded Bernard L. Madoff Investment Securities LLC as a broker-dealer.

As a broker the firm handled stocks for others; as a dealer the firm bought and sold for its own accounts. The shrewd, hardworking Madoff pioneered various technological innovations that helped to create a computerized information system that made over-the-counter trades more transparent and contributed to development of the NASDAQ stock market. Madoff's firm became a major force in the securities industry as did the gregarious Madoff. They played important roles in the development of NASD (National Association of Security Dealers) as the chief self-regulatory organization for U.S. broker-dealer firms. Madoff served as its chair for a time and was an active member of the organization's board of directors as well as sitting on numerous NASD committees.

The firm handled trades for clients who wanted to buy and sell when the stock exchanges were closed or who wanted to trade away from these exchanges. The firm's commission fees were reasonable, less than those of other brokers, and by the time that Madoff and the firm came under scrutiny the broker-dealer

Bernard Madoff (right) arrives at federal court for his hearing in New York on January 14, 2009. (AP Photo/Frank Franklin II)

business was operating at a loss and was subsidized by his supposed earnings as an investment advisor.

Madoff generally had a magical aura in the 1990s and early 2000s. Well connected with the regulatory agencies because of his political contributions, he was lauded as a man of stature in the securities industry, much admired for his many philanthropies. Those whose investments he handled commended him for producing consistent, high returns on investment that always "beat" the market. Madoff claimed that this exceptional performance resulted from a novel, secret strategy whereby the firm cut out the middleman, dealing directly with retail brokers.

In some quarters, however, Madoff's investments were viewed with suspicion as early as 1999. That year Harry Markopolis (b. 1956), an obscure New England forensic accountant and former trader, alerted the Securities and Exchange Commission (SEC), the federal agency regulating the stock markets, to what he believed were the mathematical impossibilities of Madoff's claimed return on investments. However, Markopolis's comments at the time had no impact, only seeming prescient in retrospect.

For ten years, Markopolis continued without success to file complaints with the SEC in Boston, New York, and Washington, D.C. During this period he also failed to rouse interest in other Wall Street firms that had expressed concern that Madoff's returns were too outrageous and consistent. Other suspicious aspects of Madoff's operations attracting attention included the small number of, and relative lack of independence of, the accountants responsible for signing off on the books.

Prosecutors later alleged, based on Madoff's testimony, that reports on client investments were faked and based on "trades" that never happened. A special computer system was rigged to allow the doctoring of records to account for the consistent exceptional returns supposedly achieved by Madoff. Instead of being traded, investor money was deposited in a Chase Manhattan bank account; if clients attempted to collect their "profit" Madoff paid them using funds of other clients. This is the essence of a Ponzi scheme: the scam can stay afloat as long as new investors buy in sufficient amounts. Once investments failed to increase sufficiently to meet the faked "returns," Madoff became unable to pay back clients and the scam began to fail.

Like all Ponzi schemes, Madoff's billion-dollar bluff hit a wall. In December 2008 it fell $7 billion short in redemptions; when investors attempted to collect, they were unable to do so. Madoff then admitted to his sons and wife that the firm was "one big lie" and a "Ponzi scheme"; his sons reported him to regulators, claiming they were not complicit in the fraud. Madoff was arrested on December 11, 2008, charged with numerous crimes relating to the fraud, and remained under house arrest in his penthouse on the Upper East Side for several months until remanded to the Metropolitan Correctional Center.

Madoff and his wife Ruth (b. 1941) settled with federal prosecutors in a deal that required them to turn over $85 million in assets, leaving Ruth with $2.5 million in cash, though some speculated she previously secreted away up to $15 million. Madoff pled guilty in March 2009 to 11 felonies and in June received a prison sentence of 150 years. Their son Mark (1964–2010) committed suicide in December 2010 on the second anniversary of his father's arrest. Both he and his brother Andrew (b. 1966) were the subject of intensive investigations, but as of July 2012 no charges had been filed. Some of the firm's back office staff later were prosecuted on various charges, found guilty, fined, and sentenced to short prison terms.

Estimates of the extent of Bernard Madoff's fraud have ranged from $17 billion to nearly $65 billion. The FBI investigation revealed that JPMorgan Chase also made a killing on interest and banking fees for warehousing the stolen cash, though the bank has denied any complicity. Different accounts indicate involvement at high levels by a number of the elite of the financial industry, including such prominent money managers as J. Ezra Merkin (b. 1953), who have been successfully sued for taking fees from Madoff for recommending their clients invest with him.

For various reasons, Madoff had strong personal and philanthropic ties to the Jewish community, and his fraud had a serious impact on both organizations and individuals who were part of it. The endowment of institutions like Hadassah, the Lappin Foundation, and the Jewish Community Federation of Los Angeles all suffered grievously, as did many individuals in his extensively Jewish client base, not only celebrities and Jewish country club members but many smaller investors who had believed in him and lost millions that could not be replaced.

The Madoff scheme and its repercussions became public knowledge in 2009 when the financial crisis was making headlines. The Madoff frauds became one more symbol of the failures of Wall Street and its ostensible regulators. Many commentators argued that there was little difference between the unwilling-ness of regulators to rein in Madoff despite obvious reasons for suspicion and the failed control of major financial institutions that continued to sell real estate investment products backed by subprime mortgages the marketers knew would fail.

Other critics of the high-flying 1990s and 2000s suggested that Madoff stood out among the "guilty" parties of the financial crisis—in that he was charged with crimes, prosecuted, and jailed—because his victims included the wealthy and the powerful, these critics speculated Madoff's crimes therefore were taken more seriously by authorities.

Further Reading

Henriques, Diana B. *The Wizard of Lies: Bernard Madoff and the Death of Trust*. New York: Oxford University Press, 2011.

Occupy Wall Street (OWS)

Occupy Wall Street was a protest movement against what were seen as the depredations of Wall Street's institutions on the lives of average Americans. During the fall of 2011 Occupy Wall Street (OWS) attracted thousands in New York City and hundreds elsewhere in the United States to demonstrations. By mid-2012 OWS survived as a rump protest group that lacked the flair and mas-sive support the original achieved.

Its organizers attempted to tie OWS to 2011 demonstrations such as "the Arab Spring" and Eurozone anti-austerity protests as well as previous world-wide student demonstrations. However, OWS's origins lie in the response of some New York City activists to a call for action against what was perceived as the spiritual hollowness of the society formed by consumer capitalism.

Adbusters, a provocative Canada-based bimonthly (both online and in print), called for protest demonstrations in New York City's financial district.

Responsible for this call was the magazine's founding editor, Kalle Lasn (b. 1942), and its senior editor, Micah White (b. 1982). Before starting the magazine in 1989, Vancouver-based Lasn was an Estonian immigrant to Australia, a successful market researcher in Japan, and a respected experimental Canadian filmmaker. Lasn was joined in the call by his close editorial associate, Berkeley, California–based White, a self-described "mystical anarchist" and an active radical since his Michigan high school days.

In early June 2011 they sent out the first of several mass e-mailings ("tactical briefings") to *Adbusters* subscribers and its estimated 90,000 "friends," in print and online, proposing that a "tent city" of "revolutionaries" should "swarm Wall Street," condemned as "the greatest corruptor of our democracy." On June 9 Lasn registered the web address OccupyWallstreet.org; approximately five weeks later a transgender anarchist, stimulated by the call to action, registered OccupyWallSt.org.

OWS made intelligent, extensive use of social media and continued to do so even as over time it lost support. OWS advocates understood how to sell online their charges about the disparity of wealth in the United States, the inadequacy of American health care, and the defects of a consumer-based capitalism; their ideas and slogans such as "We are the 99 percent" (the other 1 percent represented corporate influence and the wealthy) filtered into the mass media and the public consciousness.

In mid-July 2011 Lasn and White determined September 17 to be the date for action. At Lasn's instigation, *Adbusters*'s art department designed a poster whose image and message circulated widely on social media. It displayed a slim dancer atop a charging bull that duplicated the statue of the bull in Chase Manhattan Plaza at the edge of Wall Street; an iconic sculpture, it symbolized an optimistic view of Wall Street's operations. The poster asked "what is our one demand" and urged "occupy Wall Street, September 17th, Bring tents."

The poster's call to action came after failure of a strikingly similar protest, dubbed "Bloombergville." In mid-June 2011 outrage at budget cuts proposed by New York City mayor Michael Bloomberg (b. 1942) led protesters to set up a tent city by City Hall. It drew only dozens, quickly fizzled out, and garnered little media attention. But on the web some protesters presented a slide show depicting Bloomberg as a heartless Grinch and on YouTube put together a video showing him as a Godzilla destroying schools and city services.

Bloombergville's failure aroused skepticism about the possible success of a second tent city aimed at Wall Street, particularly one organized by out-of-towners over the Internet. Meanwhile, decision making moved from *Adbusters*'s editors to New York City-based seasoned protesters. Drawn in by online feeds, throughout August their plans for September 17 were formulated. Originally the protestors sought to occupy the "Charging Bull" site, but police, learning of this goal, fenced off the location.

Nearby Zuccotti Park then became the target. A small sliver of land (about 33,000 square feet), one of the few park spaces in the Financial District, it had been created (1968) in return for a company being allowed to build a taller building. After 9/11 and the destruction of the nearby World Trade Center, the space was covered by debris during the cleanup of the area.

A property company bought the park, planted trees, built lights into the ground, and put in granite tables and seating. In June 2006, the renovated park reopened, renamed after John Zuccotti (b. 1937), a former deputy mayor and prominent real estate developer. On September 17 OWS took over the park and began using it as a campground and staging area. Being privately owned the park was exempt from normal curfew hours and was open to the public 24 hours a day.

The planned occupation of Wall Street fell far short of the call for 20,000 occupiers; the protest on September 17 attracted about 1,000 demonstrators, 300 of whom decided to occupy Zuccotti Park—renamed "Liberty Square" by the protesters. Despite inclement weather and police harassment the Zuccotti Park camp began attracting numbers by word of mouth and the Internet, sparking national and international attention.

A watershed moment came on the morning of September 23 when the Zuccotti Park occupiers along with supporters marched to Union Square. New York City police corralled several young female protesters with orange crowd-control netting and then blasted them in the face with pepper spray, a moment captured on a YouTube video that went viral. The episode resulted in widespread outrage and attracted attention to the protest.

A second incident on October 1, in which 700 demonstrators were arrested with unnecessary cruelty while marching across the Brooklyn Bridge, added further momentum to the protests and won them sympathizers in the city and elsewhere. The protest on Wall Street began to spread. Facebook, tweets, and traditional message sites helped connect OWS to the larger world and to the occupations that began to spring up in other American cities and towns. At key junctures—such as the first attempt by New York City authorities to evict the protesters from Zuccotti Park—social media helped gain assistance from previously passive supporters such as municipal unionists.

Oakland, California, rapidly became OWS's West Coast center, and its encampment opposite the town's city hall was one of the first raided by police (October 25). Continuing confrontations, many violent, between police and demonstrators led Oakland occupiers to call (November 2) for a "general strike," a tactic long out of use in the United States. While the strike did not effectively suspend economic activity in Oakland it drew support from a broad spectrum of the community.

Ultimately, tent city occupations that sprang up across the country called attention to issues such as inequality, Wall Street abuses, and economic disparities, but also resulted in violent confrontations (not always initiated by the authorities) in places as disparate as Denver, Miami, and Washington, D.C.

Nationally, OWS diminished in the days following its eviction (November 15) from Zuccotti Park. Following the lead of New York City's mayor, who claimed to act in the public interest to preserve security and maintain sanitation and cleanliness, local authorities across the country moved to evict the protesters who had taken over public spaces.

During this period, occupy protesters coined the slogan "you can't evict an idea." Controversy continues about the movement's lack of goals or clear demands, but commentators across the political spectrum have noted the protestors' impact on major political issues such as American inequality and criminal financial speculation. OWS and what it represented even if no longer occupying public spaces remains very active on the web.

Further Reading

Blumenkraz, Carla, et al., eds. *Occupy: Scenes from Occupied America*. Brooklyn: Verso, 2011.

Byrne, Jane, ed. *The Occupy Handbook*. New York: Back Bay Books, 2012.

Grusky, David B., Doug McAdam, Rob Reich, and Debra Satz, eds. *Occupy the Future*. Cambridge, MA: The MIT Press, 2013.

Pelosi, Nancy (1940–)

As 60th Speaker of the House of Representatives of the Congress of the United States, serving from January 3, 2007, to January 3, 2011, Nancy Pelosi, a lifelong Democrat, was the highest-ranking elected female politician in American history. She was the first woman, the first Italian American, and the first Californian to hold that office.

Born Nancy Patricia D'Alesandro on March 26, 1940, the youngest of six children, she grew up in a political family. Her father, Thomas D'Alesandro (1903–1987), was elected to Congress (D-MD) for five terms, serving from January 3, 1939, to May 16, 1947, when he resigned, having been elected mayor of Baltimore, which office he held from May 16, 1947, to May 16, 1959. His son also was elected mayor of Baltimore as a Democrat, serving one term (1967–1971).

She interned for one of Maryland's senators while a college student in Washington, D.C. In 1962 she graduated from Trinity College (now Trinity Washington University). The next year she married Paul Pelosi (b. 1940), who has had a successful career as a businessman. The couple lived in New York City for some years before moving (1969) to San Francisco. Once there she worked her way up in the Democratic Party.

After handling some scut assignments she was elected to the Democratic National Committee (1976) and subsequently served as party chair for Northern California (1977), as chair of California's Democratic Party (1981), and finance chair of the Democratic Senatorial Campaign Committee (1985). In June 1987 after the death of Sala Burton (1925–1987), widow of long-serving (1964–1983) Democratic California congressman Phillip Burton (1926–1983) who had succeeded him in office, Nancy Pelosi won a special election for the seat, won again in 1988, and has continued to be reelected.

She represents one of the safest Democratic congressional seats. Democrats have held that seat since 1949. Nancy Pelosi served on the important Appropriations and Intelligence Committees. In 2001 she was elected House minority whip, second-in-command to the House minority leader, and the next year was elected to that position: in each case she was the first woman chosen for the post. In 2007 she became Speaker.

Pelosi was a controversial figure as Speaker, much-hated both by conservative media personalities and rank-and-file Republicans. Despite having earned a reputation for radicalism among her detractors, Pelosi as Speaker during the Bush administration had a mixed record. She strongly and effectively opposed Republican attempts to privatize Social Security but also blocked efforts by left-wing Democrats to impeach President George W. Bush (b. 1946) for "crimes" ostensibly related to the invasion of Iraq. Her position in this instance resulted in her being challenged unsuccessfully in 2008 for her seat by antiwar activist and gold-star mom Cindy Sheehan (b. 1957). In 2010, when Democrats lost the House, Pelosi returned to her former position as House minority leader.

Pelosi's unpopularity with her right-wing critics reached a peak with the 2008 financial crisis. As the financial system unraveled, controversy erupted about a proposed $700 billion bailout for Wall Street. Calls flooded congressional offices opposing the bill and voicing resentment that Wall Street, whom many held responsible for the collapse, should benefit from its own mistakes at the expense of taxpayers. Nevertheless, most observers expected the bill to pass because of a perceived need for the bailout lest credit markets freeze up. The first iteration of the bill, however, failed with 95 Democrats and 135 Republicans voting against it. Many critics cited a strident speech by Pelosi as the factor that tipped the balance to failure.

Blaming the crisis on the Bush administration's "budget recklessness," "failed economic policies," and "anything goes mentality," she contrasted them with Democratic consideration for the "free market." Sticking to a theme of Main Street pain and Wall Street bumbling, she argued that Americans losing homes

Newly elected House minority whip Nancy Pelosi holds a whip she received as a gift from outgoing House minority leader David Bonior in Washington, D.C., on October 10, 2001. Pelosi was the first woman to serve as party leader in either branch of Congress. (AP Photo/Joe Marquette)

and businesses "did not decide to dangerously weaken our regulatory and oversight policies ... did not make unwise and risky financial deals ... did not jeopardize the economic security of the nation. And ... must not pay the cost of this emergency recovery." She strongly opposed any bill that did not include provisions for mortgage renegotiation, increased regulation of financial institutions, and limits on CEO and manager salaries and bonuses, concluding "Our message to Wall Street is this: the party is over."

Her speech provoked outrage in the business press as well as among right-wing commentators, although right-wing opposition to the bill was as strong, or stronger, than the criticism she made. Other critics argued that her speech was simply a stunt aimed at improving the image of then-presidential candidate Barack Obama (b. 1961). During his presidency Pelosi took a different tack. Once a convener of the Congressional Progressive Caucus she moved in a more conservative direction. While along with the Senate Majority Leader, Nevada Democrat Harry Reid (b. 1939), she had strenuously opposed President George W. Bush's plan for a "troop surge" in Iraq, maintaining a military solution was not possible there, she did not offer any criticism of President Obama's delays on promised deadlines for bringing troops home and ending the war.

A staunch supporter of reproductive rights, women's health care, and same sex marriage, she also promoted legislation that would raise the minimum wage. However, Pelosi's reputation as a progressive fighter for the economic underdog took a major hit in November 2011 when the TV show *60 Minutes* reported that the wealthy Pelosi, among the richest members of Congress, had engaged in insider trading during the time she was vehemently castigating "Wall Street" on the House floor. Pelosi, reported *60 Minutes*, used information gleaned in the course of her official duties to identify IPOs (initial public offerings) and other deals that would have been opaque to average citizens or even to the financially savvy.

Perhaps most shocking in the report was that such deals were not illegal, though "insider trading" is generally regarded as criminal. After Pelosi's questionable trades were revealed, it came to light that various politicians had similarly enriched themselves using information gleaned during the process of developing the emergency bailout bill, and that such trades did not violate the law or congressional ethics guidelines. *60 Minutes*, while concentrating on Pelosi, revealed that other members of Congress, both Republicans and Democrats, had worked together to pass legislation exempting themselves from the letter and spirit of restrictions on insider trading.

As of this writing, the hardworking, bitterly partisan Pelosi remained one of the most effective Democrats in Congress. Whatever the criticisms leveled against her by enemies in the media and in Congress, the well-turned-out Nancy Pelosi stood by her progressive principles. One can safely assume that she will continue to be reelected by her constituents, who seem pleased by her stance on the policies that concern them.

Further Reading

"Confronting Nancy Pelosi on Insider Trading, '60 Minutes.'" cbsnews.com. November 3, 2011.

"Nancy Pelosi (D-Calif.)." *WhoRunsGov.* http://www.washingtonpost.com/politics/nancy-pelosi-d-calif/gIQAF3PM9O_topic.html [accessed March 12, 2013].

"Pelosi Defends Record after '60 Minutes' Report." cbsnews.com, November 14, 2011.

"This Is What a Speaker Looks Like." *Ms* magazine cover story for Winter 2007 issue. http://www.msmagazine.com/winter2007 [accessed March 12, 2013].

Rubin, Robert (1938–)

Robert Rubin's fascinating career has not been without considerable controversy. After 24 profitable and successful years with the investment firm Goldman Sachs, he became its co-chairman in 1990. Three years later at the behest of the newly inaugurated president Clinton (b. 1946) he became the first director of the National Economic Council, created by the president to coordinate the federal government's economic policies. In January 1995 he became secretary of the treasury, an office he held until July 1999. Serving President Clinton during both his terms of office, Rubin won accolades and severe criticism for his advice to the president and for his policies. Since then Rubin has held a series of positions; his tenure (1999–2009) with the banking giant Citigroup (which included a five week stint in November–December 2007 as chairman), was more important than and much less contentious than being cochair of the Council on Foreign Relations, a position he also assumed that year.

Rubin was born August 29, 1938, and grew up in Miami, Florida. He graduated with honors from Harvard, attended the London School of Economics, and earned (1964) a law degree from Yale. After a stint with a New York law firm, he joined Goldman Sachs and as a result of his success at risk arbitrage became a general partner in 1971. He joined the firm's management committee in 1980, was vice chairman from 1987 to 1990, and after serving two years as cochairman was asked to join the incoming administration of Bill Clinton.

During the 1990s Rubin played a central role in stemming a financial crisis sparked by the introduction of the North American Free Trade Agreement (NAFTA), as well as dealing with localized market crises in the Asian and Latin American markets. His role in containing such economic problems led him, along with his deputy Lawrence Summers (b. 1954) and Federal Reserve Board chair Alan Greenspan (b. 1926), perhaps a bit exaggeratedly, to be anointed in 1999 as "The Committee to Save the World" by *Time* magazine.

During the same period Rubin played a major role in directing the Clinton administration's policies toward deregulation of financial markets. Along with Alan Greenspan, he strongly opposed government regulation through the Commodity Futures Corporation of over-the-counter derivatives that played such a nefarious role in the fiscal crisis that began in 2008. While secretary of the treasury, Rubin successfully lobbied for the repeal of a series of banking laws initiated by the 1929 stock market crash (they were often referred to collectively as "Glass-Steagall," after the congressional sponsors of the 1933 legislation).

The absence or removal of government regulation made possible the sale of mortgage-backed securities and growth of the derivatives market that helped spread the 2008 crisis in the American real estate market. Rubin's antiregulation policies have come under severe attack. In his defense he has published an analysis that identifies various problems he believes led to the economic crisis, including undercapitalized institutions, abusive mortgage practices, and low wages, as well as the unchecked growth of derivatives and novel financial products. Interestingly, in his analysis he opines that concerted government regulation is required to prevent similar issues in the future.

President Clinton once called Rubin "the greatest Secretary of the Treasury since Alexander Hamilton" but also felt that his treasury secretary had made the ill-fated suggestion that the administration not pursue regulation of new derivative financial instruments, like those that went on to transform the real estate market crisis into a global financial catastrophe. Clinton, however, has stood by his generally positive opinion of the financial advice Rubin offered him.

On leaving the Clinton administration Rubin joined Citigroup as a board member and senior advisor, without—at his request—any line responsibilities, yet because of his capabilities, connections, and past record it seems no major decision was made without his input. During his years on the board (1999–2009) Citigroup sold itself as a "financial supermarket" that should serve as a model for all such institutions.

Rubin played no official policy role during the financial crisis that began in 2008 that would result in the megabank struggling for existence. During his years on the Citigroup board, Citigroup divided itself into two separate financial institutions, separating its trading arm from its standard banking operations. It was then restored to profitability through government intervention. Rubin's role has been criticized as being fundamentally a pay-to-play deal in which he had no managerial responsibilities other than facilitating access to the administration of Barack Obama (b. 1961). By the time Rubin stepped down from the board in January 2009, he had received more than $126 million in cash and stock over the decade served on the board.

Critics of the Obama administration's handling of the continuing financial crisis have linked it to Clinton-era economic policy, maintaining that there remain strong professional, political, and financial connections centered around ideas tied to Rubin and Goldman Sachs. *Rolling Stone* journalist Matt Taibbi (b. 1970), one prominent critic, argues that though Rubin has never worked for Obama, his philosophies have driven policy in ways that primarily benefit the financial industry in general and firms closely associated with Rubin in particular. According to Taibbi:

> Rubin probably more than any other person was responsible for the financial crisis by deregulating the economy [while] in the White House. And he had a major role in helping destroy one of the world's biggest companies in Citigroup. He has one of the worst track records you can find, but he was basically the guy who was the architect of the entire Obama policy. Obama put him in charge of everything.

Tim Geithner (b. 1961), President Obama's secretary of the treasury and a former Goldman Sachs manager, has been called a Rubin protégé by many observers; under his direction of the Treasury Department, Goldman Sachs benefited from nearly $800 billion in loans, while a major competitor (Lehman Brothers) was allowed to go bankrupt. Various commentators have pointed out that Rubin's "alumni" have influenced many Obama administration policies.

Extremely ambitious even if somewhat laid back, Rubin is an interesting combination of drive and anxiousness. He wishes to be respected but is committed to financial policies that have been very beneficial for him but less so for much of the public. The results of some of Rubin's policies have led him to revise his views. Thus, he has backpedaled from his initial stance on deregulation but remains wedded to fiscal restraint. Rubin continues to be involved with important projects but for all his accomplishments in the public and private spheres continues to have numerous detractors who highlight what they consider serious flaws in the policies he pursues.

Further Reading

"Bob Rubin Cuddles." http://www.rollingstone.com/politics/blogs/taibblog/bob-rubin-cuddles-20100501accessed March 12, 2013].

Cohen, William D. "Rethinking Robert Rubin" *Bloomberg Businessweek* September 30, 2012. http://www.businessweek.com/printer/articles/73822-rethinking-robe...

"Obama's 'Big Sellout': How the White House Is Caving to Wall Street." http://www.huffingtonpost.com/2009/12/03/matt-taibbi-obamas-big-se_n_378705.html [accessed March 12, 2013].

Rubin, Robert. "Getting the Economy Back on Track." *Newsweek.* December 28, 2009. http://www.thedailybeast.com/newsweek/2009/12/28/getting-the-economy-back-on-track.html [accessed March 12, 2013].

Rubin, Robert E., and Jacob Weisberg. *In An Uncertain World: Tough Choices from Wall Street to Washington.* New York: Random House, 2003.

Tea Party

A conservative American political movement that came into prominence after the 2008 financial collapse, the Tea Party Movement has played a significant role in local and national politics and driven Republicans to embrace more conservative positions. The central tenets of the Tea Party movement are classic tropes of the conservative wing of the Republican Party, including reduction of government spending on health, public education, unemployment benefits, food assistance programs, and housing assistance, as well as balancing the budget and cutting taxes.

When the Tea Party first appeared on the national stage in 2009 it projected an image of rebellion against a tyrannical government that overtaxed and overspent without intelligent responsible oversight. The movement claimed to have borrowed its name from the December 1773 "Boston Tea Party," when a group of protesters dumped bales of tea into Boston Harbor to protest taxes on the tea imposed by the British government on American colonists without their consent.

For members of the Tea Party, the dumping was a watershed moment in American history, dramatically popularizing the idea of "no taxation without representation" that underlay the colonists' rebellion against the Crown and led to the American Revolution and the establishment of the United States. Supporters of the contemporary Tea Party have felt that the federal government bailout of Wall Street and government spending in general represent undemocratic taxation and redistribution. It also has been said that *Tea* is an acronym for "Taxes, Enough Already."

The "Tea Party" is not really a political grouping in the traditional sense of having a centralized organizational structure or codes of proper conduct. On the contrary, the Tea Party supposedly is inspired by not having the trappings of organizations that might divert it from representing "ordinary" Americans, opposed to Washington's insider politics and deal-making. However, in reality the Tea Party, no matter to what ideal it aspires, has functioned not so much as a movement but as a "grassroots" faction within the Republican party of a broad array of predominantly white senior citizens, social and fiscal conservatives, evangelical Christians, libertarians, and constitutional literalists.

The iconic origins of the Tea Party have been attributed to an incident at the Chicago Board of Trade on February 19, 2009: Rick Santelli (b. 1953), a CNBC-TV business reporter standing on the exchange floor, ranted against what he saw as government bailing out losers (and such rants have continued on air and off over the years since then). Santelli angrily attacked as a real threat to traditional American values the Troubled Assets Relief Program (TARP), a federal program to help big financial institutions on the brink of bankruptcy but also expected to aid ordinary homeowners.

Santelli's on-camera anger was not directed at the exchange traders (who represented the big financial institutions that through their greed and avarice brought about the worst financial crisis in 70 years) but at ordinary homeowners. The only part of TARP that was supposed to benefit ordinary Americans instead of institutional players drew his venom. He claimed TARP would be "subsidiz[ing] the losers' mortgages" with public money that more usefully should be directed to society's winners. Santelli's outrage at the "losers" was inexhaustible as he ranted, "They 'drink the water' while others 'carry the water.'"

His rant included holding a tea party in July and dumping into the Chicago River financial paper underlying such mortgages. Traders who heard his rant cheered him. When the Drudge Report played a video of Santelli's rant, it went viral, and fed into and hyped the protests against the policies of the newly installed administration of President Barack Obama (b. 1961). His election and the reforms he proposed galvanized the Tea Party movement and deepened its base.

Protest meetings demanding local, state, and federal fiscal responsibility had already been held prior to Santelli's rant (which subsequently has been described as "staged"). There had been a New York meeting in January 2009 protesting an obesity tax and a "Porkulus Protest" in Seattle on February 16, 2009, protesting the stimulus. After Santelli's rant drew public attention there were conservative radio talk shows, online postings, and TV commentators mentioning a new Tea Party.

Subsequently, at the end of February 2009, a "Nationwide Chicago Tea Party" was held in over 40 U.S. cities, and soon a loose affiliation of local groups sprang up, but without central leadership. Minnesota representative Michele Bachman (b. 1956) in her quest for the 2012 Republican presidential nomination formed a Tea Party Congressional Caucus. The Tea Party's early supporters included defeated former vice presidential contender Sarah Palin (b. 1964), and conservative TV pundits Rush Limbaugh (b. 1964) and Glenn Beck (b. 1951), as well as such unique conservative political activists as "Joe the Plumber"—Samuel Joseph Wurzelbacher (b. 1973), made famous during the 2008 presidential campaign.

To further energize the Tea Party movement Beck and others—including Fox News—organized a march on Washington for August 26, 2009. Modeled on Civil Rights marches of an earlier era, the demographics indicated how unlike them it was. Made up of mostly of older, white people with above average incomes, the Tea Party continues to have such a base.

They opposed President Obama's attempt to extend health coverage to millions of uninsured Americans, dubbing the program "Obamacare" and presenting it and the other legislation the president proposed as evidence he was a "socialist" committed to income redistribution. They were outraged at his plans, arguing, for instance, that the Obamacare proposals infringed on American freedoms by involving government in health care.

For some time, many Tea Partiers were preoccupied with accusations Barack Obama was ineligible for the presidency because he had misrepresented his birthplace and was not born in U.S. territory as the Constitution requires. The issue seems to have been resolved with release of the president's Hawaii birth records. Some Tea Party critics have argued that the strenuous opposition of Tea Partiers to President Obama is rooted in a racist backlash against the nation's first black president, a charge that has been vehemently denied.

The Tea Party played a strong role in the 2010 elections and in the 2012 primaries. In 2010 it contributed to defeat in the Republican primaries of some long-serving legislators who it charged were conservatives "in name only" and helped elect their primary opponents to office. Again very active in 2012, the

Tea Party was responsible, for instance, for the primary defeat of veteran Indiana senator Richard Luger (b. 1932) and victories in the primaries for other unlikely candidates who successfully challenged Republican incumbents as RINOs (Republican In Name Only).

An English newspaper commenting on the Tea Party's impact on the 2010 elections described it as a mix of "grassroots populism, professional politics, and big money." That money came primarily from the very wealthy Koch brothers—especially David H. Koch (b. 1940)—known for their generous philanthropy but also strongly committed to a libertarian brand of politics. It was charged that the Kochs "hijacked" the Tea Party movement. The Kochs have spent millions providing financial aid and organizational support for the Tea Party movement and its candidates as well as various other conservative front groups.

A well-received, balanced, scholarly 2012 study of the Tea Party movement found it substantial (numbering about 20 percent of Americans), influential (especially in Republican Party politics), and primarily generational (predominantly white Americans averaging 60 years of age). Some commentators found the study alarming. Its authors found it startling, since they were surprised that while the Tea Partiers supported tax benefit programs like Social Security and Medicare. The Tea Baggers (as they were derisively dubbed by their enemies) seemed unwilling or unable to adapt to a modern America.

Further Reading

Skocpol, Theda, and Vanessa Williamson. *The Tea Party and the Remaking of Republican Conservatism.* New York: Oxford University Press, 2012.

"Tea Party Movement," collected news and coverage. http://hnn.us/articles/124391 .html [accessed March 12, 2013].

PRIMARY DOCUMENTS

1. The Critical Period, 1783–1789

A. Shays' Rebellion: A Schedule of Grievances (August 22–25, 1786)

Shays' Rebellion, an uprising named for one of its leaders, Daniel Shays (c. 1747–1825), erupted in Massachusetts in 1786–1787. The main causes of the rebellion were economic: many of the rebels were suffering from the ill effects of an economic depression, made worse by a lack of hard currency, which dried up access to credit; and the harsh fiscal policies of the state government, which was trying to ease its own debt problems. Reproduced here is a list of grievances drawn up at a convention held in Hampshire County, Massachusetts, in August 1786. These county protests marked the beginning of the insurrection.

At a meeting of delegates from fifty towns in the county of Hampshire, in convention held at Hatfield, in said county, on Tuesday the 22d day of August instant [1786], and continued by adjournments until the twenty fifth, &c. Voted, that this meeting is constitutional.

The convention from a thorough conviction of uneasiness, subsisting among the people of this county and Commonwealth, then went into an inquiry for the cause; and, upon mature consideration, deliberation and debate, were of opinion, that many grievances and unnecessary burdens now lying upon the people, are sources of that discontent so evidently discoverable throughout this Commonwealth. Among which the following articles were voted as such, viz.

1st. The existence of the Senate.

2d. The present mode of representation.

3d. The officers of government not being annually dependent on the representatives of the people, in General Court assembled, for their salaries.

4th. All the civil officers of government, not being annually elected by the Representatives of the people, in General Court assembled.

5th. The existence of the Courts of Common Pleas, and General Sessions of the Peace.

6th. The Fee Table as it now stands.

7th. The present mode of appropriating the impost and excise.

8th. The unreasonable grants made to some of the officers of government.

9th. The supplementary aid.

10th. The present mode of paying the governmental securities.

11th. The present mode adopted for the payment and speedy collection of the last tax.

12th. The present mode of taxation as it operates unequally between the polls and estates, and between landed and mercantile interests.

13th. The present method of practice of the attornies at law.

14th. The want of a sufficient medium of trade, to remedy the mischiefs arising from the scarcity of money.

15th. The General Court sitting in the town of Boston.

16th. The present embarrassments on the press.

17th. The neglect of the settlement of important matters depending between the Commonwealth and Congress, relating to monies and averages.

18th. Voted, This convention recommend to the several towns in this county, that they instruct their Representatives, to use their influence in the next General court, to have emitted a bank of paper money, subject to a depreciation; making it a tender in all payments, equal to silver and gold, to be issued in order to call in the Commonwealth's securities.

19th. Voted, That whereas several of the above articles of grievances, arise from defects in the constitution; therefore a revision of the same ought to take place.

20th. Voted, That it be recommended by this convention to the several towns in this county, that they petition the Govenour to call the General court immediately together, in order that the other grievances complained of, may by the legislature, be redressed.

21st. Voted, That this convention recommend it to the inhabitants of this county, that they abstain from all mobs and unlawful assemblies, until a constitutional method of redress be obtained.

22d. Voted, That Mr. Caleb West be desired to transmit a copy of the proceedings of this convention to the convention of the county of Worcester.

23d. Voted, That the chairman of this convention be desired to transmit a copy of the proceedings of this convention to the county of Berkshire.

24th. Voted, That the chairman of this convention be directed to notify a county convention, upon any motion made to him for that purpose, if he judge the reasons offered be sufficient, giving such notice, together with the reasons therefore, in the publick papers of this county.

25th. Voted, That a copy of the proceedings of this convention be sent to the press in Springfield for publication.

Source: Minot, George Richards. *The History of the Insurrection in Massachusetts in the Year MDCCLXXXVI.* Worcester, MA, 1788, pp. 34–37.

B. George Washington and Thomas Jefferson React to Shays' Rebellion (1786, 1787)

Reproduced here are two letters reacting to Shays' Rebellion—the first from November 1786 by George Washington (1732–1799) and the second from January 1787 by Thomas Jefferson (1743–1826). In his letter to Benjamin Lincoln (1733–1810), Washington expresses alarm at the damage the uprising might do to the young republic. In these excerpts from his letter to James Madison (1751–1836), Jefferson, who was then serving as ambassador to France, found nothing alarming in the rebellion, declaring to Madison "that a little rebellion now and then is a good thing."

1. The Dangers of Rebellion: George Washington's Letter to General Benjamin Lincoln (November 7, 1786)

Mount Vernon 7th. Novr. 1786.

My dear Sir

I have, I think, seen your name mentioned as President of the Society of the Cincinnati in the State of Massachusetts.—For this reason I give you the trouble of the enclosed address.

I hope your wishes were fully accomplished in your Eastern trip.—Are your people getting mad?—Are we to have the goodly fabrick that eight years were spent in rearing pulled over our heads?—What is the cause of all these commotions?—When & how is it to end?

I need not repeat to you how much I am My dear Sir

Y^r. Most Obed^t. & Affect^e. H^{ble}. Servant
G Washington

Source: National Park Service, U.S. Department of the Interior Website. http://www.nps.gov/spar/historyculture/shays-rebellion-documents.htm.

2. The Benefits of Rebellion: Thomas Jefferson's Letter to James Madison (January 30, 1787)

Dear Sir,

My last to you was of the 16th of December; since which, I have received yours of November 25 and December 4, which afforded me, as your letters always do, a treat on matters public, individual, and economical. I am impatient to learn your sentiments on the late troubles in the Eastern states. So far as I have yet seen, they do not appear to threaten serious consequences. Those states have suffered by the stoppage of the channels of their commerce, which have not yet found other issues. This must render money scarce and make the people uneasy. This uneasiness has produced acts absolutely unjustifiable; but I hope they will provoke no severities from their governments. A consciousness of those in power that their administration of the public affairs has been honest may, perhaps, produce too great a degree of indignation; and those characters, wherein fear predominates over hope, may apprehend too much from these instances of irregularity. They may conclude too hastily that nature has formed man insusceptible of any other government than that of force, a conclusion not founded in truth or experience.

Societies exist under three forms, sufficiently distinguishable: (1) without government, as among our Indians; (2) under governments, wherein the will of everyone has a just influence, as is the case in England, in a slight degree, and in our states, in a great one; (3) under governments of force, as is the case in all other monarchies, and in most of the other republics.

To have an idea of the curse of existence under these last, they must be seen. It is a government of wolves over sheep. It is a problem, not clear in my mind, that the first condition is not the best. But I believe it to be inconsistent with any great degree of population. The second state has a great deal of good in it. The mass of mankind under that enjoys a precious degree of liberty and happiness. It has its evils, too, the principal of which is the turbulence to which it is subject. But weigh this against the oppressions of monarchy, and it becomes nothing. *Malo periculosam libertatem quam quietam servitutem.* Even this evil is productive of good. It prevents the degeneracy of government and nourishes a general attention to the public affairs.

I hold it that a little rebellion now and then is a good thing, and as necessary in the political world as storms in the physical. Unsuccessful rebellions, indeed, generally establish the encroachments on the rights of the people which have produced them. An observation of this truth should render honest republican governors so mild in their punishment of rebellions as not to discourage them too much. It is a medicine necessary for the sound health of government.

If these transactions give me no uneasiness, I feel very differently at another piece of intelligence, to wit, the possibility that the navigation of the Mississippi may be abandoned to Spain. . . .

Yours affectionately,
Th. Jefferson

Source: National Park Service, U.S. Department of the Interior Website. http://www
    .nps.gov/spar/historyculture/shays-rebellion-documents.htm.

C. The Land Ordinance of 1785 (May 20, 1785) and the Northwest Ordinance (July 13, 1787)

Even before the successful conclusion of the Revolutionary War ensured American independence, the question of the western land claims of the former colonies required resolution. The cession of claims helped in the creation of the United States under the Articles of Confederation. One of the most important achievements of the Confederation government was the laying out of a plan for the integration of those lands into the United States through a series of thoughtful enactments. Reproduced here are excerpts from the Land Ordinance of 1785 and the Northwest Ordinance of 1787, two of the most important of those measures.

1. LAND ORDINANCE OF 1785

An Ordinance for ascertaining the mode of disposing of Lands in the Western Territory.

Be it ordained by the United States in Congress assembled, that the territory ceded by individual States to the United States, which has been purchased of the Indian inhabitants, shall be disposed of in the following manner:

A surveyor from each state shall be appointed by Congress, or a committee of the States, who shall take an Oath for the faithful discharge of his duty, before the Geographer of the United States. . . .

The Surveyors, as they are respectively qualified, shall proceed to divide the said territory into townships of six miles square, by lines running due north and south, and others crossing these at right angles, as near as may be, unless where the boundaries of the late Indian purchases may render the same impracticable. . . .

There shall be reserved for the United States out of every township, the four lots, being numbered 8, 11, 26, 29, and out of every fractional part of a township, so many lots of the same numbers as shall be found thereon, for future sale. There shall be reserved the lot N 16, of every township, for the maintenance of public schools, within the said township; also one third part of all gold, silver, lead and copper mines, to be sold, or otherwise disposed of as Congress shall hereafter direct. . . .

And whereas Congress by their resolutions of September 16 and 18 in the year 1776, and the 12th of August, 1780, stipulated grants of land to certain officers and soldiers of the late continental army, and by the resolution of the 22d September, 1780, stipulated grants of land to certain officers in the hospital department of the late continental army; for complying therefore with such engagements, Be it ordained, That the secretary at war, from the returns in his office, or such other evidence as the nature of the case may admit, determine who are the objects of the above resolutions and engagements, and the quantity of land to which such persons or their representatives are respectively entitled, and cause the townships, or fractional parts of townships, hereinbefore reserved for the use of the late continental army, to be drawn for in such manner as he shall deem expedient. . . .

Done by the United States in Congress assembled, the 20th day of May, in the year of our Lord 1785, and of our sovereignty and independence the ninth.

Source: Journals of the Continental Congress, 1774–1789. Vol. 28. Edited by Worthington C. Ford, et al. Washington, D.C.: U.S. Government Printing Office, 1904–1937, p. 375ff.

2. Northwest Ordinance (1787)

. . . It is hereby ordained and declared by the authority aforesaid, That the following articles shall be considered as articles of compact between the original States and the people and States in the said territory and forever remain unalterable, unless by common consent, to wit:

Art. 1. No person, demeaning himself in a peaceable and orderly manner, shall ever be molested on account of his mode of worship or religious sentiments, in the said territory.

Art. 2. The inhabitants of the said territory shall always be entitled to the benefits of the writ of habeas corpus, and of the trial by jury; of a proportionate representation of the people in the legislature; and of judicial proceedings according to the course of the common law. . . .

Art. 3. Religion, morality, and knowledge, being necessary to good government and the happiness of mankind, schools and the means of education shall forever be encouraged. The utmost good faith shall always be observed towards the Indians; their lands and property shall never be taken from them without their consent; and, in their property, rights, and liberty, they shall never be invaded or disturbed, unless in just and lawful wars authorized by Congress; but laws founded in justice and humanity, shall from time to time be made for preventing wrongs being done to them, and for preserving peace and friendship with them.

Art. 4. The said territory, and the States which may be formed therein, shall forever remain a part of this Confederacy of the United States of America, subject to the Articles of Confederation, and to such alterations therein as shall be constitutionally made; and to all the acts and ordinances of the United States in Congress assembled, conformable thereto. The inhabitants and settlers in the said territory shall be subject to pay a part of the federal debts contracted or to be contracted, and a proportional part of the expenses of government, to be apportioned on them by Congress according to the same common rule and measure by which apportionments thereof shall be made on the other States; and the taxes for paying their proportion shall be laid and levied by the authority and direction of the legislatures of the district or districts, or new States, as in the original States, within the time agreed upon by the United States in Congress assembled. . . .

Art. 5. There shall be formed in the said territory, not less than three nor more than five States; and the boundaries of the States, as soon as Virginia shall alter her act of cession, and consent to the same, shall become fixed and established. . . . And, whenever any of the said States shall have sixty thousand free inhabitants therein, such State shall be admitted, by its delegates, into the Congress of the United States, on an equal footing with the original States in all respects whatever, and shall be at liberty to form a permanent constitution and State government: Provided, the constitution and government so to be formed, shall be republican, and in conformity to the principles contained in these articles; and, so far as it can be consistent with the general interest of the confederacy, such admission shall be allowed at an earlier period, and when there may be a less number of free inhabitants in the State than sixty thousand.

Art. 6. There shall be neither slavery nor involuntary servitude in the said territory, otherwise than in the punishment of crimes whereof the party shall have been duly convicted: Provided, always, That any person escaping into the same, from whom labor or service is lawfully claimed in any one of the original States, such fugitive may be lawfully reclaimed and conveyed to the person claiming his or her labor or service as aforesaid.

Be it ordained by the authority aforesaid, That the resolutions of the 23rd of April, 1784, relative to the subject of this ordinance, be, and the same are hereby repealed and declared null and void.

Source: Journals of the Continental Congress, 1774–1789. Vol. 32. Edited by Worthington C. Ford, et al. Washington, D.C.: U.S. Government Printing Office, 1904–1937, p. 334ff.

D. Objections to the Federal Constitution: Letters from the Federal Farmer to the Republican (October 8, 1787)

The "Federal Farmer" was an anonymous anti-federalist who published two pamphlets (November 1787, May 1788) opposing ratification of the new U.S. constitution. In the following excerpts from his first pamphlet, the writer argues that the proposed constitution would destroy the authority of sovereign states and the liberties of citizens. Although the identity of the Federal Farmer is unknown, Richard Henry Lee (1732–1794), who proposed the resolution calling for independence in the Continental Congress in 1776, and Melancton Smith (1744–1798), a New York delegate to the Continental Congress, have both been suggested as possibilities. "The Republican," to whom the letters are addressed is thought to be George Clinton (1739–1812), then governor of New York.

Dear Sir,

My letters to you last winter, on the subject of a well balanced national government for the United States, were the result of free enquiry; when I passed from that subject to enquiries relative to our commerce, revenues, past administration, etc. I anticipated the anxieties I feel, on carefully examining the plan of government proposed by the convention. It appears to be a plan retaining some federal features; but to be the first important step, and to aim strongly to one consolidated government of the United States. It leaves the powers of government, and the representation of the people, so unnaturally divided between the general and state governments, that the operations of our system must be very uncertain. My uniform federal attachments, and the interest I have in the protection of property, and a steady execution of the laws, will convince you, that, if I am under any bias at all, it is in favor of any general system which shall promise those advantages. . . .

The present moment discovers a new face in our affairs. Our object has been all along, to reform our federal system, and to strengthen our governments—to establish peace, order and justice in the community—but a new object now presents. The plan of government now proposed is evidently calculated totally to change, in time, our condition as a people. Instead of being thirteen republics, under a federal head, it is clearly designed to make us one consolidated government. Of this, I think, I shall fully convince you, in my following letters on this subject. This consolidation of the states has been the object of several men in this country for some time past. Whether such a change can ever be effected in any manner; whether it can be effected without convulsions and civil wars; whether such a change will not totally destroy the liberties of this country—time only can determine. . . .

Your's &c.
The Federal Farmer.

Source: "Observations Leading to a Fair Examination of the System of Government Proposed by the Late Convention; and to Several Essential and Necessary Alterations to it, In a Number of Letters from the Federal Farmer to the Republican." [author unknown], published as a pamphlet in New York 1788. Available at http://www.constitution.org/afp/fedfar00.htm.

E. The Federalist No. 15: Alexander Hamilton's Objections to the Articles of Confederation (December 1, 1787)

The fifteenth essay of the Federalist Papers, excerpts of which are reproduced below, was written by Alexander Hamilton (c. 1755–1804)—writing under the pseudonym "Publius"—and published on December 1, 1787. Entitled "The Insufficiency of the Present Confederation to Preserve the Union," Federalist No. 15 argues that the Articles of Confederation have failed to provide strong and stable government and will, if not replaced by the new Constitution, lead to financial chaos and political disintegration.

We may indeed with propriety be said to have reached almost the last stage of national humiliation. There is scarcely anything that can wound the pride or degrade the character of an independent nation which we do not experience. Are there engagements to the performance of which we are held by every tie respectable among men? These are the subjects of constant and unblushing violation. Do we owe debts to foreigners and to our own citizens contracted in a time of imminent peril for the preservation of our political existence? These remain without any proper or satisfactory provision for their discharge. Have we valuable territories and important posts in the possession of a foreign power which, by express stipulations, ought long since to have been surrendered? These are still retained, to the prejudice of our interests, not less than of our rights. Are we in a condition to resent or to repel the aggression? We have neither troops, nor treasury, nor government. Are we even in a condition to remonstrate with dignity? The just imputations on our own faith, in respect to the same treaty, ought first to be removed. Are we entitled by nature and compact to a free participation in the navigation of the Mississippi? Spain excludes us from it. Is public credit an indispensable resource in time of public danger? We seem to have abandoned its cause as desperate and irretrievable. Is commerce of importance to national wealth? Ours is at the lowest point of declension. Is respectability in the eyes of foreign powers a safeguard against foreign encroachments? The imbecility of our government even forbids them to treat with us. Our ambassadors abroad are the mere pageants of mimic sovereignty. Is a violent and unnatural decrease in the value of land a symptom of national distress? The price of improved land in most parts of the country is much lower than can be accounted for by the quantity of waste land at market, and can only be fully explained by that want of private and public confidence, which are so alarmingly prevalent among all ranks, and which have a direct tendency to depreciate property of every kind. Is private credit the friend and patron of industry? That most useful kind which relates to borrowing and lending is reduced within the narrowest limits, and this still more from an opinion of insecurity than from the scarcity of money. To shorten an enumeration of particulars which can afford neither pleasure nor instruction, it may in general be demanded, what indication is there of national disorder, poverty, and insignificance that could befall a community so peculiarly blessed with natural advantages as we are, which does not form a part of the dark catalogue of our public misfortunes? . . . .

The great and radical vice in the construction of the existing Confederation is in the principle of LEGISLATION for STATES or GOVERNMENTS, in their CORPORATE or COLLECTIVE CAPACITIES, and as contradistinguished from the INDIVIDUALS of which they consist. Though this principle does not run through all the powers delegated to the Union, yet it pervades and governs those on which the efficacy of the rest depends. Except as to the rule of appointment, the United States has an indefinite discretion to make requisitions for men and money; but they have no authority to raise either, by regulations extending to the individual citizens of America. The consequence of this is, that though in theory their resolutions concerning those objects are laws, constitutionally binding on the members of the Union, yet in practice they are mere recommendations which the States observe or disregard at their option.

It is a singular instance of the capriciousness of the human mind, that after all the admonitions we have had from experience on this head, there should still be found men who object to the new Constitution, for deviating from a principle which has been found the bane of the old, and which is in itself evidently incompatible with the idea of GOVERNMENT; a principle, in short, which, if it is to be executed at all, must substitute the violent and sanguinary agency of the sword to the mild influence of the magistracy.

There is nothing absurd or impracticable in the idea of a league or alliance between independent nations for certain defined purposes precisely stated in a treaty regulating all the details of time, place, circumstance, and quantity; leaving nothing to future discretion; and depending for its execution on the good faith of the parties. Compacts of this kind exist among all civilized nations, subject to the usual vicissitudes of peace and war, of observance and non-observance, as the interests or passions of the contracting powers dictate. . . .

If the particular States in this country are disposed to stand in a similar relation to each other, and to drop the project of a general DISCRETIONARY SUPERINTENDENCE, the scheme would indeed be pernicious, and would entail upon us all the mischiefs which have been enumerated under the first head; but it would have the merit of being, at least, consistent and practicable Abandoning all views towards a confederate government, this would bring us to a simple alliance offensive and defensive; and would place us in a situation to be alternate friends and enemies of each other, as our mutual jealousies and rivalships, nourished by the intrigues of foreign nations, should prescribe to us.

But if we are unwilling to be placed in this perilous situation; if we still will adhere to the design of a national government, or, which is the same thing, of a superintending power, under the direction of a common council, we must resolve to incorporate into our plan those ingredients which may be considered as forming the characteristic difference between a league and a government; we must extend the authority of the Union to the persons of the citizens,—the only proper objects of government. . . .

Publius

Source: Yale Law School. The Avalon Project: Documents in Law, History, and Diplomacy. http://avalon.law.yale.edu/18th_century/fed15.asp.

F. Alexander Hamilton's First Report on the Public Credit (January 14, 1790)

Reproduced here are excerpts from the first of three reports on national economic policy that Alexander Hamilton (c. 1755–1804), President George Washington's secretary of the treasury, submitted to Congress. In this report, Hamilton proposes that all federal debts be paid at face value and that the federal government assume all debts owed by the states, the payments to be financed by the issuance of new government bonds. The large and powerful federal administration required to support the financial system Hamilton envisioned drew much criticism from opponents of strong, centralized government, such as Thomas Jefferson (1743–1826).

. . . As an additional expedient for effecting a reduction of the debt, and for other purposes, which will be mentioned, the Secretary would further propose [that the United States] to borrow . . . a sum not exceeding twelve millions of dollars, to be applied:

First.—To the payment of the interest and instalments of the foreign debt, to the end of the present year, which will require 3,491,932 dollars and 46 cents.

Secondly.—To the payment of any deficiency which may happen in the product of the funds provided for paying the interest of the domestic debt.

Thirdly.—To the effecting a change in the form of such part of the foreign debt as bears an interest of five per cent. It is conceived that for this purpose a new loan at a lower interest may be combined with other expedients. The remainder of this part of the debt, after paying the instalments which will accrue in the course of 1790, will be 3,888,888 dollars and 81 cents.

Fourthly.—To purchase of the public debt, at the price it shall bear in the market, while it continues below its true value. This measure, which would be, in the opinion of the Secretary, highly dishonorable to the Government if it were to precede a provision for funding the debt, would become altogether unexceptionable after that had been made. Its effect would be in favor of the public creditors, as it would tend to raise the value of stock; and all the difference between its true value and the actual price would be so much clear gain to the public. The payment of foreign interest on the capital to be borrowed for this purpose, should that be a necessary consequence, would not, in the judgment of the Secretary, be a good objection to the measure. The saving, by the operation, would be itself a sufficient indemnity; and the employment of that capital, in a country situated like this, would much more than compensate for it. Besides, if the Government does not undertake this operation, the same inconvenience which the objection in question supposes, would happen in another way, with a circumstance of aggravation. As long, at least, as the debt shall continue below its proper value it will be an object of speculation to foreigners, who will not only receive the interest upon what they purchase, and remit it abroad, as in the case of the loan, but will reap the additional profit of the difference in value. By the Government's entering into competition with them, it will not only reap a part of the profit itself, but will contract the extent, and lessen the extra profit of foreign purchases. That competition will accelerate the rise of stock; and whatever greater rate this obliges foreigners to pay for what they purchase, is so much clear saving to the nation. In the opinion of the Secretary, and contrary to an idea which is not without patrons, it ought to be the policy of the Government to raise the value of stock to its true standard as fast as possible. When it arrives to that point, foreign speculations (which, till then, must be deemed pernicious, further than as they serve to bring it to that point) will become beneficial. Their money, laid out in this country upon our agriculture, commerce, and manufactures, will produce much more to us than the income they will receive from it.

The Secretary contemplates the application of this money through the medium of a national bank, for which, with the permission of the House, he will submit a plan in the course of the session.

The Secretary now proceeds, in the last place, to offer to the consideration of the House his ideas of the steps which ought, at the present session, to be taken toward the assumption of the State debts.

These are, briefly, that concurrent resolutions of the two Houses, with the approbation of the President be entered into, declaring in substance:

That the United States do assume, and will, at the first session in the year 1791, provide, on the same terms with the present debt of the United States, for all such parts of the debts of the respective States, or any of them, as shall, prior to the first day of January, in the said year, 1791, be subscribed toward a loan to the United States, upon the principles of either of the plans which shall have been adopted by them, for obtaining a reloan of their present debt.

Provided, that the provision to be made, as aforesaid, shall be suspended, with respect to the debt of any State which may have exchanged the securities of the United States for others issued by itself, until the whole of the said securities shall either be re-exchanged or surrendered to the United States.

And provided, also, that the interest upon the debt assumed, be computed to the end of the year 1791; and that the interest to be paid by the United States commence on the first day of January, 1792.

That the amount of the debt of each State, so assumed and provided for, be charged to such State in account with the United States, upon the same principles upon which it shall be lent to the United States.

That subscriptions be opened for receiving loans of the said debts, at the same times and places, and under the like regulations, as shall have been prescribed in relation to the debt of the United States.

The Secretary has now completed the objects which he proposed to himself to comprise in the present report. He has for the most part omitted details, as well to avoid fatiguing the attention of the House as because more time would have been desirable, even to digest the general principles of the plan. If these should be found right, the particular modifications will readily suggest themselves in the progress of the work.

The Secretary, in the views which have directed his pursuit of the subject, has been influenced, in the first place, by the consideration that his duty, from the very terms of the resolution of the House, obliged him to propose what appeared to him an adequate provision for the support of the public credit, adapted at the same time to the real circumstances of the United States; and, in the next, by the reflection that measures which will not bear the test of future unbiased examination, can neither be productive of individual reputation nor (which is of much greater consequence) public honor or advantage.

Deeply impressed, as the Secretary is, with a full and deliberate conviction that the establishment of the public credit, upon the basis of a satisfactory provision for the public debt, is, under the present circumstances of this country, the true desideratum toward relief from individual and national embarrassments; that without it these embarrassments will be likely to press still more severely upon the community; he cannot but indulge an anxious wish that an effectual plan for that purpose may during the present session be the result of the united wisdom of the Legislature.

He is fully convinced that it is of the greatest importance that no further delay should attend the making of the requisite provision: not only because it will give a better impression of the good faith of the country, and will bring earlier relief to the creditors, both which circumstances are of great moment to public credit, but because the advantages to the community, from raising stock, as speedily as possible, to its natural value, will be incomparably greater than any that can result from its continuance below that standard. No profit which could be derived from purchases in the market, on account of the Government, to any practicable extent, would be an equivalent for the loss which would be sustained by the purchases of foreigners at a low value. Not to repeat, that governmental purchases to be honorable ought to be preceded by a provision. Delay, by disseminating doubt, would sink the price of stock; and, as the temptation to foreign speculations, from the lowness of the price, would be too great to be neglected, millions would probably be lost to the United States.

All of which is humbly submitted.

Alexander Hamilton,
Secretary of the Treasury

Source: Lodge, Henry Cabot, ed. *The Works of Alexander Hamilton.* Vol. 2. New York: G.P. Putnam's Sons, 1904.

G. Alexander Hamilton's Opinion on the Constitutionality of the Bank of the United States (1791)

On February 25, 1791 President George Washington (1732–1799) signed a bill establishing the First Bank of the United States, which, though federally chartered, was a private financial institution. Secretary of the Treasury Alexander Hamilton (c. 1755–1804) proposed and supported the creation of a central bank to stabilize credit and improve management of government finances. Opponents of strong centralized government, such as Thomas Jefferson (1743–1826), attacked the bank as unconstitutional. In the following excerpts from his written opinion upholding the constitutionality of the bank, Hamilton asserts that the federal government does have the power to take actions it deems beneficial to the country so long as they are not specifically prohibited by the Constitution.

The Secretary of the Treasury having perused with attention the papers containing the opinions of the Secretary of State and Attorney General, concerning the constitutionality of the bill for establishing a National Bank, proceeds, according to the order of the President, to submit the reasons which have induced him to entertain a different opinion. . . .

Here then, as far as concerns the reasonings of the Secretary of State and the Attorney General, the affirmative of the constitutionality of the bill might be permitted to rest. It will occur to the President, that the principle here advanced has been untouched by either of them.

For a more complete elucidation of the point, nevertheless, the arguments which they had used against the power of the government to erect corporations, however foreign they are to the great and fundamental rule which has been stated, shall be particularly examined. And after showing that they do not tend to impair its force, it shall also be shown that the power of incorporation, incident to the government in certain cases, does fairly extend to the particular case which is the object of the bill.

The first of these arguments is, that the foundation of the Constitution is laid on this ground: "That all powers not delegated to the United States by the Constitution, nor prohibited to it by the States, are reserved for the States, or to the people." Whence it is meant to be inferred, that Congress can in no case exercise any power not Included in those not enumerated in the Constitution. And it is affirmed, that the power of erecting a corporation is not included in any of the enumerated powers.

The main proposition here laid down, in its true signification is not to be questioned. It is nothing more than a consequence of this republican maxim, that all government is a delegation of power. But how much is delegated in each case, is a question of fact, to be made out by fair reasoning and construction, upon the particular provisions of the Constitution, taking as guides the general principles and general ends of governments.

It is not denied that there are implied well as express powers, and that the former are as effectually delegated as the tatter. And for the sake of accuracy it shall be mentioned, that there is another class of powers, which may be properly denominated resting powers. It will not be doubted, that if the United States should make a conquest of any of the territories of its neighbors, they would possess sovereign jurisdiction over the conquered territory. This would be rather a result, from the whole mass of the powers of the government, and from the nature of political society, than a consequence of either of the powers specially enumerated.

But be this as it may, it furnishes a striking illustration of the general doctrine contended for; it shows an extensive case in which a power of erecting corporations is either implied in or would result from, some or all of the powers vested in the national government. The jurisdiction acquired over such conquered country would certainly be competent to any species of legislation.

To return: It is conceded that implied powers are to be considered as delegated equally with express ones. Then it follows, that as a power of erecting a corporation may as well be implied as any other thing, it may as well be employed as an instrument or mean of carrying into execution any of the specified powers, as any other instrument or mean whatever. The only question must be in this, as in every other case, whether the mean to be employed or in this instance, the corporation to be erected, has a natural relation to any of the acknowledged objects or lawful ends of the government. Thus a corporation may not be erected by Congress for superintending the police of the city of Philadelphia, because they are not authorized to regulate the police of that city. But one may be erected in relation to the collection of taxes, or to the trade with foreign countries, or to the trade between the States, or with the Indian tribes; because it is the province of the federal government to regulate those objects, and because it is incident to a general sovereign or legislative power to regulate a thing, to employ all the means which relate to its regulation to the best and greatest advantage.

A strange fallacy seems to have crept into the manner of thinking and reasoning upon the subject. Imagination appears to have been unusually busy concerning it. An incorporation seems to have been regarded as some great independent substantive thing; as a political end of peculiar magnitude and moment; whereas it is truly to be considered as a quality, capacity, or mean to an end. Thus a mercantile company is formed, with a certain capital, for the purpose of carrying on a particular branch of business. Here the business to be prosecuted is the end. The association, in order to form the requisite capital, is the primary mean. Suppose that an incorporation were added to this, it would only be to add a new quality to that association, to give it an artificial capacity, by which it would be enabled to prosecute the business with more safety and convenience.

That the importance of the power of incorporation has been exaggerated, leading to erroneous conclusions, will further appear from tracing it to its origin. The Roman law is the source of it, according to which a voluntary association of individuals, at any time, or for any purpose, was capable of producing it. In England, whence our notions of it are immediately borrowed, it forms part of the executive authority, and the exercise of it has been often delegated by that authority. Whence, therefore, the ground of the supposition that it lies beyond the reach of all those very important portions of sovereign power, legislative as well as executive, which belongs to the government of the United States.

To this mode of reasoning respecting the right of employing all the means requisite to the execution of the specified powers of the government, it is objected, that none but necessary and proper means are to be employed; and the Secretary of State maintains, that no means are to be considered as necessary but those without which the grant of the power would be nugatory. Nay, so far does he go in his restrictive interpretation of the word, as even to make the case of necessity which shall warrant the constitutional exercise of the power to depend on casual and temporary circumstances; an idea which alone refutes the construction. The expediency of exercising a particular power, at a particular time, must, indeed depend on circumstances, but the constitutional right of exercising it must be uniform and invariable, the same to-day as to-morrow.

All the arguments, therefore, against the constitutionality of the bill derived from the accidental existence of certain State banks, institutions which happen to exist to-day, and, for aught that concerns the government of the United States, may disappear tomorrow, must not only be rejected as fallacious, but must be viewed as demonstrative that there is a radical source of error in the reasoning.

It is essential to the being of the national government, that so erroneous a conception of the meaning of the word necessary should be exploded.

Source: Ford, Paul Leicester, ed. *The Federalist: A Commentary on the Constitution of the United States by Alexander Hamilton, James Madison and John Jay.* New York: Henry Holt and Company, 1898; Yale Law School. The Avalon Project: Documents in Law, History, and Diplomacy. http://avalon.law.yale.edu/18th_century/bank-ah.asp.

H. Thomas Jefferson's Opinion on the Constitutionality of the Bank of the United States (1791)

Thomas Jefferson (1743–1826), supported by fellow Virginian James Madison (1751–1836), opposed the proposal of Secretary of the Treasury Alexander Hamilton (c. 1755–1804) for congressional chartering of a central bank. The Virginians believed a central bank would enhance the power of the federal government, harm state banks, and benefit commercial northern interests at the expense of the agrarian South. In the excerpts below from his written opinion on the constitutionality of the bank, Jefferson argues that the bank threatens traditional property rights and that its chartering is not within the specified powers of Congress as laid out in the Constitution. For Jefferson, any powers not so specified were reserved to the people and thus beyond the scope of Congress. President George Washington (1732–1799) signed the bill creating the First Bank of the United States in February 1791.

The bill for establishing a National Bank undertakes among other things:

1. To form the subscribers into a corporation.
2. To enable them in their corporate capacities to receive grants of land; and so far is against the laws of *Mortmain.*
3. To make alien subscribers capable of holding lands, and so far is against the laws of *Alienage.*
4. To transmit these lands, on the death of a proprietor, to a certain line of successors; and so far changes the course of *Descents.*
5. To put the lands out of the reach of forfeiture or escheat, and so far is against the laws of *Forfeiture and Escheat.*

6. To transmit personal chattels to successors in a certain line and so far is against the laws of *Distribution*.
7. To give them the sole and exclusive right of banking under the national authority; and so far is against the laws of Monopoly.
8. To communicate to them a power to make laws paramount to the laws of the States; for so they must be construed, to protect the institution from the control of the State legislatures, and so, probably, they will be construed.

I consider the foundation of the Constitution as laid on this ground: That "all powers not delegated to the United States, by the Constitution, nor prohibited by it to the States, are reserved to the States or to the people." [XIIth amendment.] To take a single step beyond the boundaries thus specially drawn around the powers of Congress, is to take possession of a boundless field of power, no longer susceptible of any definition.

The incorporation of a bank, and the powers assumed by this bill, have not, in my opinion, been delegated to the United States, by the Constitution.

I.

1. They are not among the powers specially enumerated: for these are: 1st A power to lay taxes for the purpose of paying the debts of the United States; but no debt is paid by this bill, nor any tax laid. Were it a bill to raise money, its origination in the Senate would condemn it by the Constitution.
2. "To borrow money." But this bill neither borrows money nor ensures the borrowing it. The proprietors of the bank will be just as free as any other money holders, to lend or not to lend their money to the public. The operation proposed in the bill first, to lend them two millions, and then to borrow them back again, cannot change the nature of the latter act, which will still be a payment, and not a loan, call it by what name you please.
3. To "regulate commerce with foreign nations, and among the States, and with the Indian tribes." To erect a bank, and to regulate commerce, are very different acts. He who erects a bank, creates a subject of commerce in its bills, so does he who makes a bushel of wheat, or digs a dollar out of the mines; yet neither of these persons regulates commerce thereby. To make a thing which may be bought and sold, is not to prescribe regulations for buying and selling. Besides, if this was an exercise of the power of regulating commerce, it would be void, as extending as much to the internal commerce of every State, as to its external. For the power given to Congress by the Constitution does not extend to the internal regulation of the commerce of a State, (that is to say of the commerce between

citizen and citizen,) which remain exclusively with its own legislature; but to its external commerce only, that is to say, its commerce with another State, or with foreign nations, or with the Indian tribes. Accordingly the bill does not propose the measure as a regulation of trace, but as "productive of considerable advantages to trade." Still less are these powers covered by any other of the special enumerations. . . .

Source: Ford, Paul Leicester, ed. *The Federalist: A Commentary on the Constitution of the United States by Alexander Hamilton, James Madison and John Jay.* New York: Henry Holt and Company, 1898; Yale Law School. The Avalon Project: Documents in Law, History, and Diplomacy. http://avalon.law.yale.edu/18th_century/bank-tj.asp.

2. The Embargo Era, 1807–1809

A. James Stephen's Pamphlet Arguing for Restriction of Neutral Rights (1805)

In 1805 James Stephen (1758–1832), a noted maritime lawyer and active supporter and brother-in-law of antislavery agitator William Wilberforce (1759–1833), published a pamphlet arguing the justice of restricting such neutral traders as the Americans. Stephen's pamphlet, which is excerpted below, was so influential that he is often considered the origin of the Orders in Council restricting neutral rights that were subsequently issued by the British government.

Let us next enquire what use has been made by neutral merchants, of the indulgences which the British government has thus liberally granted.—We have suffered neutrals to trade with the colonies of our enemy, directly to or from the ports of their own respective countries, but not to or from any other part of the world, England, during the last war, excepted. Have they been content to observe the restriction? . . .

The chief danger of our so far receding from the full extent of our belligerent rights, as to allow the neutral states to import directly the produce of the hostile colonies, was that it might be re-exported, and sent either to the mother country in Europe, or to neighbouring neutral ports, from which the produce itself, or its proceeds, might be easily remitted to the hostile country; in which case our enemies would scarcely feel any serious ill effect from the war. . . .

To the Americans especially, whether dealing on their own account, or as secret agents of the enemy, the profit would have been comparatively small, and the business itself inconsiderable, had they not been allowed to send forward to Europe, at least in a circuitous way, the produce they brought from the islands. The obligation of first importing into their own country, wan as inconvenience which their geographical position made of little moment; but the European, and not the American market, was that in which alone the ultimate profit could be reaped. . . .

From these causes it has naturally happened that the protection given by the American flag, to the intercourse between our European enemies and their colonies, since the instruction of January, 1794, has chiefly been in the way of a double voyage, in which America has been the half-way house, or central point of communication. The fabrics and commodities of France, Spain, and Holland, have been brought under American colours to ports in the United States; and from thence re-exported, under the same flag, for the supply of hostile colonies. Again, the produce of those colonies has been brought, in a like manner, to the American ports. . . .

By the merchants, and custom-house officers of the United States, the line of neutral duty in this case was evidently not misconceived; for the departures from it, were carefully concealed, by artful and fraudulent contrivance. When a ship arrived at one of their ports to neutralize a voyage that fell within the restriction, e.g., from a Spanish colony to Spain, all her papers were immediately sent on shore, or destroyed. Not one document was left, which could disclose the fact that her cargo had been taken in at a colonial port: and new bills of lading, invoices, clearances, and passports were put on board, all importing that it had been shipped in America. Nor were official certificates, or oaths wanting, to support the fallacious pretence. The fraudulent precaution of the agents often went so far, as to discharge all the officers and crew, and sometimes even the master, and to ship an entire new company in their stead, who, being ignorant of the former branch of the voyage, could, in case of examination or capture, support the new papers by their declarations and oaths, as far as their knowledge extended, with a safe conscience. Thus, the ship and cargo were sent to sea again, perhaps within eight and forty hours from the time of her arrival, in a condition to defy the scrutiny of any British cruiser. . . .

With such facilities, it is not strange that this fraudulent practice should have prevailed. . . .

Accordingly, in the class of cases we are considering, it was held of great importance to shew, that the cargo had been landed in the neutral port, that the duties on importation had been paid, and that the first insurance had been made for a voyage to terminate in the neutral country. . . .

The landing the cargo in America, and re-shipping it in the same bottom, were no very costly precautions for better securing the merchant against the peril of capture and detection in the latter branch of these important voyages. . . .

The laying a foundation for the necessary evidence, in regard to insurance, was a still easier work: for though at first they sometimes insured the whole intended voyage, with liberty to touch in America, it was afterwards found, in consequence perhaps of the captures and discoveries we have noticed, to be much safer for the underwriters, and consequently cheaper in point of premium to the owners, to insure separately the two branches of the voyage; in which case, America necessarily appeared by the policies on the first branch, to be the ultimate destination; and on the last, to be that of original shipment.

The payment of duties, then, was the only remaining badge of the simulated intention for which the merchants had to provide; and here they found facilities from the port officers and government of the United States, such as obviated every inconvenience. On the arrival of a cargo destined for re-exportation in the course of this indirect commerce, they were allowed to land the goods, and even to put them in private warehouses, without paying any part of the duties; and without any further trouble, than that of giving a bond, with condition that if the goods should not be re-exported the duties should be paid. On their re-shipment and exportation, official clearances were given, in which no mention was made that the cargo consisted of bonded or debentured goods, which had previously been entered for re-exportation; but the same general forms were used, as on an original shipment of goods which had actually paid duties in America. Nor was this all; for, in the event of capture and further inquiry respecting the importation into America, the collectors and other officers were accommodating enough solemnly to certify, that the duties had been actually paid or secured to the United States; withholding the fact, that the bonds had been afterwards discharged on the production of debentures, or other official instruments, certifying the re-exportation of the goods. . . .

Source: Stephen, James. *War in Disguise; or, the Frauds of the Neutral Flags.* London, 1805, 36–121 passim.

B. Napoleon's Berlin and Milan Decrees (November 21, 1806; December 17, 1807)

Issued by Napoleon I (1769–1821), emperor of France, in November 1806, the Berlin Decree banned all trade with Britain by all French, allied, and neutral vessels. Because the destruction of a Franco-Spanish fleet at the Battle of Trafalgar in 1805 ended French plans to invade Britain, Napoleon sought instead to destroy Britain's economy by crippling her trade and reducing her access to credit. The British responded to the Berlin Decree with new Orders in Council, which prohibited French trade with Britain, her allies, and neutrals, and ordered the British navy to blockade French and allied ports. Napoleon replied in December 1807 with his Milan Decree, which declared that all neutral vessels entering British ports or paying British duties would be considered British and seized. The

Napoleonic decrees and the British Orders in Council had a devastating economic impact on the United States, one of the largest neutral trading nations.

1. The Berlin Decree

From our Imperial Camp at Berlin, November 21, 1806. . . .

Art. I. The British islands are declared in a state of blockade.

II. All commerce and correspondence with the British islands are prohibited. In consequence, letters or packets, addressed either to England, to an Englishman, or in the English language, shall not pass through the post-office and shall be seized.

III. Every subject of England, of whatever rank and condition soever, who shall be found in the countries occupied by our troops, or by those of our allies, shall be made a prisoner of war.

IV. All magazines, merchandise, or property whatsoever, belonging to a subject of England, shall be declared lawful prize.

V. The trade in English merchandise is forbidden; all merchandise belonging to England, or coming from its manufactories and colonies, is declared lawful prize.

VI. One half of the proceeds of the confiscation of the merchandise and property; declared good prize by the preceding articles, shall be applied to indemnify the merchants for the losses which they have suffered by the capture of merchant vessels by English cruisers.

VII. No vessel coming directly from England, or from the English colonies, or having been there since the publication of the present decree, shall be received into any port.

VIII. Every vessel contravening the above clause, by means of a false declaration, shall be seized, and the vessel and cargo confiscated, as if they were English property.

IX. Our tribunal of prizes at Paris is charged the definitive adjudication of all the controversies, which by the French army, relative to the execution of the present decree. Our tribunal of prizes at Milan shall be charged with the definitive adjudication of the said controversies, which may arise within the extent of our kingdom of Italy.

X. The present decree shall be communicated by our minister of exterior relations, to the kings of Spain, of Naples, of Holland, and of Etruria, and to our allies, whose subjects, like ours, are the victims of the injustice and the barbarism of the English maritime laws.

XI. Our ministers of foreign affairs, of war, of the navy, of finance, of the police, and our post masters general, are charged each, in what concerns him, with the execution of the present decree.

Source: State Papers and Publick Documents of the United States. Vol. V. Boston: T.B. Wait and Sons, 1817, 478.

2. THE MILAN DECREE

Napoleon, Emperor of the French, King of Italy, Protector of the Confederation of the Rhine.

In view of the measures adopted by the British government on the 11th of November last by which vessels belonging to powers which are neutral or are friendly and even allied with England are rendered liable to be searched by British cruisers, detained at certain stations in England, and subject to an arbitrary tax of a certain per cent upon their cargo to be regulated by English legislation;

Considering that by these acts the English government has denationalized the vessels of all the nations of Europe and that no government may compromise in any degree its independence or its rights—all the rulers of Europe being jointly responsible for the sovereignty and independence of their flags—and that, if through unpardonable weakness which would be regarded by posterity as an indelible stain, such tyranny should be admitted and become consecrated by custom, the English would take steps to give it the force of law, as they have already taken advantage of the toleration of the governments to establish the infamous principle that the flag does not cover the goods and to give the right of blockade an arbitrary extension which threatens the sovereignty of every state;

We have decreed and do decree as follows:

Article 1. Every vessel of whatever nationality, which shall submit to be searched by an English vessel or shall consent to a voyage to England or shall pay any tax whatever to the English government, is ipso facto declared denationalized, loses the protection afforded by its flag, and becomes English property.

Article 2. Should such vessels which are thus denationalized through the arbitrary measures of the English government enter our ports or those of our allies or fall into the hands of our ships of war or of our privateers, they shall be regarded as good and lawful prizes.

Article 3. The British Isles are proclaimed to be in a state of blockade both by land and by sea. Every vessel of whatever nation or whatever may be its cargo that sails from the ports of England or from those of the English colonies or of countries occupied by English troops or is bound for England or for any of the English colonies or any country occupied by English troops becomes, by violating the present decree, a lawful prize and may be captured by our ships of war and adjudged to the captor.

Article 4. These measures, which are only a just retaliation against the barbarous system adopted by the English government, which models its legislation upon that of Algiers, shall cease to have any effect in the case of those nations which shall force the English to respect their flags. They shall continue in force so long as that government shall refuse to accept the principles of international law which regulate the relations of civilized states in a state of war. The provisions of the present decree shall be ipso facto abrogated and void so soon as the English government shall abide again by the principles of the law of nations, which are at the same time those of justice and honor.

Article 5. All our ministers are charged with the execution of the present decree, which shall be printed in the *Bulletin des lois.*

Napoleon

Source: State Papers and Publick Documents of the United States. Vol. VI. Boston: T.B. Wait and Sons, 1817, 74.

C. British Order in Council (January 7, 1807)

An order in council is a British government decree, roughly analogous to an American executive order, which defines and declares government policy. In American history, the Orders in Council were a series of such decrees issued between 1793 and 1812 for the purpose of restricting trade with and enforcing a blockade of Revolutionary and Napoleonic France, with which Britain was at war. British enforcement of the orders severely damaged American trade, causing much friction between the United States and Britain and becoming a chief cause of the Anglo-American War of 1812. Reproduced below is the British Order in Council of January 1807 declaring the blockade of France.

Whereas the French Government has issued certain orders, which, in violation of the usages of war, purport to prohibit the commerce of all neutral nations with His Majesty's dominions, and also to prevent such nations from trading with any other country in any articles, the growth, produce, or manufacture of His Majesty's dominions; and whereas the said Government has also taken upon itself to declare all His Majesty's dominions to be in a state of blockade, at the time when the fleets of France and her allies are themselves confined within their own ports by the superior valor and discipline of the

British navy; and whereas such attempts, on the part of the enemy, would give to His Majesty an unquestioned right or retaliation, and would warrant His Majesty in enforcing the same prohibition of all commerce with France, which that power vainly hopes to effect against the commerce of His Majesty's subjects, a prohibition which the superiority of His Majesty's naval forces might enable him to support by actually investing the ports and coasts of the enemy with numerous squadrons and cruisers, so as to make the entrance or approach thereto manifestly dangerous; and whereas His Majesty, though unwilling to follow the example of his enemies by proceeding to an extremity so distressing to all nations not engaged in the war, and carrying on their accustomed trade, yet feels himself bound, by due regard to the just defense of the rights and interests of his people not to suffer such measures to be taken by the enemy, without taking some steps on his part to restrain this violence, and to retort upon them the evils of their own injustice; His Majesty is thereupon pleased, by and with the advice of his privy council, to order, and it is hereby ordered, that no vessels shall be permitted to trade from one port to another, both which ports shall belong to or be in the possession of France or her allies, or shall be so far under their control as that British vessels may not trade freely thereat; and the commanders of His Majesty's ships of war and privateers shall be, and are hereby, instructed to warn every neutral vessel coming from any such port and destined to another such port, to discontinue her voyage, and not to proceed to any such port; and any vessel, after being so warned, or any vessel coming from any such port, after a reasonable time shall have been afforded for receiving information of this His Majesty's order, which shall be found proceeding to another such port, shall be captured and brought in, and together with her cargo shall be condemned as lawful prize; and His Majesty's principal Secretaries of State, the Lords Commissioners of the Admiralty, and the Judges of the High Court of Admiralty, and the Courts of Vice-admiralty are to take the necessary measures herein as to them shall respectively appertain.

Source: Lowrie, Walter, and Matthew St. Clair Clarke, eds. *American State Papers, Foreign Relations.* Vol. III. Washington, D.C., 1832, 267.

D. Act to Prohibit the Importation of Slaves (March 2, 1807)

In March 1807 President Thomas Jefferson (1743–1826) signed an act ending the importation of slaves into the United States. The act declared that as of January 1, 1808, the earliest date allowed by the U.S. Constitution, African slaves could no longer be transported to or sold in the country. Because the international slave trade was highly lucrative, the act was not always well enforced and, of course, slavery itself continued in the United States.

An Act to Prohibit the Importation of Slaves into any Port or Place Within the Jurisdiction of the United States, From and After the First Day of January, in the Year of our Lord One Thousand Eight Hundred and Eight

Be it enacted by the Senate and House of Representatives of the United States of America in Congress assembled, That from and after the first day of January, one thousand eight hundred and eight, it shall not be lawful to import or bring into the United States or the territories thereof from any foreign kingdom, place, or country, any negro, mulatto, or person of colour, with intent to hold, sell, or dispose of such negro, mulatto, or person of colour, as a slave, or to be held to service or labour.

SEC 2. *And be it further enacted,* That no citizen or citizens of the United States, or any other person, shall, from arid after the first day of January, in the year of our Lord one thousand eight hundred and eight, for himself, or themselves, or any other person whatsoever, either as master, factor, or owner, build, fit, equip, load or otherwise prepare any ship or vessel, in any port or place within the jurisdiction of the United States, nor shall cause any ship or vessel to sail from any port or place within the same, for the purpose of procuring any negro, mulatto, or person of colour, from any foreign kingdom, place, or country, to be transported to any port or place whatsoever, within the jurisdiction of the United States, to be held, sold, or disposed of as slaves, or to be held to service or labour: and if any ship or vessel shall be so fitted out for the purpose aforesaid, or shall be caused to sail so as aforesaid, every such ship or vessel, her tackle, apparel, and furniture, shall be forfeited to the United States, and shall be liable to be seized, prosecuted, and condemned in any of the circuit courts or district courts, for the district where the said ship or vessel may be found or seized.

SEC. 3. *And be it further enacted,* That all and every person so building, fitting out, equipping, loading, or otherwise preparing or sending away, any ship or vessel, knowing or intending that the same shall be employed in such trade or business, from and after the first day of January, one thousand eight hundred and eight, contrary to the true intent and meaning of this act, or any ways aiding or abetting therein, shall severally forfeit and pay twenty thousand dollars, one moiety thereof to the use of the United States, and the other moiety to the use of any person or persons who shall sue for and prosecute the same to effect. . . .

APPROVED, March 2, 1807.

Source: United States Statutes at Large, 9th Congress, 2nd Session, Chapter 22, 426; Yale Law School. The Avalon Project: Documents in Law, History, and Diplomacy. http://avalon.law.yale.edu/19th_century/sl004.asp.

E. Report of the *Chesapeake*'s Encounter with the *Leopard* (June 23, 1807)

On June 22, 1807, in the waters off Norfolk, Virginia, the British warship Leopard, *seeking British deserters, attacked and boarded the American frigate* Chesapeake, *commanded by James Barron (1769–1851), who was caught unprepared and surrendered his vessel after firing only one shot. The British seized and tried four members of Barron's crew for desertion from the British navy, hanging one aboard the* Leopard. *The* Chesapeake *was released, but Barron was subsequently court-martialed and removed from his command. The British refusal to end the seizure of seamen from American vessels, despite the outrage the* Chesapeake-Leopard *affair aroused in the United States, led President Thomas Jefferson (1743–1826) to propose his embargo as a way to avoid further such incidents. Reproduced here is the report written by Barron on the day after his encounter with the* Leopard.

United States frigate, Chesapeake, Chesapeake Bay, *June 23, 1807.*
Sir:

Yesterday at 6., a.m., the wind became favorable, and knowing your anxiety that the ship should sail with all possible dispatch, we weighed from our station in Hampton Roads and stood to sea. In Lynnhaven bay we passed two British men of war, one of them the Bellona, the other the Melampus; their colors flying, and their appearance friendly. Some time afterwards, we observed one of the two line-of-battle ships that lay off Cape Henry to get under way, and stand to sea; at this time the wind became light, and it was not until near four in the afternoon that the ship under way came within hail. Cape Henry then bearing northwest by west, distance three leagues, the communication, which appeared to be her commander's object for speaking the Chesapeake, he said he would send on board; on which I ordered the Chesapeake to be hove to for his convenience. On the arrival of the officer he presented me with the enclosed paper from the captain of Leopard, and a copy of an order from Admiral Berkeley, which another officer afterwards took back, to which I gave the enclosed answer, and was waiting for his reply. About this time I observed some appearance of a hostile nature, and said to Captain Gordon that it was possible they were serious, and requested him to have his men sent to their quarters with as little noise as possible, not using those ceremonies which we should have done with an avowed enemy, as I fully supposed their arrangements were more menace than any thing serious. Captain Gordon immediately gave orders to the officers and men to go to quarters, and have all things in readiness; but before a match could be lighted, or the quarter-bill of any division examined, or the lumber on the gun-deck, such as sails, cables, &c., could be cleared, the commander of the Leopard Hailed; I could not hear what he said, and was talking to him, as I supposed, when she commenced a heavy fire, which did great execution.

It is distressing to me to acknowledge, that I found the advantage they had gained over our unprepared and unsuspicious state, did not warrant a longer opposition; nor should I have exposed this ship and crew to so galling a fire had it not been with the hope of getting the gun-deck clear, so as to have made a more formidable defence; consequently our resistance was byt feeble. In about twenty minutes after I ordered the colors to be struck, and sent Lieutenant Smith on board the Leopard to inform her commander that I considered the Chesapeake her prize. To this message I received no answer; the Leopard's boat soon after came on board, and the officer who came in her demanded the muster book. I replied the ship and books were theirs, and if he expected to see the men he must find them. They called on the purser who delivered his book, and the men were examined; and the three demanded at Washington, and one man more, were taken away. On their departure from the ship I wrote the commander of the Leopard . . . . On finding that the men were his only object, and that he refused to consider the ship his prize, and the officers and crew his prisoners, I called a council of our officers, and requested their opinion relative to the conduct it was now our duty to pursue. The result was that the ship should return to Hampton Roads, and there wait your further orders, Enclosed you have a list of the unfortunate killed and wounded, as also a statement of the damage sustained . . . .

With great respect, I have the honor to be, sir, your obedient servant,

James Barron.

Hon. Robert Smith, *Secretary of the Navy, Washington.*

Source: Lowrie, Walter, and Matthew St. Clair Clarke, eds. *American State Papers.* Vol. III. Washington, D.C.: Gales and Seaton, 1832, 18.

F. Embargo Act (December 22, 1807)

President Thomas Jefferson (1743–1826) recommended an embargo of U.S. trade in a message to Congress on December 18, 1807. The administration's embargo bill passed the Senate by a vote of 22-6 on that same day and it passed the House by a vote of 82-14 on December 21. Over the strenuous objections of representatives from the commercial states, the president signed the Embargo Act, reproduced here, into law on December 22, 1807.

An Act laying an Embargo on all ships and vessels in the ports and harbors of the United States.

Be it enacted, That an embargo be, and hereby is laid on all ships and vessels in the ports and places within the limits or jurisdiction of the United States, cleared or not cleared, bound to any foreign port or place; and that no clearance be furnished to any ship or vessel bound to such foreign port or place, except vessels under the immediate direction of the President of the United States: and that the President be authorized to give such instructions to officers of the revenue, and of the navy and revenue cutters of the United States, as shall appear best adapted for carrying the same into full effect: *Provided,* that nothing herein contained shall be construed to prevent the departure of any foreign ship or vessel, either in ballast, or with the goods, wares and merchandise on board of such foreign ship or vessel, when notified of this act.

Sec. 2. That during the continuance of this act, no registered, or sea letter vessel, having on board goods, wares and merchandise, shall be allowed to depart from one port of the United States to any other within the same, unless the master, owner, consignee or factor of such vessel first give bond, with one or more sureties to the collector of the district from which she is bound to depart, in a sum of double the value of the vessel and cargo, that the said goods, wares, or merchandise shall be relanded in some port of the United States, dangers of the seas excepted, which bond, and also a certificate from the collector where the same may be relanded, shall by the collector respectively be transmitted to the Secretary of the Treasury. All armed vessels possessing public commissions from any foreign power, are not to be considered as liable to the embargo laid by this act.

Source: United States Statutes at Large. Vol. II. Edited by Richard Peters. Boston: Charles C. Little and James Brown, 1845, 451–53.

G. Secretary Madison's List of Restrictions on Foreign Trade (December 21, 1808)

In December 1808 James Madison (1751–1836), then secretary of state, composed this list of British and French restrictions on foreign trade imposed between the start of the Anglo-French war in 1793 and the end of 1808. Madison intended the list as a means of supporting the Jefferson administration's Embargo Act. Although supposedly directed indiscriminately at all neutral trade, the restrictions fell most heavily on the trade of the United States, which was by far the most active trader among the neutral nations.

Department of State, December 21, 1808

The Secretary of State, in pursuance of the resolution of the Senate of the 14th of November, respectfully reports to the President of the United States copies of such belligerent acts, decrees, orders, and proclamations as affect neutral rights of commerce, and as have been attainable in the Department of State, with the exception, however, of sundry acts, particularly blockades, of doubtful import or inferior importance, which it was supposed would have inconveniently extended the delay and the size of the report.

JAMES MADISON

I. THE ACTS, ORDERS IN COUNCIL, &C. OF GREAT BRITAIN.

1793,	March 25.	Extract from the Russian treaty.
	May 25.	" " Spanish.
	July 14.	" " Prussian.
	August 30.	" " Austrian.
1793,	June 8.	Additional instructions with respect to corn, meal &c.
	Nov. 6.	Detention of neutral vessels, laden with French colonial productions, &c.
1794,	January 8.	Revocation of the last order, and the enactment of new regulations.
1798,	January 25.	Revocation of the last one, and the enactment of new regulations.
1799,	March 22.	Blockade of all the ports of Holland.
	Nov. 27.	Suspension of the blockade of Holland.
1803,	June 24.	Direct trade between neutrals and the colonies of enemies not to be interrupted, unless, upon the outward voyage, contraband supplies shall have been furnished by the neutrals.
1804,	April 12.	Instructions concerning blockades, communicated by Mr. Merry.
	" "	Conversion of the blockade of Curaçoa onto a blockade.
	Aug. 9.	Blockade of Fécamp, &c.
1805,	Aug. 17.	Direct trade with enemy's colonies subjected to restrictions, &c.
1806,	April 8.	Blockade of the Ems, Weser, &c.
	May 16.	Blockade from the Elbe to Brest.
	Sept. 25.	Discontinuance of the last blockade in part.
1807,	January 7.	Interdiction of the trade, from port to port, of France.
	June 26.	Blockade of the Ems, &c.
	Oct. 16.	Proclamation recalling seamen.
	Nov. 11.	Three orders in council.
	" 25.	Six do. do.
1808,	Jan 2.	Blockade of Carthagena, &c.
	March 28.	Act of Parliament for carrying orders of council into effect.

April 11.	Order in council permitting neutral vessels, without papers, to carry supplies to the West Indies.
" 14.	Act of Parliament prohibiting importation of cotton, wool, &c.
" "	Act of parliament making valid certain orders in council.
May 4.	Blockade of Copenhagen and of the island of Zealand.
June 23.	Act of Parliament regulating trade between the United States and Great Britain.
Oct. 14.	Admiral Cochrane's blockade of French Leeward islands. . . .

II. THE DECREES OF FRANCE

1793, May 9. Authorizes French vessels to arrest and bring into the ports of the republic vessels laden with provisions destined for an enemy port.

1793, May 23. Exempts American vessels from the operation of the decree of the 9th.

1793, May 28. Suspends the decree of the 23d of May.

1793, July 1. The decree of the 23d again enforced.

1793, July 27. The decree of the 23d of May repealed, and that of the 9th of May enforced.

1794, November 18, (25th Brumaire 3d year.) General regulations the most important is, that merchandise belonging to the enemy is made liable to seizure in neutral vessels, until the enemy shall exempt from seizure French merchandise similarly situated.

1795, January 3, (14th Nivose 3d year.) Repeals the fifth article of the above, and exempts enemy goods from capture in neutral vessels.

1796, July 2, (14th Messidor, 4th year.) The French will treat neutral nations as they suffer themselves to be treated by the English.

1797, March 2, (17th Ventose, 5th year.) Enemy's property in neutral vessels liable to confiscation; makes necessary roles d'équipages.

1798, January 18, (29th Nivose, 6th year.) The character of vessels to be determined by that of their cargoes.

1799, March 18, (28th Ventose, 7th year.) Explains the fourth article of the decree of the 2d of March 1797.

1799, October 29, (8th Brumaire, 7th year.) Neutrals found on board enemy vessels liable to be treated as pirates.

1799, November 14, (24th Brumaire, 7th year.) Suspends the operation of the above decree of the 29th of October.

1800, December 13, (23d Frimaire, 8th year.) Repeals the first article of the law of the (29th Nivose, 6th year,) 18th January, 1798.

1800,   December 19, (29th Frimaire, 8th year.)   Enforces the regulations of
        the 26th of July, 1778.
1806,   November 21.   Berlin decree.
1807,   December 17.   Milan decree.
1808,   April 17.   Bayone decree. . . .

Source: Lowrie, Walter, and Matthew St. Clair Clarke, eds. *American State Papers,*
   Foreign Relations. Vol. III. Washington, D.C., 1832, 262–92 passim.

H. The Non-Intercourse Act (March 1, 1809)

Because of strong opposition to the Embargo Act, President Thomas Jefferson
(1743–1826) signed, only days before leaving office in 1809, the Non-Intercourse
Act, which replaced the Embargo Act's prohibition of all American trade with
prohibitions only of direct trade with Britain or France. The act was an attempt
to deprive the British and French of American trade and thus compel them to
lift their restrictions on neutral trade, which had so harmed the American econ-
omy. Like the Embargo Act, the Non-Intercourse Act, which is excerpted below,
was impossible to enforce and more detrimental to the American economy than
to the economies of either Britain or France.

An ACT to interdict the commercial intercourse between the United States
and Great Britain and France, and their dependencies; and for other purposes.

Be it enacted . . . , That from and after the passing of this act, the entrance
of the harbors and waters of the United States and of the territories thereof,
be, and the same is hereby interdicted to all public ships and vessels belonging
to Great Britain or France, excepting vessels only which may be forced in by
distress, or which are charged with despatches or business from the government to which they belong, and also packets having no cargo nor merchandise
on board And if any public ship or vessel as aforesaid, not being included in
the exception above mentioned, shall enter any harbor or waters within the
jurisdiction of the United States. or of the territories thereof, it shall be lawful
for the President of the United States, or such other person as he shall have
empowered for that purpose, to employ such part of the land and naval forces,
or of the militia of the United States, or the territories thereof, as he shall deem
necessary, to compel such ship or vessel to depart.
SEC. 2. And be it further enacted, That it shall not be lawful for any citizen
or citizens of the United States or the territories thereof, nor for any person
or persons residing or being in the same, to have any intercourse with, or to
afford any aid or supplies to any public ship or vessel as aforesaid, which shall,
contrary to the provisions of this act, have entered any harbor or waters within

the jurisdiction of the United States or the territories thereof; and if any person shall, contrary to the provisions of this act, have any intercourse with such ship or vessel, or shall afford any aid to such ship or vessel, either in repairing the said vessel or in furnishing her, her officers and crew with supplies of any kind or in any manner whatever, or if any pilot or other person shall assist in navigating or piloting such ship or vessel, unless it be for the purpose of carrying her beyond the limits and jurisdiction of the United States, every person so offending, shall forfeit and pay a sum not less than one hundred dollars, nor exceeding ten thousand dollars; and shall also be imprisoned for a term not less than one month, nor more than one year.

SEC. 3. And be it further enacted, That from and after the twentieth day of May next, the entrance of the harbors and waters of the United States and the territories thereof be, and the same is hereby interdicted to all ships or vessels sailing under the flag of Great Britain or France, or owned in whole or in part by any citizen or subject of either; vessels hired, chartered or employed by the government of either country, for the sole purpose of carrying letters or despatches, and also vessels forced in by distress or by the dangers of the sea, only excepted. And if any ship or vessel sailing under the flag of Great Britain or France, or owned in whole or in part by any citizen or subject of either, and not excepted as aforesaid, shall after the said twentieth day of May next, arrive either with or without a cargo, within the limits of the United States or of the territories thereof, such ship or vessel, together with the cargo, if any, which may be found on board, shall be forfeited, and may be seized and condemned in any court of the United States or the territories thereof, having competent jurisdiction, and all and every act and acts heretofore passed, which shall be within the purview of this act, shall be, and the same are hereby repealed.

SEC. 4. And be it further enacted, That from and after the twentieth day of May next, it shall not be lawful to import into the United States or the territories thereof, any goods, wares or merchandise whatever, from any port or place situated in Great Britain or Ireland, or in any of the colonies or dependencies of Great Britain, nor from any port or place situated in France, or in any of her colonies or dependencies, nor from any port or place in the actual possession of either Great Britain or France. Nor shall it be lawful to import into the United States, or the territories thereof, from any foreign port or place whatever, any goods, wares or merchandise whatever, being of the growth, produce or manufacture of France, or of any of her colonies or dependencies, or being of the growth, produce or manufacture of Great Britain or Ireland, or of any of the colonies or dependencies of Great Britain, or being of the growth, produce or manufacture of any place or country in the actual possession of either France or Great Britain: Provided, that nothing herein contained shall be construed to affect the cargoes of ships or vessels wholly owned by a citizen or citizens of the United States, which had cleared for any port beyond the Cape of Good Hope, prior to . . . [December 22, 1807,] . . . or which had departed for such port by permission of the President, under the acts supplementary to the act laying an embargo on all ships and vessels in the ports and harbors of the United States. . . .

Source: Rockcastle Karst Conservancy website. http://www.rkci.org/library/gsp/early /nonintercourseact.htm.

I. Joseph Story's Recollections of His Opposition to the Embargo (1809)

Joseph Story (1779–1845), who served for over 30 years as a justice of the U.S. Supreme Court, is best known for his massive learned commentaries on the U.S. Constitution. Story served one term in the U.S. House of Representatives in 1808–1809 as a Democratic-Republican representative from Massachusetts. As a member of President Thomas Jefferson's party, Story had initially supported the Embargo. However, after seeing the ill effects of the measure on New England, Story, as he recalls in this excerpt from his autobiography, written in the 1830s, became a strong advocate for repeal of the Embargo.

There is one other act of my brief career, which I notice, only because it has furnished an occasion for a remark of Mr. Jefferson in the recent post-humous publication of his Correspondence, (4th vol., p. 148). It was during the session of 1808–1809 that the embargo, unlimited in duration and extent, was passed, at the instance of Mr. Jefferson, as a retaliatory measure upon England. It prostrated the whole commerce of America, and produced a degree of distress in the New England States greater than that which followed upon the War. I always thought that it was a measure of doubtful policy, but I sustained it, however, with all my little influence for the purpose of giving it a fair experiment. A year passed away, and the evils, which it inflicted upon ourselves, were daily increasing in magnitude and extent; and in the mean time, our navigation being withdrawn from the ocean, Great Britain was enjoying a triumphant monopoly of the commerce of the world. Alive to the sufferings of my fellow-citizens, and perceiving that their necessities were driving them on to the most violent resistance of the measure,—and, indeed, to a degree which threatened the very existence of the Union,—I became convinced of the necessity of abandoning it, and as soon as I arrived at Washington I held free conversations with many distinguished members of the Republican party on the subject, which were soon followed up by consultations of a more public nature. I found that as a measure of retaliation the system had not only failed, but that Mr. Jefferson from pride of opinion, as well as from that visionary course of speculation, which often misled his judgment, was resolutely bent upon maintaining it at all hazards. He professed a firm belief that Great Britain would abandon her orders in council, if we persisted in the embargo; and having no other scheme to offer in case of the failure of this, he maintained in private conversation the indispensable necessity of closing the session of Congress without any attempt to limit the duration of the system. The consequence of this would be an aggravation for another year of all the evils which then were breaking down New England. I felt that my duty to my county called on me for a strenuous effort to prevent such calamities. And I was persuaded, that if the embargo was kept on during the year, there would be an open disregard and resistance of the laws. I was unwearied, therefore, in my endeavors to impress other members of Congress with a sense of our common dangers. Mr. Jefferson has imputed mainly to me the repeal of the embargo, in a letter to which I have already alluded, and has stigmatized me on this account with the epithet of "pseudo-republican." "Pseudo-republican" of course, I must be; as every one was in Mr. Jefferson's opinion, who dared to venture upon a doubt of his infallibility. But Mr. Jefferson has forgotten to mention the reiterated attempts made by him through a committee of his particular adherents . . . to detach me from my object. In the course of those consultations, I learned the whole policy of Mr. Jefferson; and was surprised as well as grieved to find, that in the face of the clearest proofs of the failure of his plan, he continued to hope against the facts. Mr. Jefferson has honored me by attributing to my influence the repeal of the embargo. I freely admit that I did all I could to accomplish it, though I returned home before the act passed. The very eagerness with which the repeal was supported by a majority of the Republican party ought to have taught Mr. Jefferson that it was already considered by them as a miserable and mischievous failure. It is not a little remarkable, that many years afterwards, Mr. Jefferson took great credit to himself for yielding up . . . this favorite measure, to preserve, as he intimates, New England from open rebellion. What in me was almost a crime, became, it seems in him an extraordinary virtue. The truth is, that if the measure had not been abandoned when it was, it would have overturned the Administration itself, and the Republican party would have been driven from power by the indignation of the people, goaded on the madness of their sufferings. . . .

The whole influence of the Administration was directly brought to bear upon Mr. Ezekiel Bacon and myself, to seduce us from what we considered a great duty to our country, and especially to New England. We were scolded, privately consulted, and argued with, by the Administration and its friends, on that occasion. I knew, at the time. That Mr. Jefferson had no ulterior measure in view, and was determined on protracting the embargo for an indefinite period, even for years. I was well satisfied, that such a course would not and could not be borne by New England, and would bring on a direct rebellion. It would be ruin to the whole country. Yet Mr. Jefferson, with his usual visionary obstinacy, was determined to maintain it; and the New England Republicans were to be made the instruments. Mr. Bacon and myself resisted, and measures were concerted by us, with the aid of Pennsylvania, to compel him to abandon his mad scheme. For this he never forgave me. The measure was not carried until I left Congress for home. The credit of it is due to the firmness and integrity of Mr. Bacon.

Source: Story, Joseph. *Life and Letters.* Vol. I. Edited by William W. Story. Boston, 1851, 183–87.

3. Panic of 1819

A. *Craig et al. v. Missouri* (March 12, 1830)

In 1821 the Missouri legislature authorized the issuance of paper money that the state could loan to Missouri farmers hard hit by the panic of 1819. When Hiram Craig defaulted on his loan, suit was brought against him in circuit court to force payment. Although both the circuit court and the Missouri ruled against Craig, the U.S. Supreme Court in 1830 declared in Craig et al. v. Missouri that the Missouri certificates were unconstitutional because they violated Article I, Section 10 of the U.S. Constitution prohibiting bills of credit. The bare majority opinion, written by Chief Justice John Marshall (1755–1835), is excerpted below.

WRIT of error to the supreme court of the state of Missouri.

In 1823, an action of trespass on the case was instituted in the circuit court for the county of Chariton, in the state of Missouri, by the state of Missouri, against Hiram Craig and others. The declaration sets forth the cause of action in the following terms:

'For, that whereas, heretofore, on the 1st day of August, in the year of our lord 1822, at the county of Chariton, aforesaid, the said Craig, John Moore, and Ephraim Moore, made their certain promissory note in writing, bearing date the day and year aforesaid, and now to the court here shown, and thereby, and then and there, for value received, jointly, and severally, promised to pay to the state of Missouri, on the 1st day of November 1822, at the loan office in Chariton, the sum of one hundred and ninety-nine dollars and ninety-nine cents, and the two per centum per annum, the interest accruing on the certificates borrowed, from the 1st day of October 1821. Nevertheless, the said Hiram Craig, John Moore, and Ephraim Moore, did not on the 1st day of November, or at any time before or since, pay to the state of Missouri, at the loan office in Chariton, the said sum of one hundred and ninety-nine dollars and ninety-nine cents, or the two per centum per annum, the interest accruing on the certificates borrowed, from the 1st day of October 1821; but the same to pay, &c.'

To this declaration the defendants pleaded the general issue; and neither party requiring a trial by jury, the case was submitted to the court on the evidence and the arguments of counsel. The record contained the following entry of the proceedings of the court:

'And afterwards, at a court began and held at Chariton, on Monday the 1st day of November 1824, and on the second day of said court, in open court, the parties came into court by their attorneys, and neither party requiring a jury, the cause is submitted to the court; therefore, all and singular the matter and things and evidences being seen and heard by the court, it is found by them, that the said defendants did assume upon themselves, in manner and form as the plaintiffs, by their counsel, allege: and the court also find that the consideration for which the writing declared upon, and the *assumpsit* was made, was for the loan of loan office certificates, loaned by the state at her loan office at Chariton; which certificates were issued, and the loan made in the manner pointed out by an act of the legislature of the said state of Missouri, approved the 27th day of June 1821, entitled, 'an act for the establishment of loan offices, and the acts amendatory and supplementary thereto.' And the court do further find that the plaintiff hath sustained damages by reason of the non-performance of the assumptions and undertakings of them, the said defendants, to the sum of two hundred and thirty-seven dollars and seventy-nine cents. Therefore it is considered, &c.'

The defendants in the circuit court of the county of Chariton appealed, in 1825, to the supreme court of the state of Missouri, the highest tribunal in that state; where the judgment of the circuit court was affirmed.

The defendants prosecuted this writ of error, under the twenty-fifth section of the judiciary act of 1789.

The act of the legislature of Missouri, under which the certificates were issued which formed the consideration of the note declared upon, was passed on the 27th of June 1821. It is entitled 'an act for the establishment of loan offices, &c.' The provisions of the third, thirteenth, fifteenth, sixteenth, twenty-third and twenty-fourth sections of the act, are all that have a connexion with the questions in the case which were before the court.

'Sec. 3. *Be it further enacted*, That the auditor of public accounts and treasurer, under the direction of the governor, shall, and they are hereby required to issue certificates signed by the said auditor and treasurer to the amount of two hundred thousand dollars, of denominations not exceeding ten dollars, nor less than fifty cents, (to bear such devices as they may deem the most safe) in the following form, to wit: *This certificate shall be receivable at the treasury or any of the loan offices of the state of Missouri, in the discharge of taxes or debts due to the state, for the sum of $ _____, with interest for the same, at the rate of two per centum per annum from this date, the ____ day of _____ 182*

'Sec. 13. *Be it further enacted*, That the certificates of the said loan office shall be receivable at the treasury of the state, and by all tax gatherers and other public officers, in payment of taxes or other moneys now due, or to become due to the state or any county or town therein; and the said certificates shall also be received by all officers civil and military in the state, in discharge of salaries and fees of office.

'Sec. 15. *Be it further enacted*, That the commissioners of the said loan offices shall have power to make loans of the said certificates to citizens of this state, residing within their respective districts only; and in each district a proportion shall be loaned to the citizens of each county therein, according to the number thereof, secured by mortgage or personal security: *Provided*, That the sum loaned on mortgage shall never exceed one half the real unincumbered value of the estate so mortgaged: *Provided also*, That no loans shall ever be made for a longer period than one year, nor at a greater interest than at the rate of six per cent per annum, which interest shall be always payable in advance, nor shall a loan in any case be renewed, unless the interest on such re-loan be also paid in advance: *Provided also*, That the commissioners aforesaid shall never make a call for the payment of any instalment at a greater rate than ten per centum for every six months; and that whenever any instalment to a greater amount than at the rate of ten per centum per annum be required, at least sixty days previous notice shall be given to the person or persons thus required to pay: *And provided also*, That all and every person failing to make payment shall be deprived in future of credit in such office, and be liable to suit immediately, for the whole amount by him or them due.

'Sec. 16. *Be it further enacted*, That the said commissioners of each of the said offices are further authorised to make loans on personal securities, by them deemed good and sufficient, for sums less than two hundred dollars; which securities shall be jointly and severally bound for the payment of the amount so loaned, with interest thereon, under the regulations contained in the preceding section of this act.'

'Sec. 23. *Be it further enacted*, That the general assembly shall, as soon as may be, cause the salt springs and lands attached thereto given by congress to this state, to be leased out, and it shall always be the fundamental condition in such leases, that the lessee or lessees shall receive the certificates hereby required to be issued, in payment for salt, at a price not exceeding that which may be prescribed by law; and all the proceeds of the said salt springs, the interest accruing to the state, and all estates purchased by officers of the several offices, under the provisions of this act, and all the debts now due, or hereafter to be due to this state, are hereby pledged, and constituted a fund for the redemption of the certificates hereby required to be issued; and the faith of the state is hereby also pledged for the same purpose.

'Sec. 24. *Be it further enacted,* That it shall be the duty of the auditor and treasurer to withdraw, annually, from circulation one tenth part of the certificates which are hereby required to be issued, &c.'

The case was argued by Mr Sheffey for the plaintiffs in error; and by Mr Benton for the state of Missouri.

Mr Sheffey, for the plaintiffs in error, contended,

1. That the record shows a proper case for the jurisdiction of this court, within the provisions of the twenty-fifth section of the judiciary act of 1789.

2. That the act of the legislature of Missouri, entitled 'an act for the establishment of loan offices,' is unconstitutional and void; being repugnant to the provision of the constitution of the United States, which declares that no state shall emit bills of credit.

3. That the state of Missouri has no right to recover on the promissory note which is the foundation of this suit, because the consideration was illegal.

He argued, that this case comes fully within the purpose, spirit, and letter of the twenty-fifth section of the judiciary act of 1789. The purpose of that section was, to place within the revising, controlling, and correcting power of the supreme court of the United States, any violations of the constitution of the United States, or of treaties, by state legislation. The harmony of the government, its equal operation, the preservation of its fundamental principles, the peace of the nation, rest securely upon the execution of this power of the supreme court. While this power would be cautiously used; it would be fearlessly asserted and employed, when it was required of the court, and enjoined on the judges. The government of the United States was one for the whole of 'the people of the United States.' It was formed for 'the people;' and its solemn and impressive preamble contains the declaration, that, 'we, the people of the United States, in order to form a more perfect union,' 'do ordain and establish this constitution of the United States.'

To keep the constitution perfect, and preserve it as a government for 'the whole people, the twenty-fifth section of the judiciary law of 1789 was enacted. This law brought into exercise the constitutional powers of the court, but it created no new powers.

In the case of Martin *vs.* Hunter's Lessee, 1 Wheat. 304, 330, this court have said, 'the twenty-fifth section of the judiciary act of September 24, 1799, is supported by the letter and spirit of the constitution.' And in the same case (p. 324) they say, 'the constitution of the United States was ordained and established,' not by the United States in their sovereign capacities; but, as the preamble declares, 'by *the people of the United States.*'

That a tribunal should exist, before which questions of a constitutional character may be brought, is not denied by any one; and the constitution itself has provided that which now entertains such questions. It has given to this court the powers which they exercise; great, extensive, superior and responsible as they are; that this court may stand forth as the guardians of the rights of the people claimed and declared in the constitution, and that those rights may be protected from encroachment and destruction. To this court 'the people' look for this protection; and when the invader of their rights is a sovereign state, they have not the less confidence and assurance, that the principles of the government will be preserved. This court know no parties to the cases which come before them for decision. It is the principles which are to govern their decisions in those cases, to which the court look; and they leave to those from whom their powers are derived, to 'the people of the United States,' to decide; not upon their rightful and constitutional exercise of those powers, for to the constitution they are answerable only for their exercise; but whether they shall continue so to use them. The whole people of the United States have given these powers: and they only, by a majority; and not a portion of them less than this constitutional whole; can nullify those powers, or interrupt the exercise of any which are regularly applied under the constitution. The constitution must be changed by the *whole people*, before the exercise of this power of revision can cease.

This court have never been willing to employ its powers of inquiring into the constitutionality of laws, but where the obligation was imperative, and the case was one clearly within their duties. In the case of Fletcher *vs* Peck, 6 Cranch, 128, the court declared, 'the question, whether a law be void for its repugnancy to the constitution, is a question which ought seldom, if ever, to be decided in a doubtful case. The opposition between the constitution and the law should be such, that the judge feels a clear and strong conviction of their incompatibility with each other.'

To present the question in the case now before the court, no plea was necessary; the defence arises under the general issue.

The record shows that this was a case, in the courts of the state of Missouri, in which the constitutionality of a law of that state was brought into question. The cause of action is stated to be promissory notes given for certificates issued under the act of the legislature of Missouri establishing loan offices; and the validity of these certificates must have been the whole subject of inquiry in the state courts. Their validity depended solely on the harmony of that act with the federal compact; and the courts of Missouri could only have affirmed their validity by affirming the act under which they were issued to be constitutional and valid; or in other terms, not repugnant to the constitution of the United States.

This is not a new question. It has been frequently presented to this court; and has been uniformly decided according to the views of the plaintiffs in error. Martin *vs*. Hunter's Lessee, 1 Wheat. 355. Miller *vs*. Nicholls, 4 Wheat. 311. Williams *vs*. Norris, 12 Wheat. 117. In Wilson *vs*. The Black Bird Creek

Marsh Company, 2 Peters, 251, the court say: 'it is sufficient to bring the case within the provisions of the twenty-fifth section of the judicial act, if the record shows that the constitution or a law or a treaty has been misconstrued, or the decision could not be made.'

2. The certificates issued by the state of Missouri under the law are 'bills of credit;' and thus the law conflicts with the constitution of the United States. They are issued under the authority of the state, and put into circulation by the state; as the representative of money; as a substitute for it; to perform the functions of money, by becoming the medium of circulation.

The prohibition of the constitution is in these terms; and every word in the clause is important and emphatic: 'No state shall' 'coin money,' 'emit bills of credit,' 'make any thing but gold and silver coin a tender in payment of debts.'

What is the form and meaning of these bills? They purport to be receivable at the treasury, or any loan office of the state, in discharge of taxes or debts due to the state. They are issued of different denominations, from two hundred dollars, to fifty cents, payable to no particular person; they are, by the twenty-third section of the law, to be received for salt, by the lessees of the property of the state; by the officers of the state, in discharge of their salaries and fees of office. They pass, by delivery, with every characteristic of money. It is only necessary to state these, the purposes of their issue; the character and form of the certificates; the obligation imposed on the citizens of Missouri to receive them; to establish that they are 'bills of credit;' 'emitted' 'by the state' of Missouri; or 'coined' money: and that, not being 'gold or silver,' they are 'a tender in payment of debts.'

The sufferings of the people of the United States from the issues of paper money, or 'bills of credit,' during the revolution, were yet in full operation when the constitution was formed. While it might be dangerous to deny that many of the means of the war were procured by the emission of that money; the exigencies of the country, strugling for existence, were the only safe apology for their use. When the confederated states were about to become a nation, which should owe its prosperity to sound and just and equal principles; the opportunity to reproduce the same state of things, the same wide and wasteful ruin by the acts of any of the members of the confederacy, was at once decisively and explicitly prohibited by those who formed the constitution. But, if it is contended, that the certificates issued by the state of Missouri were not 'bills of credit,' because it is said they are not declared by the act which directs their emission to be 'a legal tender;' it is asserted, that if even they are not such, it is not essential to 'a bill of credit' that it shall have that incident. The Federalist, No. 44. Many of the bills issued by the states during the war were not made a legal tender; but they circulated widely, and with equally disastrous consequences. 9 Virgin. Stat. at large, 67, 147, 223, 480, &c.

In relation to money as a circulating medium, the states are one. All and each have one and the same interest in a sound currency. These interests are a unit; not only from the neighbourhood of the states to each other, the identity of their interests, and their free and unrestrained intercourse; but because the regulations of the constitution embrace the whole subject of money as a circulating medium.

To the existence of the government, certainly to its convenient fiscal operations, a uniform currency is important, if not essential; and if the principles which may be fairly drawn from a sound construction of the provision in the constitution under examination, extend to bring into doubt the legality of bank notes circulated as money, *under the charters granted to banks by state laws;* these principles may not be the less true, or their importance of the less magnitude.

3. If the certificates for which promissory notes were given are void, and the act of the legislature of Missouri on which they are founded was against the constitution of the United States; the note upon which this action was brought in the circuit court of Missouri was without consideration, and void. The state cannot receive upon such notes.

Mr Benton for the defendant in error.

The state of Missouri has been 'summoned' by a writ from this court, under a 'penalty,' to be and appear before this court. In the language of the writ, she is 'commanded' and 'enjoined' to appear. Language of this kind does not seem proper, when addressed to a sovereign state: nor are the terms fitting, even if the only purpose of the process was to obtain the appearance of the state. They impute 'a fault' in the state; they imply an omission, or neglect by the state. The language of 'commanding and enjoining' would only be well employed if these had occurred.

The state of Missouri has done no act which was not within the full and ample powers she possesses as a free, sovereign, and independent state. She has passed a law which she considers in the proper and beneficial exercise of her legislative functions; and which had for its object the promotion of the interests of her citizens.

Mr Benton said, that he did not appear in this case for the state of Missouri, as in ordinary cases depending in this court: not as the advocate of the state; for her acts did not require the efforts of an advocate to vindicate them: he appeared rather as a 'corps of observation,' to watch what was going on.

The state had passed a law authorising the governor to employ counsel, and he had been called upon to represent the state. He had listened to what had been going on before the court; and he found a gentleman from another state, imputing to Missouri an act fraught with injustice and immorality.

Source: U.S. Supreme Court, 29 U.S. 410 (1830).

4. Panic of 1837

A. President Jackson's Bank Veto (July 10, 1832)

In the following excerpts from his 1832 veto message, President Andrew Jackson (1767–1845) explains his reasons for vetoing a bill authorizing the recharter of the Second Bank of the United States. Besides believing the bank unconstitutional, Jackson also denounces it as an institution that benefits only the wealthy and thus violates the philosophy of social equality that was the basis of Jacksonian democracy. Although the bank's supporters had attempted to use the recharter issue as a means of denying Jackson a second term, they were unsuccessful. Jackson handily defeated recharter advocate Henry Clay (1777–1852) in the election of 1832.

The bill "to modify and continue" the act entitled "An act to incorporate the subscribers to the Bank of the United States" was presented to me on the 4th July instant. Having considered it with that solemn regard to the principles of the Constitution which the day was calculated to inspire, and come to the conclusion that it ought not to become a law, I herewith return it to the Senate, in which it originated, with my objections.

A bank of the United States is in many respects convenient for the Government and useful to the people. Entertaining this opinion, and deeply impressed with the belief that some of the powers and privileges possessed by the existing bank are unauthorized by the Constitution, subversive of the rights of the States, and dangerous to the liberties of the people, I felt it my duty at an early period of my Administration to call the attention of Congress to the practicability of organizing an institution combining all its advantages and obviating these objections. I sincerely regret that in the act before me I can perceive none of those modifications of the bank charter which are necessary, in my opinion, to make it compatible with justice, with sound policy, or with the Constitution of our country.

The present corporate body, denominated the president, directors, and company of the Bank of the United States, will have existed at the time this act is intended to take effect twenty years. It enjoys an exclusive privilege of banking under the authority of the General Government, a monopoly of its favor and support, and, as a necessary consequence, almost a monopoly of the foreign and domestic exchange. The powers privileges, and favors bestowed upon it in the original charter, by increasing the value of the stock far above its par value, operated as a gratuity of many millions to the stockholders.

An apology may be found for the failure to guard against this result in the consideration that the effect of the original act of incorporation could not be certainly foreseen at the time of its passage. The act before me proposes another gratuity to the holders of the same stock, and in many cases to the same men, of at least seven millions more. This donation finds no apology in any uncertainty as to the effect of the act. On all hands it is conceded that its passage will increase at least 20 or 30 per cent more the market price of the stock, subject to the payment of the annuity of $200,000 per year secured by the act, thus adding in a moment one-fourth to its par value. It is not our own citizens only who are to receive the bounty of our Government. More than eight millions of the stock of this bank are held by foreigners. By this act the American Republic proposes virtually to make them a present of some millions of dollars. For these gratuities to foreigners and to some of our own opulent citizens the act secures no equivalent whatever. They are the certain gains of the present stockholders under the operation of this act, after making full allowance for the payment of the bonus.

Every monopoly and all exclusive privileges are granted at the expense of the public, which ought to receive a fair equivalent. The many millions which this act proposes to bestow on the stockholders of the existing bank must come directly or indirectly out of the earnings of the American people. It is due to them, therefore, if their Government sell monopolies and exclusive privileges, that they should at least exact for them as much as they are worth in open market. The value of the monopoly in this case may be correctly ascertained. The twenty-eight millions of stock would probably be at an advance of 50 per cent, and command in market at least $42,000,000, subject to the payment of the present bonus. The present value of the monopoly, therefore, is $17,000,000, and this the act proposes to sell for three millions, payable in fifteen annual installments of $200,000 each.

It is not conceivable how the present stockholders can have any claim to the special favor of the Government. The present corporation has enjoyed its monopoly during the period stipulated in the original contract. If we must have such a corporation, why should not the Government sell out the whole stock and thus secure to the people the full market value of the privileges granted? Why should not Congress create and sell twenty-eight millions of stock, incorporating the purchasers with all the powers and privileges secured in this act and putting the premium upon the sales into the Treasury?

But this act does not permit competition in the purchase of this monopoly. It seems to be predicated on the erroneous idea that the present stockholders have a prescriptive right not only to the favor but to the bounty of Government. It appears that more than a fourth part of the stock is held by foreigners and the residue is held by a few hundred of our own citizens, chiefly of the richest class. For their benefit does this act exclude the whole American people from competition in the purchase of this monopoly and dispose of it for many millions less than it is worth. This seems the less excusable because some of our citizens not now stockholders petitioned that the door of competition might be opened, and offered to take a charter on terms much more favorable to the Government and country. . . .

I have now done my duty to my country. If sustained by my fellow-citizens, I shall be grateful and happy; if not, I shall find in the motives which impel me ample grounds for contentment and peace. In the difficulties which surround us and the dangers which threaten our institutions there is cause for neither dismay nor alarm. For relief and deliverance let us firmly rely on that kind Providence which I am sure watches with peculiar care over the destinies of our Republic, and on the intelligence and wisdom of our countrymen. Through His abundant goodness and their patriotic devotion our liberty and Union will be preserved.

Source: Miller Center. University of Virginia. http://millercenter.org/scripps/archive /speeches/detail/3636.

B. President Jackson's Message to the Cabinet Regarding Removal of Public Deposits from the Bank of the United States (September 18, 1833)

President Andrew Jackson (1767–1845) interpreted his reelection in 1832 as an expression of national support for his veto of a bill authorizing recharter of the Second Bank of the United States. However, because the bank's current charter did not expire until 1836, Jackson feared that bank president Nicholas Biddle (1786–1844) would use the economic influence of his institution to generate political support for renewing the charter. To forestall such a move, Jackson ordered the removal of all federal deposits from the bank in 1833. The federal funds were eventually placed with various private banks around the country. Below are excerpts from Jackson's message to his cabinet explaining his reasons for taking this action.

Having carefully and anxiously considered all the facts and arguments which have been submitted to him relative to a removal of the public deposits from the Bank of the United States, the President deems it his duty to communicate in this manner to his Cabinet the final conclusions of his own mind and the reasons on which they are founded, in order to put them in durable form and to prevent misconceptions.

The President's convictions of the dangerous tendencies of the Bank of the United States, since signally illustrated by its own acts, were so overpowering when he entered on the duties of Chief Magistrate that he felt it his duty, notwithstanding the objections of the friends by whom he was surrounded, to avail himself of the first occasion to call the attention of Congress and the people to the question of its recharter. The opinions expressed in his annual message of December, 1829, were reiterated in those of December, 1830 and 1831, and in that of 1830 he threw out for consideration some suggestions in relation to a substitute. At the session of 1831–32 an act was passed by a majority of both Houses of Congress rechartering the present bank, upon which the President felt it his duty to put his constitutional veto. In his message returning that act he repeated and enlarged upon the principles and views briefly asserted in his annual message, declaring the bank to be, in his opinion, both inexpedient and unconstitutional, and announcing to his countrymen very unequivocally his firm determination never to sanction by his approval the continuance of that institution or the establishment of any other upon similar principles.

There are strong reasons for believing that the motive of the bank in asking for a recharter at that session of Congress was to make it a leading question in the election of a President of the United States the ensuing November, and all steps deemed necessary were taken to procure from the people a reversal of the President's decision.

Although the charter was approaching its termination, and the bank was aware that it was the intention of the Government to use the public deposit as fast as it has accrued in the payment of the public debt, yet did it extend its loans from January, 1831, to May, 1832, from $42,402,304.24 to $70,428,070.72, being an increase of $28,025,766.48 in sixteen months. It is confidently believed that the leading object of this immense extension of its loans was to bring as large a portion of the people as possible under its power and influence, and it has been disclosed that some of the largest sums were granted on very unusual terms to the conductors of the public press. In some of these cases the motive was made manifest by the nominal or insufficient security taken for the loans, by the large amounts discounted, by the extraordinary time allowed for payment, and especially by the subsequent conduct of those receiving the accommodations.

Having taken these preliminary steps to obtain control over public opinion, the bank came into Congress and asked a new charter. The object avowed by many of the advocates of the bank was to *put the President to the test,* that the country might know his final determination relative to the bank prior to the ensuing election. Many documents and articles were printed and circulated at the expense of the bank to bring the people to a favorable decision upon its pretensions. Those whom the bank appears to have made its debtors for the special occasion were warned of the ruin which awaited them should the President be sustained, and attempts were made to alarm the whole people by painting the depression in the price of property and produce and the general loss, inconvenience, and distress which it was represented would immediately follow the reelection of the President in opposition to the bank.

Can it now be said that the question of a recharter of the bank was not decided at the election which ensued? Had the veto been equivocal, or had it not covered the whole ground; if it had merely taken exceptions to the details of the bill or to the time of its passage; if it had not met the whole ground of constitutionality and expediency, then there might have been some plausibility for the allegation that the question was not decided by the people. It was to compel the President to take his stand that the question was brought forward at that particular time. He met the challenge, willingly took the position into which his adversaries sought to force him, and frankly declared his unalterable opposition to the bank as being both unconstitutional and inexpedient. On that ground the case was argued to the people; and now that the people have sustained the President, notwithstanding the array of influence and power which was brought to bear upon him, it is too late, he confidently thinks, to say that the question has not been decided. Whatever may be the opinions of others, the President considers his reelection as a decision of the people against the bank. . . .

ANDREW JACKSON.

Source: Andrew Jackson: "Message Read to the Cabinet on Removal of the Public Deposits." September 18, 1833. Online by Gerhard Peters and John T. Woolley, *The American Presidency Project.* http://www.presidency.ucsb.edu/ws/?pid=67086.

C. The Specie Circular (July 11, 1836)

Because Indian removal opened many new lands to white settlement, speculation in the sale of public lands reached a fever pitch in the mid-1830s. Many speculators purchased land with notes issued by state banks that lacked the hard currency to back their paper. Fearing the economic effects of excessive speculation, President Andrew Jackson (1767–1845) issued the following executive order, known as the Specie Circular, in 1836, the last year of his presidency. The order was so-named because it required that all payment for public lands be made in gold or silver. The Specie Circular, by accelerating the devaluation of paper money, was blamed by many at the time for the rise in prices and the severe economic downturn that occurred in 1837, the first year of Martin Van Buren's (1782–1862) presidency.

In consequence of complaints which have been made of frauds, speculations, and monopolies, in the purchase of the public lands, and the aid which is said to be given to effect these objects by excessive bank credits, and dangerous if not partial facilities, through bank drafts and bank deposites, and the general evil influence likely to result to the public interests, and especially the safety of the great amount of money in the Treasury, and the sound condition of the currency of the country from the further exchange of the national domain in this manner, and chiefly for bank credits and paper money, the President of the United States has given directions, and you are hereby instructed, after the 15th day of August next, to receive in payment of the public lands nothing excerpt what is directed by the existing laws, viz: gold and silver, and, in the proper cases, Virginia land scrip; provided that, till the 15th of December next, the same indulgence heretofore extended, as to the kind of money received, may be continued for any quantity of land not exceeding 329 acres to each purchaser who is an actual settler, or bonafide resident in the State where the sales are made.

In order to insure the faithful execution of these instructions, all receivers are strictly prohibited from accepting, for land sold, any draft, certificate, or other evidence of money, or deposite, though for specie, unless signed by the Treasurer of the United States, in conformity to the Act of April 24, 1820. And each of those officers is required to annex to his monthly returns to this Department the amount of gold and silver, respectively, as well as the bills, received under the foregoing exception; and each deposite bank is required to annex to every certificate given upon a deposite of money, the proportions of it actually paid in gold, in silver, and in bank notes. All former instructions on these subjects, except as now modified, will be considered as remaining in full force.

The principal objects of the President in adopting this measure being to repress alleged frauds, and to withhold any countenance or facilities in the power of the Government from the monopoly of the public lands in the hands of speculators and capitalists, to the injury of the actual settlers in the new States, and of emigrants in search of new homes, as well as to discourage the ruinous extension of bank issues and bank credits, by which those results are generally supposed to be promoted, your utmost vigilance is required, and relied on, to carry this order into complete execution.

LEVI WOODBURY
Secretary of the Treasury

Source: Library of Congress, American Memory. http://memory.loc.gov/cgi-bin/ampage ?collId=llrd&fileName=027/llrd027.db&recNum=511; *Register of Debates,* 24th Congress, 2nd Session.

D. *Charles River Bridge v. Warren Bridge* (February 14, 1837)

In 1785 the state of Massachusetts granted a charter to the Charles River Bridge Company to build a bridge over the Charles River to connect Boston and Cambridge. When the state granted another charter to another company to build the nearby Warren Bridge in 1828, the Charles River Bridge Company sued, claiming that its charter gave it exclusive rights, which the state had now violated. The case went eventually to the U.S. Supreme Court, which rendered its decision in Charles River Bridge v. Warren Bridge *in 1837. In the following excerpts from the majority opinion delivered by Chief Justice Roger B. Taney (1777–1864), the court sides with Warren Bridge, denying the exclusive rights claimed by the Charles River Bridge Company and warning that to sustain such rights would have serious economic consequences.*

TANEY, Ch. J., delivered the opinion of the court.

The questions involved in this case are of the gravest character, and the court have given to them the most anxious and deliberate consideration. The value of the right claimed by the plaintiffs is large in amount; and many persons may, no doubt, be seriously affected in their pecuniary interests, by any decision which the court may pronounce; and the questions which have been raised as to the power of the several states, in relation to the corporations they have chartered, are pregnant with important consequences; not only to the individuals who are concerned in the corporate franchises, but to the communities in which they exist. The court are fully sensible, that it is their duty, in exercising the high powers conferred on them by the constitution of the United States, to deal with these great and extensive interests, with the utmost caution; guarding, so far as they have the power to do so, the rights of property, and at the same time, carefully abstaining from any encroachment on the rights reserved to the states. . . .

Borrowing, as we have done, our system of jurisprudence from the English law; and having adopted, in every other case, civil and criminal, its rules for the construction of statutes; is there anything in our local situation, or in the nature of our political institutions, which should lead us to depart from the principle, where corporations are concerned? Are we to apply to acts of incorporation, a rule of construction differing from that of the English law, and, by implication, make the terms of a charter, in one of the states, more unfavorable to the public, than upon an act of parliament, framed in the same words, would be sanctioned in an English court? Can any good reason be assigned, for excepting this particular class of cases from the operation of the general principle; and for introducing a new and adverse rule of construction, in favor of corporations, while we adopt and adhere to the rules of construction known to the English common law, in every other case, without exception? We think not; and it would present a singular spectacle, if, while the courts in England are restraining, within the strictest limits, the spirit of monopoly, and exclusive privileges in nature of monopolies, and confining corporations to the privileges plainly given to them in their charter; the courts of this country should be found enlarging these privileges by implication; and construing a statute more unfavorably to the public, and to the rights of community, than would be done in a like case in an English court of justice.

But we are not now left to determine, for the first time, the rules by which public grants are to be construed in this country. The subject has already been considered in this court; and the rule of construction, above stated, fully established. In the case of the *United States* v. *Arredondo*, 8 Pet. 738, the leading cases upon this subject are collected together by the learned judge who delivered the opinion of the court; and the principle recognised, that in grants by the public, nothing passes by implication. The rule is still more clearly and plainly stated in the case of *Jackson* v. *Lamphire*, 3 Pet. 289. That was a grant of land by the state; and in speaking of this doctrine of implied covenants, in grants by the state, the court use the following language, which is strikingly applicable to the case at bar: 'The only contract made by the state, is the grant to John Cornelius, his heirs and assigns, of the land in question. The patent contains no covenant to do, or not to do, any further act in relation to the land; and we do not feel ourselves at liberty, in this case, to create one by implication. The state has not, by this act, impaired the force of the grant; it does not profess or attempt to take the land from the assigns of Cornelius, and gave it to one not claiming under him; neither does the award produce that effect; the grant remains in full force; the property conveyed is held by his grantee, and the state asserts no claim to it.' The same rule of construction is also stated in the case of *Beaty* v. *Lessee of Knowler*, 4 Pet. 168, decided in this court in 1830. In delivering their opinion in that case, the court say: 'That a corporation is strictly limited to the exercise of those powers which are specifically conferred on it, will not be denied. The exercise of the corporate franchise being restrictive of individual rights, cannot be extended beyond the letter and spirit of the act of incorporation'. . . .

Many other questions, of the deepest importance, have been raised and elaborately discussed in the argument. It is not necessary, for the decision of this case, to express our opinion upon them; and the court deem it proper to avoid volunteering an opinion on any question, involving the construction of the constitution, where the case itself does not bring the question directly before them, and make it their duty to decide upon it. Some questions, also, of a purely technical character, have been made and argued, as to the form of proceeding and the right to relief. But enough appears on the record, to bring out the great question in contest; and it is the interest of all parties concerned, that the real controversy should be settled, without further delay: and as the opinion of the court is pronounced on the main question in dispute here, and disposes of the whole case, it is altogether unnecessary to enter upon the examination of the forms of proceeding, in which the parties have brought it before the court.

The judgment of the supreme judicial court of the commonwealth of Massachusetts, dismissing the plaintiffs' bill, must, therefore, be affirmed, with costs.

Source: U.S. Supreme Court, 36 U.S. 420 (1837)

E. President Van Buren's Message to Congress Opposing Federal Action during Hard Economic Times (September 4, 1837)

As the Panic of 1837 deepened into depression, many Americans called for the government to take action to right the economy. A staunch Jacksonian, President Martin Van Buren (1782–1862) did not believe that the government should involve itself in the economy. In the following excerpts from his September 1837 message to Congress, Van Buren explains his reasons for refusing to act. As a result of this stance, Van Buren was blamed for the country's economic woes, especially the record high levels of unemployment. In 1840 Van Buren was handily defeated in his bid for reelection by his Whig opponent, William Henry Harrison (1773–1841).

The preceding suggestions and recommendations are submitted in the belief that their adoption by Congress will enable the Executive department to conduct our fiscal concerns with success, so far as their management has been committed to it. Whilst the objects and the means proposed to attain them are within its constitutional powers and appropriate duties, they will at the same time, it is hoped, by their necessary operation, afford essential aid in the transaction of individual concerns, and thus yield relief to the people at large, in a form adapted to the nature of our Government. Those who look to the action of this Government for specific aid to the citizen to relieve embarrassments arising from losses by revulsions in commerce and credit, lose sight of the ends for which it was created, and the powers with which it is clothed. It was established to give security to us all in our lawful and honorable pursuits, under the lasting safeguard of republican institutions. It was not intended to confer special favors on individuals, or on any classes of them; to create systems of agriculture, manufactures, or trade; or to engage in them, either separately or in connexion with individual citizens or organized associations. If its operations were to be directed for the benefit of any one class, equivalent favors must, in justice, be extended to the rest; and the attempt to bestow such favors with an equal hand, or even to select those who should most deserve them, would never be successful. All communities are apt to look to Government for too much. Even in our own country, where its powers and duties are so strictly limited, we are prone to do so, especially at periods of sudden embarrassment and distress. But this ought not to be. The framers of our excellent constitution, and the people who approved it with calm and sagacious deliberation, acted at the time on a sounder principle. They wisely judged that the less Government interferes with private pursuits, the better for the general prosperity. It is not its legitimate object to make men rich, or to repair, by direct grants of money or legislation in favor of particular pursuits, losses not incurred in the public service. This would be substantially to use the property of some for the benefit of others. But its real duty—that duty the performance of which makes a good Government the most precious of human blessings—is to enact and enforce a system of general laws commensurate with, but not exceeding, the objects of its establishment, and to leave every citizen and every interest to reap, under its benign protection, the rewards of virtue, industry, and prudence.

I cannot doubt that on this, as on all similar occasions, the Federal Government will find its agency most conducive to the security and happiness of the people, when limited to the exercise of its conceded powers. In never assuming, even for a well-meant object, such powers as were not designed to be conferred upon it, we shall in reality do most for the general welfare. To avoid every unnecessary interference with the pursuits of the citizen, will result in more benefit than to adopt measures which could only assist limited interests, and are eagerly, but perhaps naturally, sought for, under the pressure of temporary circumstances. If, therefore, I refrain from suggesting to Congress any specific plan for regulating the exchanges of the country, relieving mercantile embarrassments, or interfering with the ordinary operations of foreign or domestic commerce, it is from a conviction that such measures are not within the constitutional province of the General Government, and that their adoption would not promote the real and permanent welfare of those they might be designed to aid.

The difficulties and distresses of the times, though unquestionably great, are limited in their extent, and cannot be regarded as affecting the permanent prosperity of the nation. Arising, in a great degree, from the transactions of foreign and domestic commerce, it is upon them that they have chiefly fallen. The great agricultural interest has, in many parts of the country, suffered comparatively little; and, as if Providence intended to display the munificence of its goodness at the moment of our greatest need, and indirect contrast to the evils occasioned by the waywardness of man, we have been blessed throughout our extended territory with a season of general health and of uncommon fruitfulness. The proceeds of our great staples will soon furnish the means of liquidating debts at home and abroad, and contribute equally to the revival of commercial activity, and the restoration of commercial credit. The banks, established avowedly for its support, deriving their profits from it, and resting under obligations to it which cannot be overlooked, will feel at once the necessity and justice of uniting their energies with those of the mercantile interest. The suspension of specie payments, at such a time and under such circumstances as we have lately witnessed, could not be other than a temporary measure; and we can scarcely err in believing that the period must soon arrive when all that are solvent will redeem their issues in gold and silver. Dealings abroad naturally depend on resources and prosperity at home. If the debt of our merchants has accumulated, or their credit is impaired, these are fluctuations always incident to extensive or extravagant mercantile transactions. But the ultimate security of such obligations does not admit of question. They are guarantied by the resources of a country, the fruits of whose industry afford abundant means of ample liquidation, and by the evident interest of every merchant to sustain a credit, hitherto high, by promptly applying these means for its preservation.

I deeply regret that events have occurred which require me to ask your consideration of such serious topics. I could have wished that, in making my first communication to the assembled Representatives of my country, I had nothing to dwell upon but the history of her unalloyed prosperity. Since it is otherwise, we can only feel more deeply the responsibility of the respective trusts that have been confided to us, and, under the pressure of difficulties, unite in invoking the guidance and aid of the Supreme Ruler of nations, and in laboring with zealous resolution to overcome the difficulties by which we are environed. . . .

M. VAN BUREN.

Source: James D. Richardson, ed., *A Compilation of the Messages and Papers of the Presidents 1789–1897*, vol. 3, 1920, 324–46.

F. William Harper's "Memoir on Slavery" (1837)

William Harper (1790–1847), a prominent South Carolina politician, is best known as an early advocate of slavery as a positive social good. Reproduced here are excerpts from Harper's "Memoir on Slavery," a speech first read before the South Carolina Society for the Advancement of Learning in 1837 and later published in the Southern Literary Messenger. *Harper argues that slavery allows the South to achieve steady, balanced economic and technological progress without the social inequality and political radicalism that was developing in the growing industrial cities of Britain and the North.*

Slavery was forced upon us by the extremest exigency of circumstances in a struggle for existence. Without it, it is doubtful whether a white man would be now existing on this continent—certain that, if there were, they would be in a state of the utmost destitution, weakness, and misery. I neither deprecate nor resent the gift of slavery.

The Africans brought to us have been slaves in their own country and only underwent a change of masters.

That there are great evils in a society where slavery exists, and that the institution is liable to great abuse, I have already said. But the whole of human life is a system of evils and compensations. The free laborer has few real guarantees from society, while security is one of the compensations of the slave's humble position. There have been fewer murders of slaves than of parents, children, and apprentices in society where slavery does not exist. The slave offers not temptation to the murderer, nor does he realy suffer injury from his master. Who but a driveling fanatic has thought of the necessity of protecting domestic animals from the cruelty of their owners?

. . . It is true that the slave is driven to labor by stripes; and if the object of punishment be to produce obedience or reformation with the least permanent injury, it is the best method of punishment. Men claim that this is intolerable. It is not degrading to a slave, nor is it felt to be so. Is it degrading to a child?

Odium has been cast upon our legislation on account of its forbidding the elements of education to be communicated to slaves. But in truth what injury has been done them by this? He who works during the day with his hands does not read in intervals of leisure for his amusement or the improvement of his mind—or the exception is so rare as scarcely to need the being provided for. If there were any chance of elevating their rank, the denial of the rudiments of education might be a matter of hardship. But this they know cannot be and that further attainments would be useless to them. . . .

It has been said that marriage does not exist among our slaves. But we know that marriages among slaves are solemnized; but the law does not make them indissoluble, nor could it be so. . . . Some suppose that a slaveholding country is one wide stew [brothel] for the indulgence of unbridled lust, and there are particular instances of brutal and shameless debauches in every country. It is even true that in this respect the morals of this class [slave women] are very loose and that the passions of men of the superior caste tempt and find gratification in the easy chastity of the females. . . .

[In countries where free labor prevails] the unmarried woman who becomes a mother is an outcast from society—and though sentimentalists lament the hardship of the case, it is justly and necessarily so. But with us this female slave has a different status. She is not a less useful member of society than before. She has not impaired her means of support nor materially impaired her character or lowered her station in society; she has done no great injury to herself or any other human beings. Her offspring is not a burden but an acquisition to her owner. . . .

Supposing finally that the abolitionists should effect their purpose. What would be the result? The first and most obvious effect would be to put an end to the cultivation of our great Southern staple [cotton]. . . . The cultivation of the great staple crops cannot be carried out . . . in any portion of our country where there are not slaves. . . . Even if it were possible to procure laborers at all, what planter would venture to carry on his operations? Imagine an extensive rice or cotton plantation cultivated by free laborers who might perhaps strike for an increase in wages at a season when the neglect of a few days would insure the destruction of the whole crop. I need hardly say that these staples cannot be produced to any extent where the proprietor of the soil cultivates it with his own hands.

And what would be the effect of putting an end to the cultivation of these staples and thus annihilating, at a blow, two-thirds or three-fourths of our foreign commerce? Can any sane mind contemplate such a result without terror? Our slavery has not only given existence to millions of slaves within our own territories; it has given the means of subsistence, and therefore of existence, to millions of freemen in our Confederate [United] States, enabling them to send forth their swarms to overspread the plains and forests of the West and appear as the harbingers of civilization. Not only on our continent but on the other it has given existence [in textile mills] to hundreds of thousands and the means of comfortable subsistence to millions. A distinguished citizen of our state has lately stated that our great staple, cotton, has contributed more than anything else of later times to the progress of civilization. By enabling the poor to obtain cheap and becoming clothing, it has inspired a taste for comfort, the first stimulus to civilization.

Source: McLaughlin, A. C., et al., eds. *Source Problems in United States History.* New York: Harper & Brothers, 1918, 419–24.

G. Theodore Weld's *American Slavery As It Is: Testimony of a Thousand Witnesses* (1839)

Theodore Dwight Weld (1803–1895), a leading American abolitionist, is best known as the coauthor, with his wife, Angelina Grimké (1805–1879), and her sister, Sarah Moore Grimké (1792–1873), of American Slavery As It Is: Testimony of a Thousand Voices, *a compendium of stories detailing the horrors of slave life. Published in 1839,* American Slavery As It Is *had great influence on the growth and development of the abolitionist movement, even serving later as a source for Harriet Beecher Stowe's (1811–1896)* Uncle Tom's Cabin. *Weld and his coauthors drew most of their material from articles and notices in southern newspapers. Reproduced below are excerpts from the "Introduction" to* American Slavery As It Is.

READER, you are empannelled as a juror to try a plain case and bring in an honest verdict. The question at issue is not one of law, but of fact—"What is the actual condition of the slaves in the United States?" A plainer case never went to a jury. Look at it. TWENTY-SEVEN HUNDRED THOUSAND PERSONS in this country, men, women, and children, are in SLAVERY. Is slavery, as a condition for human beings, good, bad, or indifferent? We submit the question without argument. You have common sense, and conscience, and a human heart;—pronounce upon it. You have a wife, or a husband, a child, a father, a mother, a brother or a sister—make the case your own, make it theirs, and bring in your verdict. The case of Human Rights against Slavery has been adjudicated in the court of conscience times innumerable. The same verdict has always been rendered—"Guilty;" the same sentence has always been pronounced, "Let it be accursed;" and human nature, with her million echoes, has rung it round the world in every language under heaven, "Let it be accursed. Let it be accursed." His heart is false to human nature, who will not say "Amen." There is not a man on earth who does not believe that slavery is a curse. Human beings may be inconsistent, but human *nature* is true to herself. She has uttered her testimony against slavery with a shriek ever since the monster was begotten; and till it perishes amidst the execrations of the universe, she will traverse the world on its track, dealing her bolts upon its head, and dashing against it her condemning brand. We repeat it, every man knows that slavery is a curse. Whoever denies this, his lips libel his heart. Try him; clank the chains in his ears, and tell him they are for *him;* give him an hour to prepare his wife and children for a life of slavery; bid him make haste and get ready their necks for the yoke, and their wrists for the coffle chains, then look at his pale lips and trembling knees, and you have *nature's* testimony against slavery.

Two millions seven hundred thousand persons in these States are in this condition. They were made slaves and are held such by force, and by being put in fear, and this for no crime! Reader, what have you to say of such treatment? Is it right, just, benevolent? Suppose I should seize you, rob you of your liberty, drive you into the field, and make you work without pay as long as you live, would that be justice and kindness, or monstrous injustice and cruelty? Now, every body knows that the slaveholders do these things to the slaves every day, and yet it is stoutly affirmed that they treat them well and kindly, and that their tender regard for their slaves restrains the masters from inflicting cruelties upon them. We shall go into no metaphysics to show the absurdity of this pretence. The man who *robs* you every day, is, forsooth, quite too tender-hearted ever to cuff or kick you! True, he can snatch your money, but he does it gently lest he should hurt you. He can empty your pockets without qualms, but if your *stomach* is empty, it cuts him to the quick. He can make you work a life time without pay, but loves you too well to let you go hungry. He fleeces you of your *rights* with a relish, but is shocked if you work bareheaded in summer, or in winter without warm stockings. He can make you go without your *liberty,* but never without a shirt. He can crush, in you, all hope of bettering your condition, by vowing that you shall die his slave, but though he can coolly torture your feelings, he is too compassionate to lacerate your back—he can break your heart, but he is very tender of your skin. He can strip you of all protection and thus expose you to all outrages, but if you are exposed to the *weather,* half clad and half sheltered, how yearn his tender bowels! What! slaveholders talk of treating men well, and yet not only rob them of all they get, and as fast as they get it, but rob them of *themselves,* also; their very hands and feet, all their muscles, and limbs, and senses, their bodies and minds, their time and liberty and earnings, their free speech and rights of conscience, their right to acquire knowledge, and property, and reputation;—and yet they, who plunder them of all these, would fain make us believe that their soft hearts ooze out so lovingly toward their slaves that they always keep them well housed and well clad, never push them too hard in the field, never make their dear backs smart, nor let their dear stomachs get empty.

But there is no end to these absurdities. Are slaveholders dunces, or do they take all the rest of the world to be, that they think to bandage our eyes with such thin gauzes? Protesting their kind regard for those whom they hourly plunder of all they have and all they get! What! when they have seized their victims, and annihilated all their *rights,* still claim to be the special guardians of their *happiness!* Plunderers of their liberty, yet the careful suppliers of their wants? Robbers of their earnings, yet watchful sentinels round their interests, and kind providers for their comfort? Filching all their time, yet granting generous donations for rest and sleep? Stealing the use of their muscles, yet thoughtful of their ease? Putting them under *drivers,* yet careful that they are not hard-pushed? Too humane forsooth to stint the stomachs of their slaves, yet force their *minds* to starve, and brandish over them pains and penalties, if they dare to reach forth for the smallest crumb of knowledge, even a letter of the alphabet!

Source: Weld, Theodore D. *American Slavery As It Is: Testimony of a Thousand Witnesses.* New York: American Anti-Slavery Society, 1839, 7–10.

5. Panic of 1857

A. Independent Treasury Act (August 6, 1846)

In 1833 President Andrew Jackson (1767–1845), a Democrat, removed federal funds from the Bank of the United States, an institution that he believed to be unconstitutional and harmful to the national economy. The opposition Whig Party sought to reverse this policy after it won the presidency in 1840. However, the election of Democrat James K. Polk (1795–1849) as president in 1844 allowed Jackson's party to pass the Independent Treasury Act of 1846, which mandated the holding of government funds in the U.S. Treasury in Washington, D.C., and in various subtreasuries in cities around the country. Under the act, which is excerpted below, the Treasury paid out and received all government funds and operated independently of the country's banking and financial system. The Independent Treasury system existed in some form until 1921.

An Act to provide for the better Organization of the Treasury, and for the Collection, Safe keeping, Transfer, and Disbursement of the public Revenue.

Be it enacted . . . , That the rooms prepared and provided in the new treasury building at the seat of government for the use of the treasurer of the United States, his assistants, and clerks, and occupied by them, and also the fireproof vaults and safes erected in said rooms for the keeping of the public moneys in the possession and under the immediate control of said treasurer, and such other apartments as are provided for in this act as places of deposit of the public money, are hereby constituted and declared to be the treasury of the United States. And all moneys paid into the same shall be subject to the draft of the treasurer, drawn agreeably to appropriations made by law.

[Sections 2–4 of the act declared the mint at Philadelphia, the branch mint at New Orleans, and the places provided for use of receivers general of public money at New York, Boston, Charleston, and St. Louis, under the Independent Treasury Act of July 4, 1840, which was repealed in 1841, shall be places of deposit.]

SEC. 5. And be it further enacted, That the President shall nominate, and by and with the advice and consent of the Senate appoint, four officers to be denominated "assistant treasurers of the United States," which said officers shall hold their respective offices for the term of four years unless sooner removed therefrom; one of which shall be located at the city of New York . . . ; one . . . at the city of Boston . . . ; one . . . at the city of Charleston . . . ; and one other at St. Louis . . .

SEC. 6. And be it further acted, That the treasurer of the United States, the treasurer of the mint of the United States, the treasurers, and those acting as such, of the various branch mints, all collectors of the customs, all surveyors of the customs acting also as collectors, all assistant treasurers, all receivers of public moneys at the several land offices, all postmasters, and all public officers of whatsoever character, be, and they are hereby, required to keep safely, without loaning, using, depositing in bank, or exchanging for other funds than as allowed by this act, all the public money collected by them, or otherwise at any time placed in their possession and custody, till the same is ordered, by the proper department or officer of the government, to be transferred or paid out; and when such orders for transfer or payment are received, faithfully and promptly to make the same as directed, and to do and perform all other duties as fiscal agents of the government which may be imposed by this or any other acts of Congress, or by any regulation of the treasury department made in conformity to law; and also to do and perform all acts and duties required by law, or by direction of any of the Executive departments of the government, as agents for paying pensions, or for making any other disbursements which either of the heads of these departments may be required by law to make, and which are of a character to be made by the depositories hereby constituted, consistently with the other official duties imposed upon them. . . .

SEC. 9. And be it further enacted, That all collectors and, receivers of public money, of every character and description, within the District of Columbia, shall, as frequently as they may be directed by the Secretary of the Treasury, or the Postmaster general so to do, pay over to the treasurer of the United States, at the treasury, all public moneys collected by them, or in their hands; that all such collectors and receivers of public moneys within the cities of Philadelphia and New Orleans shall, upon the same direction, pay over to the treasurers of the mints in their respective cities, at the said mints, all public moneys collected by them, or in their hands; and that all such collectors and receivers of public moneys within the cities of New York, Boston, Charleston, and St. Louis, shall, upon the same direction, pay over to the assistant treasurers in their respective cities, at their offices, respectively, all the public moneys collected by them, or in their hands, to be safely kept by the said respective depositories until otherwise disposed of according to law and it shall be the duty of the said Secretary and Postmaster general respectively to direct such payments by the said collectors and receivers at all the said places, at least as often as once in each week, and as much more frequently, in all cases, as they in their discretion may think proper. . . .

SEC. 18. Be it further enacted, That on . . . [January 1, 1847] . . . , and thereafter, all duties, taxes, sales of public lands, debts, and sums of money accruing or becoming due to the United States, and also all sums due for postages or otherwise, to the general post office department, shall be paid in gold and silver coin only, or in treasury notes issued under the authority of the United States. . . .

SEC. 19. And be it further enacted, That on . . . [April 1, 1847] . . . , and thereafter, every officer or agent engaged in making disbursements on account of the United States, or of the general post-office, shall make all payments in gold and silver coin, or in treasury notes, if the creditor agree to receive said notes in payment.

Source: U.S. Statutes at Large, Vol IX, Session I, Ch. 90, p. 59.

B. Joseph Glover Baldwin's *Flush Times* (1853)

Joseph Glover Baldwin (1815–1864), an Alabama lawyer and Whig politician, was best known as the author of The Flush Times of Alabama and Mississippi, *which contained a series a humorous sketches of life on the southwestern frontier in the antebellum era. Baldwin believed that frontier society was fluid and chaotic, allowing for people to rise above the economic and social positions they might have been forced into by older, more stratified societies. In the excerpts from* Flush Times *reproduced below, Baldwin describes the conditions that he believed made for this economic freedom.*

In the fullness of time the new era had set in—the era of the second great experiment of independence: the experiment, namely, of credit without capital, and enterprise without honesty. The Age of Brass had succeeded the Arcadian period when men got rich by saving a part of their earnings, and lived at their own cost and in ignorance of the new plan of making fortunes on the profits of what they owed. A new theory, not found in the works on political economy, was broached. It was found out that the prejudice in favor of the metals (brass excluded) was an absurd superstition; and that, in reality, any thing else, which the parties interested in giving it currency chose, might serve as a representative of value and medium for exchange of property; and as gold and silver had served for a great number of years as representatives, the republican doctrine of rotation in office required they should give way. Accordingly it was decided that Rags, a very familiar character, and very popular and easy of access, should take their place. Rags belonged to the school of progress. He was representative of the then Young America. His administration was not tame. It was *very* spirited. It was based on the Bonapartist idea of keeping the imagination of the people excited. The leading fiscal idea of his system was to *democratize* capital, and to make, for all purposes of trade, credit and enjoyment of wealth, the man that had *no* money a little richer, if any thing, than the man that had a million. The principle of success and basis of operation, though inexplicable in the hurry of the time, is plain enough now: it was faith. Let the public believe that a smutted rag is money, it is money: in other words; it was a sort of financial biology, which made, at night, the thing conjured for, the thing that was seen, so far as the patient was concerned, while the fit was on him—except that now a man does not do his trading when under the mesmeric influence: in the flush times he did.

This country was just settling up. Marvellous accounts had gone forth of the fertility of its virgin lands; and the productions of the soil were commanding a price remunerating to slave labor as it had never been remunerated before. Emigrants came flocking in from all quarters of the Union, especially from the slaveholding States. The new country seemed to be a reservoir, and every road leading to it a vagrant stream of enterprise and adventure. Money, or what passed for money, was the only cheap thing to be had. Every cross-road and every avocation presented an opening,—through which a fortune was seen by the adventurer in near perspective. Credit was a thing of course. To refuse it—if the thing was ever done—were an insult for which a bowie-knife were not a too summary or exemplary a means of redress. The State banks were issuing their bills by the sheet, like a patent steam printing-press *its* issues; and no other showing was asked of the applicant for the loan than an authentication of his great distress for money. Finance, even in its most exclusive quarter, had thus already got, in this wonderful revolution, to work upon the principles of the charity hospital. If an overseer grew tired of supervising a plantation and felt a call to the mercantile life, even if he omitted the compendious method of buying out a merchant wholesale, stock, house and good will, and laying down, at once, his bull-whip for the yard-stick—all he had to do was to go on to New-York, and present himself in Pearlstreet with a letter avouching his citizenship, and a clean shirt, and he was regularly given a through ticket to speedy bankruptcy.

Under this stimulating process prices rose like smoke. Lots in obscure villages were held at city prices; lands, bought at the minimum cost of government, were sold at from thirty to forty dollars per acre, and considered dirt cheap at that. In short, the country had got to be a full ante-type of California, in all except the gold. Society was wholly unorganized: there was no restraining public opinion: the law was well-nigh powerless—and religion scarcely was heard of except as furnishing the oaths and *technics* of profanity. The world saw a fair experiment of what it would have been, if the fiat had never been pronounced which decreed subsistence as the price of labor.

Money, got without work, by those unaccustomed to it, turned the heads of its possessors, and they spent it with a recklessness like that with which they gained it. The pursuits of industry neglected, riot and coarse debauchery filled up the vacant hours. "Where the carcass is, there will the eagles be gathered together;" and the eagles that flocked to the Southwest, were of the same sort as the *black eagles* the Duke of Saxe-Weimar saw on his celebrated journey to the Natural Bridge. "The cankers of a long peace and a calm world"—there were no

Mexican wars and filibuster expeditions in those days—gathered in the villages and cities by scores.

Even the little boys caught the taint of the general infection of morals; and I knew one of them—Jim Ellett by name—to give a man ten dollars to hold him up to bet at the table of a faro-bank. James was a fast youth; and I sincerely hope he may not fulfil his early promise, and some day be *assisted up still higher.*

Source: Baldwin, Joseph G. *The Flush Times of Alabama and Mississippi: A Series of Sketches.* New York: D. Appleton and Co., 1854, 81–92.

C. *Dred Scott v. Sandford* (March 6, 1857)

In Dred Scot v. Sandford, *a landmark case known in American history as the Dred Scott Decision, the U.S. Supreme Court declared that the descendants of Africans brought into the United States as slaves were not U.S. citizens and not protected by the U.S. Constitution. The court also concluded that Congress had no authority to prohibit slavery in federal territories; that slaves, as non-citizens, could not sue in U.S. courts; and that slave owners could not be denied their property in slaves without due process. The court's opinion in the 1857 case, written by Chief Justice Roger B. Taney (1777–1864) and excerpted below, caused a firestorm of controversy and sharpened the divisions between North and South in the last years before the Civil War. The decision was overturned by the ratification of 14th Amendment in 1868.*

. . . The counsel then filed the following agreed statement of facts, viz:

In the year 1834, the plaintiff was a negro slave belonging to Dr. Emerson, who was a surgeon in the army of the United States. In that year, 1834, said Dr. Emerson took the plaintiff from the State of Missouri to the military post at Rock Island, in the State of Illinois, and held him there as a slave until the month of April or May, 1836. At the time last mentioned, said Dr. Emerson removed the plaintiff from said military post at Rock Island to the military post at Fort Snelling, situate on the west bank of the Mississippi river, in the Territory known as Upper Louisiana, acquired by the United States of France, and situate north of the latitude of thirty-six degrees thirty minutes north, and north of the State of Missouri. Said Dr. Emerson held the plaintiff in slavery at said Fort Snelling, from said last-mentioned date until the year 1838.

In the year 1835, Harriet, who is named in the second count of the plaintiff's declaration, was the negro slave of Major Taliaferro, who belonged to the army of the United States. In that year, 1835, said Major Taliaferro took said Harriet to said Fort Snelling, a military post, situated as hereinbefore stated, and kept her there as a slave until the year 1836, and then sold and delivered her as a slave at said Fort Snelling unto the said Dr. Emerson hereinbefore named. Said Dr. Emerson held said Harriet in slavery at said Fort Snelling until the year 1838.

In the year 1836, the plaintiff and said Harriet at said Fort Snelling, with the consent of said Dr. Emerson, who then claimed to be their master and owner, intermarried, and took each other for husband and wife. Eliza and Lizzie, named in the third count of the plaintiff's declaration, are the fruit of that marriage. Eliza is about fourteen years old, and was born on board the steamboat Gipsey, north of the north line of the State of Missouri, and upon the river Mississippi. Lizzie is about seven years old, and was born in the State of Missouri, at the military post called Jefferson Barracks.

In the year 1838, said Dr. Emerson removed the plaintiff and said Harriet and their said daughter Eliza from said Fort Snelling to the State of Missouri, where they have ever since resided.

Before the commencement of this suit, said Dr. Emerson sold and conveyed the plaintiff, said Harriet, Eliza, and Lizzie, to the defendant, as slaves, and the defendant has ever since claimed to hold them and each of them as slaves.

At the times mentioned in the plaintiff's declaration, the defendant, claiming to be owner as aforesaid, laid his hands upon said plaintiff, Harriet, Eliza, and Lizzie, and imprisoned them, doing in this respect, however, no more than what he might lawfully do if they were of right his slaves at such times.

Further proof may be given on the trial for either party.

It is agreed that Dred Scott brought suit for his freedom in the Circuit Court of St. Louis county; that there was a verdict and judgment in his favor; that, on a writ of error to the Supreme Court, the judgment below was reversed, and the same remanded to the Circuit Court, where it has been continued to await the decision of this case.

In May, 1854, the cause went before a jury, who found the following verdict, viz:

As to the first issue joined in this case, we of the jury find the defendant not guilty; and as to the issue secondly above joined, we of the jury find that before and at the time when, &c., in the first count mentioned, the said Dred Scott was a negro slave, the lawful property of the defendant; and as to the issue thirdly above joined, we, the jury, find that before and at the time when, &c., in the second and third counts mentioned, the said Harriet, wife of [p399] said Dred Scott, and Eliza and Lizzie, the daughters of the said Dred Scott, were negro slaves, the lawful property of the defendant.

Whereupon, the court gave judgment for the defendant.

After an ineffectual motion for a new trial, the plaintiff filed the following bill of exceptions.

On the trial of this cause by the jury, the plaintiff, to maintain the issues on his part, read to the jury the following agreed statement of facts, (see agreement above.) No further testimony was given to the jury by either party. Thereupon the plaintiff moved the court to give to the jury the following instruction, viz:

"That, upon the facts agreed to by the parties, they ought to find for the plaintiff. The court refused to give such instruction to the jury, and the plaintiff, to such refusal, then and there duly excepted."

The court then gave the following instruction to the jury, on motion of the defendant:

The jury are instructed, that upon the facts in this case, the law is with the defendant.

The plaintiff excepted to this instruction.

Upon these exceptions, the case came up to this court.

Source: Dred Scott v. Sandford, 60 U.S. 393 (1857).

D. George Fitzhugh's *Cannibals All!* (1857)

In 1857 George Fitzhugh (1806–1881), a Virginia writer and planter, published Cannibals All!, *a widely read defense of slavery as an economic and social good. In the excerpts reproduced below, Fitzhugh argues that black slaves in the South were freer and happier than wage laborers in the North. Slaves, declared Fitzhugh, were allowed a greater share of the fruits of their labor by their owners than free laborers were allowed by their bosses. During the Civil War, Fitzhugh worked for the Confederate Treasury in Richmond.*

The negro slaves of the South are the happiest, and, in some sense, the freest people in the world. The children and the aged and infirm work not at all, and yet have all the comforts and necessaries of life provided for them. They enjoy liberty, because they are oppressed neither by care nor labor. The women do little hard work, and are protected from the despotism of their husbands by their masters. The negro men and stout boys work, on the average, in good weather, not more than nine hours a day. The balance of their time is spent in perfect abandon. Besides, they have their Sabbaths and holidays. White men, with so much of license and liberty, would die of ennui; but negroes luxuriate in corporeal and mental repose. With their faces upturned to the sun, they can sleep at any hour; and quiet sleep is the greatest of human enjoyments. "Blessed be the man who invented sleep." 'Tis happiness in itself—and results from contentment with the present, and confident assurance of the future. We do not know whether free laborers ever sleep. They are fools to do so; for, whilst they sleep, the wily and watchful capitalist is devising means to ensnare and exploitate them. The free laborer must work or starve. He is more of a slave than the negro, because he works longer and harder for less allowance than the slave, and has no holiday, because the cares of life with him begin when its labors end. He has no liberty, and not a single right. We know, 'tis often said, air and water, are common property, which all have equal right to participate and enjoy; but this is utterly false. The appropriation of the lands carries with it the appropriation of all on or above the lands, *usque ad coelumm aut ad inferos.* A man cannot breathe the air, without a place to breathe it from, and all places are appropriated. All water is private property "to the middle of the stream," except the ocean, and that is not fit to drink.

Free laborers have not a thousandth part of the rights and liberties of negro slaves. Indeed, they have not a single right or a single liberty, unless it be the right or liberty to die. But the reader may think that he and other capitalists and employers are freer than negro slaves. Your capital would soon vanish, if you dared indulge in the liberty and abandon of negroes. You hold your wealth and position by the tenure of constant watchfulness, care and circumspection. You never labor; but you are never free.

Where a few own the soil, they have unlimited power over the balance of society, until domestic slavery comes in, to compel them to permit this balance of society to draw a sufficient and comfortable living from "terra mater." Free society, asserts the right of a few to the earth—slavery, maintains that it belongs, in different degrees, to all. . . .

Until the lands of America are appropriated by a few, population becomes dense, competition among laborers active, employment uncertain, and wages low, the personal liberty of all the whites will continue to be a blessing. We has have vast unsettled territories; population may cease to increase, or increase slowly, as in most countries, and many centuries may elapse before the question will be practically suggested, whether slavery to capital be preferable to slavery to human masters. But the negro has neither energy nor enterprise, and, even in our sparser population, finds, with his improvident habits, that his liberty is a curse to himself, and a greater curse to the society around him. These considerations, and others equally obvious, have induced the South to attempt to defend negro slavery as an exceptional institution, admitting, nay asserting; that slavery, in the general or in the abstract, is morally wrong, and against common right. With singular inconsistency, after making this admission, which admits away the authority of the Bible, of profane history, and of the almost universal practice of mankind—they turn round and attempt to bolster up the cause of negro slavery by these very exploded authorities. If we mean not to repudiate all divine, and almost all human authority in favor of slavery, we must vindicate that institution in the abstract.

To insist that a status of society, which has been almost universal, and which is expressly and continually justified by Holy Writ, is its natural, normal, and necessary status, under the ordinary circumstances, is on its face a plausible and probable proposition. To insist on less, is to yield our cause, and to give up our religion; for if white slavery be morally wrong, be a violation of natural rights, the Bible cannot be true. Human and divine authority do seem in the general to concur, in establishing the expediency of having masters and slaves of different races. The nominal servitude of the Jews to each other, in its temporary character, and no doubt in its mild character, more nearly resembled our wardship and apprenticeship, than ordinary domestic slavery. In very many nations of antiquity, and in some of modern times, the law has permitted the native citizens to become slaves to each other. But few take advantage of such laws; and the infrequency of the practice, establishes the general truth that master and slave should be of different national descent. In some respects, the wider the difference the better, as the slave will feel less mortified by his position. In other respects, it may be that too wide a difference hardens the hearts and brutalizes the feelings of both master and slave. The civilized man hates the savage, and the savage returns the hatred with interest. Hence, West India slavery, of newly caught negroes, is not a very humane, affectionate or civilizing institution. Virginia negroes have become moral and intelligent. They love their master and his family, and the attachment is reciprocated. Still, we like the idle, but intelligent house-servants, better than the hard-used, but stupid outhands; and we like the mulatto better than the negro; yet the negro is generally more affectionate, contented and faithful.

Source: Fitzhugh, George. *Cannibals All!, or, Slaves without Masters.* Richmond, VA: A. Morris, Publisher, 1857, 29–31, 294–99.

E. Hinton Rowan Helper's *The Impending Crisis of the South* (1857)

Although a native of North Carolina, Hinton Rowan Helper (1829–1909) was a staunch critic of the institution of slavery. In his 1857 book, The Impending Crisis of the South, *Helper argued that slavery retarded the development of the South and particularly harmed the economic prospects of the region's non-slaveholders. In the excerpts reproduced below, Helper explains how slavery has caused the South to fall far behind the North in terms of economic growth. Widely read, the book made Helper famous in the North and hated in the South, where merely circulating a copy could bring criminal charges.*

WHY THE NORTH HAS SURPASSED THE SOUTH.

And now that we have come to the very heart and soul of our subject, we feel no disposition to mince matters, but mean to speak plainly, and to the point, without any equivocation, mental reservation, or secret evasion whatever. The son of a venerated parent, who, while he lived, was a considerate and merciful slaveholder, a native of the South, born and bred in North Carolina, of a family whose home has been in the valley of the Yadkin for nearly a century and a half, a Southerner by instinct and by all the influences of thought, habits, and kindred, and with the desire and fixed purpose to reside permanently within the limits of the South, and with the expectation of dying there also—we feel that we have the right to express our opinion, however humble or unimportant it may be, on any and every question that affects the public good; and, so help us God, "sink or swim, live or die, survive or perish," we are determined to exercise that right with manly firmness, and without fear, favor or affection.

And now to the point. In our opinion, an opinion which has been formed from data obtained by assiduous researches, and comparisons, from laborious investigation, logical reasoning, and earnest reflection, the causes which have impeded the progress and prosperity of the South, which have dwindled our commerce, and other similar pursuits, into the most contemptible insignificance; sunk a large majority of our people in galling poverty and ignorance, rendered a small minority conceited and tyrannical, and driven the rest away from their homes; entailed upon us a humiliating dependence on the Free States; disgraced us in the recesses of our own souls, and brought us under reproach in the eyes of all civilized and enlightened nations—may all be traced to one common source, and there find solution in the most hateful and horrible word, that was ever incorporated into the vocabulary of human economy—*Slavery!*

Reared amidst the institution of slavery, believing it to be wrong both in principle and in practice, and having seen and felt its evil influences upon individuals, communities and states, we deem it a duty, no less than a privilege, to enter our protest against it, and to use our most strenuous efforts to overturn and abolish it! Then we are an abolitionist? Yes! not merely a freesoiler, but an abolitionist, in the fullest sense of the term. We are not only in favor of keeping slavery out of the territories, but, carrying our opposition to the institution a step further, we here unhesitatingly declare ourself in favor of its immediate and unconditional abolition, in every state in this confederacy, where it now exists! Patriotism makes us a freesoiler; state pride makes us an emancipationist; a profound sense of duty to the South makes us an abolitionist; a reasonable degree of fellow feeling for the negro, makes us a colonizationist. With the free state men in Kansas and Nebraska, we sympathize with all our heart We love the whole country, the great family of states and territories, one and inseparable, and would have the word Liberty engraved as an appropriate and truthful motto, on the escutcheon of every member of the confederacy. We love freedom, we hate slavery, and rather than give up the one or submit to the other, we will forfeit the pound of flesh nearest our heart. Is this sufficiently explicit and categorical? If not, we hold ourself in readiness at all times, to return a prompt reply to any proper question that may be propounded.

Our repugnance to the institution of slavery, springs from no one-sided idea, or sickly sentimentality. We have not been hasty in making up our mind on the subject; we have jumped at no conclusions; we have acted with perfect calmness and deliberation; we have carefully considered, and examined the reasons for and against the institution, and have also taken into account the propable consequences of our decision. The more we investigate the matter, the deeper becomes the conviction that we are right; and with this to impel and sustain us, we pursue our labor with love, with hope, and with constantly renewing vigor.

That we shall encounter opposition we consider as certain; perhaps we may even be subjected to insult and violence. From the conceited and cruel oligarchy of the South, we could look for nothing less. But we shall shrink from no responsibility, and do nothing unbecoming a man; we know how to repel indignity, and if assaulted, shall not fail to make the blow recoil upon the aggressor's head. The road we have to travel may be a rough one, but no impediment shall cause us to falter in our course. The line of our duty is clearly defined, and it is our intention to follow it faithfully, or die in the attempt.

But, thanks to heaven, we have no ominous forebodings of the result of the contest now pending between Liberty and Slavery in this confederacy. Though neither a prophet nor the son of a prophet, our vision is sufficiently penetrative to divine the future so far as to be able to see that the "peculiar institution" has but a short, and as heretofore, inglorious existence before it. Time, the righter of every wrong, is ripening events for the desired consummation of our labors and the fulfillment of our cherished hopes. Each revolving year brings nearer the inevitable crisis. The sooner it comes the better; may heaven, through our humble efforts, hasten its advent.

Source: Helper, Hinton Rowan. *The Impending Crisis of the South.* New York: Burdick Brothers, 1857, 24–33.

F. Frederick Law Olmsted's *The Cotton Kingdom* (1861)

In 1852 the New York Daily Times *sent journalist Frederick Law Olmsted (1822–1903) traveling through the South to record his impressions and experiences for publication in the newspaper. Olmstead's dispatches, written between 1852 and 1857, were collected and published in three volumes between 1856 and 1860. Reproduced below is an account of a December 1852 trip from Petersburg, Virginia, taken from a one-volume abridgement published in 1861 at the start of the Civil War and entitled* Journeys and Explorations in the Cotton Kingdom *(often shortened to* The Cotton Kingdom*). Olmsted's observations led him to conclude that slavery harmed the economy of the South, making the region inefficient and underdeveloped and robbing non-slaveholders of any chance for economic improvement.*

First, we had picked our way from the store down to the brook, through a deeply corrugated clay-road; then there was the swamp, with the fallen trees and thick underwood, beaten down and barked in the miry parts by waggons making a road for themselves, no traces of which road could we find in the harder, pebbly ground. At length, when we came to drier land, and among pine trees, we discovered a clear way cut through them, and a distinct road before us again; and this brought us soon to an old clearing, just beginning to be grown over with pines, in which was the old cabin of rotten logs, one or two of them falling out of rank on the door side, and the whole concern having a dangerous lurch to one comer, as if too much whisky had been drunk in it: then a more recent clearing, with a fenced field and another cabin, the residence of the white man we were told of, probably. No white people, however, were to be seen, but two negroes sat in the mouth of a wigwam, husking maize, and a couple of hungry bounds came bounding over the zigzag, gateless fence, as if they bad agreed with each other that they would wait no longer for the return of their master, but would straightway pull down the first traveller that passed, and have something to eat before they were quite famished. They stopped short, however, when they had got within a good cart-whip's length of us, and contented themselves with dolefully youping as long as we continued in sight. We turned the comer, following some slight traces of a road, and shortly afterwards met a curious vehicular establishment, probably belonging to the master of the hounds. It consisted of an axle-tree and wheels, and a pair of shafts made of unbarked saplings, in which was harnessed, by attachments of raw bide and rope, a single small black ox. There was a bit, made of telegraph wire, in his mouth, by which he was guided, through the mediation of a pair of much-knotted rope reins, by a white man—a dignified sovereign, wearing a brimless crown—who sat upon a two-bushel sack (of meal, I trust, for the hounds' sake), balanced upon the axle-tree, and who saluted me with a frank "How are you?" as we came opposite each other.

Soon after this, we reached a small grove of much older and larger pines than we had seen before, with long and horizontally stretching branches, and duller and thinner foliage. In the middle of it was another log cabin, with a door in one of the gable ends, a stove pipe, half rusted away, protruding from the other, and, in the middle of one of the sides, a small square port-hole, closed by a wooden shutter. This must have been the schoolhouse; but there were no children then about it, and no appearance of there having been any lately. Near it was a long string of fence, and a gate and lane, which gave entrance, probably, to a large plantation, though there was no cultivated land within sight of the road.

I could remember hardly anything after this, except a continuation of pine trees, big, little, and medium in size, and hogs, and a black, crooked, burnt sapling, that we had made believe was a snake springing at us and bad jumped away from, and then we had gone on at a trot—it must have been some time ago, that—and then I was paying attentions to Jane (the filly's name was Jane Gillan), and finally my thoughts had gone wool-gathering, and we must have travelled some miles out of our way and—"Never mind," said Jane, lifting her head, and turning in the direction we had been going, "I don't think it's any great matter if we are lost; such a fine day—so long since I've been out; if you don't care, I'd just as lief be lost as not; let's go on and see what we shall come to."

"Very well, my beauty; you know the country better than I do. If you'll risk your dinner, I'm quite ready to go anywhere you choose to take me. It's quite certain we have not passed any meeting-house, or creek, or saw-mill, or negro-quarters, and, as we have been two hours on the road, it's evident we are not going straight to Mr. W.'s; I must see what we do pass after this," and I stood up in the stirrups as we walked on, to see what the country around us was like.

"Old fields"—a coarse, yellow, sandy soil, bearing scarcely anything but pine trees and broom-sedge. In some places, for acres, the pines would not be above five feet high-that was land that had been in cultivation, used up and "turned out," not more than six or eight years before; then there were patches of every age; sometimes the trees were a hundred feet high. At long intervals, there were fields in which the pine was just beginning to spring in beautiful green plumes from the ground, and was yet hardly noticeable among the dead brown grass and sassafras bushes and blackberry vines, which nature first sends to hide *the nakedness of the impoverished earth.*

Of living creatures, for miles, not one was to be seen (not even a crow or a snow-bird), except hogs. *These long, lank, bony, snake-headed, hairy, wild beasts*—would come dashing across our path, in packs of from three to a dozen, with short, hasty grunts, almost always at a gallop, and looking neither to right nor left, as if they were in pursuit of a fox, and were quite certain to catch him in the next hundred yards; or droves of little pigs would rise up suddenly in the sedge, and scamper off squealing into cover, while their heroic mothers would turn round and make a stand, looking fiercely at us, as if they were quite ready to fight if we advanced any further, but always breaking, as we came near, with a loud boosch!

Source: Olmsted, Frederick Law. *The Cotton Kingdom.* New York: Mason Brothers, 1961, 51–52.

6. Panic of 1873

A. *Veazie Bank v. Fenno* (1869)

In 1866 Congress passed legislation imposing a 10 percent tax on notes issued by state banks and state banking associations. The Veazie Bank in Maine filed suit in the state circuit court to recover its tax payment, claiming that Congress had no authority to impose such a tax. The case eventually came before the U.S. Supreme Court, which in 1869 in its Veazie Bank v. Fenno *decision declared the tax constitutional. Below are excerpts from the court's opinion, written by Chief Justice Salmon P. Chase (1808–1873), who concluded that Congress could impose the tax under its power to regulate the circulation of coin. Congress, the court determined, could limit the circulation of notes issued by state banks or individuals to ensure that the country had a sound and uniform currency.*

THE CHIEF JUSTICE delivered the opinion of the Court.

. . . The difficulty of defining with accuracy the terms used in the clause of the Constitution which confers the power of taxation upon Congress was felt in the Convention which framed that instrument, and has always been experienced by courts when called upon to determine their meaning.

The general intent of the Constitution, however, seems plain. The general government, administered by the Congress of the Confederation, had been reduced to the verge of impotency by the necessity of relying for revenue upon requisitions on the states, and it was a leading object in the adoption of the Constitution to relieve the government to be organized under it from this necessity and confer upon it ample power to provide revenue by the taxation of persons and property. And nothing is clearer from the discussions in the Convention and the discussions which preceded final ratification by the necessary number of states than the purpose to give this power to Congress as to the taxation of everything except exports in its fullest extent.

This purpose is apparent also from the terms in which the taxing power is granted. The power is "to lay and collect taxes, duties, imposts, and excises, to pay the debt and provide for the common defense and general welfare of the United States." More comprehensive words could not have been used. Exports only are by another provision excluded from its application.

There are indeed certain virtual limitations arising from the principles of the Constitution itself. It would undoubtedly be an abuse of the power if so exercised as to impair the separate existence and independent self-government [Footnote 14] of the states, or if exercised for ends inconsistent with the limited grants of power in the Constitution.

And there are directions as to the mode of exercising the power. If Congress sees fit to impose a capitation, or other direct tax, it must be laid in proportion to the census; if Congress determines to impose duties, imposts, and excises, they must be uniform throughout the United States. These are not strictly limitations of power. They are rules prescribing the mode in which it shall be exercised. It still extends to every object of taxation except exports, and may be applied to every object of taxation, to which it extends, in such measure as Congress may determine.

The comprehensiveness of the power thus given to Congress may serve to explain at least the absence of any attempt by members of the Convention to define, even in debate, the terms of the grant. The words used certainly describe the whole power, and it was the intention of the Convention that the whole power should be conferred. The definition of particular words therefore became unimportant.

It may be said indeed that this observation, however just in its application to the general grant of power, cannot be applied to the rules by which different descriptions of taxes are directed to be laid and collected.

Direct taxes must be laid and collected by the rule of apportionment; duties, imposts, and excises must be laid and collected under the rule of uniformity.

Must diversity of opinion has always prevailed upon the question what are direct taxes? Attempts to answer it by reference to the definitions of political economists have been frequently made, but without satisfactory results. The enumeration of the different kinds of taxes which Congress was authorized to impose was probably made with very little reference to their speculations. The great work of Adam Smith, the first comprehensive treatise on political economy in the English language, had then been recently published, but in this work, though there are passages which refer to the characteristic difference between direct and indirect taxation, there is nothing which affords any valuable light on the use of the words "direct taxes" in the Constitution. . . .

It cannot be doubted that under the Constitution, the power to provide a circulation of coin is given to Congress. And it is settled by the uniform practice of the government and by repeated decisions that Congress may constitutionally authorize the emission of bills of credit. It is not important here to decide whether the quality of legal tender, in payment of debts, can be constitutionally imparted to these bills; it is enough to say that there can be no question of the power of the government to emit them, to make them receivable in payment of debts to itself, to fit them for use by those who see fit to use them in all the transactions of commerce, to provide for their redemption, to make them a currency, uniform in value and description, and convenient and useful for circulation. These powers until recently were only partially and occasionally exercised. Lately, however, they have been called into full activity, and Congress has undertaken to supply a currency for the entire country.

The methods adopted for the supply of this currency were briefly explained in the first part of this opinion. It now consists of coin, of United States notes, and of the notes of the national banks. Both descriptions of notes may be properly described as bills of credit, for both are furnished by the government, both are issued on the credit of the government, and the government is responsible for the redemption of both, primarily as to the first description, and immediately upon default of the bank as to the second. When these bills shall be made convertible into coin at the will of the holder, this currency will perhaps satisfy the wants of the community in respect to a circulating medium as perfectly as any mixed currency that can be devised.

Having thus, in the exercise of undisputed constitutional powers, undertaken to provide a currency for the whole country, it cannot be questioned that Congress may constitutionally secure the benefit of it to the people by appropriate legislation. To this end, Congress has denied the quality of legal tender to foreign coins, and has provided by law against the imposition of counterfeit and base coin on the community. To the same end, Congress may restrain by suitable enactments the circulation as money of any notes not issued under its own authority. Without this power, indeed, its attempts to secure a sound and uniform currency for the country must be futile.

Viewed in this light as well as in the other light of a duty on contracts or property, we cannot doubt the constitutionality of the tax under consideration.

Source: Justia.com. U.S. Supreme Court Center. http://supreme.justia.com/cases /federal/us/75/533/case.html. *Veazie Bank v. Fenno*, 75 U.S. 8 Wall. 533 533 (1869).

B. President Grant's Veto of the Inflation Bill of 1874 (April 22, 1874)

To ease the effects of the Panic of 1873 Secretary of the Treasury William A. Richardson (1821–1896) released $26 million in greenbacks into an economy hungry for capital. Continuing this inflationary policy to stimulate the economy, Congress in 1874 passed the Inflation Bill, which would have released another $18 million in greenbacks. Southern and western farmers and workers favored the measure, but eastern bankers and businessmen opposed it. On April 22, 1874, President Ulysses S. Grant (1822–1885) confounded expectations and the stated policy of his Republican Party by vetoing the bill. In his veto message, which is reproduced below, Grant argued that the bill would damage the nation's credit.

To the Senate of the United States:

Herewith I return, Senate bill No. 617, entitled "An act to fix the amount of United States notes and the circulation of national banks, and for other purposes," without my approval.

In doing so I must express my regret at not being able to give my assent to a measure which has received the sanction of a majority of the legislators chosen by the people to make laws for their guidance, and have studiously sought to find sufficient arguments to justify such assent, but unsuccessfully.

Practically it is a question whether the measure under discussion would give an additional dollar to the irredeemable paper currency of the country or not, and whether by requiring three-fourths of the reserve to be retained by the banks and prohibiting interest to be received on the balance it might not prove a contraction.

But the fact can not be concealed that theoretically the bill increases the paper circulation $100,000,000, less only the amount of reserves restrained from circulation by the provision of the second section. The measure has been supported on the theory that it would give increased circulation. It is a fair inference, therefore, that if in practice the measure should fail to create the abundance of circulation expected of it the friends of the measure, particularly those out of Congress, would clamor for such inflation as would give the expected relief.

The theory, in my belief, is a departure from true principles of finance, national interest, national obligations to creditors, Congressional promises, party pledges (on the part of both political parties), and of personal views and promises made by me in every annual message sent to Congress and in each inaugural address.

In my annual message to Congress in December, 1869, the following passages appear:

Among the evils growing out of the rebellion, and not yet referred to, is that of an irredeemable currency. It is an evil which I hope will receive your most earnest attention. It is a duty, and one of the highest duties, of Government to secure to the citizen a medium of exchange of fixed, unvarying value. This implies a return to a specie basis, and no substitute for it can be devised. It should be commenced now and reached at the earliest practicable moment consistent with a fair regard to the interests of the debtor class. Immediate resumption, if practicable, would not be desirable. It would compel the debtor class to pay, beyond their contracts, the premium on gold at the date of their purchase, and would bring bankruptcy and ruin to thousands. Fluctuation, however, in the paper value of the measure of all values (gold) is detrimental to the interests of trade. It makes the man of business an involuntary gambler, for in all sales where future payment is to be made both parties speculate as to what will be the value of the currency to be paid and received. I earnestly recommend to you, then, such legislation as will insure a gradual return to specie payments and put an immediate stop to fluctuations in the value of currency.

I still adhere to the views then expressed.

As early as December 4, 1865, the House of Representatives passed a resolution, by a vote of 144 yeas to 6 nays, concurring "in the views of the Secretary of the Treasury in relation to the necessity of a contraction of the currency, with a view to as early a resumption of specie payments as the business interests of the country will permit," and pledging "cooperative action to this end as speedily as possible."

The first act passed by the Forty-first Congress, (approved) on the 18th day of March, 1869, was as follows:

AN ACT to strengthen the public credit

Be it enacted, etc., That in order to remove any doubt as to the purpose of the Government to discharge all just obligations to the public creditors, and to settle conflicting questions and interpretations of the law by virtue of which such obligations have been contracted, it is hereby provided and declared that the faith of the United States is solemnly pledged to the payment in coin or its equivalent of all the obligations of the United States not bearing interest, known as United States notes, and all the interest-bearing obligations of the United States, except in cases where the law authorizing the issue of any such obligation has expressly provided that the same may be paid in lawful money or in other currency than gold and silver; but none of the said interest-bearing obligations not already due shall be redeemed or paid before maturity unless at such time United States notes shall be convertible into coin at the option of the holder, or unless at such time bonds of the United States bearing a lower rate of interest than the bonds to be redeemed can be sold at par in coin. And the United States also solemnly pledges its faith to make provision at the earliest practicable period for the redemption of the United States notes in coin.

This act still remains as a continuing pledge of the faith of the United States "to make provision at the earliest practicable period for the redemption of the United States notes in coin."

A declaration contained in the act of June 30, 1864, created an obligation that the total amount of United States notes issued or to be issued should never exceed $400,000,000. The amount in actual circulation was actually reduced to $356,000,000, at which point Congress passed the act of February 4, 1868, suspending the further reduction of the currency. The forty-four millions have ever been regarded as a reserve, to be used only in case of emergency, such as has occurred on several occasions, and must occur when from any cause revenues suddenly fall below expenditures; and such a reserve is necessary, because the fractional currency, amounting to fifty millions, is redeemable in legal tender on call.

It may be said that such a return of fractional currency for redemption is impossible; but let steps be taken for a return to a specie basis and it will be found that silver will take the place of fractional currency as rapidly as it can be supplied, when the premium on gold reaches a sufficiently low point. With the amount of United States notes to be issued permanently fixed within proper limits and the Treasury so strengthened as to be able to redeem them in coin on demand it will then be safe to inaugurate a system of free banking with such provisions as to make compulsory redemption of the circulating notes of the banks in coin, or in United States notes, themselves redeemable and made equivalent to coin.

As a measure preparatory to free banking, and for placing the Government in a condition to redeem its notes in coin "at the earliest practicable period," the revenues of the country should be increased so as to pay current expenses, provide for the sinking fund required by law, and also a surplus to be retained in the Treasury in gold.

I am not a believer in any artificial method of making paper money equal to coin when the coin is not owned or held ready to redeem the promises to pay, for paper money is nothing more than promises to pay, and is valuable exactly in proportion to the amount of coin that it can be converted into. While coin is not used as a circulating medium, or the currency of the country is not convertible into it at par, it becomes an article of commerce as much as any other product. The surplus will seek a foreign market as will any other surplus. The balance of trade has nothing to do with the question. Duties on imports being required in coin creates a limited demand for gold. About enough to satisfy that demand remains in the country. To increase this supply I see no way open but by the Government hoarding through the means above given, and possibly by requiring the national banks to aid.

It is claimed by the advocates of the measure herewith returned that there is an unequal distribution of the banking capital of the country. I was disposed to give great weight to this view of the question at first, but on reflection it will be remembered that there still remains $4,000,000 of authorized bank-note circulation assigned to States having less than their quota not yet taken. In addition to this the States having less than their quota of bank circulation have the option of twenty-five millions more to be taken from those States having more than their proportion. When this is all taken up, or when specie payments are fully restored or are in rapid process of restoration, will be the time to consider the question of "more currency."

Source: Ulysses S. Grant: "Veto Message," April 22, 1874. Online by Gerhard Peters and John T. Woolley, *The American Presidency Project.* http://www.presidency.ucsb.edu/ws/?pid=70417.

C. Dangers Presented by the Current Management of the Rail System: James Dabney McCabe's *History of the Grange Movement* (1874)

In the following excerpt from his History of the Grange Movement; or, The Farmer's War Against Monopolies, *James Dabney McCabe (1842–1883) lists the many dangers presented to farmers and to the country by the national railway system as it was managed in the early 1870s. McCabe's main point was that the railroads, rather than providing people with an efficient, affordable means of transportation and shipping, had become monopolistic enterprises seeking to force people to pay the highest rates possible for their services.*

WE have now examined hastily some of the evils of the present system of railroad management, and have pointed out some of the troubles likely to arise therefrom. Our purpose in doing so is not to excite unnecessary or ill-advised hostility to the railroad system of the country, but to arouse the people to a sense of the danger with which the mismanagement of this system threatens them. That there is danger, we presume no one will deny.

Looking back over what we have been considering, we find:

I. That the railroad system of the United States, which was intended to give the people rapid and cheap communication and transportation, and which was designed as the servant of the people, has grown into a powerful combination of monopolies, each and all animated by a common object.

II. That the object of these monopolies is to compel the people to pay whatever rates they may see fit to establish for the service rendered them, and to keep these rates at the highest possible point.

III. That the corporations have a decided advantage over the public in this struggle, and that they are determined to resist, and do resist, all efforts on the part of the latter to obtain cheap transportation.

IV. That they are utterly regardless of the rights of the people, either as individuals, or as a community, and that they resent and punish to the extent of their power, any attempt on the part of an individual to dispute their regulations, however arbitrary and unjust the said rules may be.

V. That they are practically irresponsible for their action, and resist any and all efforts to render them amenable to the law.

VI. That they pursue a systematic course of plunder, robbing the nation of its property, and levying exorbitant rates upon individuals and freight, to pay "fancy dividends" upon their fictitious stock.

VII. That in order to secure the success of their schemes, they do not hesitate to resort to the most corrupt practices. They have done what they could to debauch the men placed in positions of public trust by the people, bribing legislators, and taking them into their pay, literally purchasing courts of justice, and thus closing the means of obtaining justice once open to the people.

VIII. That they are directly responsible for a large share of the corruption that is fast demoralizing our public service, and are seeking to render themselves the masters of the National and State governments.

IX. That they have introduced an element of reckless gambling in stocks into the monetary affairs of the country, which is utterly destructive of all sound business management, and have succeeded in demoralizing this portion of our financial system to such an extent that great evils must follow unless they are compelled to desist.

X. That they are growing bolder and more audacious in their designs upon the people, caring for nothing but an increase in their gains, and that the liberties, the free institutions, the property, and the national existence of the American people are seriously endangered by the unlawful designs and the insolent acts of the railroad corporations.

Source: McCabe, James Dabney. *History of the Grange Movement; or, The Farmer's War Against Monopolies.* Chicago et al.: National Publishing Company, 1874, 236–38.

D. President Grant's Message Approving the Specie Payment Resumption Act (January 14, 1875)

In 1861 the U.S. government suspended specie payments in an effort to fund the Civil War without exhausting the country's supplies of gold and silver. By the end of the war in 1865, the government had issued over $400 million in unbacked notes, known as greenbacks, and over $50 in small denomination notes known as fractional currency. When the Panic of 1873 hit, many western and southern farmers and workingmen demanded a continuation of inflationary monetary policies, while eastern banking and business interests advocated a return to the gold standard and a constriction of the money supply. In January 1875 Congress passed the Specie Payment Resumption Act, which replaced fractional currency with silver coins and directed the Treasury to redeem in coin any greenbacks presented to it after January 1, 1879. President Ulysses Grant's (1822–1885) message to Congress approving the act is reproduced below. Many *supporters of an inflationary policy denounced the act as a main cause of the five-year depression that followed the Panic of 1873.*

To the Senate of the United States:

Senate bill No. 1044, "to provide for the resumption of specie payments," is before me, and this day receives my signature of approval.

I venture upon this unusual method of conveying the notice of approval to the "House in which the measure originated" because of its great importance to the country at large and in order to suggest further legislation which seems to me essential to make this law effective.

It is a subject of congratulation that a measure has become law which fixes a date when specie resumption shall commence and implies an obligation on the part of Congress, if in its power, to give such legislation as may prove necessary to redeem this promise.

To this end I respectfully call your attention to a few suggestions:

First. The necessity of an increased revenue to carry out the obligation of adding to the sinking fund annually 1 per cent of the public debt, amounting now to about $34,000,000 per annum, and to carry out the promises of this measure to redeem, under certain contingencies, eighty millions of the present legal-tenders, and, without contingency, the fractional currency now in circulation.

How to increase the surplus revenue is for Congress to devise, but I will venture to suggest that the duty on tea and coffee might be restored without permanently enhancing the cost to the consumers, and that the 10 per cent horizontal reduction of the tariff on articles specified in the law of June 6, 1872, be repealed. The supply of tea and coffee already on hand in the United States would in all probability be advanced in price by adopting this measure. But it is known that the adoption of free entry to those articles of necessity did not cheapen them, but merely added to the profits of the countries producing them, or of the middlemen in those countries, who have the exclusive trade in them.

Second. The first section of the bill now under consideration provides that the fractional currency shall be redeemed in silver coin as rapidly as practicable. There is no provision preventing the fluctuation in the value of the paper currency. With gold at a premium of anything over 10 per cent above the currency in use, it is probable, almost certain, that silver would be bought up for exportation as fast as it was put out, or until change would become so scarce as to make the premium on it equal to the premium on gold, or sufficiently high to make it no longer profitable to buy for export, thereby causing a direct loss to the community at large and great embarrassment to trade.

As the present law commands final resumption on the 1st day of January, 1879, and as the gold receipts by the Treasury are larger than the gold payments and the currency receipts are smaller than the currency payments, thereby making monthly sales of gold necessary to meet current currency expenses, it occurs to me that these difficulties might be remedied by authorizing the Secretary of the Treasury to redeem legal-tender notes, whenever presented in sums of not less than $100 and multiples thereof, at a premium for gold of 10 per cent, less interest at the rate of 2 1/2 per cent per annum from the 1st day of January, 1875, to the date of putting this law into operation, and diminishing this premium at the same rate until final resumption, changing the rate of premium demanded from time to time as the interest amounts to one-quarter of 1 per cent. I suggest this rate of interest because it would bring currency at par with gold at the date fixed by law for final resumption. I suggest 10 per cent as the demand premium at the beginning because I believe this rate would insure the retention of silver in the country for change.

The provisions of the third section of the act will prevent combinations being made to exhaust the Treasury of coin.

With such a law it is presumable that no gold would be called for not required for legitimate business purposes. When large amounts of coin should be drawn from the Treasury, correspondingly large amounts of currency would be withdrawn from circulation, thus causing a sufficient stringency in currency to stop the outward flow of coin.

The advantages of a currency of a fixed known value would also be reached. In my opinion, by the enactment of such a law business and industries would revive and the beginning of prosperity on a firm basis would be reached.

Other means of increasing revenue than those suggested should probably be devised, and also other legislation.

In fact, to carry out the first section of the act another mint becomes a necessity. With the present facilities for coinage, it would take a period probably beyond that fixed by law for final specie resumption to coin the silver necessary to transact the business of the country.

There are now smelting furnaces, for extracting the silver and gold from the ores brought from the mountain territories, in Chicago, St. Louis, and Omaha—three in the former city—and as much of the change required will be wanted in the Mississippi Valley States, and as the metals to be coined come from west of those States, and, as I understand, the charges for transportation of bullion from either of the cities named to the mint in Philadelphia or to New York City amount to $4 for each $1,000 worth, with an equal expense for transportation back, it would seem a fair argument in favor of adopting one or more of those cities as the place or places for the establishment of new coining facilities.

I have ventured upon this subject with great diffidence, because it is so unusual to approve a measure—as I most heartily do this, even if no further legislation is attainable at this time—and to announce the fact by message. But

I do so because I feel that it is a subject of such vital importance to the whole country that it should receive the attention of and be discussed by Congress and the people through the press, and in every way, to the end that the best and most satisfactory course may be reached of executing what I deem most beneficial legislation on a most vital question to the interests and prosperity of the nation.

U.S. GRANT.

Source: Ulysses S. Grant: "Special Message," January 14, 1875. Online by Gerhard Peters and John T. Woolley, *The American Presidency Project.* http://www.presidency.ucsb.edu/ws/?pid=70441.

E. Bland-Allison Act (February 28, 1878)

The Coinage Act of 1873 tied the national currency to the gold standard and demonetized silver, an act that cheap money advocates decried as the "Crime of '73." The depression that followed the Panic of 1873 led to calls for a return to bimetallism, that is, the use of both silver and gold as a monetary standard. The Bland-Allison Act, introduced by Congressman Richard P. Bland (D-MO) (1835–1899) and Senator William B. Allison (R-IA) (1829–1908), required the U.S. Treasury to buy a certain amount of silver to coin and circulate as silver dollars. Pressured by conservative eastern banking interests that strongly opposed bimetallism, President Rutherford B. Hayes (1822–1893) vetoed the bill. However, in February 1878 Congress overrode his veto and the Bland-Allison Act became law.

"An act to authorize the coinage of the standard silver dollar, and to restore its legal-tender character.

"Be it enacted by the Senate and House of Representatives of the United States of America in Congress assembled, That there shall be coined, at the several mints of the United States, silver dollars of the weight of four hundred and twelve and a half grains troy of standard silver, as provided in the act of January eighteenth, eighteen hundred thirty-seven, on which shall be the devices and superscriptions provided by said act; which coins together with all silver dollars heretofore coined by the United States, of like weight and fineness, shall be a legal tender at their nominal value, for all debts and dues public and private, except where otherwise expressly stipulated in the contract. And the Secretary of the Treasury is authorized and directed to purchase, from time to time, silver bullion, at the market price thereof, not less than two million dollars worth per month, nor more than four million dollars worth per month, and cause the same to be coined monthly, as fast as so purchased, into such dollars; and a sum sufficient to carry out the foregoing provision of this act is hereby appropriated out of any money in the Treasury not otherwise appropriated. And any gain or seigniorage arising from this coinage shall be accounted for and paid into the Treasury, as provided under existing laws relative to the subsidiary coinage: *Provided,* That the amount of money at any one time invested in such silver bullion, exclusive of such resulting coin, shall not exceed five million dollars: *And provided further,* That nothing in this act shall be construed to authorize the payment in silver of certificates of deposit issued under the provisions of section two hundred and fifty-four of the Revised Statutes.

"SEC. 2. That immediately after the passage of this act the President shall invite the governments of the countries composing the Latin Union, so-called, and of such other European nations as he may deem advisable, to join the United States in s conference to adopt a common ratio between gold and silver, for the purpose of establishing internationally, the use of bimetallic money, and securing fixity of relative value between those metals; such conference to be held at such place, in Europe or in the United States, at such time within six months, as may be mutually agreed upon by the executives of the governments joining in the same, whenever the governments so invited, or any three of them, shall have signified their willingness to unite in the same.

"The President shall, by and with the advice and consent of the Senate, appoint three commissioners, who shall attend such conference on behalf of the United States, and shall report the doings thereof to the President, who shall transmit the same to Congress.

"Said commissioners shall each receive the sum of two thousand five hundred dollars and their reasonable expenses, to be approved by the Secretary of State; and the amount necessary to pay such compensation and expenses is hereby appropriated out of any money in the Treasury not otherwise appropriated.

"SEC. 3. That any holder of the coin authorized by this act may deposit the same with the Treasurer or any assistant treasurer of the United States, in sums not less than ten dollars, and receive therefor certificates of not less than ten dollars each, corresponding with the denominations of the United States notes. The coin deposited for or representing the certificates shall be retained in the Treasury for the payment of the same on demand. Said certificates shall be receivable for customs, taxes, and all public dues, and, when so received, may be reissued.

"SEC. 4. All acts and parts of acts inconsistent with the provisions of this act are hereby repealed.
"SAM. J. RANDALL,
"Speaker of the House of Representatives.
"W. A. WHEELER,
"Vice-President of the United States and "President of the Senate."
Passed over President's veto.

7. Depression of the 1890s

A. Sherman Antitrust Act (July 2, 1890)

Written by Republican senator John Sherman (1823–1900) of Ohio and signed by President Benjamin Harrison (1833–1901) in July 1890, the Sherman Antitrust Act prohibits business arrangements that might create monopolies or cartels that tend to reduce competition and increase costs to consumers. The act also requires the federal government to investigate and act against any trusts or companies suspected of being in violation of the act. The act was the first federal law limiting monopolies and is still the basis of most federal antitrust action. Little used for its first decade, the Sherman Antitrust Act was widely used after 1901 by Theodore Roosevelt (1858–1919) and subsequent presidents to break up monopolistic trusts.

An act to protect trade and commerce against unlawful restraints and monopolies.

Be it enacted by the Senate and House of Representatives of the United States of America in Congress assembled,

Sec. 1. Every contract, combination in the form of trust or other-wise, or conspiracy, in restraint of trade or commerce among the several States, or with foreign nations, is hereby declared to be illegal. Every person who shall make any such contract or engage in any such combination or conspiracy, shall be deemed guilty of a misdemeanor, and, on conviction thereof, shall be punished by fine not exceeding five thousand dollars, or by imprisonment not exceeding one year, or by both said punishments, at the discretion of the court.

Sec. 2. Every person who shall monopolize, or attempt to monopolize, or combine or conspire with any other person or persons, to monopolize any part of the trade or commerce among the several States, or with foreign nations, shall be deemed guilty of a misdemeanor, and, on conviction thereof; shall be punished by fine not exceeding five thousand dollars, or by imprisonment not exceeding one year, or by both said punishments, in the discretion of the court.

Sec. 3. Every contract, combination in form of trust or otherwise, or conspiracy, in restraint of trade or commerce in any Territory of the United States or of the District of Columbia, or in restraint of trade or commerce between any such Territory and another, or between any such Territory or Territories and any State or States or the District of Columbia, or with foreign nations, or between the District of Columbia and any State or States or foreign nations, is hereby declared illegal. Every person who shall make any such contract or engage in any such combination or conspiracy, shall be deemed guilty of a misdemeanor, and, on conviction thereof, shall be punished by fine not exceeding five thousand dollars, or by imprisonment not exceeding one year, or by both said punishments, in the discretion of the court.

Sec. 4. The several circuit courts of the United States are hereby invested with jurisdiction to prevent and restrain violations of this act; and it shall be the duty of the several district attorneys of the United States, in their respective districts, under the direction of the Attorney-General, to institute proceedings in equity to prevent and restrain such violations. Such proceedings may be by way of petition setting forth the case and praying that such violation shall be enjoined or otherwise prohibited. When the parties complained of shall have been duly notified of such petition the court shall proceed, as soon as may be, to the hearing and determination of the case; and pending such petition and before final decree, the court may at any time make such temporary restraining order or prohibition as shall be deemed just in the premises.

Sec. 5. Whenever it shall appear to the court before which any proceeding under section four of this act may be pending, that the ends of justice require that other parties should be brought before the court, the court may cause them to be summoned, whether they reside in the district in which the court is held or not; and subpoenas to that end may be served in any district by the marshal thereof.

Sec. 6. Any property owned under any contract or by any combination, or pursuant to any conspiracy (and being the subject thereof) mentioned in section one of this act, and being in the course of transportation from one State to another, or to a foreign country, shall be—forfeited to the United States, and may be seized and condemned by like proceedings as those provided by law for the forfeiture, seizure, and condemnation of property imported into the United States contrary to law.

Sec. 7. Any person who shall be injured in his business or property by any other person or corporation by reason of anything forbidden or declared to be unlawful by this act, may sue therefor in any circuit court of the United States in the district in which the defendant resides or is found, without. respect to the amount in controversy, and shall recover three fold the damages by him sustained, and the costs of suit, including a reasonable attorney's fee.

Sec. 8. That the word "person," or " persons," wherever used in this act shall be deemed to include corporations and associations existing under or authorized by the laws of either the United States, the laws of any of the Territories, the laws of any State, or the laws of any foreign country.

Source: Statutes at Large, 51st Cong., 1st sess., vol. 26, ch. 647: 209.

B. *United States v. Debs et al.* (December 14, 1894)

In 1894 the U.S. government obtained an injunction against a strike by workers of the Pullman Company on the grounds that the strikers were inter-fering with the U.S. mail, some of which was carried on Pullman railcars. The government then charged several union leaders, including Eugene V. Debs (1855–1926), a founder of the Industrial Workers of the World (IWW), with contempt for violating the injunction. The U.S. Circuit Court for the Northern District of Illinois, which had issued the injunction, found Debs and the others guilty of contempt and sentenced them to prison terms. Debs's lawyers argued that the court lacked the authority to issue the injunction or sentence the men to prison without a jury trial. In the following excerpts from his opinion in United States v. Debs et al., *Judge William A. Woods (1837–1901) found that the court acted properly and that the Sherman Antitrust Act of 1890 gave it the authority to act against labor unions, as well as corporate trusts, if they obstructed interstate commerce. In 1895, in its* In Re Debs *decision, the U.S. Supreme Court upheld the right of the circuit court to issue the injunction.*

The question here, therefore, is whether the case presented by the petition was of a class which in a federal court admits of remedy by injunction.

Without going into the details of averment, the charge made against the defendants was that they were engaged in a conspiracy to hinder and interrupt interstate commerce and the carriage of the mails upon railroads centering in Chicago, by means and in a manner to constitute, within the recognized definitions, a public nuisance. . . .

Accordingly, it is contended, and numerous decisions and texts are cited to show, that "equity had jurisdiction to restrain public nuisances upon bill or information filed by the attorney general on behalf of the people." . . .

But while the reasons to justify, on the grounds considered, the issuing of the injunction for the purpose of protecting, against obstruction or interruption, either the mails alone or interstate commerce, of which the carrying of the mails is a part, are strong, and perhaps ought to be accepted as convincing, there seems to be no precedent for so holding, and the responsibility of making a precedent need not now be assumed.

While, however, the point is not decided, the authorities on the subject have been brought forward so fully because, in part, of their bearing upon the question now to be considered,—whether or not the injunction was authorized by the act of July 2, 1890. It was under that act that the order was asked and was granted; but it has been seriously questioned in this proceeding, as well as by an eminent judge and by lawyers elsewhere, whether the statute is by its terms applicable, or consistently with constitutional guaranties can be applied, to cases like this. . . .

It is therefore the privilege and duty of the court, uncontrolled by considerations drawn from other sources, to find the meaning of the statute in the terms of its provisions, interpreted by the settled rules of construction. That the original design to suppress trusts and monopolies created by contract or combination in the form of trust, which of course would be of a "contractual character," was adhered to, is clear; but it is equally clear that a further and more comprehensive purpose came to be entertained, and was embodied in the final form of the enactment. Combinations are condemned, not only when they take the form of trusts, but in whatever form found, if they be in restraint of trade. That is the effect of the words "or otherwise." . . .

I have not failed, I think, to appreciate the just force of the argument to the contrary of my opinion,—it has sometimes entangled me in doubt,—but my conclusion is clear that, under the act of 1890, the court had jurisdiction of the case presented in the application, and that the injunction granted was not without authority of law, nor for any reason invalid.

This brings me to the question of fact: Did the defendants violate the injunction? The evidence upon the question is voluminous, but need not be reviewed in detail. . . .

[The defendants'] original intention, it is true, was only to prevent the use of Pullman cars, but finding, as they did, immediately, that that aim would be thwarted by the discharge from service of men who refused to handle those cars, they began as early as June 27th, the day after the boycott was proclaimed, to issue orders to strike; and from that time to the end, to the extent of their ability, they conducted and controlled the strike with persistent consistency of purpose; and with unchanged methods of action. . . .

The evidence leaves no feature of the case in doubt. The substance of it, briefly stated, is that the defendants, in combination with members of the American Railway Union and others, who were prevailed upon to co-operate, were engaged in a conspiracy in restraint or hindrance of interstate commerce over the railroads entering Chicago, and, in furtherance of their design, those actively engaged in the strike were using threats, violence, and other unlawful means of interference with the operations of the roads; that by the injunction they were commanded to desist, but, instead of respecting the order, they persisted in their purpose, without essential change of conduct, until compelled to yield to superior force.

Much has been said, but without proof, of the wrongs of the workmen at Pullman, of an alliance between the Pullman Company and the railway managers to depress wages, and generally of corporate oppression and arrogance. But it is evident that these things, whatever the facts might have been proved or imagined to be, could furnish neither justification nor palliation for giving up a city to disorder, and for paralyzing the industries and commerce of the country.

Source: United States v. Debs et al., 64 Federal Reporter 724 (1894); Federal Judicial website. http://www.fjc.gov/history/home.nsf/page/tu_debs_doc_4.html.

C. President Cleveland's Message to Congress Calling for Action to Restore the Financial Soundness of the Economy (January 28, 1895)

President Grover Cleveland (1837–1908), believing that excessive coinage of silver was a main cause of the Panic of 1893, called Congress into special session and engineered, in the face of strong opposition from the silverite wing of his own Democratic Party, the repeal of the Sherman Silver Purchase Act of 1890. Although the repeal helped restore business confidence, it did not stem runs on the Treasury, whereby heavy exchange of silver for gold led to near depletion of the Treasury's gold reserves. In January 1895 Cleveland sent the following message to Congress recommending that the secretary of the treasury be authorized to issue government bonds to build and maintain a sufficient gold reserve and to redeem and cancel United States legal-tender notes and Treasury notes issued for the purchase of silver under the Sherman Silver Purchase Act. The sale of these bonds helped stabilize the gold reserve but led to a silverite takeover of the Democratic Party, which in 1896 repudiated Cleveland's adherence to the gold standard and nominated the silverite William Jennings Bryan (1860–1925) for president.

To the Senate and House of Representatives:

In my last annual message I commended to the serious consideration of the Congress the condition of our national finances, and in connection with the subject indorsed a plan of currency legislation which at that time seemed to furnish protection against impending danger. This plan has not been approved by the Congress. In the meantime the situation has so changed and the emergency now appears so threatening that I deem it my duty to ask at the hands of the legislative branch of the Government such prompt and effective action as will restore confidence in our financial soundness and avert business disaster and universal distress among our people.

Whatever may be the merits of the plan outlined in my annual message as a remedy for ills then existing and as a safeguard against the depletion of the gold reserve then in the Treasury, I am now convinced that its reception by the Congress and our present advanced stage of financial perplexity necessitate additional or different legislation.

With natural resources unlimited in variety and productive strength and with a people whose activity and enterprise seek only a fair opportunity to achieve national success and greatness, our progress should not be checked by a false financial policy and a heedless disregard of sound monetary laws, nor should the timidity and fear which they engender stand in the way of our prosperity.

It is hardly disputed that this predicament confronts us to-day. Therefore no one in any degree responsible for the making and execution of our laws should fail to see a patriotic duty in honestly and sincerely attempting to relieve the situation. Manifestly this effort will not succeed unless it is made untrammeled by the prejudice of partisanship and with a steadfast determination to resist the temptation to accomplish party advantage. We may well remember that if we are threatened with financial difficulties all our people in every station of life are concerned; and surely those who suffer will not receive the promotion of party interests as an excuse for permitting our present troubles to advance to a disastrous conclusion. It is also of the utmost importance that we approach the study of the problems presented as free as possible from the tyranny of preconceived opinions, to the end that in a common danger we may be able to seek with unclouded vision a safe and reasonable protection.

The real trouble which confronts us consists in a lack of confidence, widespread and constantly increasing, in the continuing ability or disposition of the Government to pay its obligations in gold. This lack of confidence grows to some extent out of the palpable and apparent embarrassment attending the efforts of the Government under existing laws to procure gold and to a greater extent out of the impossibility of either keeping it in the Treasury or canceling obligations by its expenditure after it is obtained.

The only way left open to the Government for procuring gold is by the issue and sale of its bonds. The only bonds that can be so issued were authorized nearly twenty-five years ago and are not well calculated to meet our present needs. Among other disadvantages, they are made payable in coin instead of specifically in gold, which in existing conditions detracts largely and in an increasing ratio from their desirability as investments. It is by no means certain that bonds of this description can much longer be disposed of at a price creditable to the financial character of our Government.

The most dangerous and irritating feature of the situation, however, remains to be mentioned. It is found in the means by which the Treasury is despoiled of the gold thus obtained without canceling a single Government obligation and solely for the benefit of those who find profit in shipping it abroad or whose fears induce them to hoard it at home. We have outstanding about five hundred millions of currency notes of the Government for which gold may be demanded, and, curiously enough, the law requires that when presented and, in fact, redeemed and paid in gold they shall be reissued. Thus the same notes may do duty many times in drawing gold from the Treasury; nor can the process be arrested as long as private parties, for profit or otherwise, see an advantage in repeating the operation. More than $300,000,000 in these notes have already been redeemed in gold, and notwithstanding such redemption they are all still outstanding.

Since the 17th day of January, 1894, our bonded interest-bearing debt has been increased $100,000,000 for the purpose of obtaining gold to replenish our coin reserve. Two issues were made amounting to fifty millions each, one in January and the other in November. As a result of the first issue there was realized something more than $58,000,000 in gold. Between that issue and the succeeding one in November, comprising a period of about ten months, nearly $103,000,000 in gold were drawn from the Treasury. This made the second issue necessary, and upon that more than fifty-eight millions in gold was again realized. Between the date of this second issue and the present time, covering a period of only about two months, more than $69,000,000 in gold have been drawn from the Treasury. These large sums of gold were expended without any cancellation of Government obligations or in any permanent way benefiting our people or improving our pecuniary situation.

The financial events of the past year suggest facts and conditions which should certainly arrest attention.

More than $172,000,000 in gold have been drawn out of the Treasury during the year for the purpose of shipment abroad or hoarding at home.

While nearly $103,000,000 of this amount was drawn out during the first ten months of the year, a sum aggregating more than two-thirds of that amount, being about $69,000,000, was drawn out during the following two months, thus indicating a marked acceleration of the depleting process with the lapse of time.

The obligations upon which this gold has been drawn from the Treasury are still outstanding and are available for use in repeating the exhausting operation with shorter intervals as our perplexities accumulate.

Conditions are certainly supervening tending to make the bonds which may be issued to replenish our gold less useful for that purpose.

An adequate gold reserve is in all circumstances absolutely essential to the upholding of our public credit and to the maintenance of our high national character.

Our gold reserve has again reached such a stage of diminution as to require its speedy reenforcement.

The aggravations that must inevitably follow present conditions and methods will certainly lead to misfortune and loss, not only to our national credit and prosperity and to financial enterprise, but to those of our people who seek employment as a means of livelihood and to those whose only capital is their daily labor.

It will hardly do to say that a simple increase of revenue will cure our troubles. The apprehension now existing and constantly increasing as to our financial ability does not rest upon a calculation of our revenue. The time has passed when the eyes of investors abroad and our people at home were fixed upon the revenues of the Government. Changed conditions have attracted their attention to the gold of the Government. There need be no fear that we can not pay our current expenses with such money as we have. There is now in the Treasury a comfortable surplus of more than $63,000,000, but it is not in gold, and therefore does not meet our difficulty.

I can not see that differences of opinion concerning the extent to which silver ought to be coined or used in our currency should interfere with the counsels of those whose duty it is to rectify evils now apparent in our financial situation. They have to consider the question of national credit and the consequences that will follow from its collapse. Whatever ideas may be insisted upon as to silver or bimetallism, a proper solution of the question now pressing upon us only requires a recognition of gold as well as silver and a concession of its importance, rightfully or wrongfully acquired, as a basis of national credit, a necessity in the honorable discharge of our obligations payable in gold, and a badge of solvency. I do not understand that the real fiends of silver desire a condition that might follow inaction or neglect to appreciate the meaning of the present exigency if it should result in the entire banishment of gold from our financial and currency arrangements.

Besides the Treasury notes, which certainly should be paid in gold, amounting to nearly $500,000,000, there will fall due in 1904 one hundred millions of bonds issued during the last year, for which we have received gold, and in 1907 nearly six hundred millions of 4 per cent bonds issued in 1877. Shall the payment of these obligations in gold be repudiated? If they are to be paid in such a manner as the preservation of our national honor and national solvency demands, we should not destroy or even imperil our ability to supply ourselves with gold for that purpose.

While I am not unfriendly to silver and while I desire to see it recognized to such an extent as is consistent with financial safety and the preservation of national honor and credit, I am not willing to see gold entirely banished from our currency and finances. To avert such a consequence I believe thorough and radical remedial legislation should be promptly passed. I therefore beg the Congress to give the subject immediate attention.

In my opinion the Secretary of the Treasury should be authorized to issue bonds of the Government for the purpose of procuring and maintaining a sufficient gold reserve and the redemption and cancellation of the United States legal-tender notes and the Treasury notes issued for the purchase of silver under the law of July 14, 1890. We should be relieved from the humiliating process of issuing bonds to procure gold to be immediately and repeatedly drawn out on these obligations for purposes not related to the benefit of our Government or our people. The principal and interest of these bonds should be payable on their face in gold, because they should be sold only for gold or its representative, and because there would now probably be difficulty in favorably disposing of bonds not containing this stipulation. I suggest that the bonds be issued in denominations of twenty and fifty dollars and their multiples and that they bear interest at a rate not exceeding 3 per cent per annum. I do not see why they should not be payable fifty years from their date. We of the present generation have large amounts to pay if we meet our obligations, and long bonds are most salable. The Secretary of the Treasury might well be permitted at his discretion to receive on the sale of bonds the legal-tender and Treasury notes to be retired, and of course when they are thus retired or redeemed in gold they should be canceled.

These bonds under existing laws could be deposited by national banks as security for circulation, and such banks should be allowed to issue circulation up to the face value of these or any other bonds so deposited, except bonds outstanding bearing only 2 per cent interest and which sell in the market at less than par. National banks should not be allowed to take out circulating notes of a less denomination than $10, and when such as are now outstanding reach the Treasury, except for redemption and retirement, they should be canceled and notes of the denomination of $10 and upward issued in their stead. Silver certificates of the denomination of $10 and upward should be replaced by certificates of the denominations under $10.

As a constant means for the maintenance of a reasonable supply of gold in the Treasury, our duties on imports should be paid in gold, allowing all other dues to the Government to be paid in any other form of money.

I believe all the provisions I have suggested should be embodied in our laws if we are to enjoy a complete reinstatement of a sound financial condition. They need not interfere with any currency scheme providing for the increase of the circulating medium through the agency of national or State banks that may commend itself to the Congress, since they can easily be adjusted to such a scheme. Objection has been made to the issuance of interest-bearing obligations for the purpose of retiring the noninterest-bearing legal-tender notes. In point of fact, however, these notes have burdened us with a large load of interest, and it is still accumulating. The aggregate interest on the original issue of bonds, the proceeds of which in gold constituted the reserve for the payment of these notes, amounted to $70,326,250 on January 1, 1895, and the annual charge for interest on these bonds and those issued for the same purpose during the last year will be $9,145,000, dating from January 1, 1895.

While the cancellation of these notes would not relieve us from the obligations already incurred on their account, these figures are given by way of suggesting that their existence has not been free from interest charges and that the longer they are outstanding, judging from the experience of the last year, the more expensive they will become.

In conclusion I desire to frankly confess my reluctance to issuing more bonds in present circumstances and with no better results than have lately followed that course. I can not, however, refrain from adding to an assurance of my anxiety to cooperate with the present Congress in any reasonable measure of relief an expression of my determination to leave nothing undone which furnishes a hope for improving the situation or checking a suspicion of our disinclination or disability to meet with the strictest honor every national obligation.

GROVER CLEVELAND.

Source: Grover Cleveland: "Message to Congress on the Need for Action to Restore Confidence in Financial Soundness," January 28, 1895. Online by Gerhard Peters and John T. Woolley, *The American Presidency Project.* http://www.presidency.ucsb .edu/ws/?pid=70650.

D. William Jennings Bryan's "Cross of Gold" Speech (July 9, 1896)

Speaking at the Democratic Convention in Chicago in July 1896, 36-year-old William Jennings Bryan (1860–1925), a former congressman from Nebraska, delivered one of the most famous political speeches in American history. Bryan, a strong and dynamic speaker, passionately advocates the free coinage of silver as the best way to expand the amount of money in circulation and thereby relieve the cash-poor, debt-laden farmers of the South and West. After building to a powerful crescendo, Bryan concludes with the dramatic line, "You shall not crucify mankind upon a cross of gold." The convention was electrified, and the next day the delegates nominated Bryan for president on a free silver platform. Reproduced below are excerpts from what came to be known as the "Cross of Gold" speech.

I would be presumptuous, indeed, to present myself against the distinguished gentlemen to whom you have listened if this were but a measuring of ability; but this is not a contest among persons. The humblest citizen in all the land when clad in the armor of a righteous cause is stronger than all the whole hosts of error that they can bring. I come to speak to you in defense of a cause as holy as the cause of liberty—the cause of humanity. When this debate is concluded, a motion will be made to lay upon the table the resolution offered in commendation of the administration and also the resolution in condemnation of the administration. I shall object to bringing this question down to a level of persons. The individual is but an atom; he is born, he acts, he dies; but principles are eternal; and this has been a contest of principle.

Never before in the history of this country has there been witnessed such a contest as that through which we have passed. Never before in the history of American politics has a great issue been fought out as this issue has been by the voters themselves.

On the 4th of March, 1895, a few Democrats, most of them members of Congress, issued an address to the Democrats of the nation asserting that the money question was the paramount issue of the hour; asserting also the right of a majority of the Democratic Party to control the position of the party on this paramount issue; concluding with the request that all believers in free coinage of silver in the Democratic Party should organize and take charge of and control the policy of the Democratic Party. Three months later, at Memphis, an organization was perfected, and the silver Democrats went forth openly and boldly and courageously proclaiming their belief and declaring that if successful they would crystallize in a platform the declaration which they had made; and then began the conflict with a zeal approaching the zeal which inspired the crusaders who followed Peter the Hermit. Our silver Democrats went forth from victory unto victory, until they are assembled now, not to discuss, not to debate, but to enter up the judgment rendered by the plain people of this country.

But in this contest, brother has been arrayed against brother, and father against son. The warmest ties of love and acquaintance and association have been disregarded. Old leaders have been cast aside when they refused to give expression to the sentiments of those whom they would lead, and new leaders have sprung up to give direction to this cause of freedom. Thus has the contest been waged, and we have assembled here under as binding and solemn instructions as were ever fastened upon the representatives of a people.

We do not come as individuals. Why, as individuals we might have been glad to compliment the gentleman from New York [Senator Hill], but we knew that the people for whom we speak would never be willing to put him in a position where he could thwart the will of the Democratic Party. I say it was not a question of persons; it was a question of principle; and it is not with gladness, my friends, that we find ourselves brought into conflict with those who are now arrayed on the other side. The gentleman who just preceded me [Governor Russell] spoke of the old state of Massachusetts. Let me assure him that not one person in all this convention entertains the least hostility to the people of the state of Massachusetts.

But we stand here representing people who are the equals before the law of the largest cities in the state of Massachusetts. When you come before us and tell us that we shall disturb your business interests, we reply that you have disturbed our business interests by your action. We say to you that you have made too limited in its application the definition of a businessman. The man who is employed for wages is as much a businessman as his employer. The attorney in a country town is as much a businessman as the corporation counsel in a great metropolis. The merchant at the crossroads store is as much a businessman as the merchant of New York. The farmer who goes forth in the morning and toils all day, begins in the spring and toils all summer, and by the application of brain and muscle to the natural resources of this country creates wealth, is as much a businessman as the man who goes upon the Board of Trade and bets upon the price of grain. The miners who go 1,000 feet into the earth or climb 2,000 feet upon the cliffs and bring forth from their hiding places the precious metals to be poured in the channels of trade are as much businessmen as the few financial magnates who in a backroom corner the money of the world. . . .

I want to suggest this truth, that if the gold standard is a good thing we ought to declare in favor of its retention and not in favor of abandoning it; and if the gold standard is a bad thing, why should we wait until some other nations are willing to help us to let it go?

Here is the line of battle. We care not upon which issue they force the fight. We are prepared to meet them on either issue or on both. If they tell us that the gold standard is the standard of civilization, we reply to them that this, the most enlightened of all nations of the earth, has never declared for a gold standard, and both the parties this year are declaring against it. If the gold standard is the standard of civilization, why, my friends, should we not have it? So if they come to meet us on that, we can present the history of our nation. More than that, we can tell them this, that they will search the pages of history in vain to find a single instance in which the common people of any land ever declared themselves in favor of a gold standard. They can find where the holders of fixed investments have.

Mr. Carlisle said in 1878 that this was a struggle between the idle holders of idle capital and the struggling masses who produce the wealth and pay the taxes of the country; and my friends, it is simply a question that we shall decide upon which side shall the Democratic Party fight. Upon the side of the idle holders of idle capital, or upon the side of the struggling masses? That is the question that the party must answer first; and then it must be answered by each individual hereafter. The sympathies of the Democratic Party, as described by the platform, are on the side of the struggling masses, who have ever been the foundation of the Democratic Party.

There are two ideas of government. There are those who believe that if you just legislate to make the well-to-do prosperous, that their prosperity will leak through on those below. The Democratic idea has been that if you legislate to make the masses prosperous their prosperity will find its way up and through every class that rests upon it.

You come to us and tell us that the great cities are in favor of the gold standard. I tell you that the great cities rest upon these broad and fertile prairies. Burn down your cities and leave our farms, and your cities will spring up again as if by magic. But destroy our farms and the grass will grow in the streets of every city in the country.

My friends, we shall declare that this nation is able to legislate for its own people on every question without waiting for the aid or consent of any other nation on earth, and upon that issue we expect to carry every single state in the Union.

I shall not slander the fair state of Massachusetts nor the state of New York by saying that when citizens are confronted with the proposition, "Is this nation able to attend to its own business?"—I will not slander either one by saying that the people of those states will declare our helpless impotency as a nation to attend to our own business. It is the issue of 1776 over again. Our ancestors, when but 3 million, had the courage to declare their political independence of every other nation upon earth. Shall we, their descendants, when we have grown to 70 million, declare that we are less independent than our forefathers? No, my friends, it will never be the judgment of this people. Therefore, we care not upon what lines the battle is fought. If they say bimetallism is good but we cannot have it till some nation helps us, we reply that, instead of having a gold standard because England has, we shall restore bimetallism, and then let England have bimetallism because the United States have.

If they dare to come out in the open field and defend the gold standard as a good thing, we shall fight them to the uttermost, having behind us the producing masses of the nation and the world. Having behind us the commercial interests and the laboring interests and all the toiling masses, we shall answer their demands for a gold standard by saying to them, you shall not press down upon the brow of labor this crown of thorns. You shall not crucify mankind upon a cross of gold.

Source: Official Proceedings of the Democratic National Convention Held in Chicago, Illinois, July 7, 8, 9, 10, and 11, 1896. Logansport, IN, 1896, 226–34.

8. Panic of 1907

A. *Adair v. United States* (January 27, 1908)

In 1898 Congress passed the Erdman Act, which provided for arbitration between railroad companies and their unionized employees and forbade the railroads from preventing workers from joining a union as a condition of employment, "yellow-dog" employment contracts. In 1906 William Adair, a supervisor on the Louisville and Nashville Railroad, fired an employee for joining a union. In circuit court in Kentucky, Adair was found guilty of violating the Erdman Act and fined $100. However, in Adair v. United States, *the U.S. Supreme Court declared the Erdman Act unconstitutional because it contravened the due process clause of the Fifth Amendment by limiting freedom of contract. Reproduced below are excerpts of the court's opinion written by Justice John M. Harlan (1833–1911).*

. . . Let us inquire what is commerce, the power to regulate which is given to Congress?

This question has been frequently propounded in this court, and the answer has been—and no more specific answer could well have been given—that commerce among the several States comprehends traffic, intercourse, trade, navigation, communication, the transit of persons and the transmission of messages by telegraph—indeed, every species of commercial intercourse among the several States, but not to that commerce "completely internal, which is carried on between man and man, in a State, or between different parts of the same State, and which does not extend to or affect other States."

The power to regulate interstate commerce is the power to prescribe rules by which such commerce must be governed. Of course, as has been often said, Congress has a large discretion in the selection or choice of the means to be employed in the regulation of interstate commerce, and such discretion is not to be interfered with except where that which is done is in plain violation of the Constitution. *Northern Securities Co. v. United States*, 193 U. S. 197, and authorities there cited. In this connection, we may refer to *Johnson v. Railroad*, 196 U. S. 1, relied on in argument, which case arose under the act of Congress of March 2, 1893, 27 Stat. 531, c. 196. That act required carriers engaged in interstate commerce to equip their cars used in such commerce with automatic couplers and continuous brakes, and their locomotives with driving wheel brakes. But the act, upon its face, showed that its object was to promote the safety of employees and travelers upon railroads, and this court sustained its validity upon the ground that it manifestly had reference to interstate commerce, and was calculated to subserve the interests of such commerce by affording protection to employees and travelers. It was held that there was a substantial connection between the object sought to be attained by the act and the means provided to accomplish that object. So, in regard to *Employers' Liability Cases*, 207 U. S. 63, decided at the present term. In that case, the court sustained the authority of Congress, under its power to regulate interstate commerce, to prescribe the rule of liability, as between interstate carriers and its employees in such interstate commerce, in cases of personal injuries received by employees while actually engaged in such commerce. The decision on this point was placed on the ground that a rule of that character would have direct reference to the conduct of interstate commerce, and would, therefore, be within the competency of Congress to establish for commerce among the States, but not as to commerce completely internal to a State. Manifestly, any rule prescribed for the conduct of interstate commerce, in order to be within the competency of Congress under its power to regulate commerce among the States, must have some real or substantial relation to or connection with the commerce regulated. But what possible legal or logical connection is there between an employee's membership in a labor organization and the carrying on of interstate commerce? Such relation to a labor organization cannot have, in itself, and in the eye of the law, any bearing upon the commerce with which the employee is connected by his labor and services. Labor associations, we assume, are organized for the general purpose of improving or bettering the conditions and conserving the interests of its members as wage-earners—an object entirely legitimate and to be commended, rather than condemned. But surely those associations, as labor organizations, have nothing to do with interstate commerce as such. One who engages in the service of an interstate carrier will, it must be assumed, faithfully perform his duty, whether he be a member or not a member of a labor organization. His fitness for the position in which he labors and his diligence in the discharge of his duties cannot, in law or sound reason, depend in any degree upon his being or not being a member of a labor organization. It cannot be assumed that his fitness is assured, or his diligence increased, by such membership, or that he is less fit or less diligent because of his not being a member of such an organization. It is the employee as a man, and not as a member of a labor organization, who labors in the service of an interstate carrier. Will it be said that the provision in question had its origin in the apprehension, on the part of Congress, that, if it did not show more consideration for members of labor organizations than for wage-earners who were not members of such organizations, or if it did not insert in the statute some such provision as the one here in question, members of labor organizations would, by illegal or violent measures, interrupt or impair the freedom of commerce among the States? We will not indulge in any such conjectures, nor make them, in whole or in part, the basis of our decision. We could not do so consistently with the respect due to a coordinate department of the Government. We could not do so without imputing to Congress the purpose to accord to one class of wage-earners privileges withheld from another class of wage-earners engaged, it may be, in the same kind of labor and serving the same employer. Nor will we assume, in our consideration of this case, that members of labor organizations will, in any considerable numbers, resort to illegal methods for accomplishing any particular object they have in view.

Looking alone at the words of the statute for the purpose of ascertaining its scope and effect, and of determining its validity, we hold that there is no such connection between interstate commerce and membership in a labor organization as to authorize Congress to make it a crime against the United States for an agent of an interstate carrier to discharge an employee because of such membership on his part. If such a power exists in Congress, it is difficult to perceive why it might not, by absolute regulation, require interstate carriers, under penalties, to employ in the conduct of its interstate business *only* members of labor organizations, or *only* those who are *not* members of such organizations—a power which could not be recognized as existing under the Constitution of the United States. No such rule of criminal liability as that to which we have referred can be regarded as, in any just sense, a regulation of interstate commerce. We need scarcely repeat what this court has more than once said, that the power to regulate interstate commerce, great and paramount as that power is, cannot be exerted in violation of any fundamental right secured by other provisions of the Constitution. *Gibbons v. Ogden*, 9 Wheat. 1, 22 U. S. 196; *Lottery Case*, 188 U. S. 321, 188 U. S. 353.

It results, on the whole case, that the provision of the statute under which the defendant was convicted must be held to be repugnant to the Fifth Amendment, and as not embraced by nor within the power of Congress to regulate interstate commerce, but, under the guise of regulating interstate commerce and as applied to this case, it arbitrarily sanctions an illegal invasion of the personal liberty as well as the right of property of the defendant Adair.

We add that, since the part of the act of 1898 upon which the first count of the indictment is based, and upon which alone the defendant was convicted, is severable from its other parts, and, as what has been said is sufficient to dispose of the present case, we are not called upon to consider other and independent provisions of the act, such, for instance, as the provisions relating to arbitration. This decision is therefore restricted to the question of the validity of the particular provision in the act of Congress making it a crime against the United States for an agent or officer of an interstate carrier to discharge an employee from its service because of his being a member of a labor organization.

The judgment must be reversed, with directions to set aside the verdict and judgment of conviction, sustain the demurrer to the indictment, and dismiss the case.

It is so ordered.

Source: *Adair v. United States*, 208 U.S. 161 (1908).

B. *Loewe v. Lawlor* (February 3, 1908)

In 1901 D.E. Loewe and Company, a Connecticut hat manufacturer, pro-claimed itself an "open shop," meaning that employees were not required to join a union to work there. The United Hatters of North America, which had unionized much of the hat making industry, organized a strike and boycott to persuade other firms and individuals to refrain from doing business with D.E. Loewe. The company sued the union, alleging that the boycott violated the Sher-man Antitrust Act by preventing the company from engaging in interstate com-merce. In Loewe v. Lawlor *(also known as the Danbury Hatters Case) the U.S. Supreme Court sided with the company, declaring that secondary boycotts vio-lated the Sherman Antitrust Act. The court also declared that individual union members could be held personally liable for damages incurred as a result of the union's actions. Reproduced below are excerpts from the court's opinion written by Chief Justice Melville Fuller (1833–1910).*

This was an action brought in the Circuit Court for the District of Con-necticut under § 7 of the Anti-Trust Act of July 2, 1890, c. 647, 26 Stat. 209, claiming threefold damages for injuries inflicted on plaintiffs by a combination or conspiracy declared to be unlawful by the act.

Defendants filed a demurrer to the complaint, assigning general and spe-cial grounds. The demurrer was sustained as to the first six paragraphs, which rested on the ground that the combination stated was not within the Sherman Act, and this rendered it unnecessary to pass upon any other questions in the case, and, upon plaintiffs declining to amend their complaint, the court dis-missed it with costs.

The case was then carried by writ of error to the Circuit Court of Appeals for the Second Circuit, and that court, desiring the instruction of this court upon a question arising on the writ of error, certified that question to this court. The certificate consisted of a brief statement of facts, and put the question thus: "Upon this state of facts, can plaintiffs maintain an action against defendants under section 7 of the Anti-Trust Act of July 2, 1890?"

After the case on certificate had been docketed here, plaintiffs in error applied, and defendants in error joined in the application, to this court to require the whole record and cause to be sent up for its consideration. The application was granted, and the whole record and cause being thus brought before this court, it devolved upon the court, under § 6 of the Judiciary Act of 1891, to "decide the whole matter in controversy in the same manner as if it had been brought there for review by writ of error or appeal."

The case comes up, then, on complaint and demurrer, and we give the complaint in the margin.

The question is whether, upon the facts therein averred and admitted by the demurrer, this action can be maintained under the Anti-Trust Act.

The first, second and seventh sections of that act are as follows:

"1. Every contract, combination in the form of trust or otherwise, or conspiracy, in restraint of trade or commerce among the several States, or with foreign nations, is hereby declared to be illegal. Every person who shall make any such contract or engage in any such combination or conspiracy, shall be deemed guilty of a misdemeanor, and, on conviction thereof, shall be punished by fine not exceeding five thousand dollars, or by imprisonment not exceeding one year, or by both said punishments, in the discretion of the court."

"2. Every person who shall monopolize, or attempt to monopolize, or combine or conspire with any other person or persons, to monopolize any part of the trade or commerce among the several States, or with foreign nations, shall be deemed guilty of a misdemeanor, and, on conviction thereof, shall be punished by fine not exceeding five thousand dollars, or by imprisonment not exceeding one year, or by both said punishments, in the discretion of the court. . . ."

"7. Any person who shall be injured in his business or property by any other person or corporation by reason of anything forbidden or declared to be unlawful by this act may sue therefor in any Circuit Court of the United States in the district in which the defendant resides or is found, without respect to the amount in controversy, and shall recover three fold the damages by him sustained, and the costs of suit; including a reasonable attorney's fee."

In our opinion, the combination described in the declaration is a combination "in restraint of trade or commerce among the several States," in the sense in which those words are used in the act, and the action can be maintained accordingly.

And that conclusion rests on many judgments of this court, to the effect that the act prohibits any combination whatever to secure action which essentially obstructs the free flow of commerce between the States, or restricts, in that regard, the liberty of a trader to engage in business.

The combination charged falls within the class of restraints of trade aimed at compelling third parties and strangers involuntarily not to engage in the course of trade except on conditions that the combination imposes, and there is no doubt that (to quote from the well known work of Chief Justice Erle on Trade Unions), "at common law, every person has individually, and the public also, has collectively, a right to require that the course of trade should be kept free from unreasonable obstruction."

But the objection here is to the jurisdiction, because, even conceding that the declaration states a case good at common law, it is contended that it does not state one within the statute. Thus, it is said that the restraint alleged would operate to entirely destroy plaintiffs' business, and thereby include intrastate trade as well; that physical obstruction is not alleged as contemplated, and that defendants are not themselves engaged in interstate trade.

We think none of these objections is tenable, and that they are disposed of by previous decisions of this court.

United States v. Trans-Missouri Freight Association, 166 U. S. 290; *United States v. Joint Traffic Association,* 171 U. S. 505, and *Northern Securities Company v. United States,* 193 U. S. 197, hold, in effect, that the Anti-Trust law has a broader application than the prohibition of restraints of trade unlawful at common law. Thus, in the *Trans-Missouri Case,* 166 U. S. 290, it was said that, "assuming that agreements of this nature are not void at common law, and that the various cases cited by the learned courts below show it, the answer to the statement of their validity is to be found in the terms of the statute under consideration;" and, in the *Northern Securities Case,* 193 U. S. 331, that "the act declares illegal every contract, combination or conspiracy, in whatever form, of whatever nature, and whoever may be the parties to it, which directly or necessarily operates in restraint of trade or commerce among the several States."

We do not pause to comment on cases, such as *United States v. Knight,* 156 U. S. 1; *Hopkins v. United States,* 171 U. S. 578, and *Anderson v. United States,* 171 U. S. 60; in which the undisputed facts showed that the purpose of the agreement was not to obstruct or restrain interstate commerce. The object and intention of the combination determined its legality.

In *Swift v. United States,* 196 U. S. 375, a bill was brought against a number of corporations, firms and individuals of different States alleging that they were engaged in interstate commerce in the purchase, sale, transportation and delivery, and subsequent resale at the point of delivery of meats, and that they combined to refrain from bidding against each other in the purchase of cattle; to maintain a uniform price at which the meat should be sold, and to maintain uniform charges in delivering meats thus sold through the channels of interstate trade to the various dealers and consumers in other States.

And that, thus, they artificially restrained commerce in fresh meats from the purchase and shipment of livestock from the plains to the final distribution of the meats to the consumers in the markets of the country.

Source: Loewe v. Lawlor—208 U.S. 274 (1908).

9. Economic Downturn of 1913-1914

A. Report of the Pujo Committee (1912-1913)

The Pujo committee was a subcommittee of the House Committee on Banking and Currency chaired by Congressman Arsène Pujo (D-LA) (1861-1939) and charged with investigating the "money trust," that is, a community of Wall Street bankers and financiers that supposedly controlled the nation's markets and banking system. The committee conducted hearings between May 1912 and January 1913. In its final report, issued on February 28, 1913, the committee concluded that 18 different financial firms controlled large sections of the country's manufacturing, mining, transportation, telecommunications, and finance industries. The committee's report helped spur ratification of the 16th Amendment and passage of the Federal Reserve Act in 1913. The following excerpt from the committee's report provides testimony elicited on the practice of short-selling.

SECTION 16. SHORT SELLING.

In the usual acceptation of the term one sells short when he sells stock not owned by him, but which he borrows for delivery in the expectation that the price will fall, thereby enabling him to buy and return the borrowed stock at a profit to himself. The operation is not peculiar to the stock exchange, but is also familiar to the commodity markets. The extent to which it is practiced on the New York Stock Exchange could not be definitely ascertained. Whilst your committee has not been impressed with the contention that short selling performs a valuable function in checking a rapid ascent of prices, it is enough to say that there seems no greater reason for prohibiting speculation by way of selling securities in the expectation of buving them back at lower prices than by way of purchasing them in the expectation of at once reselling at higher prices.

That is not to say, however, that means for facilitating short selling should be countenanced, since all speculation, whether for the rise or for the fall, needs to be curbed rather than stimulated. Therefore brokers should not be allowed to lend their customers' stocks to persons who have sold short and need stock with which to make deliveries.

The following extract from Mr. Sturgis's testimony fairly represents the stock exchange view of short selling and the arguments that are advanced to support it:

Q. Certainly. What is the purpose of short selling?
A. Generally speaking, to make a profit.
Q. To make a profit by what process?
A. By repurchasing the short sale at a declining price.

Q. That is, by selling a security that you have not got and gambling on the proposition that you can get it cheaper and deliver the thing that if sold? Is not that it?

A. That is the usual process—selling when you think the price is too high and repurchasing when you think it has reached the proper level.

Q. But is it, or not, the process of selling a thing you have not got?

A. It is.

Q. And is it, or not, with the idea that it will go lower, or can be depressed lower, and bought cheaper and delivered?

A. Truly.

Q. Do I understand that you regard that as legitimate and defensible?

A. Do you wish my personal expression of opinion?

Q. Yes.

A. I think it depends entirely upon circumstances.

Q. Under what circumstances would you regard that sort of short selling as legitimate and proper?

A. I would regard it so if there was a panic raging over the country and it was desirable to protect interests which could not be sold. I think it would be a perfectly legitimate thing to do.

Q. Let us see about that. If there was a panic raging over the country and a man sold stocks short, would not that simply add to the panic?

A. It might. Self-preservation is the first law of nature.

* * * * * *

Q. But, as I understand it, if there is a panic raging over the country, you think it is defensible for a man to depress stocks by selling stocks ho has not got, with the idea of adding to the panic?

A. Mr. Untermyer, if a person has property which is absolutely unsalable and he can, so to speak, protect his position by selling something for which there is a broad market—

Q. That he has not got?

A. (continuing). I do not consider it wrong.

Q. Mr. Sturgis, let us just analyze that, because I do not think I understand you. You do not want to be misunderstood, do you?

A. It is not my wish.

Q. And I do not want you to be misunderstood. Do you mean to say that if there is a panic raging it is a defensible thing for a man, under any circumstances, to sell stock that he has not got, with the idea of getting it back cheaper?

A. I do think it is defensible. I certainly think it is defensible.

Q. For what purposes does he do that except to try to make money?

A. To try to save his credit, perhaps.

Q. How does he save his credit in a panic by selling stocks that he has not got with the idea of adding to the panic and getting them cheaper?

A. Because if he can make a profit on that sale it may repair the losses that he has made on stocks he can not sell.

Q. I see. You know that that would simply accentuate the fierceness of the panic, do you not?

A. It could not be otherwise.

Q. Certainly. And his only purpose in doing a tiling of that kind in time of panic would be to make money, would it not?

A. To protect himself.

Q. It would be to make money, would it not?

A. Yes; and that would protect him.

Q. Of course it always protects a man to make money, no matter how he makes it, does it not?

A. Yes, sir.

Q. And that, you think, is justifiable?

A. I think under those circumstances it is.

Q. You do not want to make any further explanation of that proposition, do you?

A. I do not.

Q. Is it any more justifiable for a man to sell short in a panic than in a normal market?

A. It depends very much upon his financial necessities.

Q. Do you regard it as justifiable in a normal market for a man to sell *a* thing he has not got, with the idea of depressing prices in order to buy in the stock at a lower level?

A. I think it is a question between a man and his own conscience.

Q. I am asking for your judgment. You have been many years in the exchange, and you are a careful observer, and I would like to know your judgment.

Q. Do you approve of it?

A. You ask me personally?

Q. Yes.

A. I never sold a share of stock short in my life.

Q. Then you do not approve of it, do you?

A. I just happen not to have done it. My private business, if you please, I beg you to omit.

Q. I have not asked you your private business.

A. Yes; you asked me what I did myself.

Q. 1 did not ask you that, sir; I asked you what you thought about it.

Q. Do you approve of short selling in others?

A. Under what conditions?

Q. Under any conditions.

A. Yes; under some conditions.

Q. Do you approve of short selling in a normal market?

A. I will answer that question by saying it is a moral question—with the individual himself. It is not up to me to express my opinion upon it.

Q. Do you personally approve of short selling in a normal market?

A. Not I, personally; no.

Q. You do not. And is it or not the fact that the bulk of the short selling is done in a normal market?

A. I should say no; more often on an excited market.

Q. It is done every day, is it not?

A. Oh, yes; to some extent.

Q. And it is done in large volume, is it not?

A. At times.

Q. The stock exchange does not discourage it, does it?

A. The stock exchange does not enter into it at all.

Q. The stock exchange does not discourage short selling, does it?

A. The stock exchange takes no position in the matter at all.

Q. Has the stock exchange any rule or regulation against short selling?

A. None.

Q. Why is it not just as simple a matter for them to have a regulation against short selling as to have a regulation against a broker splitting his commissions?

A. There is no regulation against short selling; that is all I can say to you about it.

Source: Report of the Committee Appointed Pursuant to House Resolutions 429 and 504 to Investigate the Concentration of Control of Money and Credit. Submitted by Mr. Pujo, February 28, 1913. Washington, D.C.: Government Printing Office, 1913, 52–54; Fraser Reserve Archive website. http://fraser.stlouisfed.org/docs/historical /house/money_trust/montru_report.pdf.

B. Sixteenth Amendment (February 3, 1913)

The 16th Amendment to the U.S. Constitution permits Congress to levy an income tax without apportioning it among the states as the Constitution had hereto required for all direct taxes. In its 1895 Pollock v. Farmers' Loan and Trust Company *decision, the U.S. Supreme Court had declared certain income taxes, such as those on interest, rests, and dividends, to be direct taxes and thus subject to the requirement of being apportioned. This meant that some income taxes, which Congress had been levying since the start of the Civil War in 1861, were unconstitutional because they were unapportioned. The 16th Amendment superseded this requirement for all income taxes.*

Amendment XVI
The Congress shall have power to lay and collect taxes on incomes, from whatever source derived, without apportionment among the several states, and without regard to any census or enumeration.

Source: Cornell University Law School. Legal Information Institute Website. http://www.law.cornell.edu/constitution/amendmentxvi.

C. Federal Reserve Act (December 23, 1913)

After the expiration of the Second Bank of the United States in 1836, the country did not have a central bank. Because of the hardship caused by a series of financial panics, particularly the Panic of 1907, many Americans in the first decade of the 20th century became convinced of the need for major banking and currency reform. What was required was some means whereby credit and currency could be expanded or restricted as needed to see the economy through future financial downturns. The Federal Reserve Act, which was passed by Congress and signed by President Woodrow Wilson (1856–1924) in 1913, created the Federal Reserve system as the central banking system of the United States. The Federal Reserve was empowered to issue federal reserve notes (U.S. dollars) as legal tender. In the following excerpts from the act, the composition and powers of the Federal Reserve Board are defined.

Sec 10. A Federal Reserve Board is hereby created which shall consist of seven members, including the Secretary of the Treasury and the Comptroller of the Currency, who shall be members ex officio, and five members appointed by the President of the United States, by and with the advice and consent of the Senate. In selecting the five appointive members of the Federal Reserve Board not more than one of whom shall be selected from any one Federal reserve district, the President shall have due regard to a fair representation of the different commercial, industrial and geographical divisions of the country. The five members of the federal Reserve Board appointed by the President and confirmed as aforesaid shall devote their entire time to the business of the Federal Reserve Board and shall each receive an annual salary of $12,000, payable monthly together with actual necessary traveling expenses, and the Comptroller of the Currency, as ex officio member of the Federal Reserve Board, shall, in addition to the salary now paid nun as Comptroller of the Currency, receive the sum of $7 000 annually for his services as a member of said Board.

The members of said board, the Secretary of the Treasury the Assistant Secretaries of the Treasury, and the Comptroller of the Currency shall be ineligible during the time they are in office and for two years thereafter to hold any office, position, or employment in any member bank. Of the five members thus appointed by the President at least two shall be persons experienced in banking or finance. One shall be designated by the President to serve for two, one for four one for six, one for eight, and one for ten years, and thereafter 'each member so appointed shall serve for a term of ten years unless sooner removed for cause by the President. Of the five persons thus appointed, one shall be designated by the President as governor and one as vice governor of the Federal Reserve Board. The governor of the Federal Reserve Board, subject to its supervision, shall be the active executive officer. The Secretary of the Treasury may assign offices in the Department of the Treasury for the use of the Federal Reserve Board. Each member of the Federal Reserve Board shall within fifteen days after notice of appointment make and subscribe to the oath of office.

The Federal Reserve Board shall have power to levy semiannually upon the Federal reserve banks, in proportion to their capital stock and surplus, an assessment sufficient to pay its estimated expenses and the salaries of its members and employees for the half year succeeding the levying of such assessment, together with any deficit carried forward from the preceding half year.

The first meeting of the Federal Reserve Board shall be held in Washington, District of Columbia, as soon as may be after the passage of this Act, at a date to be fixed by the Reserve Bank Organization Committee. The Secretary of the Treasury shall be ex officio chair man of the Federal Reserve Board. No member of the Federal Reserve Board shall be an officer or director of any bank, banking institution trust company, or Federal reserve bank nor hold stock in any bank, banking institution, or trust company; and before entering upon his duties as a member of the Federal Reserve Board he shall certify under oath to the Secretary of the Treasury that he has complied with this requirement. Whenever a vacancy shall occur, other than by expiration of term, among the five members of the Federal Reserve Board appointed by the President, as above provided, a successor shall be appointed by the President, with the advice and consent of the Senate, to fill such vacancy, and when appointed he shall hold office for the unexpired term of the member whose place he is selected to fill.

The President shall have the power to fill all vacancies that may happen on the Federal Reserve Board during the recess of the Senate, by granting commissions which shall expire thirty days after the next session of the Senate convenes.

Nothing in this Act contained shall be construed as taking away any powers heretofore vested by law in the Secretary of the Treasury which relate to the supervision, management, and control of the Treasury Department and bureaus under such department, and wherever any power vested by this Act in the Federal Reserve Board or the Federal reserve agent appears to conflict with the powers of the Secretary of the Treasury, such powers shall be exercised subject to the supervision and control of the Secretary.

The Federal Reserve Board shall annually make a full report of its operations to the Speaker of the House of Representatives, who shall cause the same to be printed for the information of the Congress. . . .

Sec. 11. The Federal Reserve Board shall be authorized and empowered:

(a) to examine at its discretion the accounts, books and affairs of each Federal reserve bank and of each member bank and to require such statements and reports as it may deem necessary. The said board shall publish once each week a statement showing the condition of each Federal reserve bank and a consolidated statement for all Federal reserve banks. Such statements shall show in detail the assets and liabilities of the Federal reserve banks, single and combined, and shall furnish full information regarding the character of the money held as reserve and the amount, nature and maturities of the paper and other investments owned or held by Federal reserve banks.

(b) To permit, or, on the affirmative vote of at least five members of the Reserve Board to require Federal reserve banks to rediscount the discounted paper of other Federal reserve banks at rates of interest to be fixed by the Federal Reserve Board.

(c) To suspend for a period not exceeding thirty days, and from time to time to renew such suspension for periods not exceeding fifteen days any reserve requirement specified in this Act: Provided, that it shall establish a graduated tax upon the amounts by which the reserve requirements of this Act may be permitted to fall below the level hereinafter specified: And provided further, That when the gold reserve held against Federal reserve notes falls below forty per centum, the Federal Reserve Board shall establish a graduated tax of not more than one per centum per annum upon such deficiency until the reserves fall to thirty-two and one-half per centum, and when said reserve falls below thirty-two and one-half per centum, a tax at the rate increasingly of not less than one and one-half per centum per annum upon each two and one-half per centum or fraction thereof that such reserve falls below thirty-two and one-half per centum, the tax shall be paid by the reserve bank, but the reserve bank shall add an amount equal to said tax to the rates of interest and discount fixed by the Federal Reserve Board.

(d) To supervise and regulate through the bureau under the charge of the Comptroller of the Currency the issue and retirement of Federal reserve notes, and to prescribe rules and regulations under which such notes may be delivered by the Comptroller to the Federal reserve agents applying therefor.

(e) To add to the number of cities classified as reserve and central reserve cities under existing law in which national banking associations are subject to the reserve requirements set forth in section twenty of this Act; or to reclassify existing reserve and central reserve cities or to terminate their designation as such.

(f) To suspend or remove any officer or director of any Federal reserve bank, the cause of such removal to be forthwith communicated in writing by the Federal Reserve Board to the removed officer or director and to said bank.

(g) To require the writing off of doubtful or worthless assets upon the books and balance sheets of Federal reserve banks.

(h) To suspend, for the violation of any of the provisions of this Act, the operations of any Federal reserve bank, to take possession thereof, administer the same during the period of suspension, and, when deemed advisable, to liquidate or reorganize such bank.

(i) To require bonds of Federal reserve agents, to make regulations for the safeguarding of all collateral, bonds, Federal reserve notes, money or property of any kind deposited in the hands of such agents, and said board shall perform the duties, functions, or services specified in this Act, and make all rules and regulations necessary to enable said board effectively to perform the same.

(j) To exercise general supervision over said Federal reserve banks.

(k) To grant by special permit to national banks applying therefor, when not in contravention of State or local law, the right to act as trustee, executor, administrator, or registrar of stocks and bonds under such rules and regulations as the said board may prescribe.

(l) To employ such attorneys, experts, assistants, clerks, or other employees as may be deemed necessary to conduct the business of the board. All salaries and fees shall be fixed in advance by said board and shall be paid in the same manner as the salaries of the members of said board. All such attorneys, experts, assistants, clerics, and other employees shall be appointed without regard to the provisions of the Act of January sixteenth, eighteen hundred and eighty-three . . . and amendments thereto, or any rule or regulation made in pursuance thereof: Provided, That nothing herein shall prevent the President from placing said employees in the classified service.

Source: Federal Reserve Act (ch. 6, 38 Stat. 251, enacted December 23, 1913, 12 U.S.C. ch. 3).

10. Recession of 1920–1921

A. *United States v. United States Steel Corporation* (March 1, 1920)

In 1901 J. P. Morgan (1837–1913) and Elbert H. Gary (1846–1927) founded U.S. Steel by combining several large steel companies, including Gary's Federal Steel Company and Andrew Carnegie's (1835–1919) Carnegie Steel Company. Because the new concern controlled almost 90 percent of the market, the government in 1911 sued the company as a monopoly that violated the Sherman Antitrust Act of 1890. In 1920 the U.S. Supreme Court declared in United States v. United States Steel Corporation *that U.S. Steel did not violate the act because its size was the result of natural growth rather than an attempt to monopolize the market. Also, by 1920, the company's market share had dropped to about 50 percent, leading the court to conclude that U.S. Steel had in fact not achieved a monopoly and had thus not harmed the economy despite its size. Below are excerpts from the court's opinion written by Justice Joseph McKenna (1843–1926).*

Suit against the Steel Corporation and certain other companies which it directs and controls by reason of the ownership of their stock, it and they being separately and collectively charged as violators of the Sherman Anti-Trust Act.

It is prayed that it and they be dissolved because engaged in illegal restraint of trade and the exercise of monopoly.

Special charges of illegality and monopoly are made, and special redresses and remedies are prayed—among others, that there be a prohibition of stock ownership and exercise of rights under such ownership, and that there shall be such orders and distribution of the stock and other properties as shall be in accordance with equity and good conscience and "shall effectuate the purpose of the Anti-Trust Act." General relief is also prayed.

The Steel Corporation is a holding company only; the other companies are the operating ones, manufacturers in the iron and steel industry, twelve in number. There are, besides, other corporations and individuals, more or less connected in the activities of the other defendants, that are alleged to be instruments or accomplices in their activities and offendings, and that these activities and offendings (speaking in general terms) extend from 1901 to 1911, when the bill was filed, and have illustrative periods of significant and demonstrated illegality.

Issue is taken upon all these charges, and we see at a glance what detail of circumstances may be demanded, and we may find ourselves puzzled to compress them into an opinion that will not be of fatiguing prolixity. . . .

The corporation was formed in 1901, no act of aggression upon its competitors is charged against it, it confederated with them at times in offense against the law, but abandoned that before this suit was brought, and, since 1911, no act in violation of law can be established against it except its existence be such an act. This is urged, as we have seen, and that the interest of the public is involved, and that such interest is paramount to corporation or competitors. Granted—though it is difficult to see how there can be restraint of trade when there is no restraint of competitors in the trade nor complaints by customers—how can it be worked out of the situation, and through what proposition of law? Of course, it calls for nothing other than a right application of the law, and, to repeat what we have said above, shall we declare the law to be that size is an offense, even though it minds its own business, because what it does is imitated? The corporation is undoubtedly of impressive size, and it takes an effort of resolution not to be affected by it or to exaggerate its influence. But we must adhere to the law, and the law does not make mere size an offense, or the existence of unexerted power an offense. It, we repeat, requires overt acts, and trusts to its prohibition of them and its power to repress or punish them. It does not compel competition, nor require all that is possible.

Admitting, however, that there is pertinent strength in the propositions of the government, and in connection with them, we recall the distinction we made in the *Standard Oil* case, 221 U. S. 1, between acts done in violation of the statute and a condition brought about which, "in and of itself, is not only a continued attempt to monopolize, but also a monopolization." In such case, we declared, "the duty to enforce the statute" required "the application of broader and more controlling" remedies than in the other. And the remedies applied conformed to the declaration; there was prohibition of future acts and there was dissolution of "the combination found to exist in violation of the statute" in order to "neutralize the extension and continually operating force which the possession of the power unlawfully obtained" had "brought" and would "continue to bring about."

Are the case and its precepts applicable here? The Steel Corporation by its formation, united under one control competing companies, and thus, it is urged, a condition was brought about in violation of the statute, and therefore illegal, and became a "continually operating force" with the "possession of power unlawfully obtained."

But there are countervailing considerations. We have seen whatever there was of wrong intent could not be executed; whatever there was of evil effect was discontinued before this suit was brought, and this, we think, determines the decree. We say this in full realization of the requirements of the law. It is clear in its denunciation of monopolies, and equally clear in its direction that the courts of the nation shall prevent and restrain them (its language is "to prevent and restrain violations of" the act); but the command is necessarily submissive to the conditions which may exist and the usual powers of a court of equity to adapt its remedies to those conditions. In other words, it is not expected to enforce abstractions, and do injury thereby, it may be, to the purpose of the law. It is this flexibility of discretion—indeed, essential function—that makes its value in our jurisprudence—value in this case as in others. We do not mean to say that the law is not its own measure, and that it can be disregarded, but only that the appropriate relief in each instance is remitted to a court of equity to determine, not, and let us be explicit in this, to advance a policy contrary to that of the law, but in submission to the law and its policy, and in execution of both. And it is certainly a matter for consideration that there was no legal attack on the corporation until 1911, ten years after its formation and the commencement of its career. We do not, however, speak of the delay simply as to its time, or say that there is estoppel in it because of its time, but on account of what was done during that time—the many millions of dollars spent, the development made, and the enterprises undertaken; the investments by the public that have been invited, and are not to be ignored. And what of the foreign trade that has been developed and exists? The government, with some inconsistency, it seems to us, would remove this from the decree of dissolution. Indeed, it is pointed out that, under congressional legislation in the Webb Act, the foreign trade of the corporation is reserved to it. And further, it is said that the corporation has constructed a company called the Products Company, which can be "very easily preserved as a medium through which the steel business might reach the balance of the world," and that, in the decree of "dissolution, that could be provided." This is supplemented by the suggestion that not only the Steel Corporation, "but other steel makers of the country could function through an instrumentality created under the Webb Act."

The propositions and suggestions do not commend themselves. We do not see how the Steel Corporation can be such a beneficial instrumentality in the trade of the world, and its beneficence be preserved, and yet be such an evil instrumentality in the trade of the United States that it must be destroyed. And by whom and how shall all the adjustments of preservation or destruction be made? How can the corporation be sustained, and its power of control over its subsidiary companies be retained and exercised in the foreign trade, and given up in the domestic trade? The government presents no solution of the problem. Counsel realize the difficulty, and seem to think that its solution or its evasion is in the suggestion that the Steel Corporation and "other steel makers could function through an instrumentality created under the Webb Act." But we are confronted with the necessity of immediate judicial action under existing laws, not action under conceptions which may never be capable of legal execution.

We must now decide, and we see no guide to decision in the propositions of the government.

The government, however, tentatively presents a proposition which has some tangibility. It submits that certain of the subsidiary companies are so mechanically equipped and so officially directed as to be released and remitted to independent action and individual interests and the competition to which such interests prompt, without any disturbance to business. The companies are enumerated. They are the Carnegie Steel Company (a combination of the old Carnegie Company, the National Steel Company, and the American Steel Company), the Federal Steel Company, the Tennessee Company, and the Union Steel Company (a combination of the Union Steel Company of Donora, Pennsylvania, Sharon Steel Company of Sharon, Pennsylvania, and Sharon Tin Plate Company). They are fully integrated, it is said—possess their own supplies, facilities of transportation, and distribution. They are subject to the Steel Corporation, is in effect the declaration, in nothing but its control of their prices. We may say parenthetically that they are defendants in the suit and charged as offenders, and we have the strange circumstance of violators of the law being urged to be used as expedients of the law.

But let us see what guide to a procedure of dissolution of the corporation and the dispersion as well of its subsidiary companies, for they are asserted to be illegal combinations, is prayed. And the fact must not be overlooked or underestimated. The prayer of the government calls for not only a disruption of present conditions, but the restoration of the conditions of twenty years ago, if not literally, substantially. Is there guidance to this in the *Standard Oil* case and the *Tobacco* case, [221 U.S. 1, 221 U. S. 106]? As an element in determining the answer, we shall have to compare the cases with that at bar, but this can only be done in a general way. And the law necessarily must be kept in mind. No other comment of it is necessary. It has received so much exposition that it and all it prescribes and proscribes should be considered as a consciously directing presence.

The Standard Oil Company had its origin in 1882, and, through successive forms of combinations and agencies, it progressed in illegal power to the day of the decree, even attempting to circumvent by one of its forms the decision of a court against it. And its methods in using its power was of the kind that Judge Woolley described as "brutal," and of which practices, he said, the Steel Corporation was absolutely guiltless. We have enumerated them, and this reference to them is enough. And of the practices, this Court said no disinterested mind could doubt that the purpose was "to drive others from the field, and to exclude them from their right to trade, and thus accomplish the mastery which was the end in view." It was further said that what was done and the final culmination "in the plan of the New Jersey corporation" made "manifest the continued existence of the intent . . . and impelled the expansion of the New Jersey corporation." It was to this corporation, which represented the power and purpose of all that preceded, that the suit was addressed and the decree of the court was to apply. What we have quoted contrasts that case with this. The contrast is further emphasized by pointing out how, in the case of the New Jersey corporation, the original wrong was reflected in and manifested by the acts which followed the organization, as described by the court. It said:

"The exercise of the power which resulted from that organization fortifies the foregoing conclusions [as to monopoly, etc.], since the development which came, the acquisition here and there which ensued of every efficient means by which competition could have been asserted, the slow but resistless methods which followed by which means of transportation were absorbed and brought under control, the system of marketing which was adopted, by which the country was divided into districts and the trade in each district in oil was turned over to the designated corporation within the combination and all others were excluded, all lead the mind up to a conviction of a purpose and intent which we think is so certain as practically to cause the subject not to be within the domain of reasonable contention."

The *Tobacco Company* case has the same bad distinctions as the *Standard Oil* case. The illegality in which it was formed (there were two American Tobacco Companies, but we use the name as designating the new company as representing the combinations of the suit) continued—indeed, progressed in intensity and defiance to the moment of decree. And it is the intimation of the opinion, if not its direct assertion, that the formation of the company (the word "combination" is used) was preceded by the intimidation of a trade war "inspired by one or more of the minds which brought about and became parties to that combination." In other words, the purpose of the combination was signaled to competitors, and the choice presented to them was submission or ruin, to become parties to the illegal enterprise or be driven "out of the business." This was the purpose, and the achievement, and the processes by which achieved, this Court enumerated to be the formation of new companies, taking stock in others to obscure the result actually attained, but always to monopolize and retain power in the hands of the few and mastery of the trade, putting control in the hands of seemingly independent corporations as barriers to the entry of others into the trade; the expenditure of millions upon millions in buying out plants not to utilize them, but to close them; by constantly recurring stipulations by which numbers of persons, whether manufacturers, stockholders, or employees, were required to bind themselves, generally for long periods, not to compete in the future. In the *Tobacco* case, therefore, as in the *Standard Oil* case, the Court had to deal with a persistent and systematic lawbreaker masquerading under legal forms, and which not only had to be stripped of its disguises, but arrested in its illegality. A decree of dissolution was the manifest instrumentality, and inevitable. We think it would be a work of sheer supererogation to point out that a decree in that case or in the *Standard Oil* case furnishes no example for a decree in this.

In conclusion, we are unable to see that the public interest will be served by yielding to the contention of the government respecting the dissolution of the company or the separation from it of some of its subsidiaries, and we do see in a contrary conclusion a risk of injury to the public interest, including a material disturbance of, and, it may be serious detriment to, the foreign trade. And, in submission to the policy of the law and its fortifying prohibitions, the public interest is of paramount regard.

We think, therefore, that the decree of the district court should be affirmed. *So ordered.*

Source: United States v. United States Steel Corp., 251 U.S. 417 (1920).

11. Great Depression, 1929–1933

A. Wickersham Commission Report on Alcohol Prohibition (January 7, 1931)

In May 1929 President Herbert Hoover (1874–1964) established the National Commission on Law Observance and Enforcement to investigate the growing number of violations of national prohibition and to suggest modification of the 18th Amendment to make it more enforceable. Headed by George W. Wickersham (1858–1936), a former attorney general, the commission became known as the Wickersham Commission. Reproduced below are the commission's conclusions and recommendations as embodied in its final report, known as the Wickersham Report, which was issued in January 1931. Although the commission did not support repeal of prohibition, it did find much evasion of prohibition, much lax or effective enforcement of prohibition, and much police corruption. To improve the situation, the commission suggested revision of the 18th Amendment and more aggressive action by police to make prohibition more effective.

X—CONCLUSIONS AND RECOMMENDATIONS
1. The Commission is opposed to repeal of the Eighteenth Amendment.
2. The Commission is opposed to the restoration in any manner of the legalized saloon.
3. The Commission is opposed to the federal or state governments, as such, going into the liquor business.

4. The Commission is opposed to the proposal to modify the National Prohibition Act so as to permit manufacture and sale of light wines or beer.

5. The Commission is of opinion that the cooperation of the states is an essential element in the enforcement of the Eighteenth Amendment and the National Prohibition Act throughout the territory of the United States; that the support of public opinion in the several states is necessary in order to insure such cooperation.

6. The Commission is of opinion that prior to the enactment of the Bureau of Prohibition Act, 1927, the agencies for enforcement were badly organized and inadequate; that subsequent to that enactment there has been continued improvement in organization and effort for enforcement.

7. The Commission is of opinion that there is yet no adequate observance or enforcement.

8. The Commission is of opinion that the present organization for enforcement is still inadequate.

9. The Commission is of opinion that the federal appropriations for enforcement of the Eighteenth Amendment should be substantially increased and that the vigorous and better organized efforts which have gone on since the Bureau of Prohibition Act, 1927, should be furthered by certain improvements in the statutes and in the organization, personnel, and equipment of enforcement, so as to give to enforcement the greatest practicable efficiency.

10. Some of the Commission are not convinced that Prohibition under the Eighteenth Amendment is unenforceable and believe that a further trial should be made with the help of the recommended improvements, and that if after such trial effective enforcement is not secured there should be a revision of the Amendment. Others of the Commission are convinced that it has been demonstrated that Prohibition under the Eighteenth Amendment is unenforceable and that the Amendment should be immediately revised, but recognizing that the process of amendment will require some time, they unite in the recommendations of Conclusion No. 9 for the improvement of the enforcement agencies.

11. All the Commission agree that if the Amendment is revised it should be made to read substantially as follows:
Section 1. The Congress shall have power to regulate or to prohibit the manufacture, traffic in or transportation of intoxicating liquors within, the importation thereof into and the exportation thereof from the United States and all territory subject to the jurisdiction thereof for beverage purposes.

12. The recommendations referred to in conclusion Number 9 are:
1. Removal of the, causes of irritation and resentment on the part of the medical profession by:
(a) Doing away with the statutory fixing of the amount which may be prescribed and the number of prescriptions;

(b) Abolition of the requirement of specifying the ailment for which liquor is prescribed upon a blank to go into the public files;

(c) Leaving as much as possible to regulations rather than fixing details by statute.

2. Removal of the anomalous provisions in Section 29, National Prohibition Act, as to cider and fruit juices by making some uniform regulation for a fixed alcoholic content.

3. Increase of the number of agents, storekeeper-gaugers, prohibition investigators, and special agents; increase in the personnel of the Customs Bureau and in the equipment of all enforcement organizations.

4. Enactment of a statute authorizing regulations permitting access to the premises and records of wholesale and retail dealers so as to make it possible to trace products of specially denatured alcohol to the ultimate consumer.

5. Enactment of legislation to prohibit independent denaturing plants.

6. The Commission is opposed to legislation allowing more latitude for federal searches and seizures.

7. The Commission renews the recommendation contained in its previous reports for codification of the National Prohibition Act and the acts supplemental to and in amendment thereof.

8. The Commission renews its recommendation of legislation for making procedure in the so-called padlock injunction cases more effective.

9. The Commission recommends legislation providing a mode of prosecuting petty offenses in the federal courts and modifying the Increased Penalties Act of 1929, as set forth in the Chairman's letter to the Attorney General dated May 23, 1930, H. R. Rep. 1699.

There are differences of view among the members of the Commission as to certain of the conclusions stated and as to some matters included in or omitted from this report. The report is signed subject to individual reservation of the right to express these individual views in separate or supplemental reports to be annexed hereto.

Geo W. Wickersham, Chairman

Source: Schaffer Library of Drug Policy website. http://www.druglibrary.org/schaffer /library/studies/wick/wick10.html.

B. Franklin D. Roosevelt's Commonwealth Club Address (September 23, 1932)

On September 23, 1932, in the midst of the 1932 presidential campaign, Governor Franklin D. Roosevelt (1882–1945) of New York, the Democratic candidate, delivered an address at the Commonwealth Club in San Francisco that laid out the basic philosophy behind the "New Deal" that he proposed for a country mired in the Great Depression. In the speech, which is excerpted below, Roosevelt explains the stark philosophical differences that he has with his Republican opponent, President Herbert Hoover (1874–1964). Roosevelt argues that growing abuses of industrial and corporate power have brought the United States into a new era in which individual liberty and opportunity can best be protected by an activist government, not the limited government and voluntary action advocated by Hoover.

I want to speak not of politics but of government. I want to speak not of parties, but of universal principles. They are not political, except in that larger sense in which a great American once expressed a definition of politics, that nothing in all of human life is foreign to the science of politics. . . .

The issue of government has always been whether individual men and women will have to serve some system of government of economics, or whether a system of government and economics exists to serve individual men and women. This question has persistently dominated the discussion of government for many generations. On questions relating to these things men have differed, and for time immemorial it is probable that honest men will continue to differ. . . .

A glance at the situation today only too clearly indicates that equality of opportunity as we have known it no longer exists. Our industrial plant is built; the problem just now is whether under existing conditions it is not overbuilt. Our last frontier has long since been reached, and there is practically no more free land. More than half of our people do not live on the farms or on lands and cannot derive a living by cultivating their own property. There is no safety valve in the form of a Western prairie to which those thrown out of work by the Eastern economic machines can go for a new start. We are not able to invite the immigration from Europe to share our endless plenty. We are now providing a drab living for our own people.

Our system of constantly rising tariffs has at last reacted against us to the point of closing our Canadian frontier on the north, our European markets on the east, many of our Latin American markets to the south, and a goodly proportion of our Pacific markets on the west, through the retaliatory tariffs of those countries. It has forced many of our great industrial institutions who exported their surplus production to such countries, to establish plants in such countries within the tariff walls. This has resulted in the reduction of the operation of their American plants, and opportunity for employment.

Just as freedom to farm has ceased, so also the opportunity in business has narrowed. It still is true that men can start small enterprises, trusting to native shrewdness and ability to keep abreast of competitors; but area after area has been preempted altogether by the great corporations, and even in the fields which still have no great concerns, the small man starts with a handicap. The unfeeling statistics of the past three decades show that the independent business man is running a losing race. Perhaps he is forced to the wall; perhaps he cannot command credit; perhaps he is "squeezed out," in Mr. Wilson's words, by highly organized corporate competitors, as your corner grocery man can tell you.

Recently a careful study was made of the concentration of business in the United States. It showed that our economic life was dominated by some six hundred odd corporations who controlled two-thirds of American industry. Ten million small business men divided the other third. More striking still, it appeared that if the process of concentration goes on at the same rate, at the end of another century we shall have all American industry controlled by a dozen corporations, and run by perhaps a hundred men. Put plainly, we are steering a steady course toward economic oligarchy, if we are not there already.

Clearly, all this calls for a re-appraisal of values. A mere builder of more industrial plants, a creator of more railroad systems, and organizer of more corporations, is as likely to be a danger as a help. The day of the great promoter or the financial Titan, to whom we granted anything if only he would build, or develop, is over. Our task now is not discovery or exploitation of natural resources, or necessarily producing more goods. It is the soberer, less dramatic business of administering resources and plants already in hand, of seeking to reestablish foreign markets for our surplus production, of meeting the problem of under consumption, of adjusting production to consumption, of distributing wealth and products more equitably, of adapting existing economic organizations to the service of the people. The day of enlightened administration has come.

Just as in older times the central government was first a haven of refuge, and then a threat, so now in a closer economic system the central and ambitious financial unit is no longer a servant of national desire, but a danger. I would draw the parallel one step farther. We did not think because national government had become a threat in the 18th century that therefore we should abandon the principle of national government. Nor today should we abandon the principle of strong economic units called corporations, merely because their power is susceptible of easy abuse. In other times we dealt with the problem of an unduly ambitious central government by modifying it gradually into a constitutional democratic government. So today we are modifying and controlling our economic units.

As I see it, the task of government in its relation to business is to assist the development of an economic declaration of rights, an economic constitutional order. This is the common task of statesman and business man. It is the minimum requirement of a more permanently safe order of things.

Every man has a right to life; and this means that he has also a right to make a comfortable living. He may by sloth or crime decline to exercise that right; but it may not be denied him. We have no actual famine or death; our industrial and agricultural mechanism can produce enough and to spare. Our government formal and informal., political and economic, owes to every one an avenue to possess himself of a portion of that plenty sufficient for his needs, through his own work.

Every man has a right to his own property; which means a right to be assured, to the fullest extent attainable, in the safety of his savings. By no other means can men carry the burdens of those parts of life which, in the nature of things afford no chance of labor; childhood, sickness, old age. In all thought of property, this right is paramount; all other property rights must yield to it. If, in accord with this principle, we must restrict the operations of the speculator, the manipulator, even the financier, I believe we must accept the restriction as needful, not to hamper individualism but to protect it.

These two requirements must be satisfied, in the main, by the individuals who claim and hold control of the great industrial and financial combinations which dominate so large a part of our industrial life. They have undertaken to be, not business men, but princes-princes of property. I am not prepared to say that the system which produces them is wrong. I am very clear that they must fearlessly and competently assume the responsibility which goes with the power. So many enlightened business men know this that the statement would be little more than a platitude, were it not for an added implication.

This implication is, briefly, that the responsible heads of finance and industry instead of acting each for himself, must work together to achieve the common end. They must, where necessary, sacrifice this or that private advantage; and in reciprocal self-denial must seek a general advantage. It is here that formal government-political government, if you choose, comes in. Whenever in the pursuit of this objective the lone wolf, the unethical competitor, the reckless promoter, the Ishmael or Insull whose hand is against every man's, declines to join in achieving and end recognized as being for the public welfare, and threatens to drag the industry back to a state of anarchy, the government may properly be asked to apply restraint. Likewise, should the group ever use its collective power contrary to public welfare, the government must be swift to enter and protect the public interest.

The government should assume the function of economic regulation only as a last resort, to be tried only when private initiative, inspired by high responsibility, with such assistance and balance as government can give, has finally failed. As yet there has been no final failure, because there has been no attempt, and I decline to assume that this nation is unable to meet the situation.

The final term of the high contract was for liberty and the pursuit of happiness. We have learnt a great deal of both in the past century. We know that individual liberty and individual happiness mean nothing unless both are ordered in the sense that one man's meat is not another man's poison. We know that the old "rights of personal competency"—the right to read, to think, to speak to choose and live a mode of life, must be respected at all hazards. We know that liberty to do anything which deprives others of those elemental rights is outside the protection of any compact; and that government in this regard is the maintenance of a balance, within which every individual may have a place if he will take it; in which every individual may find safety if he wishes it; in which every individual may attain such power as his ability permits, consistent with his assuming the accompanying responsibility. . . .

Faith in America, faith in our tradition of personal responsibility, faith in our institutions, faith in ourselves demands that we recognize the new terms of the old social contract. We shall fulfill them, as we fulfilled the obligation of the apparent Utopia which Jefferson imagined for us in 1776, and which Jefferson, Roosevelt and Wilson sought to bring to realization. We must do so, lest a rising tide of misery engendered by our common failure, engulf us all. But failure is not an American habit; and in the strength of great hope we must all shoulder our common load.

Source: Speech given to the Commonwealth Club of San Francisco. Available at http://www.ucs.louisiana.edu/~ras2777/conlaw/fdr.html.

C. President Hoover's Madison Square Garden Address (October 31, 1932)

On October 31, 1932, during the last days of the 1932 presidential campaign, President Herbert Hoover (1874–1964) delivered an address to over 20,000 people at New York's Madison Square Garden. Hoover used the speech to emphasize the differences in governing philosophy between himself and his Democratic opponent, Governor Franklin D. Roosevelt (1882–1945) of New York. Stressing the superiority of a philosophy based on individualism and voluntary cooperation over one based on coercive government action, Hoover declared his opponent's proposed "New Deal" reflected "the same philosophy of government that has poisoned Europe." On November 8, Hoover was overwhelmingly defeated, winning less than 40 percent of the popular vote.

. . . This campaign is more than a contest between two men. It is more than a contest between two parties. It is a contest between two philosophies of government.

We are told by the opposition that we must have a change, that we must have a new deal. It is not the change that comes from normal development of national life to which I object or you object, but the proposal to alter the whole foundations of our national life which have been builded through generations of testing and struggle, and of the principles upon which we have made this Nation. The expressions of our opponents must refer to important changes in our economic and social system and our system of government; otherwise they would be nothing but vacuous words. And I realize that in this time of distress many of our people are asking whether our social and economic system is incapable of that great primary function of providing security and comfort of life to all of the firesides of 25 million homes in America, whether our social system provides for the fundamental development and progress of our people, and whether our form of government is capable of originating and sustaining that security and progress.

This question is the basis upon which our opponents are appealing to the people in their fear and their distress. They are proposing changes and so-called new deals which would destroy the very foundations of the American system of life.

Our people should consider the primary facts before they come to the judgment—not merely through political agitation, the glitter of promise, and the discouragement of temporary hardships—whether they will support changes which radically affect the whole system which has been builded during these six generations of the toil of our fathers. They should not approach the question in the despair with which our opponents would clothe it.

Our economic system has received abnormal shocks during the last 3 years which have temporarily dislocated its normal functioning. These shocks have in a large sense come from without our borders, and I say to you that our system of government has enabled us to take such strong action as to prevent the disaster which would otherwise have come to this Nation. It has enabled us further to develop measures and programs which are now demonstrating their ability to bring about restoration and progress.

We must go deeper than platitudes and emotional appeals of the public platform in the campaign if we will penetrate to the full significance of the changes which our opponents are attempting to float upon the wave of distress and discontent from the difficulties through which we have passed. We can find what our opponents would do after searching the record of their appeals to discontent, to group and sectional interest. To find that, we must search for them in the legislative acts which they sponsored and passed in the Democratic-controlled House of Representatives in the last session of Congress. We must look into both the measures for which they voted and in which they were defeated. We must inquire. whether or not the Presidential and Vice-Presidential candidates have disavowed those acts. If they have not, we must conclude that they form a portion and are a substantial indication of the profound changes in the new deal which is proposed.

And we must look still further than this as to what revolutionary changes have been proposed by the candidates themselves.

We must look into the type of leaders who are campaigning for the Democratic ticket, whose philosophies have been well known all their lives and whose demands for a change in the American system are frank and forceful. I can respect the sincerity of these men in their desire to change our form of government and our social and our economic system, though I shall do my best tonight to prove they are wrong. I refer particularly to Senator Norris, Senator La Follette, Senator Cutting, Senator Huey Long, Senator Wheeler, William Randolph Hearst, and other exponents of a social philosophy different from the traditional philosophies of the American people. Unless these men have felt assurance of support to their ideas they certainly would not be supporting these candidates and the Democratic Party. The zeal of these men indicates that they must have some sure confidence that they will have a voice in the administration of this Government.

I may say at once that the changes proposed from all these Democratic principals and their allies are of the most profound and penetrating character. If they are brought about, this will not be the America which we have known in the past.

Now, I may pause for a moment and examine the American system of government and of social and economic life which it is now proposed that we should alter. Our system is the product of our race and of our experience in building a Nation to heights unparalleled in the whole history of the world. It is a system peculiar to the American people. It differs essentially from all others in the world. It is an American system. It is rounded on the conception that only through ordered liberty, through freedom to the individual, and equal opportunity to the individual will his initiative and enterprise be summoned to spur the march of national progress.

It is by the maintenance of an equality of opportunity and therefore of a society absolutely fluid in the movement of its human particles that our individualism departs from the individualism of Europe. We resent class distinction because there can be no rise for the individual through the frozen strata of classes, and no stratification of classes can take place in a mass that is livened by the free rise of its human particles. Thus in our ideals the able and ambitious are able to rise constantly from the bottom to leadership in the community. We denounce any attempt to stir class feeling or class antagonisms in the United States.

This freedom of the individual creates of itself the necessity and the cheerful willingness of men to act cooperatively in a thousand ways and for every purpose as the occasion requires, and it permits such voluntary cooperations to be dissolved as soon as it has served its purpose and to be replaced by new voluntary associations for new purposes.

There has thus grown within us, to gigantic importance, a new conception. That is the conception of voluntary cooperation within the community; cooperation to perfect the social organizations; cooperation for the care of those in distress; cooperation for the advancement of knowledge, of scientific research, of education; cooperative action in a thousand directions for the advancement of economic life. This is self-government by the people outside of the Government. It is the most powerful development of individual freedom and equality of opportunity that has taken place in the century and a half since our fundamental institutions were founded.

It is in the further development of this cooperation and in a sense of its responsibility that we should find solution for many of the complex problems, and not by the extension of the Government into our economic and social life. The greatest function a government can perform is to build up that cooperation, and its most resolute action should be to deny the extension of bureaucracy. We have developed great agencies of cooperation by the assistance of the Government which do promote and protect the interests of individuals and the smaller units of business: the Federal Reserve System, in its strengthening and support of the smaller banks; the Farm Board, in its strengthening and support of the farm cooperatives; the home loan banks, in the mobilizing of building and loan associations and savings banks; the Federal land banks, in giving independence and strength to land mortgage associations; the great mobilization of relief to distress, the mobilization of business and industry in measures of recovery from this depression, and a score of other activities that are not socialism, and they are not the Government in business. They are the essence of protection to the development of free men. I wish to explore this point a little further. The primary conception of this whole American system is not the ordering of men but the cooperation of free men. It is rounded upon the conception of responsibility of the individual to the community, of the responsibility of local government to the State, of the State to the National Government. . . .

It is a tribute to America and its past and present leaders, and even more a tribute to this younger generation, that, contrary to the experience of other countries, we can say tonight that the youth of America are more staunch than many of their elders. I can ask no higher tribute to the Republican Party, no greater aid in the maintenance of the American system and the program of this administration than the support being given by the younger men and women of our country. It has just been communicated to me that in every county and almost every precinct of our country, 3 million members of the Young Republican League are meeting tonight to listen to this address and to rally their support for the party on November 8. That in itself is a victory for the American system.

My countrymen, the proposals of our opponents represent a profound change in American life—less in concrete proposal, bad as that may be, than by implication and by evasion. Dominantly in their spirit they represent a radical departure from the foundations of 150 years which have made this the greatest Nation in the world. This election is not a mere shift from the ins to the outs. It means the determining of the course of our Nation over a century to come.

Now, my conception of America is a land where men and women may walk in ordered liberty, where they may enjoy the advantages of wealth not concentrated in the hands of a few but diffused through the opportunity of all, where they build and safeguard their homes, give to their children the full opportunities of American life, where every man shall be respected in the faith that his conscience and his heart direct him to follow, and where people secure in their liberty shall have leisure and impulse to seek a fuller life. That leads to the release of the energies of men and women, to the wider vision and higher hope. It leads to opportunity for greater and greater service not alone of man to man in our country but from our country to the world. It leads to health in body and a spirit unfettered, youthful, eager with a vision stretching beyond the farthest horizons with a mind open and sympathetic and generous. But that must be builded upon our experience with the past, upon the foundations which have made this country great. It must be the product of the development of our truly American system.

Source: Herbert Hoover: "Address at Madison Square Garden in New York City." October 31, 1932. Online by Gerhard Peters and John T. Woolley, *The American Presidency Project.* http://www.presidency.ucsb.edu/ws/?pid=23317.

D. Twentieth Amendment (January 23, 1933)

Prior to 1933 presidential terms and congressional sessions had always begun on March 4, four months after federal elections. This delay was justified in the early 19th century when a newly elected president would need the time to put his personal affairs in order and travel to Washington. However, by the 20th century, this delay only served to prevent an incoming administration from tackling urgent problems in a timely manner. In 1933 the delay between the election of Franklin D. Roosevelt (1882–1945) in November and the end of Herbert Hoover's (1874–1964) term in March allowed the Great Depression to worsen, since Hoover, as a lame duck, had no mandate to act and Roosevelt, as president-elect, had no power to act. The 20th Amendment, which was ratified in January 1933, moved the start of new presidential terms to January 20 and of new congressional sessions to January 3. The first presidential term to begin under the amendment was Roosevelt's second term, which started on January 20, 1937.

Amendment XX

Section 1.
The terms of the President and Vice President shall end at noon on the 20th day of January, and the terms of Senators and Representatives at noon on the 3d day of January, of the years in which such terms would have ended if this article had not been ratified; and the terms of their successors shall then begin.

Section 2.
The Congress shall assemble at least once in every year, and such meeting shall begin at noon on the 3d day of January, unless they shall by law appoint a different day.

Section 3.
If, at the time fixed for the beginning of the term of the President, the President elect shall have died, the Vice President elect shall become President. If a President shall not have been chosen before the time fixed for the beginning of his term, or if the President elect shall have failed to qualify, then the Vice President elect shall act as President until a President shall have qualified; and the Congress may by law provide for the case wherein neither a President elect nor a Vice President elect shall have qualified, declaring who shall then act as President, or the manner in which one who is to act shall be selected, and such person shall act accordingly until a President or Vice President shall have qualified.

Section 4.
The Congress may by law provide for the case of the death of any of the persons from whom the House of Representatives may choose a President whenever the right of choice shall have devolved upon them, and for the case of the death of any of the persons from whom the Senate may choose a Vice President whenever the right of choice shall have devolved upon them.

Section 5.
Sections 1 and 2 shall take effect on the 15th day of October following the ratification of this article.

Section 6.
This article shall be inoperative unless it shall have been ratified as an amendment to the Constitution by the legislatures of three-fourths of the several states within seven years from the date of its submission.

Source: Cornell University Law School. Legal Information Institute. http://www.law.cornell.edu/constitution/amendmentxx.

12. Great Depression, 1933–1939

A. President Roosevelt's First Inaugural Address (March 4, 1933)

In 1933 newly inaugurated president Franklin D. Roosevelt (1882–1945) devoted most of his 20-minute inaugural address to the devastating economic crisis then gripping the nation. Opening with the now famous line that the only thing Americans had to fear was "fear itself," the president went on to condemn the "stubbornness" and "incompetence" of unscrupulous bankers and business-men as a main cause of the Great Depression. With unemployment nearing 25 percent, the president sought to reassure his listeners, admitting the seriousness of the situation but promising that he would take swift and determined action to bring relief. With this speech, which is reproduced below, Roosevelt assured the tens of millions of Americans listening to it on the radio that the days of government refusal to intervene in economic affairs were over.

I am certain that my fellow Americans expect that on my induction into the Presidency I will address them with a candor and a decision which the present situation of our Nation impels. This is preeminently the time to speak the truth, the whole truth, frankly and boldly. Nor need we shrink from honestly facing conditions in our country today. This great Nation will endure as it has endured, will revive and will prosper. So, first of all, let me assert my firm belief that the only thing we have to fear is fear itself—nameless, unreasoning, unjustified terror which paralyzes needed efforts to convert retreat into advance. In every dark hour of our national life a leadership of frankness and vigor has met with that understanding and support of the people themselves which is essential to victory. I am convinced that you will again give that support to leadership in these critical days.

In such a spirit on my part and on yours we face our common difficulties. They concern, thank God, only material things. Values have shrunken to fantastic levels; taxes have risen; our ability to pay has fallen; government of all kinds is faced by serious curtailment of income; the means of exchange are frozen in the currents of trade; the withered leaves of industrial enterprise lie on every side; farmers find no markets for their produce; the savings of many years in thousands of families are gone.

More important, a host of unemployed citizens face the grim problem of existence, and an equally great number toil with little return. Only a foolish optimist can deny the dark realities of the moment.

Yet our distress comes from no failure of substance. We are stricken by no plague of locusts. Compared with the perils which our forefathers conquered because they believed and were not afraid, we have still much to be thankful for. Nature still offers her bounty and human efforts have multiplied it. Plenty is at our doorstep, but a generous use of it languishes in the very sight of the supply. Primarily this is because rulers of the exchange of mankind's goods have failed through their own stubbornness and their own incompetence, have admitted their failure, and have abdicated. Practices of the unscrupulous money changers stand indicted in the court of public opinion, rejected by the hearts and minds of men.

True they have tried, but their efforts have been cast in the pattern of an outworn tradition. Faced by failure of credit they have proposed only the lending of more money. Stripped of the lure of profit by which to induce our people to follow their false leadership, they have resorted to exhortations, pleading tearfully for restored confidence. They know only the rules of a generation of self-seekers. They have no vision, and when there is no vision the people perish.

The money changers have fled from their high seats in the temple of our civilization. We may now restore that temple to the ancient truths. The measure of the restoration lies in the extent to which we apply social values more noble than mere monetary profit.

Happiness lies not in the mere possession of money; it lies in the joy of achievement, in the thrill of creative effort. The joy and moral stimulation of work no longer must be forgotten in the mad chase of evanescent profits. These dark days will be worth all they cost us if they teach us that our true destiny is not to be ministered unto but to minister to ourselves and to our fellow men.

Recognition of the falsity of material wealth as the standard of success goes hand in hand with the abandonment of the false belief that public office and high political position are to be valued only by the standards of pride of place and personal profit; and there must be an end to a conduct in banking and in business which too often has given to a sacred trust the likeness of callous and selfish wrongdoing. Small wonder that confidence languishes, for it thrives only on honesty, on honor, on the sacredness of obligations, on faithful protection, on unselfish performance; without them it cannot live. Restoration calls, however, not for changes in ethics alone. This Nation asks for action, and action now.

Our greatest primary task is to put people to work. This is no unsolvable problem if we face it wisely and courageously. It can be accomplished in part by direct recruiting by the Government itself, treating the task as we would treat the emergency of a war, but at the same time, through this employment, accomplishing greatly needed projects to stimulate and reorganize the use of our natural resources.

Hand in hand with this we must frankly recognize the overbalance of population in our industrial centers and, by engaging on a national scale in a redistribution, endeavor to provide a better use of the land for those best fitted for the land. The task can be helped by definite efforts to raise the values of agricultural products and with this the power to purchase the output of our cities. It can be helped by preventing realistically the tragedy of the growing loss through foreclosure of our small homes and our farms. It can be helped by insistence that the Federal, State, and local governments act forthwith on the demand that their cost be drastically reduced. It can be helped by the unifying of relief activities which today are often scattered, uneconomical, and unequal. It can be helped by national planning for and supervision of all forms of trans-portation and of communications and other utilities which have a definitely public character. There are many ways in which it can be helped, but it can never be helped merely by talking about it. We must act and act quickly.

Finally, in our progress toward a resumption of work we require two safe-guards against a return of the evils of the old order: there must be a strict supervision of all banking and credits and investments, so that there will be an end to speculation with other people's money; and there must be provision for an adequate but sound currency.

These are the lines of attack. I shall presently urge upon a new Congress, in special session, detailed measures for their fulfillment, and I shall seek the immediate assistance of the several States.

Through this program of action we address ourselves to putting our own national house in order and making income balance outgo. Our international trade relations, though vastly important, are in point of time and necessity sec-ondary to the establishment of a sound national economy. I favor as a practical policy the putting of first things first. I shall spare no effort to restore world trade by international economic readjustment, but the emergency at home can-not wait on that accomplishment.

The basic thought that guides these specific means of national recovery is not narrowly nationalistic. It is the insistence, as a first considerations, upon the interdependence of the various elements in and parts of the United States—a recognition of the old and permanently important manifestation of the Amer-ican spirit of the pioneer. It is the way to recovery. It is the immediate way. It is the strongest assurance that the recovery will endure.

In the field of world policy I would dedicate this Nation to the policy of the good neighbor—the neighbor who resolutely respects himself and, because he does so, respects the rights of others—the neighbor who respects his obligations and respects the sanctity of his agreements in and with a world of neighbors.

If I read the temper of our people correctly, we now realize as we have never realized before our interdependence on each other; that we cannot merely take but we must give as well; that if we are to go forward, we must move as a trained and loyal army willing to sacrifice for the good of a common discipline, because without such discipline no progress is made, no leadership becomes effective. We are, I know, ready and willing to submit our lives and property to such discipline, because it makes possible a leadership which aims at a larger good. This I propose to offer, pledging that the larger purposes will bind upon us all as a sacred obligation with a unity of duty hitherto evoked only in time of armed strife.

With this pledge taken, I assume unhesitatingly the leadership of this great army of our people dedicated to a disciplined attack upon our common problems.

Action in this image and to this end is feasible under the form of government which we have inherited from our ancestors. Our Constitution is so simple and practical that it is possible always to meet extraordinary needs by changes in emphasis and arrangement without loss of essential form. That is why our constitutional system has proved itself the most superbly enduring political mechanism the modern world has produced. It has met every stress of vast expansion of territory, of foreign wars, of bitter internal strife, of world relations.

It is to be hoped that the normal balance of Executive and legislative authority may be wholly adequate to meet the unprecedented task before us. But it may be that an unprecedented demand and need for undelayed action may call for temporary departure from that normal balance of public procedure.

I am prepared under my constitutional duty to recommend the measures that a stricken Nation in the midst of a stricken world may require. These measures, or such other measures as the Congress may build out of its experience and wisdom, I shall seek, within my constitutional authority, to bring to speedy adoption.

But in the event that the Congress shall fail to take one of these two courses, and in the event that the national emergency is still critical, I shall not evade the clear course of duty that will then confront me. I shall ask the Congress for the one remaining instrument to meet the crisis—broad Executive power to wage a war against the emergency, as great as the power that would be given to me if we were in fact invaded by a foreign foe.

For the trust reposed in me I will return the courage and the devotion that befit the time. I can do no less.

We face the arduous days that lie before us in the warm courage of national unity; with the clear consciousness of seeking old and precious moral values; with the clean satisfaction that comes from the stern performance of duty by old and young alike. We aim at the assurance of a rounded and permanent national life.

We do not distrust the future of essential democracy. The people of the United States have not failed. In their need they have registered a mandate that they want direct, vigorous action. They have asked for discipline and direction under leadership. They have made me the present instrument of their wishes. In the spirit of the gift I take it.

In this dedication of a Nation we humbly ask the blessing of God. May He protect each and every one of us. May He guide me in the days to come.

Source: Franklin D. Roosevelt: "Inaugural Address," March 4, 1933. Online by Gerhard Peters and John T. Woolley, *The American Presidency Project.* http://www.presidency.ucsb.edu/ws/?pid=14473.

B. Senator Long's "Share the Wealth" Program (February 5, 1934)

Senator Huey P. Long (1893–1935) was a flamboyant, Populist politician who dominated the politics of his home state of Louisiana, where he was wildly popular. In February 1934, in the following statement that Long had read into the congressional record, he laid out his "Share the Wealth" program for lifting the country out of the Great Depression. The plan contained some elements in common with President Franklin D. Roosevelt's (1882–1945) New Deal, such as old-age pensions for persons over 60 and public works projects to provide employment. However, it also proposed caps on how much net worth an individual could accumulate and limits on annual incomes and inheritances as well as higher taxes on the wealthy. Many viewed the Share the Wealth Society that Long founded to promote the program as merely a vehicle for a possible third-party challenge to Roosevelt in 1936. Whether this was true or not, Long's assassination in September 1935 ended any such ambitions.

People of America: In every community get together at once and organize a share-our-wealth society—Motto: Every man a king

Principles and platform:

1. To limit poverty by providing that every deserving family shall share in the wealth of America for not less than one third of the average wealth, thereby to possess not less than $5,000 free of debt.
2. To limit fortunes to such a few million dollars as will allow the balance of the American people to share in the wealth and profits of the land.
3. Old-age pensions of $30 per month to persons over 60 years of age who do not earn as much as $1,000 per year or who possess less than $10,000 in cash or property, thereby to remove from the field of labor in times of unemployment those who have contributed their share to the public service.
4. To limit the hours of work to such an extent as to prevent overproduction and to give the workers of America some share in the recreations, conveniences, and luxuries of life.

5. To balance agricultural production with what can be sold and consumed according to the laws of God, which have never failed.
6. To care for the veterans of our wars.
7. Taxation to run the Government to be supported, first, by reducing big fortunes from the top, thereby to improve the country and provide employment in public works whenever agricultural surplus is such as to render unnecessary, in whole or in part, any particular crop.

Simple and Concrete—Not an Experiment

To share our wealth by providing for every deserving family to have one third of the average wealth would mean that, at the worst, such a family could have a fairly comfortable home, an automobile, and a radio, with other reasonable home conveniences, and a place to educate their children. Through sharing the work, that is, by limiting the hours of toil so that all would share in what is made and produced in the land, every family would have enough coming in every year to feed, clothe, and provide a fair share of the luxuries of life to its members. Such is the result to a family, at the worst.

From the worst to the best there would be no limit to opportunity. One might become a millionaire or more. There would be a chance for talent to make a man big, because enough would be floating in the land to give brains its chance to be used. As it is, no matter how smart a man may be, everything is tied up in so few hands that no amount of energy or talent has a chance to gain any of it.

Would it break up big concerns? No. It would simply mean that, instead of one man getting all the one concern made, that there might be 1,000 or 10,000 persons sharing in such excess fortune, any one of whom, or all of whom, might be millionaires and over.

I ask somebody in every city, town, village, and farm community of America to take this as my personal request to call a meeting of as many neighbors and friends as will come to it to start a share-our-wealth society. Elect a president and a secretary and charge no dues. The meeting can be held at a courthouse, in some town hall or public building, or in the home of someone.

It does not matter how many will come to the first meeting. Get a society organized, if it has only two members. Then let us get to work quick, quick, quick to put an end by law to people starving and going naked in this land of too much to eat and too much to wear. The case is all with us. It is the word and work of the Lord. The Gideons had but two men when they organized. Three tailors of Tooley Street drew the Magna Carta of England. The Lord says: "For where two or three are gathered together in My name, there am I in the midst of them."

We propose to help our people into the place where the Lord said was their rightful own and no more.

We have waited long enough for these financial masters to do these things. They have promised and promised. Now we find our country $10 billion further in debt on account of the depression, and big lenders even propose to get 90 percent of that out of the hides of the common people in the form of a sales tax.

There is nothing wrong with the United States. We have more food than we can eat. We have more clothes and things out of which to make clothes than we can wear. We have more houses and lands than the whole 120 million can use if they all had good homes. So what is the trouble? Nothing except that a handful of men have everything and the balance of the people have nothing if their debts were paid. There should be every man a king in this land flowing with milk and honey instead of the lords of finance at the top and slaves and peasants at the bottom.

Now be prepared for the slurs and snickers of some high-ups when you start your local spread-our-wealth society. Also when you call your meeting be on your guard for some smart-aleck tool of the interests to come in and ask questions. Refer such to me for an answer to any question, and I will send you a copy. Spend your time getting the people to work to save their children and to save their homes, or to get a home for those who have already lost their own.

To explain the title, motto, and principles of such a society I give the full information, viz:

Title: Share-our-wealth society is simply to mean that God's creatures on this lovely American continent have a right to share in the wealth they have created in this country. They have the right to a living, with the conveniences and some of the luxuries of this life, so long as there are too many or enough for all. They have a right to raise their children in a healthy, wholesome atmosphere and to educate them, rather than to face the dread of their under-nourishment and sadness by being denied a real life.

Motto: "Every man a king" conveys the great plan of God and of the Declaration of Independence, which said: "All men are created equal." It conveys that no one man is the lord of another, but that from the head to the foot of every man is carried his sovereignty.

Now to cover the principles of the share-our-wealth society, I give them in order:

1. To limit poverty:

We propose that a deserving family shall share in our wealth of America at least for one third the average. An average family is slightly less than five persons. The number has become less during depression. The United States total wealth in normal times is about $400 billion or about $15,000 to a family. If there were fair distribution of our things in America, our national wealth would be three or four or five times the $400 billion, because a free, circulating wealth is worth many times more than wealth congested and frozen into a few hands as is America's wealth. But, figuring only on the basis of wealth as valued when frozen into a few hands, there is the average of $15,000 to the family. We say that we will limit poverty of the deserving people. One third of the average wealth to the family, or $5,000, is a fair limit to the depths we will allow any one man's family to fall. None too poor, none too rich.

2. To limit fortunes:

The wealth of this land is tied up in a few hands. It makes no difference how many years the laborer has worked, nor does it make any difference how many dreary rows the farmer has plowed, the wealth he has created is in the hands of manipulators. They have not worked any more than many other people who have nothing. Now we do not propose to hurt these very rich persons. We simply say that when they reach the place of millionaires they have everything they can use and they ought to let somebody else have something. As it is, 0.1 of 1 percent of the bank depositors nearly half of the money in the banks, leaving 99.9 of bank depositors owning the balance. Then two thirds of the people do not even have a bank account. The lowest estimate is that 4 percent of the people own 85 percent of our wealth. The people cannot ever come to light unless we share our wealth, hence the society to do it.

3. Old-age pensions:

Everyone has begun to realize something must be done for our old people who work out their lives, feed and clothe children and are left penniless in their declining years. They should be made to look forward to their mature years for comfort rather than fear. We propose that, at the age of 60, every person should begin to draw a pension from our Government of $30 per month, unless the person of 60 or over has an income of over $1,000 per year or is worth $10,000, which is two thirds of the average wealth in America, even figured on a basis of it being frozen into a few hands. Such a pension would retire from labor those persons who keep the rising generations from finding employment.

4. To limit the hours of work:

This applies to all industry. The longer hours the human family can rest from work, the more it can consume. It makes no difference how many labor-saving devices we may invent, just as long as we keep cutting down the hours and sharing what those machines produce, the better we become. Machines can never produce too much if everybody is allowed his share, and if it ever got to the point that the human family could work only 15 hours per week and still produce enough for everybody, then praised be the name of the Lord. Heaven would be coming nearer to earth. All of us could return to school a few months every year to learn some things they have found out since we were there: All could be gentlemen: Every man a king.

5. To balance agricultural production with consumption:

About the easiest of all things to do when financial masters and market manipulators step aside and let work the law of the Lord. When we have a supply of anything that is more than we can use for a year or two, just stop planting that particular crop for a year either in all the country or in a part of it. Let the Government take over and store the surplus for the next year. If there is not something else for the farmers to plant or some other work for them to do to live on for the year when the crop is banned, then let that be the year for the public works to be done in the section where the farmers need work. There is plenty of it to do and taxes of the big fortunes at the top will supply plenty of money without hurting anybody. In time we would have the people not struggling to raise so much when all were well fed and clothed. Distribution of wealth almost solves the whole problem without further trouble.

6. To care for the veterans of our wars:

A restoration of all rights taken from them by recent laws and further, a complete care of any disabled veteran for any ailment, who has no means of support.

7. Taxation:

Taxation is to be levied first at the top for the Governments support and expenses. Swollen fortunes should be reduced principally through taxation. The Government should be run through revenues it derives after allowing persons to become well above millionaires and no more. In this manner the fortunes will be kept down to reasonable size and at the same time all the works of the Government kept on a sound basis, without debts.

Things cannot continue as they now are. America must take one of three choices, viz:

1. A monarchy ruled by financial masters—a modern feudalism.
2. Communism.
3. Sharing of the wealth and income of the land among all the people by limiting the hours of toil and limiting the size of fortunes.

The Lord prescribed the last form. It would preserve all our gains, share them among our population, guarantee a greater country and a happy people.

The need for such share-our-wealth society is to spread the truth among the people and to convey their sentiment to their Members of Congress.

Whenever such a local society has been organized, please send me notice of the same, so that I may send statistics and data which such local society can give out in their community, either through word of mouth in meetings, by circulars, or, when possible, in local newspapers.

Please understand that the Wall Street controlled public press will give you as little mention as possible and will condemn and ridicule your efforts. Such makes necessary the organizations to share the wealth of this land among the people, which the financial masters are determined they will not allow to be done. Where possible, I hope those organizing a society in one community will get in touch with their friends in other communities and get them to organize societies in them. Anyone can have copies of this article reprinted in circular form to distribute wherever they may desire, or, if they want me to have them printed for them, I can do so and mail them to any address for 60 cents per hundred or $4 per thousand copies.

I introduced in Congress and supported other measures to bring about the sharing of our wealth when I first reached the United States Senate in January 1932. The main efforts to that effect polled about six votes in the Senate at first. Last spring my plan polled the votes of nearly twenty United States Senators, becoming dangerous in proportions to the financial lords. Since then I have been abused in the newspapers and over the radio for everything under the sun. Now that I am pressing this program, the lies and abuse in the big news-papers and over the radio are a matter of daily occurrence. It will all become greater with this effort. Expect that. Meantime go ahead with the work to orga-nize a share-our-wealth society.

Source: Social Security online website. http://www.ssa.gov/history/longsen.html.

C. *Schechter Poultry Corp. v. United States* (May 27, 1935)

Enacted in June 1933, the National Industrial Recovery Act (NIRA) was a centerpiece of President Franklin D. Roosevelt's (1882–1945) New Deal legisla-tion. The act empowered the president to regulate industries by promulgating fair codes of competition and created the Public Works Administration to pro-vide the unemployed with work on public projects. The Schechter Poultry Corpo-ration of Brooklyn, New York, sued to invalidate some of the regulations imposed under the act on the poultry industry; these regulations included the fixing of wages and prices and requirements regarding the sale of chickens. Because the

government accused Schechter of selling unhealthy poultry, the resulting U.S.
Supreme Court case, Schechter Poultry Corp. v. United States, *was often called*
the "sick chicken case." In its unanimous decision, written by Chief Justice
Charles Evans Hughes (1862–1948), the court declared the NIRA unconstitu-
tional because Congress had no power to authorize the president to issue such
regulations. Reproduced below is the court's syllabus to the case summarizing
its findings.

1. Extraordinary conditions, such as an economic crisis, may call for extraordinary remedies, but they cannot create or enlarge constitutional power. P.
   295 U.S. 528.
2. Congress is not permitted by the Constitution to abdicate, or to transfer to
   others, the essential legislative functions with which it is vested. Art. I, § 1;
   Art. I, § 8, par. 18. *Panama Refining Co. v. Ryan,* 293 U.S. 388. P. 295 U.S. 529.
3. Congress may leave to selected instrumentalities the making of subordinate
   rules within prescribed limits, and the determination of facts to which the
   policy, as declared by Congress, is to apply; but it must itself lay down the
   policies and establish standards.
4. The delegation of legislative power sought to be made to the President by § 3
   of the National Industrial Recovery Act of June 16, 1933, is unconstitutional
   (pp. 295 U.S. 529 *et seq.*), and the Act is also unconstitutional, as applied in
   this case, because it exceeds the power of Congress to regulate interstate
   commerce and invades the power reserved exclusively to the States (pp. 295
   U.S. 542 *et seq.*).
5. Section 3 of the National Industrial Recovery Act provides that "codes of
   fair competition," which shall be the " standards of fair competition" for the
   trades and industries to which they relate, may be approved by the President
   upon application of representative associations of the trades or industries
   to be affected, or may be prescribed by him on his own motion. Their provisions are to be enforced by injunctions from the federal courts, and "any
   violation of any of their provisions in any transaction in or affecting interstate commerce" is to be deemed an unfair method of competition within
   the meaning of the Federal Trade Commission Act, and is to be punished as
   a crime against the United States. Before approving, the President is to make
   certain findings as to the character of the association presenting the code
   and absence of design to promote monopoly or oppress small enterprises,
   and must find that it will "tend to effectuate the policy of this title." Codes
   permitting monopolies or monopolistic practices are forbidden. The President may "impose such conditions (including requirements for the making of reports and the keeping of accounts) for the protection of consumers,
   competitors, employees and others, and in the furtherance of the public

interest, and may provide such exceptions and exemptions from the provisions of such code," as he, in his discretion, deems necessary "to effectuate
the policy herein declared." A code prescribed by him is to have the same
effect as one approved on application.

Held:

(1) The statutory plan is not simply one of voluntary effort; the "codes of fair
competition" are meant to be codes of laws. P. 295 U.S. 529.

(2) The meaning of the term "fair competition" (not expressly defined in the
Act) is clearly not the mere antithesis of "unfair competition," as known to
the common law, or of "unfair methods of competition" under the Federal
Trade Commission Act. P. 295 U.S. 531.

(3) In authorizing the President to approve codes which "will tend to effectuate
the policy of this title," § 3 of the Act refers to the Declaration of Policy in
§ 1. The purposes declared in § 1 are all directed to the rehabilitation of
industry and the industrial recovery which was the major policy of Congress in adopting the Act. P. 295 U.S. 534.

(4) That this is the controlling purpose of the code now before the Court appears
both from its repeated declarations to that effect and from the scope of its
requirements. P. 295 U.S. 536.

(5) The authority sought to be conferred by § 3 was not merely to deal with
"unfair competitive practices" which offend against existing law, or to create administrative machinery for the application of established principles
of law to particular instances of violation. Rather, the purpose is clearly
disclosed to authorize new and controlling prohibitions through codes of
laws which would embrace what the formulators would propose, and what
the President would approve or prescribe, as wise and beneficent measures
for the government of trades and industries, in order to bring about their
rehabilitation, correction and improvement, according to the general declaration of policy in § 1. Codes of laws of this sort are styled " codes of fair
competition." P. 295 U.S. 535.

(6) A delegation of its legislative authority to trade or industrial associations,
empowering them to enact laws for the rehabilitation and expansion of their
trades or industries, would be utterly inconsistent with the constitutional
prerogatives and duties of Congress. P. 295 U.S. 537.

(7) Congress cannot delegate legislative power to the President to exercise an
unfettered discretion to make whatever laws he thinks may be needed or
advisable for the rehabilitation and expansion of trade and industry. P. 295
U.S. 537.

(8) The only limits set by the Act to the President's discretion are that he
shall find, first, that the association or group proposing a code imposes no

inequitable restrictions on admission to membership and is truly representative; second, that the code is not designed to promote monopolies or to eliminate or oppress small enterprises and will not operate to discriminate against them, and third, that it "will tend to effectuate the policy of this title"—this last being a mere statement of opinion. These are the only findings which Congress has made essential in order to put into operation a legislative code having the aims described in the "Declaration of Policy." P. 295 U.S. 538.

(9) Under the Act, the President, in approving a code, may impose his own conditions, adding to or taking from what is proposed, as "in his discretion" he thinks necessary "to effectuate the policy" declared by the Act. He has no less liberty when he prescribes a code on his own motion or on complaint, and he is free to prescribe one if a code has not been approved. P. 295 U.S. 538.

(10) The acts and reports of the administrative agencies which the President may create under the Act have no sanction beyond his will. Their recommendations and findings in no way limit the authority which § 3 undertakes to vest in him. And this authority relates to a host of different trades and industries, thus extending the President's discretion to all the varieties of laws which he may deem to be beneficial in dealing with the vast array of commercial activities throughout the country. P. 295 U.S. 539.

(11) Such a sweeping delegation of legislative power finds no support in decisions of this Court defining and sustaining the powers granted to the Interstate Commerce Commission, to the Radio Commission, and to the President when acting under the "flexible tariff" provisions of the Tariff Act of 1922. P. 295 U.S. 539.

(12) Section 3 of the Recovery Act is without precedent. It supplies no standards for any trade, industry or activity. It does not undertake to prescribe rules of conduct to be applied to particular states of fact determined by appropriate administrative procedure. Instead, it authorizes the making of codes to prescribe them. For that legislative undertaking, it sets up no standards, aside from the statement of the general aims of rehabilitation, correction and expansion found in § 1. In view of the broad scope of that declaration, and of the nature of the few restrictions that are imposed, the discretion of the President in approving or prescribing codes, and thus enacting laws for the government of trade and industry throughout the country, is virtually unfettered. The code-making authority thus sought to be conferred is an unconstitutional delegation of legislative power. P. 295 U.S. 541.

6. Defendants were engaged in the business of slaughtering chickens and selling them to retailers. They bought their fowls from commission men in a

market where most of the supply was shipped in from other States, transported them to their slaugterhouses, and there held them for slaughter and local sale to retail dealers and butchers, who in turn sold directly to consumers. They were indicted for disobeying the requirements of a "Code of Fair Competition for the Live Poultry Industry of the Metropolitan Area in and about the City of New York," approved by the President under § 3 of the National Industrial Recovery Act. The alleged violations were: failure to observe in their place of business provisions fixing minimum wages and maximum hours for employees; permitting customers to select individual chickens from particular coops and half-coops; sale of an unfit chicken; sales without compliance with municipal inspection regulations and to slaughterers and dealers not licensed under such regulations; making false reports, and failure to make reports relating to range of daily prices and volume of sales.

Held:
(1) When the poultry had reached the defendants' slaughterhouses, the interstate commerce had ended, and subsequent transactions in their business, including the matters charged in the indictment, were transactions in intrastate commerce. P. 295 U.S. 542.
(2) Decisions which deal with a stream of interstate commerce—where goods come to rest within a State temporarily and are later to go forward in interstate commerce—and with the regulation of transactions involved in that practical continuity of movement, are inapplicable in this case. P. 295 U. S. 543.
(3) The distinction between intrastate acts that directly affect interstate commerce, and therefore are subject to federal regulation, and those that affect it only indirectly, and therefore remain subject to the power of the States exclusively, is clear in principle, though the precise line can be drawn only as individual cases arise. Pp. 295 U.S. 544, 295 U.S. 546.
(4) If the commerce clause were construed to reach all enterprises and transactions which could be said to have an indirect effect upon interstate commerce, the federal authority would embrace practically all the activities of the people, and the authority of the State over its domestic concerns would exist only by sufferance of the Federal Government. Indeed, on such a theory, even the development of the State's commercial facilities would be subject to federal control. P. 295 U.S. 546.
(5) The distinction between direct and indirect effects has long been clearly recognized in the application of the Anti-Trust Act. It is fundamental and essential to the maintenance of our constitutional system. P. 295 U.S. 547.

(6) The Federal Government cannot regulate the wages and hours of labor of persons employed in the internal commerce of a State. No justification for such regulation is to be found in the fact that wages and hours affect costs and prices, and so indirectly affect interstate commerce, nor in the fact that failure of some States to regulate wages and hours diverts commerce from the States that do regulate them. P. 295 U.S. 548.

(7) The provisions of the code which are alleged to have been violated in this case are not a valid exercise of federal power. P. 295 U.S. 550.

Source: A. L. A. Schechter Poultry Corp. v. United States, 29 U.S. 495 (1935).

D. National Labor Relations Act (Wagner Act) (July 5, 1935)

The National Labor Relations Act, which was signed by President Franklin D. Roosevelt (1882–1945) in July 1935, protects the rights of private-sector workers to form unions, engage in collective bargaining, participate in strikes, and take any other concerted action in regard to their employment. Also known as the Wagner Act, for its sponsor, Senator Robert F. Wagner (D-NY) (1877–1953), the statute, which is excerpted below, defined unfair labor practices and created a National Labor Relations Board to oversee the process by which employees decide to unionize and to prosecute violations of the act. Agricultural employees, domestic employees, and government workers were not covered by the act. The National Labor Relations Act, despite many criticisms and challenges, was declared constitutional by the U.S. Supreme Court in National Labor Relations Board v. Jones & Laughlin Steel Corporation *(1937).*

FINDINGS AND POLICIES

Section 1. [§151.] The denial by some employers of the right of employees to organize and the refusal by some employers to accept the procedure of collective bargaining lead to strikes and other forms of industrial strife or unrest, which have the intent or the necessary effect of burdening or obstructing commerce by (a) impairing the efficiency, safety, or operation of the instrumentalities of commerce; (b) occurring in the current of commerce; (c) materially affecting, restraining, or controlling the flow of raw materials or manufactured or processed goods from or into the channels of commerce, or the prices of such materials or goods in commerce; or (d) causing diminution of employment and wages in such volume as substantially to impair or disrupt the market for goods flowing from or into the channels of commerce.

The inequality of bargaining power between employees who do not possess full freedom of association or actual liberty of contract and employers who are organized in the corporate or other forms of ownership association substantially burdens and affects the flow of commerce, and tends to aggravate recurrent business depressions, by depressing wage rates and the purchasing power of wage earners in industry and by preventing the stabilization of competitive wage rates and working conditions within and between industries.

Experience has proved that protection by law of the right of employees to organize and bargain collectively safeguards commerce from injury, impairment, or interruption, and promotes the flow of commerce by removing certain recognized sources of industrial strife and unrest, by encouraging practices fundamental to the friendly adjustment of industrial disputes arising out of differences as to wages, hours, or other working conditions, and by restoring equality of bargaining power between employers and employees.

Experience has further demonstrated that certain practices by some labor organizations, their officers, and members have the intent or the necessary effect of burdening or obstructing commerce by preventing the free flow of goods in such commerce through strikes and other forms of industrial unrest or through concerted activities which impair the interest of the public in the free flow of such commerce. The elimination of such practices is a necessary condition to the assurance of the rights herein guaranteed.

It is declared to be the policy of the United States to eliminate the causes of certain substantial obstructions to the free flow of commerce and to mitigate and eliminate these obstructions when they have occurred by encouraging the practice and procedure of collective bargaining and by protecting the exercise by workers of full freedom of association, self-organization, and designation of representatives of their own choosing, for the purpose of negotiating the terms and conditions of their employment or other mutual aid or protection. . . .

NATIONAL LABOR RELATIONS BOARD

Sec. 3. [§ 153.] (a) [Creation, composition, appointment, and tenure; Chairman; removal of members] The National Labor Relations Board (hereinafter called the "Board") created by this Act [subchapter] prior to its amendment by the Labor Management Relations Act, 1947 [29 U.S.C. § 141 et seq.], is continued as an agency of the United States, except that the Board shall consist of five instead of three members, appointed by the President by and with the advice and consent of the Senate. Of the two additional members so provided for, one shall be appointed for a term of five years and the other for a term of two years. Their successors, and the successors of the other members, shall be appointed for terms of five years each, excepting that any individual chosen to fill a vacancy shall be appointed only for the unexpired term of the member whom he shall succeed. The President shall designate one member to serve as Chairman of the Board. Any member of the Board may be removed by the President, upon notice and hearing, for neglect of duty or malfeasance in office, but for no other cause.

(b) [Delegation of powers to members and regional directors; review and stay of actions of regional directors; quorum; seal] The Board is authorized to delegate to any group of three or more members any or all of the powers which it may itself exercise. The Board is also authorized to delegate to its regional directors its powers under section 9 [section 159 of this title] to determine the unit appropriate for the purpose of collective bargaining, to investigate and provide for hearings, and determine whether a question of representation exists, and to direct an election or take a secret ballot under subsection (c) or (e) of section 9 [section 159 of this title] and certify the results thereof, except that upon the filling of a request therefore with the Board by any interested person, the Board may review any action of a regional director delegated to him under this paragraph, but such a review shall not, unless specifically ordered by the Board, operate as a stay of any action taken by the regional director. A vacancy in the Board shall not impair the right of the remaining members to exercise all of the powers of the Board, and three members of the Board shall, at all times, constitute a quorum of the Board, except that two members shall constitute a quorum of any group designated pursuant to the first sentence hereof. The Board shall have an official seal which shall be judicially noticed.

(c) [Annual reports to Congress and the President] The Board shall at the close of each fiscal year make a report in writing to Congress and to the President summarizing significant case activities and operations for that fiscal year.

(d) [General Counsel; appointment and tenure; powers and duties; vacancy] There shall be a General Counsel of the Board who shall be appointed by the President, by and with the advice and consent of the Senate, for a term of four years. The General Counsel of the Board shall exercise general supervision over all attorneys employed by the Board (other than administrative law judges and legal assistants to Board members) and over the officers and employees in the regional offices. He shall have final authority, on behalf of the Board, in respect of the investigation of charges and issuance of complaints under section 10 [section 160 of this title], and in respect of the prosecution of such complaints before the Board, and shall have such other duties as the Board may prescribe or as may be provided by law. In case of vacancy in the office of the General Counsel the President is authorized to designate the officer or employee who shall act as General Counsel during such vacancy, but no person or persons so designated shall so act (1) for more than forty days when the Congress is in session unless a nomination to fill such vacancy shall have been submitted to the Senate, or (2) after the adjournment sine die of the session of the Senate in which such nomination was submitted.

Sec. 4. [§ 154. Eligibility for reappointment; officers and employees; payment of expenses] (a) Each member of the Board and the General Counsel of the Board shall be eligible for reappointment, and shall not engage in any other business, vocation, or employment. The Board shall appoint an executive secretary, and such attorneys, examiners, and regional directors, and such other employees as it may from time to time find necessary for the proper performance of its duties. The Board may not employ any attorneys for the purpose of reviewing transcripts of hearings or preparing drafts of opinions except that any attorney employed for assignment as a legal assistant to any Board member may for such Board member review such transcripts and prepare such drafts. No administrative law judge's report shall be reviewed, either before or after its publication, by any person other than a member of the Board or his legal assistant, and no administrative law judge shall advise or consult with the Board with respect to exceptions taken to his findings, rulings, or recommendations. The Board may establish or utilize such regional, local, or other agencies, and utilize such voluntary and uncompensated services, as may from time to time be needed. Attorneys appointed under this section may, at the direction of the Board, appear for and represent the Board in any case in court. Nothing in this Act [subchapter] shall be construed to authorize the Board to appoint individuals for the purpose of conciliation or mediation, or for economic analysis.

(b) All of the expenses of the Board, including all necessary traveling and subsistence expenses outside the District of Columbia incurred by the members or employees of the Board under its orders, shall be allowed and paid on the presentation of itemized vouchers therefore approved by the Board or by any individual it designates for that purpose.

Sec. 5. [§ 155. Principal office, conducting inquiries throughout country; participation in decisions or inquiries conducted by member] The principal office of the Board shall be in the District of Columbia, but it may meet and exercise any or all of its powers at any other place. The Board may, by one or more of its members or by such agents or agencies as it may designate, prosecute any inquiry necessary to its functions in any part of the United States. A member who participates in such an inquiry shall not be disqualified from subsequently participating in a decision of the Board in the same case.

Sec. 6. [§ 156. Rules and regulations] The Board shall have authority from time to time to make, amend, and rescind, in the manner prescribed by the Administrative Procedure Act [by subchapter II of chapter 5 of title 5], such rules and regulations as may be necessary to carry out the provisions of this Act [subchapter].

RIGHTS OF EMPLOYEES

Sec. 7. [§ 157.] Employees shall have the right to self-organization, to form, join, or assist labor organizations, to bargain collectively through representatives of their own choosing, and to engage in other concerted activities for the purpose of collective bargaining or other mutual aid or protection, and shall also have the right to refrain from any or all such activities except to the extent that such right may be affected by an agreement requiring membership in a labor organization as a condition of employment as authorized in section 8(a) (3) [section 158(a)(3) of this title].

UNFAIR LABOR PRACTICES

Sec. 8. [§ 158.] (a) [Unfair labor practices by employer] It shall be an unfair labor practice for an employer—

(1) to interfere with, restrain, or coerce employees in the exercise of the rights guaranteed in section 7 [section 157 of this title];

(2) to dominate or interfere with the formation or administration of any labor organization or contribute financial or other support to it: Provided, That subject to rules and regulations made and published by the Board pursuant to section 6 [section 156 of this title], an employer shall not be prohibited from permitting employees to confer with him during working hours without loss of time or pay;

(3) by discrimination in regard to hire or tenure of employment or any term or condition of employment to encourage or discourage membership in any labor organization: Provided, That nothing in this Act [subchapter], or in any other statute of the United States, shall preclude an employer from making an agreement with a labor organization (not established, maintained, or assisted by any action defined in section 8(a) of this Act [in this subsection] as an unfair labor practice) to require as a condition of employment membership therein on or after the thirtieth day following the beginning of such employment or the effective date of such agreement, whichever is the later, (i) if such labor organization is the representative of the employees as provided in section 9(a) [section 159(a) of this title], in the appropriate collective-bargaining unit covered by such agreement when made, and (ii) unless following an election held as provided in section 9(e) [section 159(e) of this title] within one year preceding the effective date of such agreement, the Board shall have certified that at least a majority of the employees eligible to vote in such election have voted to rescind the authority of such labor organization to make such an agreement: Provided further, That no employer shall justify any discrimination against an employee for non-membership in a labor organization (A) if he has reasonable grounds for believing that such membership was not available to the employee on the same terms and conditions generally applicable to other members, or (B) if he has reasonable grounds for believing that membership was denied or terminated for reasons other than the failure of the employee to tender the periodic dues and the initiation fees uniformly required as a condition of acquiring or retaining membership. . . .

Source: National Labor Relations Act. U.S. Code 29, §§ 151 et seq.

E. President Roosevelt's Statement upon Signing the Social Security Act (August 14, 1935)

Enacted as part of President Franklin D. Roosevelt's (1882–1945) New Deal program, the Social Security Act provided federal benefits to the retired and the unemployed. As the first president to support federal assistance to the elderly, Roosevelt saw the act as a means for relieving the economic hardships of 20th-century society, which had been so starkly highlighted by the Great Depression. Benefits for retirees were to be funded by a payroll tax on the wages of current workers, with half raised by the tax and half contributed by employers. The Social Security Act was a distinct break from the limited government philosophy that had dominated American governance in the 18th and 19th centuries and was still a cornerstone of Republican principles. Reproduced below are Roosevelt's remarks upon signing the act.

Today a hope of many years' standing is in large part fulfilled. The civilization of the past hundred years, with its startling industrial changes, has tended more and more to make life insecure. Young people have come to wonder what would be their lot when they came to old age. The man with a job has wondered how long the job would last.

This social security measure gives at least some protection to thirty millions of our citizens who will reap direct benefits through unemployment compensation, through old-age pensions and through increased services for the protection of children and the prevention of ill health.

We can never insure one hundred percent of the population against one hundred percent of the hazards and vicissitudes of life, but we have tried to frame a law which will give some measure of protection to the average citizen and to his family against the loss of a job and against poverty-ridden old age.

This law, too, represents a cornerstone in a structure which is being built but is by no means complete. It is a structure intended to lessen the force of possible future depressions. It will act as a protection to future Administrations against the necessity of going deeply into debt to furnish relief to the needy. The law will flatten out the peaks and valleys of deflation and of inflation. It is, in short, a law that will take care of human needs and at the same time provide for the United States an economic structure of vastly greater soundness.

I congratulate all of you ladies and gentlemen, all of you in the Congress, in the executive departments and all of you who come from private life, and I thank you for your splendid efforts in behalf of this sound, needed and patriotic legislation.

If the Senate and the House of Representatives in this long and arduous session had done nothing more than pass this Bill, the session would be regarded as historic for all time.

Source: Franklin D. Roosevelt: "Statement on Signing the Social Security Act." August 14, 1935. Online by Gerhard Peters and John T. Woolley. *The American Presidency Project.* http://www.presidency.ucsb.edu/ws/?pid=14916.

F. President Roosevelt's Forbes Field Speech (October 1, 1936)

In October 1936, in the midst of his first reelection campaign, President Franklin D. Roosevelt (1882–1945) delivered the following campaign speech at Forbes Field in Pittsburgh. In the speech, the president, taking advantage of the sports setting, provides a "box score" of the New Deal's successes to date in curbing the Great Depression. Declaring the fight against the Depression "in the bag," Roosevelt lists the successes of his administration as he sees them, including a declining federal deficit and an end to bank failures. On November 3, 1936, Roosevelt was overwhelmingly reelected, defeating Republican Alf Landon (1887–1987) by a total of 523-8 in the Electoral College.

Mr. Chairman, Governor Earle, my friends of Pennsylvania:

A baseball park is a good place to talk about box scores. Tonight I am going to talk to you about the box score of the Government of the United States. I am going to tell you the story of our fight to beat down the depression and win recovery. From where I stand it looks as though the game is pretty well "in the bag."

I am convinced that when Government finance or any other kind of finance is honest, and when all the cards are on the table, there is no higher mathematics about it. It is just plain, scoreboard arithmetic.

When the present management of your team took charge in 1933, the national scoreboard looked pretty bad. In fact, it looked so much like a shutout for the team that you voted a change of management in order to give the country a chance to win the game. And today we are winning it.

When the new management came to Washington, we began to make our plans—plans to meet the immediate crisis and plans that would carry the people of the country back to decent prosperity.

You and I and everybody else saw the millions out of work, saw the business concerns running in the red, saw the banks closing. Our national income had declined over 50 percent—and, what was worse, it showed no prospect of recuperating by itself. By national income I mean the total of all income of all the 125,000,000 people in this country—the total of all the pay envelopes, all the farm sales, all the profits of all the businesses and all the individuals and corporations in America.

During the four lean years before this Administration took office, that national income had declined from eighty-one billions a year to thirty-eight billions a year. In short, you and I, all of us together, were making forty-three billions—spelled with a "b," not an "m"—forty-three billion dollars less in 1932 than we made in 1929.

Now, the rise and fall of national income—since they tell the story of how much you and I and everybody else are making—are an index of the rise and fall of national prosperity. They are also an index of the prosperity of your Government. The money to run the Government comes from taxes; and the tax revenue in turn depends for its size on the size of the national income. When the incomes and the values and transactions of the country are on the downgrade, then tax receipts go on the down-grade too. If the national income continues to decline, then the Government cannot run without going into the red. The only way to keep the Government out of the red is to keep the people out of the red. And so we had to balance the budget of the American people before we could balance the budget of the national Government.

That makes common sense, doesn't it?

The box score when the Democratic Administration came to bat in 1933 showed a net deficit in our national accounts of about $3,000,000,000, accumulated in the three previous years under my predecessor.

National income was in a downward spiral. Federal Government revenues were in a downward spiral. To pile on vast new taxes would get us nowhere because values were going down—and that makes sense too.

On top of having to meet the ordinary expenses of Government, I recognized the obligation of the Federal Government to feed and take care of the growing army of homeless and destitute unemployed.

Something had to be done. A national choice had to be made. We could do one of two things. Some people who sat across my desk in those days urged me to let Nature take its course and to continue a policy of doing nothing. I rejected that advice because Nature was in an angry mood.

To have accepted that advice would have meant the continued wiping out of people of small means—the continued loss of their homes and farms and small businesses into the hands of people who still had enough capital left to pick up those homes and farms and businesses at bankruptcy prices. It would have meant, in a very short time, the loss of all the resources of a multitude of individuals and families and small corporations. You would have seen, throughout thpre Nation, a concentration of property ownership in the hands of one or two percent of the population, a concentration unequaled in any great Nation since the days of the later Roman Empire.

And so the program of this Administration set out to protect the small business, the small corporation, the small shop, and the small individual from the wave of deflation that threatened them. We realized then, as we do now, that the vast army of small business men and factory owners and shop owners—together with our farmers and workers—form the backbone of the industrial life of America. In our long-range plan we recognized that the prosperity of America depended upon, and would continue to depend upon, the prosperity of them all.

I rejected the advice that was given to me to do nothing for an additional reason. I had promised, and my Administration was determined, to keep the people of the United States from starvation.

I refused to leave human needs solely in the hands of local communities—local communities which themselves were almost bankrupt.

To have accepted that advice would have been to offer breadlines again to the American people, knowing this time, however, that in many places the lines would last far longer than the bread. In those dark days, between us and a balanced budget stood millions of needy Americans, denied the promise of a decent American life.

To balance our budget in 1933 or 1934 or 1935 would have been a crime against the American people. To do so we should either have had to make a capital levy that would have been confiscatory, or we should have had to set our face against human suffering with callous indifference. When Americans suffered, we refused to pass by on the other side. Humanity came first.

No one lightly lays a burden on the income of a Nation. But this vicious tightening circle of our declining national income simply had to be broken. The bankers and the industrialists of the Nation cried aloud that private business was powerless to break it. They turned, as they had a right to turn, to the Government. We accepted the final responsibility of Government, after all else had failed, to spend money when no one else had money left to spend.

I adopted, therefore, the other alternative. I cast aside a do nothing or a wait-and-see policy.

As a first step in our program we had to stop the quick spiral of deflation and decline in the national income. Having stopped them, we went on to restore purchasing power, to raise values, to put people back to work, and to start the national income going up again.

In 1933 we reversed the policy of the previous Administration. For the first time since the depression you had a Congress and an Administration in Washington which had the courage to provide the necessary resources which private interests no longer had or no longer dared to risk.

This cost money. We knew, and you knew, in March, 1933, that it would cost money. We knew, and you knew, that it would cost money for several years to come. The people understood that in 1933. They understood it in 1934, when they gave the Administration a full endorsement of its policy. They knew in 1935, and they know in 1936, that the plan is working.

All right, my friends, let us look at the cost. Since we could not get the money by taxes we borrowed it, and increased the public debt.

President Hoover's Administration increased the national debt in the net amount of over three billion dollars in three depression years, and there was little to show for it. My Administration has increased the national debt in the net amount of about eight billion dollars and there is much to show for it.

Put that figure of eight billions out here on the scoreboard, and let me tell you where the dollars went.

Over a billion and a half went for payment of the World War Veterans' Bonus this year instead of in 1945. That payment is now out of the way, and is no longer a future obligation of the Government.

As for the other six and a half billions of the deficit we did not just spend money; we spent it for something. America got something for what we spent—conservation of human resources through C.C.C. camps and through work relief; conservation of natural resources of water, soil and forest; billions for security and a better life. While many who criticize today were selling America short, we were investing in the future of America.

Contrast those expenditures and what we got for them with certain other expenditures of the American people in the years between 1920 and 1930. During that period not merely eight billions but many more billions came out of American pockets and were sent abroad—to foreign countries where the money was used for increasing foreign armaments, for building foreign factories to compete with us, for building foreign dwellings, swimming pools, and slaughter houses, for giving employment to the foreign unemployed—foreign boondoggling, if you will.

Those dollars, billions of them, were just as good American money—just as hard-earned—just as much the reward of our thrift—as the dollars we have spent during these three years at home giving work to the unemployed. Most of those dollars sent abroad are gone for good. Those billions, lost to us under previous Administrations, do not, by the way, include the other billions loaned by the United States to foreign Governments during and immediately after the War.

I ask you the simple question: Has it not been a sounder investment for us during these past three years to spend eight billion dollars for American industry, American farms, American homes and the care of American citizens?

I have used the figure of eight billion dollars as representing the net increase in our national debt. Immediately people will rush into print or run to the microphone to tell you that my arithmetic is all wrong. They will tell you that the increase in the national debt is thirteen billions instead of eight. That is technically and morally just as correct as if someone were to try to scare you about the condition of your bank by telling you all about its liabilities and not telling you about its assets.

That is technically and morally just as correct as telling you good people here in Pennsylvania that none of your bank deposits or insurance policies is sound.

When you are told that the United States Treasury has thirteen billions more of liabilities than it had in 1933, you should also be told that it has six billion dollars of increased assets to set off against these liabilities.

In three years our net national debt has increased eight billions of dollars. But in two years of the recent war it increased as much as twenty-five billion dollars. National defense and the future of America were involved in 1917. National defense and the future of America were also involved in 1933. Don't you believe that the saving of America has been cheap at that price? It was more than defense—it was more than rescue. It was an investment in the future of America.

And, incidentally, tonight is an anniversary in the affairs of our Government which I wish to celebrate with you and the American people. It is October first, and it marks the end of a whole year in which there has been not a single national bank failure in all the United States. It has been fifty-five years since that kind of record has been established. You and I can take this occasion to rejoice in that record. It is proof that the program has worked.

Compare the scoreboard which you have in Pittsburgh now with the scoreboard which you had when I stood here at second base in this field four years ago. At that time, as I drove through these great valleys, I could see mile after mile of this greatest mill and factory area in the world, a dead panorama of silent black structures and smokeless stacks. I saw idleness and hunger instead of the whirl of machinery. Today as I came north from West Virginia, I saw mines operating, I found bustle and life, the hiss of steam, the ring of steel on steel—the roaring song of industry.

And now a word as to this foolish fear about the crushing load the debt will impose upon your children and mine. This debt is not going to be paid by oppressive taxation on future generations. It is not going to be paid by taking away the hard-won savings of the present generation.

It is going to be paid out of an increased national income and increased individual incomes produced by increasing national prosperity.

The deficit of the national Government has been steadily declining for three years running, although technically this year it did not decline, because we paid the Bonus this year instead of 1945. Without the Bonus the deficit would have declined this year also.

The truth is that we are doing better than we anticipated in 1933. The national income has gone up faster than we dared then to hope. Deficits have been less than we expected. Treasury receipts are increasing. The national debt today in relation to the national income is much less than it was in 1933, when this Administration took office.

The national income was thirty-eight billions in 1932. In 1935 it was fifty-three billions and this year it will be well over sixty billions. If it keeps on rising at the present rate, as I am confident that it will, the receipts of the Government, without imposing any additional taxes, will, within a year or two, be sufficient to care for all ordinary and relief expenses of the Government—in other words, to balance the budget.

The Government of this great Nation, solvent, sound in credit, is coming through a crisis as grave as war without having sacrificed American democracy or the ideals of American life.

Source: Franklin D. Roosevelt Library, http://www.fdrlibrary.marist.edu/aboutfdr/pdfs /smCampaign_10-1-1936.pdf.

13. Economic Downturns, 1974–1984

A. President Nixon's Message Transmitting the 1972 *Economic Report of the President* to Congress (January 27, 1972)

Prepared by the Council of Economic Advisors, the Economic Report of the President *is mandated by the Employment Act of 1946 and has been submitted annually to Congress since 1947. In this excerpt from his message accompanying the 1972 report, President Richard Nixon (1913–1994) describes the measures his administration took in the previous year to curb inflation and lower unemployment.*

To the Congress of the United States:
The American economy is beginning to feel the effects of the new policies launched last August.

I undertook the New Economic Policy because it was becoming clear that not enough was being done to meet our ambitious goals for the American economy. The new measures are designed to bring the Nation to higher employment, greater price stability, and a stronger international position.

The essence of the New Economic Policy is not the specific list of measures we announced on August 15; it is the determination to do all that is necessary to achieve the Nation's goals.

Nineteen hundred and seventy-one was in many ways a good economic year. Total employment, total output, output per person, real hourly earnings, and real income after tax per person all reached new highs. The inflation which had plagued the country since 1965 began to subside. In the first 8 months of the year the rate of inflation was 30 percent less than in the same months of 1970.

But I did not believe this was enough to meet the Nation's needs. Although the rate of inflation had declined before August, it was still too high. Although unemployment stopped rising, it remained near 6 percent. In the first part of the year, our international balance-of-payments deficit—the excess of our payments to the rest of the world over their payments to us—had risen far too high.

The conditions called for decisive actions. On August 15, I announced these actions.

First, I imposed a 90-day freeze on prices, wages, and rents.

Second, I suspended conversion of dollars into gold and other reserve assets.

Third, I imposed a temporary surcharge on imports generally at the rate of 10 percent.

Fourth, I proposed a number of tax changes intended to stimulate the economy, including repeal of the excise tax on automobiles, a tax credit for investment, and reduction of income taxes on individuals. At the same time I took steps to keep the budget under control.

The package of measures was unprecedented in scope and degree. My Administration had struggled for 2 1/2 years in an effort to check the inflation we inherited by means more consistent with economic freedom than price-wage controls. But the inflationary momentum generated by the policy actions and in actions of 1965–68 was too stubborn to be eradicated by these means alone. Or at least it seemed that it could only be eradicated at the price of persistent high unemployment—and this was a price we would not ask the American people to pay.

Similarly, more than a decade of balance-of-payments deficits had built up an overhang of obligations and distrust which no longer left time for the gradual methods of correction which had been tried earlier.

The measures begun on August 15 will have effects continuing long into the future. They cannot be fully evaluated by what has happened in the little over 5 months since that date. Still the results up to this point have been extremely encouraging.

The freeze slowed down the rate of inflation dramatically. In the 3 months of its duration the index of consumer prices rose only 0.4 percent, compared to 1.0 percent in the previous 3 months. The freeze was a great testimonial to the public spirit of the American people, because that result could have been achieved with the small enforcement staff we had only if the people had been cooperating voluntarily.

The freeze was followed by a comprehensive, mandatory system of controls, with more flexible and equitable standards than were possible during the first

90 days. General principles and specific regulations have been formulated, staffs have been assembled and cases are being decided. This effort is under the direction of citizens on the Price Commission and Pay Board, with advice from other citizens on special panels concerned with health services, State and local government, and rent. These citizens are doing a difficult job, doing it well, and the Nation is in their debt.

While this inflation-control system was being put in place, vigorous action was going forward on the international front. The suspension of the convertibility of the dollar was a shock felt around the world. The surcharge emphasized the need to act swiftly and decisively to improve our position. Happily, the process of adjustment began promptly, without disrupting the flow of international business. Other currencies rose in cost relative to the U.S. dollar. As a result, the cost of foreign goods increased relative to the cost of U.S. goods, improving the competitive position of American workers and industries. International negotiations were begun to stabilize exchange rates at levels that would help in correcting the worldwide disequilibrium, of which the U.S. balance of-payments deficit was the most obvious symptom. These negotiations led to significant agreements on a number of points:

1. Realignment of exchange rates, with other currencies rising in cost relative to the dollar, as part of which we agreed to recommend to Congress that the price of gold in dollars be raised when progress had been made in trade liberalization.
2. Commitment to discussion of more general reform of the international monetary system.
3. Widening of the permitted range of variation of exchange rates, pending other measures of reform.
4. Commitment to begin discussions to reduce trade barriers, including some most harmful to the United States.
5. Assumption of a larger share of the costs of common defense by some of our allies.
6. Elimination of the temporary U.S. surcharge on imports.

The third part of the August 15 action was the stimulative tax program. Enactment of this package by Congress, although not entirely in the form I had proposed, put in place the final part of my New Economic Policy.

In part as a result of this program, economic activity rose more rapidly in the latter part of the year. In the fourth quarter real output increased at the annual rate of 6 percent, compared with about 3 percent in the 2 previous quarters. Employment rose by about 1.1 million from July to December, and only an extraordinarily large rise of the civilian labor force—1.3 million kept unemployment from falling. . . .

RICHARD NIXON

Source: Richard Nixon: "Annual Message to the Congress: The Economic Report of the President." January 27, 1972. Online by Gerhard Peters and John T. Woolley. *The American Presidency Project.* http://www.presidency.ucsb.edu/ws/?pid=3530.

B. President Ford's Message Transmitting the 1976 *Economic Report of the President* to Congress (January 26, 1976)

Reproduced here is an excerpt from the presidential message accompanying the 1976 Economic Report of the President, *which, by law, is submitted annually to Congress. In the message, President Gerald Ford (1913–2006) admits that the problems of inflation and unemployment, which were the main economic problems confronting the Nixon administration five years earlier, are still serious issues for the U.S. economy in 1976. Among the measures outlined by Ford to deal with these issues is a tax cut of almost $30 billion.*

To the Congress of the United States:

As we enter 1976, the American public still confronts its two greatest personal concerns: inflation and unemployment. As valid as those concerns are, we should not let them overshadow the very genuine progress we have made in the past year. The underlying fact about our economy is that it is steadily growing healthier. My policies for 1976 are intended to keep us on that upward path.

A year ago the economy was in the midst of a severe recession with no immediate end in sight. Exceptionally strong inflationary forces were just beginning to abate, and the prospects for containing unemployment were not bright.

It is now clear that we have made notable progress. The sharpest recession in the post-World War II period hit bottom last spring, and a substantial recovery is now under way. There were 85.4 million Americans at work in December, 1.3 million more than during March of 1975. While the rate of unemployment remains far too high, it is slowly moving in the right direction. There have also been appreciable advances in reducing the rate of inflation. The increase in the consumer price index was 7 percent between December 1974 and December 1975, down from a rate of more than 12 percent during the previous 12 months.

In reviewing 1975 it is also wise to remember the large number of potentially serious economic problems that did not materialize. The financial crisis that some predicted did not occur. The recession did not deepen into a cumulative depression. There was no collapse in international trade and investment.

The price of bread never rose to a dollar, nor did the price of gasoline. We did not experience corrosive social unrest as a consequence of our economic difficulties. While I do not regard the events of 1975 as fully satisfactory by any measure, we should find it reassuring that our economic system withstood severe strains and displayed inherent strengths during the year. I am confident that with responsible and appropriate policies we can achieve sustained economic progress in the future.

Unfortunately there is no simple formula or single act that will quickly produce full economic health. It has taken many years for excessive stimulation, combined with external shocks like the quintupling of international oil prices, to create the economic difficulties of 1974 and 1975, and it will take several years of sound policies to restore sustained, noninflationary growth. I will not make promises which I know, and you know, cannot be kept. We must restore the strength of the American economy as quickly as we can; but in so doing we cannot ignore the dangers of refueling inflationary forces, because unchecked inflation makes steady growth and full employment impossible. The events of the past several years have once again convincingly demonstrated that accelerating inflation causes instability and disruptions, increases unemployment, and ultimately precludes real prosperity.

It is often said that we must choose between inflation and unemployment, and that the only way to reduce unemployment is to accept chronic inflation or rigid controls. I reject this view. Inflation and unemployment are not opposites but are related symptoms of an unhealthy economy. The latter months of 1974 illustrate the relationship between inflation and unemployment. Sharply rising prices created a climate of uncertainty and were to blame for part of the massive reduction in the purchasing power of household assets placed in savings accounts and investment securities. In turn, consumers cut back on expenditures; and consequently inventories, already swollen by speculative buying, backed up in distribution channels. By the early months of 1975 there were sharp cutbacks in production and employment. Thus inflation played a significant part in the surge of unemployment, and if we have a new round of inflation it is likely to bring still more unemployment. Chronically high unemployment is an intolerable waste of human resources and entails an unacceptable loss of material production. Clearly, we must attack inflation and unemployment at the same time; our policies must be balanced.

My economic program for 1976 has three parts: First, a long-term continuation of the effort to revive the American economy; second, implementation of the many programs necessary to provide cushions for the unemployed during the transition to a healthy economy; and third, the elimination of Government policies and institutions that interfere with price flexibility and vigorous competition.

I. My key economic goal is to create an economic environment in which sustainable, noninflationary growth can be achieved.

When private spending is depressed, Government can properly absorb private savings and provide fiscal stimulus to the economy. But in the longer run, a viable, steady increase in prosperity is only possible if we have a vigorous private sector. My policies are designed to support the long-term growth of the economy by fostering an environment in which the private sector can flourish.

Increased capital formation is essential to meeting our long-term goals of full employment and noninflationary growth. Although there is no shortage of industrial capacity at the present time, many of our current priorities—to become independent in energy, to improve the environment, to create more jobs, and to raise our living standards—require increased investment. This means that business investment in plant and equipment as a share of gross national product must increase. We must also slow the growth of Federal spending in the years immediately ahead, so that mounting claims by the Federal Government on our economic resources will not prevent an adequate flow of savings into capital investments.

Accordingly, I am recommending that budget savings be refunded to the American taxpayer by means of tax cuts. I have proposed an annual tax cut of $28 billion from 1974 levels, effective July 1, 1976. If we continue in the years ahead to pursue the kind of budgetary restraint which I am recommending, another major tax cut will be feasible by 1979. I strongly believe that the individual wage earner has the right to spend his own money on the goods and services he wants, rather than having the Government increase its control over the disposition of his income. . . .

GERALD R. FORD

Source: Gerald R. Ford: "Annual Message to the Congress: The Economic Report of the President." January 26, 1976. Online by Gerhard Peters and John T. Woolley. *The American Presidency Project.* http://www.presidency.ucsb.edu/ws/?pid=5811.

C. President Carter Addresses the Nation on Energy (November 8, 1977)

In the following excerpts from his speech of November 8, 1977, President Jimmy Carter (1924–) presses for congressional passage of the national energy plan that he had proposed in an address delivered on April 18, 1977. In this speech, Carter describes the seriousness of America's energy problem and seeks to convince the American people of the need for a national energy policy that includes energy conservation, development of alternatives to oil, and creation of a Department of Energy.

Good evening.

. . . Tonight, at this crucial time, I want to emphasize why it is so important that we have an energy plan and what we will risk, as a nation, if we are timid or reluctant to face this challenge. It's crucial that you understand how serious this challenge is.

With every passing month, our energy problems have grown worse. This summer we used more oil and gasoline than ever before in our history. More of our oil is coming from foreign countries. Just since April, our oil imports have cost us $23 billion—about $350 worth of foreign oil for the average American family.

A few weeks ago, in Detroit, an unemployed steelworker told me something that may reflect the feelings of many of you. "Mr. President," he said, "I don't feel much like talking about energy and foreign policy. I'm concerned about how I'm going to live. . . . I can't be too concerned about other things when I have a 10-year-old daughter to raise and I don't have a job and I'm 56 years old."

Well, I understand how he felt, but I must tell you the truth. And the truth is that you cannot talk about economic problems now or in the future without talking about energy.

Let me try to describe the size and the effect of the problem. Our farmers are the greatest agricultural exporters the world has ever known, but it now takes all the food and fiber that we export in 2 years just to pay for 1 year of imported oil—about $45 billion.

This excessive importing of foreign oil is a tremendous and rapidly increasing drain on our national economy. It hurts every American family. It causes unemployment. Every $5 billion increase in oil imports costs us 200,000 American jobs. It costs us business investments. Vast amounts of American wealth no longer stay in the United States to build our factories and to give us a better life.

It makes it harder for us to balance our Federal budget and to finance needed programs for our people. It unbalances our Nation's trade with other countries. This year, primarily because of oil, our imports will be at least $25 billion more than all the American goods that we sell overseas.

It pushes up international energy prices because excessive importing of oil by the United States makes it easier for foreign producers to raise their prices. It feeds serious inflationary pressures in our own economy.

If this trend continues, the excessive reliance on foreign oil could make the very security of our Nation increasingly dependent on uncertain energy supplies. Our national security depends on more than just our Armed Forces; it also rests on the strength of our economy, on our national will, and on the ability of the United States to carry out our foreign policy as a free and independent nation. America overseas is only as strong as America at home. . . .

Our biggest problem, however, is that we simply use too much and waste too much energy. Our imports have more than tripled in the last 10 years. Although all countries could, of course, be more efficient, we are the worst offender. Since the great price rise in 1973, the Japanese have cut their oil imports, the Germans, the French, the British, the Italians have all cut their oil imports. Meanwhile, although we have large petroleum supplies of our own and most of them don't, we in the United States have increased our imports more than 40 percent.

This problem has come upon us suddenly. Ten years ago, when foreign oil was cheap, we imported just 2 1/2 million barrels of oil a day, about 20 percent of what we used. By 1972, we were importing about 30 percent. This year, when foreign oil is very expensive, we are importing nearly 9 million barrels a day—almost one-half of all the oil we use. Unless we act quickly, imports will continue to go up, and all the problems that I've just described will grow even worse.

There are three things that we must do to avoid this danger: first, cut back on consumption; second, shift away from oil and gas to other sources of energy; and third, encourage production of energy here in the United States. These are the purposes of the new energy legislation. . . .

Now the energy proposal that I made to Congress last April has three basic elements to ensure that it is well balanced. First, it's fair both to the American consumers and to the energy producers, and it will not disrupt our national economy. Second, as I've said before, it's designed to meet our important goals for energy conservation, to promote a shift to more plentiful and permanent energy supplies and encourage increased production of energy in the United States. And third, it protects our Federal budget from any unreasonable burden. These are the three standards by which the final legislation must be judged. I will sign the energy bills only if they meet these tests.

During the next few weeks, the Congress will make a judgment on these vital questions. I will be working closely with them. And you are also deeply involved in these decisions. This is not a contest of strength between the President and the Congress, nor between the House and the Senate. What is being measured is the strength and will of our Nation—whether we can acknowledge a threat and meet a serious challenge together.

I'm convinced that we can have enough energy to permit the continued growth of our economy, to expand production and jobs, and to protect the security of the United States—if we act wisely. . . .

Source: Miller Center, University of Virginia. http://millercenter.org/president/speeches /detail/3400.

D. President Carter's State of the Union Address (January 19, 1978)

The president's annual State of the Union message is mandated by Article II, Section 3 of the U.S. Constitution. Between 1801 and 1912, the State of the Union message was delivered to Congress in written form, but since 1913 most State of the Union messages have been delivered orally to Congress by the president. In the following excerpt from his 1978 State of the Union address, President Jimmy Carter (1924–) discusses the serious consequences for the U.S. economy of American dependence on foreign oil to meet the country's growing energy needs.

Mr. President, Mr. Speaker, Members of the 95th Congress, ladies and gentlemen:

Two years ago today we had the first caucus in Iowa, and one year ago tomorrow, I walked from here to the White House to take up the duties of President of the United States. I didn't know it then when I walked, but I've been trying to save energy ever since. [Laughter]

I return tonight to fulfill one of those duties of the Constitution: to give to the Congress—and to the Nation—information on the state of the Union.

Militarily, politically, economically, and in spirit, the state of our Union is sound.

We are a great country, a strong country, a vital and a dynamic country— and so we will remain.

We are a confident people and a hardworking people, a decent and a compassionate people—and so we will remain.

I want to speak to you tonight about where we are and where we must go, about what we have done and what we must do. And I want to pledge to you my best efforts and ask you to pledge yours.

Each generation of Americans has to face circumstances not of its own choosing, but by which its character is measured and its spirit is tested.

There are times of emergency, when a nation and its leaders must bring their energies to bear on a single urgent task. That was the duty Abraham Lincoln faced when our land was torn apart by conflict in the War Between the States. That was the duty faced by Franklin Roosevelt when he led America out of an economic depression and again when he led America to victory in war.

There are other times when there is no single overwhelming crisis, yet profound national interests are at stake.

At such times the risk of inaction can be equally great. It becomes the task of leaders to call forth the vast and restless energies of our people to build for the future.

That is what Harry Truman did in the years after the Second World War, when we helped Europe and Japan rebuild themselves and secured an international order that has protected freedom from aggression.

We live in such times now, and we face such duties.

We've come through a long period of turmoil and doubt, but we've once again found our moral course, and with a new spirit, we are striving to express our best instincts to the rest of the world.

There is all across our land a growing sense of peace and a sense of common purpose. This sense of unity cannot be expressed in programs or in legislation or in dollars. It's an achievement that belongs to every individual American. This unity ties together, and it towers over all our efforts here in Washington, and it serves as an inspiring beacon for all of us who are elected to serve.

This new atmosphere demands a new spirit, a partnership between those of us who lead and those who elect. The foundations of this partnership are truth, the courage to face hard decisions, concern for one another and the common good over special interests, and a basic faith and trust in the wisdom and strength and judgment of the American people.

For the first time in a generation, we are not haunted by a major international crisis or by domestic turmoil, and we now have a rare and a priceless opportunity to address persistent problems and burdens which come to us as a nation—quietly and steadily getting worse over the years.

As President, I've had to ask you, the Members of Congress, and you, the American people, to come to grips with some of the most difficult and hard questions facing our society.

We must make a maximum effort, because if we do not aim for the best, we are very likely to achieve little. I see no benefit to the country if we delay, because the problems will only get worse.

We need patience and good will, but we really need to realize that there is a limit to the role and the function of government. Government cannot solve our problems, it can't set our goals, it cannot define our vision. Government cannot eliminate poverty or provide a bountiful economy or reduce inflation or save our cities or cure illiteracy or provide energy. And government cannot mandate goodness. Only a true partnership between government and the people can ever hope to reach these goals.

Those of us who govern can sometimes inspire, and we can identify needs and marshal resources, but we simply cannot be the managers of everything and everybody.

We here in Washington must move away from crisis management, and we must establish clear goals for the future—immediate and the distant future—which will let us work together and not in conflict. Never again should we neglect a growing crisis like the shortage of energy, where further delay will only lead to more harsh and painful solutions.

Every day we spend more than $120 million for foreign oil. This slows our economic growth, it lowers the value of the dollar overseas, and it aggravates unemployment and inflation here at home.

Now we know what we must do—increase production. We must cut down on waste. And we must use more of those fuels which are plentiful and more permanent. We must be fair to people, and we must not disrupt our Nation's economy and our budget.

Now, that sounds simple. But I recognize the difficulties involved. I know that it is not easy for the Congress to act. But the fact remains that on the energy legislation, we have failed the American people. Almost 5 years after the oil embargo dramatized the problem for us all, we still do not have a national energy program. Not much longer can we tolerate this stalemate. It undermines our national interest both at home and abroad. We must succeed, and I believe we will.

Our main task at home this year, with energy a central element, is the Nation's economy. We must continue the recovery and further cut unemployment and inflation. . . .

Source: Jimmy Carter: "The State of the Union Address Delivered before a Joint Session of the Congress." January 19, 1978. Online by Gerhard Peters and John T. Woolley. *The American Presidency Project.* http://www.presidency.ucsb.edu/ws/?pid=30856.

E. California Proposition 13: The People's Initiative to Limit Property Taxation (Approved June 6, 1978)

Brought to the ballot by means of the initiative process, Proposition 13 proposed an amendment to the California state constitution that limited the tax rate for real estate, decreased property taxes, and required a two-thirds majority in both houses of the state legislature for any future increases in state tax rates. Approved by almost 63 percent of the voters in June 1978, Proposition 13 was embodied in Article 13A of the California constitution. Although Proposition 13 received much attention around the country, and generated much controversy in California, it was upheld by the U.S. Supreme Court in 1992.

CALIFORNIA CONSTITUTION

ARTICLE 13A [TAX LIMITATION]

SECTION 1. (a) The maximum amount of any ad valorem tax on real property shall not exceed one percent (1%) of the full cash value of such property. The one percent (1%) tax to be collected by the counties and apportioned according to law to the districts within the counties.

(b) The limitation provided for in subdivision (a) shall not apply to ad valorem taxes or special assessments to pay the interest and redemption charges on any of the following:

(1) Indebtedness approved by the voters prior to July 1, 1978.

(2) Bonded indebtedness for the acquisition or improvement of real property approved on or after July 1, 1978, by two-thirds of the votes cast by the voters voting on the proposition.

(3) Bonded indebtedness incurred by a school district, community college district, or county office of education for the construction, reconstruction, rehabilitation, or replacement of school facilities, including the furnishing and equipping of school facilities, or the acquisition or lease of real property for school facilities, approved by 55 percent of the voters of the district or county, as appropriate, voting on the proposition on or after the effective date of the measure adding this paragraph. This paragraph shall apply only if the proposition approved by the voters and resulting in the bonded indebtedness includes all of the following accountability requirements:

(A) A requirement that the proceeds from the sale of the bonds be used only for the purposes specified in Article XIII A, Section 1(b) (3), and not for any other purpose, including teacher and administrator salaries and other school operating expenses.

(B) A list of the specific school facilities projects to be funded and certification that the school district board, community college board, or county office of education has evaluated safety, class size reduction, and information technology needs in developing that list.

(C) A requirement that the school district board, community college board, or county office of education conduct an annual, independent performance audit to ensure that the funds have been expended only on the specific projects listed.

(D) A requirement that the school district board, community college board, or county office of education conduct an annual, independent financial audit of the proceeds from the sale of the bonds until all of those proceeds have been expended for the school facilities projects.

(c) Notwithstanding any other provisions of law or of this Constitution, school districts, community college districts, and county offices of education may levy a 55 percent vote ad valorem tax pursuant to subdivision (b). . . .

SEC. 3. (a) Any change in state statute which results in any taxpayer paying a higher tax must be imposed by an act passed by not less than two-thirds of all members elected to each of the two houses of the Legislature, except that no new ad valorem taxes on real property, or sales or transaction taxes on the sales of real property may be imposed.

(b) As used in this section, "tax" means any levy, charge, or exaction of any kind imposed by the State, except the following:

(1) A charge imposed for a specific benefit conferred or privilege granted directly to the payor that is not provided to those not charged, and which does not exceed the reasonable costs to the State of conferring the benefit or granting the privilege to the payor.

(2) A charge imposed for a specific government service or product provided directly to the payor that is not provided to those not charged, and which does not exceed the reasonable costs to the State of providing the service or product to the payor.

(3) A charge imposed for the reasonable regulatory costs to the State incident to issuing licenses and permits, performing investigations, inspections, and audits, enforcing agricultural marketing orders, and the administrative enforcement and adjudication thereof.

(4) A charge imposed for entrance to or use of state property, or the purchase, rental, or lease of state property, except charges governed by Section 15 of Article XI.

(5) A fine, penalty, or other monetary charge imposed by the judicial branch of government or the State, as a result of a violation of law.

(c) Any tax adopted after January 1, 2010, but prior to the effective date of this act, that was not adopted in compliance with the requirements of this section is void 12 months after the effective date of this act unless the tax is reenacted by the Legislature and signed into law by the Governor in compliance with the requirements of this section.

(d) The State bears the burden of proving by a preponderance of the evidence that a levy, charge, or other exaction is not a tax, that the amount is no more than necessary to cover the reasonable costs of the governmental activity, and that the manner in which those costs are allocated to a payor bear a fair or reasonable relationship to the payor's burdens on, or benefits received from, the governmental activity.

Section 4. Cities, Counties and special districts, by a two-thirds vote of the qualified electors of such district, may impose special taxes on such district, except ad valorem taxes on real property or a transaction tax or sales tax on the sale of real property within such City, County or special district.

Section 5. This article shall take effect for the tax year beginning on July 1 following the passage of this Amendment, except Section 3 which shall become effective upon the passage of this article.

Section 6. If any section, part, clause, or phrase hereof is for any reason held to be invalid or unconstitutional, the remaining sections shall not be affected but will remain in full force and effect.

SEC. 7. Section 3 of this article does not apply to the California Children and Families First Act of 1998.

Source: California Constitution, Article 13A. http://www.leginfo.ca.gov/.const/.article _13A.

F. Full Employment and Balanced Growth Act (Humphrey-Hawkins Full Employment Act) (October 27, 1978)

Proposed by Representative Augustus Hawkins (D-CA) (1907–2007) and Senator Hubert Humphrey (D-MN) (1911–1978), and signed by President Jimmy Carter (1924–) in October 1978, the Full Employment and Balanced Growth Act (informally known as Humphrey-Hawkins) was an attempt to clarify and strengthen federal economic policy as a means of fighting the main economic problems of the late 1970s—inflation and unemployment. The act directed the federal government to actively encourage private enterprise to attain four goals: full employment, increased productivity, price stability, and balanced trade and budgets.

General Findings

Section 2.

(a) The Congress finds that the Nation has suffered substantial unemployment and underemployment, idleness of other productive resources, high rates of inflation, and inadequate productivity growth, over prolonged periods of time, imposing numerous economic and social costs on the Nation. Such costs include the following:

    (1) The Nation is deprived of the full supply of goods and services, the full utilization of labor and capital resources, and the related increases in economic well-being that would occur under conditions of genuine full employment, production, and real income, balanced growth, a balanced Federal budget, and the effective control of inflation.

    (2) The output of goods and services is insufficient to meet pressing national priorities.

    (3) Workers are deprived of the job security, income, skill development, and productivity necessary to maintain and advance their standards of living.

    (4) Business and industry are deprived of the production, sales, capital flow, and productivity necessary to maintain adequate profits, undertake new investment, create jobs, compete internationally, and contribute to meeting society's economic needs. These problems are especially acute for smaller businesses. Variations in the business cycle and low-level operations of the economy are far more damaging to smaller businesses than to larger business concerns because smaller businesses have fewer available resources, and less access to resources, to withstand nation-wide economic adversity. A decline in small business enterprises contributes to unemployment by reducing employment opportunities and contributes to inflation by reducing competition.

(5) Unemployment exposes many families to social, psychological, and physiological costs, including disruption of family life, loss of individual dignity and self-respect, and the aggravation of physical and psychological illnesses, alcoholism and drug abuse, crime, and social conflicts.

(6) Federal, State, and local government budgets are undermined by deficits due to shortfalls in tax revenues and in increases in expenditures for unemployment compensation, public assistance, and other recession-related services in the areas of criminal justice, alcoholism and drug abuse, and physical and mental health.

(b) The Congress further finds that:

(1) High unemployment may contribute to inflation by diminishing labor training and skills, underutilizing capital resources, reducing the rate of productivity advance, increasing unit labor costs, and reducing the general supply of goods and services.

(2) Aggregate monetary and fiscal policies alone have been unable to achieve full employment and production, increased real income, balanced growth, a balanced Federal budget, adequate productivity growth, proper attention to national priorities, achievement of an improved trade balance, and reasonable price stability, and therefore must be supplemented by other measures designed to serve these ends.

(3) Attainment of these objectives should be facilitated by setting explicit short-term and medium-term economic goals, and by improved coordination among the President, the Congress, and the Board of Governors of the Federal Reserve System.

(4) Increasing job opportunities and full employment would greatly contribute to the elimination of discrimination based upon sex, age, race, color, religion, national origin, handicap, or other improper factors.

(c) The Congress further finds that an effective policy to promote full employment and production, increased real income, balanced growth, a balanced Federal budget, adequate productivity growth, proper attention to national priorities, achievement of an improved trade balance, and reasonable price stability should

(1) be based on the development of explicit economic goals and policies involving the President, the Congress, and the Board of Governors of the Federal Reserve System, with maximum reliance on the resources and ingenuity of the private sector of the economy,

(2) include programs specifically designed to reduce high unemployment due to recessions, and to reduce structural unemployment within regional areas and among particular labor force groups, and

(3) give proper attention to the role of increased exports and improvement in the international competitiveness of agriculture, business, and industry in providing productive employment opportunities and achieving an improved trade balance.

(d) The Congress further finds that full employment and production, increased real income, balanced growth, a balanced Federal budget, adequate productivity growth, proper attention to national priorities, achievement of an improved trade balance through increased exports and improvement in the international competitiveness of agriculture, business, and industry, and reasonable price stability are important national requirements and will promote the economic security and well-being of all citizens of the Nation.

(e) The Congress further finds that the United States is part of an interdependent world trading and monetary system and that attainment of the requirements specified in subsection (d) of this section is dependent upon policies promoting a free and fair international trading system and a sound and stable international monetary system.

Report

Sec. 3.

Not later than one year after October 27, 1978, the Committee on Labor and Human Resources of the Senate and the Committee on Education and Labor of the House of Representatives each shall conduct a study and submit a report, including findings and recommendations, to the Committee on Rules and Administration of the Senate and the Committee on Rules of the House, respectively, on the subject of establishing a full employment goal in connection with the provisions of this chapter.

National Employment Conference

Sec. 4.

(a) Organization and implementation

A National Employment Conference may be convened in the District of Columbia within a reasonable period of time after October 27, 1978.

Responsibility for the organization and implementation of this conference shall rest with the President or the appropriate department or agency of the Federal Government, and the conference shall bring together leaders of small and larger business, labor, government, and all other interested parties.

(b) Subject matter

The subject of the conference shall be employment, with particular attention to structural unemployment and the plight of disadvantaged youth. The conference shall also focus on issues such as implementation of adequate and effective incentives for private sector employers to hire the hard-core unemployed. Special attention shall be given to the creation of jobs through the use of targeted employment tax credits, wage vouchers, and other incentives to private sector businesses.

Source: 15 USC, Chapter 58 § 3103; Pub. L. 95-523, Oct. 27, 1978, 92 Stat. (1887–89). Cornell University law School, Legal Information Institute. http://www.law.cornell.edu/uscode/text/15/3103.

G. President Carter's "Crisis of Confidence" or "Malaise" Speech (July 15, 1979)

Faced in the summer of 1979 with continuing energy shortages and deepening economic recession, President Jimmy Carter (1924–) saw his approval ratings decline below those of President Richard Nixon (1913–1994) during the Watergate scandal. In a major televised speech, excerpted below, Carter described the energy crisis as a "crisis of the spirit in our country," and asked people to sacrifice to reduce energy consumption and adjust to new limits in energy availability. Known thereafter as the "malaise" speech, even though Carter never used the word in his address, the speech drew much criticism for its pessimistic tone, which, when contrasted with the optimistic visions offered by his Republican challenger, Ronald Reagan (1911–2004), helped lead to Carter's massive reelection defeat in 1980.

Good evening.

This is a special night for me. Exactly 3 years ago, on July 15, 1976, I accepted the nomination of my party to run for President of the United States. I promised you a President who is not isolated from the people, who feels your pain, and who shares your dreams and who draws his strength and his wisdom from you.

During the past 3 years I've spoken to you on many occasions about national concerns, the energy crisis, reorganizing the Government, our Nation's

economy, and issues of war and especially peace. But over those years the subjects of the speeches, the talks, and the press conferences have become increasingly narrow, focused more and more on what the isolated world of Washington
thinks is important. Gradually, you've heard more and more about what the
Government thinks or what the Government should be doing and less and less
about our Nation's hopes, our dreams, and our vision of the future.

Ten days ago I had planned to speak to you again about a very important
subject—energy. For the fifth time I would have described the urgency of the
problem and laid out a series of legislative recommendations to the Congress.
But as I was preparing to speak, I began to ask myself the same question that I
now know has been troubling many of you. Why have we not been able to get
together as a nation to resolve our serious energy problem?

It's clear that the true problems of our Nation are much deeper—deeper
than gasoline lines or energy shortages, deeper even than inflation or recession.
And I realize more than ever that as President I need your help. So, I decided to
reach out and listen to the voices of America.

I invited to Camp David people from almost every segment of our society—
business and labor, teachers and preachers, Governors, mayors, and private
citizens. And then I left Camp David to listen to other Americans, men and
women like you. It has been an extraordinary 10 days, and I want to share with
you what I've heard.

First of all, I got a lot of personal advice. Let me quote a few of the typical
comments that I wrote down. . . .

. . . [T]his from a young Chicano: "Some of us have suffered from recession
all our lives." . . .

And I like this one particularly from a black woman who happens to be the
mayor of a small Mississippi town: "The big-shots are not the only ones who are
important. Remember, you can't sell anything on Wall Street unless someone
digs it up somewhere else first."

This kind of summarized a lot of other statements: "Mr. President, we are
confronted with a moral and a spiritual crisis." . . .

Several of our discussions were on energy, and I have a notebook full of
comments and advice. . . .

These 10 days confirmed my belief in the decency and the strength and the
wisdom of the American people, but it also bore out some of my longstanding
concerns about our Nation's underlying problems.

I know, of course, being President, that government actions and legislation
can be very important. That's why I've worked hard to put my campaign promises into law—and I have to admit, with just mixed success. But after listening
to the American people I have been reminded again that all the legislation in
the world can't fix what's wrong with America. So, I want to speak to you first

tonight about a subject even more serious than energy or inflation. I want to talk to you right now about a fundamental threat to American democracy.

I do not mean our political and civil liberties. They will endure. And I do not refer to the outward strength of America, a nation that is at peace tonight everywhere in the world, with unmatched economic power and military might.

The threat is nearly invisible in ordinary ways. It is a crisis of confidence. It is a crisis that strikes at the very heart and soul and spirit of our national will. We can see this crisis in the growing doubt about the meaning of our own lives and in the loss of a unity of purpose for our Nation.

The erosion of our confidence in the future is threatening to destroy the social and the political fabric of America.

The confidence that we have always had as a people is not simply some romantic dream or a proverb in a dusty book that we read just on the Fourth of July. It is the idea which founded our Nation and has guided our development as a people. Confidence in the future has supported everything else—public institutions and private enterprise, our own families, and the very Constitution of the United States. Confidence has defined our course and has served as a link between generations. We've always believed in something called progress. We've always had a faith that the days of our children would be better than our own.

Our people are losing that faith, not only in government itself but in the ability as citizens to serve as the ultimate rulers and shapers of our democracy. As a people we know our past and we are proud of it. Our progress has been part of the living history of America, even the world. We always believed that we were part of a great movement of humanity itself called democracy, involved in the search for freedom, and that belief has always strengthened us in our purpose. But just as we are losing our confidence in the future, we are also beginning to close the door on our past.

In a nation that was proud of hard work, strong families, close-knit communities, and our faith in God, too many of us now tend to worship self-indulgence and consumption. Human identity is no longer defined by what one does, but by what one owns. But we've discovered that owning things and consuming things does not satisfy our longing for meaning. We've learned that piling up material goods cannot fill the emptiness of lives which have no confidence or purpose.

The symptoms of this crisis of the American spirit are all around us. For the first time in the history of our country a majority of our people believe that the next 5 years will be worse than the past 5 years. Two-thirds of our people do not even vote. The productivity of American workers is actually dropping, and the willingness of Americans to save for the future has fallen below that of all other people in the Western world.

As you know, there is a growing disrespect for government and for churches and for schools, the news media, and other institutions. This is not a message of happiness or reassurance, but it is the truth and it is a warning. . . .

Source: Carter, Jimmy. *Public Papers of the Presidents: Jimmy Carter, 1979,* Book 2. Washington, D.C.: Government Printing Office, 1979.

H. President Reagan's Program for Economic Recovery (February 18, 1981)

Below are excerpts from a document titled "America's New Beginning: A Program for Economic Recovery," which was issued by President Ronald Reagan (1911–2004) in February 1981, only weeks after he took office. Attempting to combat what he described as a "debilitating combination of sustained inflation and economic distress," Reagan proposed tax cuts, spending cuts, and regulatory relief as the best way to get the economy moving again. Although the economic recession deepened in 1982, forcing Reagan to accept some tax increases, by late 1983 a strong recovery had taken hold, helping Reagan win a massive reelection victory in 1984.

I. A Program for Economic Recovery

Today the Administration is proposing a national recovery plan to reverse the debilitating combination of sustained inflation and economic distress which continues to face the American economy. Were we to stay with existing policies, the results would be readily predictable: a rising government presence in the economy, more inflation, stagnating productivity, and higher unemployment. Indeed, there is reason to fear that if we remain on this course, our economy may suffer even more calamitously.

The program we have developed will break that cycle of negative expectations. It will revitalize economic growth, renew optimism and confidence, and rekindle the Nation's entrepreneurial instincts and creativity.

The benefits to the average American will be striking. Inflation—which is now at double digit rates—will be cut in half by 1986. The American economy will produce 13 million new jobs by 1986, nearly 3 million more than if the status quo in government policy were to prevail. The economy itself should break out of its anemic growth patterns to a much more robust growth trend of 4 to 5 percent a year. These positive results will be accomplished simultaneously with reducing tax burdens, increasing private saving, and raising the living standard of the American family.

The plan is based on sound expenditure, tax, regulatory, and monetary policies. It seeks properly functioning markets, free play of wages and prices, reduced government spending and borrowing, a stable and reliable monetary framework, and reduced government barriers to risk-taking and enterprise. This agenda for the future recognizes that sensible policies which are consistently applied can release the strength of the private sector, improve economic growth, and reduce inflation.

We have forgotten some important lessons in America. High taxes are not the remedy for inflation. Excessively rapid monetary growth cannot lower interest rates. Well-intentioned government regulations do not contribute to economic vitality. In fact, government spending has become so extensive that it contributes to the economic problems it was designed to cure. More government intervention in the economy cannot possibly be a solution to our economic problems.

We must remember a simple truth. The creativity and ambition of the American people are the vital forces of economic growth. The motivation and incentive of our people—to supply new goods and services and earn additional income for their families—are the most precious resources of our Nation's economy. The goal of this Administration is to nurture the strength and vitality of the American people by reducing the burdensome, intrusive role of the Federal Government; by lowering tax rates and cutting spending; and by providing incentives for individuals to work, to save, and to invest. It is our basic belief that only by reducing the growth of government can we increase the growth of the economy.

The U.S. economy faces no insurmountable barriers to sustained growth. It confronts no permanently disabling tradeoffs between inflation and unemployment, between high interest rates and high taxes, or between recession and hyperinflation. We can revive the incentives to work and save. We can restore the willingness to invest in the private capital required to achieve a steadily rising standard of living. Most important, we can regain our faith in the future.

The plan consists of four parts: (1) a substantial reduction in the growth of Federal expenditures; (2) a significant reduction in Federal tax rates; (3) prudent relief of Federal regulatory burdens; and (4) a monetary policy on the part of the independent Federal Reserve System which is consistent with those policies. These four complementary policies form an integrated and comprehensive program.

It should be clear from the most cursory examination of the economic program of this Administration that we have moved from merely talking about the economic difficulties facing the American people to taking the strong action necessary to turn the economy around.

The leading edge of our program is the comprehensive reduction in the rapid growth of Federal spending. As shown in detail below, our budget restraint is more than "cosmetic" changes in the estimates of Federal expenditures. But we have not adopted a simple-minded "meat ax" approach to budget reductions.

Rather, a careful set of guidelines has been used to identify lower-priority programs in virtually every department and agency that can be eliminated, reduced, or postponed.

The second element of the program, which is equally important and urgent, is the reduction in Federal personal income tax rates by 10 percent a year for 3 years in a row. Closely related to this is an incentive to greater investment in production and job creation via faster tax write-offs of new factories and production equipment.

The third key element of our economic expansion program is an ambitious reform of regulations that will reduce the government-imposed barriers to investment, production, and employment. We have suspended for 2 months the unprecedented flood of last-minute rulemaking on the part of the previous Administration. We have eliminated the ineffective and counterproductive wage and price standards of the Council on Wage and Price Stability, and we have taken other steps to eliminate government interference in the marketplace.

The fourth aspect of this comprehensive economic program is a monetary policy to provide the financial environment consistent with a steady return to sustained growth and price stability. During the first week of this Administration its commitment to the historic independence of the Federal Reserve System was underscored. It is clear, of course, that monetary and fiscal policy are closely interrelated. Success in one area can be made more difficult—or can be reinforced—by the other. Thus, a predictable and steady growth in the money supply at more modest levels than often experienced in the past will be a vital contribution to the achievement of the economic goals described in this Report. The planned reduction and subsequent elimination of Federal deficit financing will help the Federal Reserve System perform its important role in achieving economic growth and stability.

The ultimate importance of this program for sustained economic growth will arise not only from the positive effects of the individual components, important as they are. Rather, it will be the dramatic improvement in the underlying economic environment and outlook that will set a new and more positive direction to economic decisions throughout the economy. Protection against inflation and high tax burdens will no longer be an overriding motivation. Once again economic choices—involving working, saving, and investment—will be based primarily on the prospect for real rewards for those productive activities which improve the true economic well-being of our citizens. . . .

Source: Ronald Reagan: "White House Report on the Program for Economic Recovery." February 18, 1981. Online by Gerhard Peters and John T. Woolley. *The American Presidency Project.* http://www.presidency.ucsb.edu/ws/?pid=43427.

14. Great Recession of 2008–2009

A. Barack Obama's Victory Speech (November 4, 2008)

*Barack Obama (1961–), the 2008 Democratic candidate for president, deliv-
ered the following address in Chicago on the evening of November 4, 2008, after
receiving a call from his Republican opponent, John McCain (1936–), who conceded defeat and congratulated Obama on his election as 44th president of the
United States. In his speech, Obama acknowledges that the country is in the grip
of the "worst financial crisis in a century," and that solving the crisis will take
time, perhaps longer than one presidential term.*

If there is anyone out there who still doubts that America is a place where
all things are possible; who still wonders if the dream of our founders is alive
in our time; who still questions the power of our democracy, tonight is your
answer.

It's the answer told by lines that stretched around schools and churches in
numbers this nation has never seen; by people who waited three hours and four
hours, many for the very first time in their lives, because they believed that this
time must be different; that their voice could be that difference.

It's the answer spoken by young and old, rich and poor, Democrat and
Republican, black, white, Latino, Asian, Native American, gay, straight, disabled and not disabled—Americans who sent a message to the world that we
have never been a collection of Red States and Blue States: we are, and always
will be, the United States of America.

It's the answer that led those who have been told for so long by so many to
be cynical, and fearful, and doubtful of what we can achieve to put their hands
on the arc of history and bend it once more toward the hope of a better day.

It's been a long time coming, but tonight, because of what we did on this
day, in this election, at this defining moment, change has come to America.

I just received a very gracious call from Senator McCain. He fought long and
hard in this campaign, and he's fought even longer and harder for the country
he loves. He has endured sacrifices for America that most of us cannot begin to
imagine, and we are better off for the service rendered by this brave and self-
less leader. I congratulate him and Governor Palin for all they have achieved,
and I look forward to working with them to renew this nation's promise in the
months ahead.

I want to thank my partner in this journey, a man who campaigned from
his heart and spoke for the men and women he grew up with on the streets of
Scranton and rode with on that train home to Delaware, the Vice President-
elect of the United States, Joe Biden.

I would not be standing here tonight without the unyielding support of my best friend for the last sixteen years, the rock of our family and the love of my life, our nation's next First Lady, Michelle Obama. Sasha and Malia, I love you both so much, and you have earned the new puppy that's coming with us to the White House. And while she's no longer with us, I know my grandmother is watching, along with the family that made me who I am. I miss them tonight, and know that my debt to them is beyond measure.

To my campaign manager David Plouffe, my chief strategist David Axelrod, and the best campaign team ever assembled in the history of politics—you made this happen, and I am forever grateful for what you've sacrificed to get it done.

But above all, I will never forget who this victory truly belongs to—it belongs to you.

I was never the likeliest candidate for this office. We didn't start with much money or many endorsements. Our campaign was not hatched in the halls of Washington—it began in the backyards of Des Moines and the living rooms of Concord and the front porches of Charleston.

It was built by working men and women who dug into what little savings they had to give five dollars and ten dollars and twenty dollars to this cause. It grew strength from the young people who rejected the myth of their generation's apathy; who left their homes and their families for jobs that offered little pay and less sleep; from the not-so-young people who braved the bitter cold and scorching heat to knock on the doors of perfect strangers; from the millions of Americans who volunteered, and organized, and proved that more than two centuries later, a government of the people, by the people and for the people has not perished from this Earth. This is your victory.

I know you didn't do this just to win an election and I know you didn't do it for me. You did it because you understand the enormity of the task that lies ahead. For even as we celebrate tonight, we know the challenges that tomorrow will bring are the greatest of our lifetime—two wars, a planet in peril, the worst financial crisis in a century. Even as we stand here tonight, we know there are brave Americans waking up in the deserts of Iraq and the mountains of Afghanistan to risk their lives for us. There are mothers and fathers who will lie awake after their children fall asleep and wonder how they'll make the mortgage, or pay their doctor's bills, or save enough for college. There is new energy to harness and new jobs to be created; new schools to build and threats to meet and alliances to repair.

The road ahead will be long. Our climb will be steep. We may not get there in one year or even one term, but America—I have never been more hopeful than I am tonight that we will get there. I promise you—we as a people will get there.

There will be setbacks and false starts. There are many who won't agree with every decision or policy I make as President, and we know that government can't solve every problem. But I will always be honest with you about the challenges we face. I will listen to you, especially when we disagree. And above all, I will ask you join in the work of remaking this nation the only way it's been done in America for two-hundred and twenty-one years—block by block, brick by brick, calloused hand by calloused hand.

What began twenty-one months ago in the depths of winter must not end on this autumn night. This victory alone is not the change we seek—it is only the chance for us to make that change. And that cannot happen if we go back to the way things were. It cannot happen without you.

So let us summon a new spirit of patriotism; of service and responsibility where each of us resolves to pitch in and work harder and look after not only ourselves, but each other. Let us remember that if this financial crisis taught us anything, it's that we cannot have a thriving Wall Street while Main Street suffers—in this country, we rise or fall as one nation; as one people.

Let us resist the temptation to fall back on the same partisanship and pettiness and immaturity that has poisoned our politics for so long. Let us remember that it was a man from this state who first carried the banner of the Republican Party to the White House—a party founded on the values of self-reliance, individual liberty, and national unity. Those are values we all share, and while the Democratic Party has won a great victory tonight, we do so with a measure of humility and determination to heal the divides that have held back our progress. As Lincoln said to a nation far more divided than ours, "We are not enemies, but friends . . . though passion may have strained it must not break our bonds of affection." And to those Americans whose support I have yet to earn—I may not have won your vote, but I hear your voices, I need your help, and I will be your President too.

And to all those watching tonight from beyond our shores, from parliaments and palaces to those who are huddled around radios in the forgotten corners of our world—our stories are singular, but our destiny is shared, and a new dawn of American leadership is at hand. To those who would tear this world down—we will defeat you. To those who seek peace and security—we support you. And to all those who have wondered if America's beacon still burns as bright—tonight we proved once more that the true strength of our nation comes not from our the might of our arms or the scale of our wealth, but from the enduring power of our ideals: democracy, liberty, opportunity, and unyielding hope.

For that is the true genius of America—that America can change. Our union can be perfected. And what we have already achieved gives us hope for what we can and must achieve tomorrow.

This election had many firsts and many stories that will be told for generations. But one that's on my mind tonight is about a woman who cast her ballot in Atlanta. She's a lot like the millions of others who stood in line to make their voice heard in this election except for one thing—Ann Nixon Cooper is 106 years old.

She was born just a generation past slavery; a time when there were no cars on the road or planes in the sky; when someone like her couldn't vote for two reasons—because she was a woman and because of the color of her skin.

And tonight, I think about all that she's seen throughout her century in America—the heartache and the hope; the struggle and the progress; the times we were told that we can't, and the people who pressed on with that American creed: Yes we can.

At a time when women's voices were silenced and their hopes dismissed, she lived to see them stand up and speak out and reach for the ballot. Yes we can.

When there was despair in the dust bowl and depression across the land, she saw a nation conquer fear itself with a New Deal, new jobs and a new sense of common purpose. Yes we can.

When the bombs fell on our harbor and tyranny threatened the world, she was there to witness a generation rise to greatness and a democracy was saved. Yes we can.

She was there for the buses in Montgomery, the hoses in Birmingham, a bridge in Selma, and a preacher from Atlanta who told a people that "We Shall Overcome." Yes we can.

A man touched down on the moon, a wall came down in Berlin, a world was connected by our own science and imagination. And this year, in this election, she touched her finger to a screen, and cast her vote, because after 106 years in America, through the best of times and the darkest of hours, she knows how America can change. Yes we can.

America, we have come so far. We have seen so much. But there is so much more to do. So tonight, let us ask ourselves—if our children should live to see the next century; if my daughters should be so lucky to live as long as Ann Nixon Cooper, what change will they see? What progress will we have made?

This is our chance to answer that call. This is our moment. This is our time—to put our people back to work and open doors of opportunity for our kids; to restore prosperity and promote the cause of peace; to reclaim the American Dream and reaffirm that fundamental truth—that out of many, we are one; that while we breathe, we hope, and where we are met with cynicism, and doubt, and those who tell us that we can't, we will respond with that timeless creed that sums up the spirit of a people:

Yes We Can. Thank you, God bless you, and may God Bless the United States of America.

Source: Barack Obama: "Address in Chicago Accepting Election as the 44th President of the United States." November 4, 2008. Online by Gerhard Peters and John T.

Woolley. *The American Presidency Project.* http://www.presidency.ucsb.edu/ws /?pid=84750.

B. President Obama's Message Transmitting the 2011 *Economic Report of the President* to Congress (February 23, 2011)

The Employment Act of 1946 requires the president to submit an economic report to Congress each year. Prepared by the Council of Economic Advisors, the Economic Report of the President *is always sent to Congress within 10 days of the submission of the annual budget. Reproduced below is the message from President Barack Obama (1961–) that accompanied the 2011 report. In this message, the president notes what he deems to be the progress made by his administration in combating what he calls "the worst recession in generations."*

To the Congress of the United States:

As we begin a new year, the country is still emerging from the worst recession in generations. Across the nation, millions lost their jobs, their businesses, and their sense of security about the future. Many have had to put off their plans for a better life: going to college, buying a new home, or retiring after a long career.

At the same time, we've seen encouraging signs that the recovery is beginning to take hold. An economy that had been shrinking for a year is now growing again. After two years of job losses, our economy added more than one million private sector jobs in 2010. Yet, as we all are too well aware, the recovery is not happening fast enough. Millions of Americans—our neighbors, friends, family members—are still looking for jobs. this means that the most immediate task must be to get our fellow Americans back to work by accelerating economic growth and job creation by the private sector.

That's why, at the end of last year, I signed into law a measure to prevent taxes from rising on middle-class families and to create new incentives for businesses to create jobs. This bipartisan compromise cut payroll taxes for 155 million workers, prevented a $3,000 tax increase from going into effect on the typical working family, and extended important tax credits to help families make ends meet and send their kids to college. The law also extended unemployment insurance, preventing 7 million Americans from losing their benefits as they look for new work, and gave businesses two powerful incentives to invest and create jobs. These were 100 percent expensing of investment expenditures and an extension of the research and experimentation tax credit.

I proposed an up-front investment in building new roads, rails, and runways to upgrade our infrastructure and create new jobs. And last month, I laid out a commonsense approach to regulation that is pragmatic, based on evidence, and driven by data that will help lay the groundwork for economic growth and job creation while continuing to protect our health, safety, and environment. In addition, my Administration has moved aggressively to open markets abroad and boost exports of American goods and services.

These steps will help the economy this year. But it is also essential that we take stock and look to the future—to what kind of America we want to see emerge from this crisis and take shape for the generations of Americans to come.

We know what it takes to compete for the jobs and industries of our time. We know what we have to do to win the future. We need to out-innovate, out-educate, and out-build the rest of the world. We have to make America the best place on Earth to do business. We need to rein in deficits after a decade of rising debt, and reform our government. This is the way to robust and widely shared prosperity.

The first step in winning the future is encouraging American innovation. That is ultimately driven by free enterprise. But public support also plays an essential role in encouraging innovative research and development. It holds incredible promise for our future. That is why, throughout history our government has provided cutting-edge scientists and inventors with the support that they need. This is what planted the seeds for the Internet. This is what helped make possible breakthroughs like computer chips and GPS.

Two years ago, I set a goal for America: that we needed to reach a level of research and development we haven't seen since the height of the Space Race. And this year, my budget helps us meet that goal. We'll invest in biomedical research, information technology, and especially clean energy technology—an investment that will strengthen our security, protect our planet, and create countless new jobs for our people.

We've begun to reinvent our energy policy. We're telling America's scientists and engineers that if they assemble teams of the best minds in their fields, and focus on the hardest problems in clean energy, we'll fund the Apollo Projects of our time. We're doing this through investments in innovation hubs across America. These are teams of scientists focused on one difficult problem. We're also supporting the Advanced Research Projects Agency for Energy, modeled on a successful defense agency that has developed cutting-edge technologies for decades.

In addition, clean energy breakthroughs will only translate into clean energy jobs if businesses know there will be a market for what they're selling. So in my State of the Union, I called on Congress to join me in setting a new goal: by 2035, 80 percent of America's electricity will come from clean energy sources.

The second part of our strategy is education. Over the next ten years, nearly half of all new jobs will require education that goes beyond a high school degree. And yet, as many as a quarter of our students aren't even finishing high school. The quality of our math and science education lags behind many other nations. And so the question is whether all of us—as citizens, and as parents—are willing to do what's necessary to give every child a chance to succeed.

Of course, our schools share this responsibility. When a child walks into a classroom, it should be a place of high expectations and high performance. Yet too many schools in our country don't meet this threshold test. That's why we launched a competition called Race to the top. Race to the top is the most meaningful reform of our public schools in a generation. For less than one percent of what we spend on education each year, it has led over 40 states to raise their standards for teaching and learning.

Next, because an increasing number of jobs require more than a high school diploma, higher education must be within reach of every American. So we've ended the taxpayer subsidies that went to banks to act as a middleman in the student loan process, and used the savings to make college affordable for millions of students. And this year, we will work to make permanent our tuition tax credit—worth $10,000 for four years of college. We are also revitalizing America's community colleges, which will help us reach the goal I set two years ago: by the end of the decade, America will once again have the highest proportion of college graduates in the world.

The third step in winning the future is rebuilding America. To attract new businesses to our shores, we need the fastest, most reliable ways to move people, goods, and information—from high-speed rail to high-speed internet. That is why, over the last two years, we have begun rebuilding for the 21st century, a project that has meant thousands of good jobs for the hard-hit construction industry.

We will put more Americans to work repairing crumbling roads and bridges. We will make sure this is fully paid for, attract private investment, and pick projects based on what's best for the economy, not politicians. Within 25 years, our goal is to give 80 percent of Americans access to highspeed rail, which could allow you to go places in half the time it takes to travel by car. Routes in California and the Midwest are already underway. And within the next five years, we will also make it possible for business to deploy the next generation of high-speed wireless coverage to 98 percent of all Americans.

All these investments—in innovation, education, and infrastructure—will make America a better place to do business and create jobs. But to help our companies compete, we also have to knock down barriers that stand in the way of their success.

To help businesses sell more products abroad, we set a goal of doubling our exports by 2014. My Administration has worked to knock down barriers our exporters face and advocated for U.S. exporters abroad—resulting in signing important deals to sell more American goods and services to China and India. And in December, we finalized a trade agreement with South Korea that will support at least 70,000 American jobs. This agreement has unprecedented support from business and labor, Democrats and Republicans, and I've asked Congress to pass it as soon as possible. Finally, we are also pursuing agreements with Panama and Colombia, and continuing our Asia Pacific and global trade talks.

To reduce barriers to growth and investment, I've ordered a review of government regulations. When we find rules that put an unnecessary burden on businesses, we will fix them. But I will not hesitate to create or enforce commonsense safeguards to protect the American people. That's what we've done in this country for more than a century, from child labor laws to protections for our air and water. It's why last year, we put in place consumer protections against hidden fees and penalties by credit card companies, and new rules to prevent another financial crisis. And it's why we passed reform that finally prevents the health insurance industry from exploiting patients.

The final step in winning the future is to make sure we aren't buried under a mountain of debt. We are living with a legacy of deficit-spending that began almost a decade ago. And in the wake of the financial crisis, some of that was necessary to keep credit flowing, save jobs, and put money in people's pockets.

That is why in my Budget, I've proposed that government live within its means while investing in the future. I have promised to veto any bill that contains earmarks. I've proposed freezing annual domestic spending for the next five years. This would reduce the deficit by more than $400 billion over the next decade, and will bring discretionary spending to the lowest share of our economy since Dwight Eisenhower was President.

Yet, at the same time, we cannot solve our fiscal problems on the backs of our most vulnerable citizens. And it would also be a mistake to cut the deficit by gutting our investments in innovation and education, which are so critical for our future prosperity. The fact is, priorities like education, innovation, and infrastructure have traditionally commanded bipartisan support. There are no inherent ideological differences that should prevent Democrats and Republicans from improving our economy. We are all Americans, and we are all in this race together—we can focus on what is necessary for America to win the future.

For as difficult as the times may be, the good news is that we know what the future could look like for the United States. We can see it in the classrooms that are experimenting with groundbreaking reforms, and giving children new math and science skills at an early age. We can see it in the wind farms, solar plants, and advanced battery plants that are opening across America. We can see it in the laboratories and research facilities all over this country that are churning out discoveries and turning them into new start-ups and new jobs.

Our job is simply to harness the potential that exists all across this country, and this economic report lays out the policies that will help our nation succeed by doing exactly that. In the subsequent chapters, we will look at the progress that has been made over the past year. In addition, this report will lay out many of the policies that will foster growth and make our economy more competitive. That is our great challenge today. And I am absolutely confident it is one we will meet.

BARACK OBAMA

Source: Barack Obama: "Message to Congress Transmitting the Economic Report of the President." February 23, 2011. Online by Gerhard Peters and John T. Woolley. *The American Presidency Project.* http://www.presidency.ucsb.edu/ws/?pid=99367.

C. President Obama's Message Transmitting the 2012 *Economic Report of the President* to Congress (February 17, 2012)

Below is President Barack Obama's (1961–) message accompanying the 2012 Economic Report of the President, *a summary of the economic state of the country that, by law, must be submitted to Congress each year. In this message, President Obama describes the measures taken since he entered office in January 2009 to lift the U.S. economy out of the Great Recession and his plans for sustaining economic recovery in the future.*

To the Congress of the United States:

One of the fundamental tenets of the American economy has been that if you work hard, you can do well enough to raise a family, own a home, send your kids to college, and put a little money away for retirement. That's the promise of America.

The defining issue of our time is how to keep that promise alive. We can either settle for a country where a shrinking number of people do very well while a growing number of Americans barely get by, or we can restore an economy where everyone gets a fair shot, everyone does their fair share, and everyone plays by the same set of rules.

Long before the recession that began in December 2007, job growth was insufficient for our growing population. Manufacturing jobs were leaving our shores. Technology made businesses more efficient, but also made some jobs obsolete. The few at the top saw their incomes rise like never before, but most hardworking Americans struggled with costs that were growing, paychecks that were not, and personal debt that kept piling up.

In 2008, the house of cards collapsed. We learned that mortgages had been sold to people who could not afford them or did not understand them. Banks had made huge bets and doled out big bonuses with other people's money. Regulators had looked the other way, or did not have the authority to stop the bad behavior. It was wrong. It was irresponsible. And it plunged our economy into a crisis that put millions out of work, saddled us with more debt, and left innocent, hardworking Americans holding the bag.

In the year before I took office, we lost nearly 5 million private sector jobs. And we lost almost another 4 million before our policies were in full effect.

Those are the facts. But so are these: In the last 23 months, businesses have created 3.7 million jobs. Last year, they created the most jobs since 2005. American manufacturers are hiring again, creating jobs for the first time since the late 1990s. And we have put in place new rules to hold Wall Street accountable, so a crisis like this never happens again.

Some, however, still advocate going back to the same economic policies that stacked the deck against middle-class Americans for way too many years. And their philosophy is simple: We are better off when everybody is left to fend for themselves and play by their own rules.

That philosophy is wrong. The more Americans who succeed, the more America succeeds. These are not Democratic values or Republican values. They are American values. And we have to reclaim them.

This is a make-or-break moment for the middle class, and for all those who are working to get into the middle class. It is a moment when we can go back to the ways of the past—to growing deficits, stagnant incomes and job growth, declining opportunity, and rising inequality—or we can make a break from the past. We can build an economy by restoring our greatest strengths: American manufacturing, American energy, skills for American workers, and a renewal of American values—an economy built to last.

When it comes to the deficit, we have already agreed to more than $2 trillion in cuts and savings. But we need to do more, and that means making choices. Right now, we are poised to spend nearly $1 trillion more on what was supposed to be a temporary tax break for the wealthiest 2 percent of Americans. Right now, because of loopholes and shelters in the tax code, a quarter of all millionaires pay lower tax rates than millions of middle-class households. I believe that tax reform should follow the Buffett Rule. If you make more than $1 million a year, you should not pay less than 30 percent in taxes. In fact, if you are earning a million dollars a year, you should not get special tax subsidies or deductions. On the other hand, if you make under $250,000 a year, like 98 percent of American families do, your taxes should not go up.

Americans know that this generation's success is only possible because past generations felt a responsibility to each other, and to the future of their country. Now it is our turn. Now it falls to us to live up to that same sense of shared responsibility.

This year's *Economic Report of the President*, prepared by the Council of Economic Advisers, describes the emergency rescue measures taken to end the recession and support the ongoing recovery, and lays out a blueprint for an economy built to last. It explains how we are restoring our strengths as a Nation—our innovative economy, our strong manufacturing base, and our workers—by investing in the technologies of the future, in companies that create jobs here in America, and in education and training programs that will prepare our workers for the jobs of tomorrow. We must ensure that these investments benefit everyone and increase opportunity for all Americans or we risk threatening one of the features that defines us as a Nation—that America is a country in which anyone can do well, regardless of how they start out.

No one built this country on their own. This Nation is great because we built it together. If we remember that truth today, join together in common purpose, and maintain our common resolve, then I am as confident as ever that our economic future is hopeful and strong.

BARACK OBAMA

Source: Barack Obama: "Message to Congress Transmitting the Economic Report of the President." February 17, 2012. Online by Gerhard Peters and John T. Woolley. *The American Presidency Project.* http://www.presidency.ucsb.edu/ws/index.php?pid=99711.

SELECTED BIBLIOGRAPHY

Brands. H. W. *Masters of Enterprise: Giants of American Business from John Jacob Astor and J.P. Morgan to Bill Gates and Oprah Winfrey.* New York: The Free Press, 1999.

Lind, Michael. *Land of Promise: An Economic History of the United States.* New York: HarperCollins, 2012.

Livesay, Harold C. *American Made: Shapers of the American Economy.* 2nd ed. New York: Pearson, Longman, 2007.

Malsberger, John W., and James N. Marshall, eds. *The American Economic History Reader: Documents and Readings.* New York and London: Routledge, 2009.

Nelson, Scott Reynolds. *A Nation of Deadbeats: An Uncommon History of America's Financial Disasters.* New York: Knopf, 2012.

Seavoy, Ronald E. *An Economic History of the United States: From 1607 to the Present.* New York: Routledge, 2006.

Sobel, Robert. *Panic on Wall Street: A Classic History of America's Financial Disasters. With a New Exploration of the Crash of 1987.* New York: Truman Talley/E.P. Dutton, 1988 (1984).

The Critical Period, 1783–1789

Barrow, Clyde W. *More Than a Historian: The Political and Economic Thought of Charles A. Beard.* New Brunswick, NJ: Transaction Books, 2000.

Beeman, Richard R., Stephen Botein, and Edward C. Carter, eds. *Beyond Confederation: Origins of the Constitution and American National Identity.* Chapel Hill: University of North Carolina Press, 1987.

Boyd, Thomas. *Poor John Fitch: Inventor of the Steamboat.* Freeport, NY: Books for Libraries Press, 1971 (1935).

Brunhouse, Robert L. *The Counter-Revolution in Pennsylvania, 1776–1790.* New York: Octagon Books, 1971 (1942).

Carpenter, Francis Ross. *The Old China Trade: Americans in Canton, 1764–1843*. New York: Coward, McCann, & Geoghegan, 1976.

Dowd, Gregory Evans. *A Spirited Resistance: The North American Indian Struggle for Unity, 1745–1815*. Baltimore: Johns Hopkins University Press, 1989.

Dulles, Foster Rhea. *The Old China Trade*. New York: AMS Press, 1970 (1930).

Hofstadter, Richard. *The Progressive Historians: Turner, Beard, Parrington*. New York: Knopf, 1958.

Holton, Woody. *Unruly Americans and the Origin of the Constitution*. New York: Hill & Wang, 2007.

Jensen, Merrill. *The Articles of Confederation: An Interpretation of the Social-Constitutional History of the American Revolution, 1774–1781*. Madison: University of Wisconsin Press, 1970 (1940).

Jensen, Merrill. *The New Nation: A History of the United States during the Confederation, 1781–1789*. New York: Knopf, 1950.

Kulikoff, Allan. *Tobacco and Slaves: The Development of Southern Cultures in the Chesapeake, 1680–1800*. Chapel Hill: University of North Carolina Press, 1986.

Matson, Cathy, and Peter S. Onuf. *A Union of Interests: Political and Economic Thought in Revolutionary America*. Lawrence: University Press of Kansas, 1990.

McDonald, Forrest. *We the People: The Economic Origins of the Constitution*. Chicago: University of Chicago Press, 1958.

Menard, Russell R. "The Tobacco Industry in the Chesapeake Colonies, 1617–1730." *Research in Economic History* 5 (1980): 109–77.

Morris, Richard B. *The Forging of the Union, 1781–1789*. New York: Harper & Row, 1987.

Nettels, Curtis P. *The Emergence of a National Economy*. New York: Harper Torchbooks, 1969 (1962).

Nuxoll, Elizabeth. "The Bank of North America and Robert Morris's Management of the Nation's First Fiscal Crisis." *Business and Economic History*, 2nd Series, 13 (1984): 159–70.

Onuf, Peter. *Statehood and Union: A History of the Northwest Ordinance*. Bloomington: University of Indiana Press, 1987.

"A Pictorial History of Flatboats on the Western Rivers." *Steamboat Times* (2007); http://steamboattimes.com/flatboats.html.

Prager, Frank D., ed. *The Autobiography of John Fitch*. Philadelphia: American Philosophical Society, 1976.

Price, Jacob M. *France and the Chesapeake: A History of the French Tobacco Monopoly 1674–1791, and Its Relationship to the British and American Trades*. 2 vols. Ann Arbor: University of Michigan Press, 1973.

Rappleye, Charles. *Robert Morris: Financier of the American Revolution.* New York: Simon & Schuster, 2010.

Richards, Leonard L. *Shays's Rebellion: The American Revolution's Final Battle.* Philadelphia: University of Pennsylvania Press, 2002.

Slauter, Eric. *The State as a Work of Art: The Cultural Origins of the Constitution.* Chicago: University of Chicago Press, 2009.

Starkey, Marion. *A Little Rebellion.* New York: Knopf, 1955.

Waldstreicher, David. *Slavery's Constitution: From Revolution to Ratification.* New York: Hill & Wang, 2009.

Williams, Frederick, ed. *The Northwest Ordinance: Essays on Its Formulation, Provisions, and Legacy.* East Lansing: Michigan State University Press, 1989.

Wood, Gordon S. *The Creation of the American Republic, 1776–1787.* Chapel Hill: University of North Carolina Press, 1969.

The Embargo Era, 1807–1809

Adams, Henry. *History of the United States during the Administrations of Thomas Jefferson.* New York: Library of America, 1986 (1889–1890).

Adams, Henry. *The Life of Albert Gallatin.* Philadelphia: J.B. Lippincott & Co., 1879.

DiFilippo, Thomas J. *Stephen Girard: The Man, His College and Estate.* 2nd ed. 1999; http://www.girardweb.com/girard/bookcover.htm.

Dolin, Eric Jay. *Fur, Fortune, and Empire: The Epic History of the Fur Trade in America.* New York: Norton, 2010.

Dungan, Nicholas. *Gallatin: America's Swiss Founding Father.* New York: New York University Press, 2010.

Egan, Clifford. *Neither Peace nor War: Franco-American Relations. 1803–1812.* Baton Rouge: Louisiana State University Press, 1983.

Frankel, Jeffrey A. "The 1807–1809 Embargo against Great Britain." *Journal of Economic History* 42 (1982): 291–308.

Green, Constance M. *Eli Whitney and the Birth of American Technology.* New York: Longman, 1997.

Harris, C. M. "Fulton, Robert." *American National Biography Online*, February 2000.

Holmberg, Tom. "The Acts, Order in Council, &c. of Great Britain (on Trade), 1793–1812." http://www.napoleon-series.org/research'government/british /decrees/.

Levy. Leonard. *Jefferson and Civil Liberties: The Darker Side.* Chicago: Ivan R. Dee, 1989 (1963).

Lomask, Milton. *Aaron Burr: The Conspiracy and Years of Exile, 1898–1836.* New York: Farrar, Straus, and Giroux, 1982.

Madsen, Axel. *John Jacob Astor: America's First Multimillionaire.* New York: Wiley, 2001.

Malone, Dumas. *Jefferson the President: Second Term. 1805–1809.* Charlottesville: University of Virginia Press, 2005.

Mannix, Richard. "Gallatin, Jefferson, and the Embargo of 1808." *Diplomatic History* 3 (1979): 151–72.

Markham, Jerry. *A Financial History of the United States.* Armonk, NY: M.E. Sharpe, 2001.

Philip, Cynthia Owen. *Robert Fulton: A Biography.* New York: Franklin Watts, 1985.

Phillips, Paul C. *The Fur Trade.* With concluding chapters by J. W. Smurr. 2 vols. Norman: University of Oklahoma Press, 1961.

Steward, David O. *American Emperor: Aaron Burr's Challenge to Jefferson's America.* New York: Simon & Schuster, 2011.

Strum, Harvey. "Rhode Island and the Embargo of 1897." *Rhode Island History* 52 (1994): 58–67.

Tucker, Spencer C., and Frank T. Reuter. *Injured Honor: The Chesapeake-Leopard Affair, June 22, 1807.* Annapolis, MD: U.S. Naval Institute Press, 1996.

Wilson, George. *Stephen Girard: America's First Tycoon.* Conshohocken, PA: Combined Books, 1995.

Wood, Gordon S. *Empire of Liberty: A History of the Early Republic.* New York: Oxford University Press, 2009.

Panic of 1819

Baxter, Maurice J. *Henry Clay and the American System.* Lexington: University Press of Kentucky, 1995.

Beerman, Kenton. "The Beginning of a Revolution: Waltham and the Boston Manufacturing Company." *The Concord Review* 5 (Summer 1994): 141–57.

Blackson, Robert M. "Pennsylvania Banks and the Panic of 1819: A Reinterpretation." *Journal of the Early Republic* 9 (1989): 335–58.

Cornog, Evan. *The Birth of Empire: DeWitt Clinton and the American Experience, 1769–1828.* New York: Oxford University Press, 2000.

Dupre, Daniel S. "The Panic of 1819 and the Political Economy of Sectionalism." In Cathy Matson, ed., *The Economy of Early America: Historical Perspectives and New Directions.* University Park: Pennsylvania State University Press, 2006.

Green, James N. *Mathew Carey: Publisher and Patriot.* Philadelphia: Library Company of Philadelphia, 1985.

Haeger, John Denis. *John Jacob Astor: Business and Finance in the Early Republic.* Detroit: Wayne State University Press, 1991.

Haulman, Clyde A. *Virginia and the Panic of 1819: The First Great Depression and the Commonwealth*. London: Pickering & Chatto, 2008.

Heidler, David S., and Jeanne T. Heidler. *Henry Clay: The Essential American*. New York: Random House, 2010.

Killenbeck, Mark R. M'Culloch v. Maryland: *Securing a Nation*. Lawrence: University Press of Kansas, 2006.

Koeppel, Gerard. *Bond of Union: Building the Erie Canal and the American Empire*. Cambridge, MA: Da Capo Press, 2009.

Larson, John Loritz. *Internal Improvements: National Public Works and the Promise of Popular Government in the Early United States*. Chapel Hill: The University of North Carolina Press, 2001.

"The National Road." *History Magazine* 1, no. 1 (1999); http://www.history -magazine.com/natroad.html.

Perkins, Edwin J. "Langdon Cheves and the Panic of 1819: A Reassessment." *The Journal of Economic History* 44 (1984): 455–61.

Raitz, Karl B., ed. *The National Road*. Baltimore: Johns Hopkins University Press, 1996.

Remini, Robert. *Andrew Jackson and the Bank War*. New York: Norton, 1967.

Rosenberg, Chaim M. *The Life and Times of Francis Cabot Lowell, 1775–1817*. Lanham, MD: Lexington Books, 2011.

Rothbard, Murray M. *The Panic of 1819: Reactions and Policies*. New York: Columbia University Press, 1962.

Sellers, Charles. *The Market Revolution: Jacksonian America 1815–1846*. New York: Oxford University Press, 1991.

Shaw, Ronald. *Erie Water West: A History of the Erie Canal, 1792–1854*. Lexington: University Press of Kentucky, 1990.

Panic of 1837

Broehl, Wayne G., Jr. *John Deere's Company: A History of Deere and Company and Its Times*. New York: Doubleday, 1984.

Byrdsall, Fitzwilliam. *The History of the Loco-foco or Equal Rights Party, Its Movements, Conventions, and Proceedings, with Short Characteristic Sketches of Its Prominent Men*. Cranbury, NJ: Scholars Bookshelf, 2007 (1842).

Dahlstrom, Neil, and Jeremy Dahlstrom. *The John Deere Story: A Biography of Plowmakers John & Charles Deere*. DeKalb: Northern Illinois University Press, 2005.

Davis, William C. *Lone Star Rising: The Revolutionary Birth of the Texas Republic*. New York: Free Press, 2004.

Delano, Sterling F. *Brook Farm: The Dark Side of Utopia*. Cambridge, MA: The Belknap Press, 2004.

Dillon, Merton. *Elijah P. Lovejoy: Abolitionist Editor.* Urbana: University of Illinois Press, 1961.

"Elijah Parish Lovejoy, 1802-1837"; http://www.state.il.us/hpa/lovejoy/bio.htm.

Eno, Arthur L., ed. *Cotton Was King: A History of Lowell, Massachusetts.* Somersworth, NH: New Hampshire Publishing Company, 1976.

Holt, Michael F. *The Rise and Fall of the American Whig Party: Jacksonian Politics and the Onset of the Civil War.* New York: Oxford University Press, 1999.

Jenkins, Jeffrey A., and Charles Stewart III. "The Gag Rule, Congressional Politics, and the Growth of Anti-Slavery Popular Politics." July 10, 2003; http://th.myweb.uga.edu/gagrule.pdf.

Kim, Namsuk, and John Joseph Wallis. "The Market for American State Government Bonds in Britain and the United States, 1830–43." *The Economic History Review,* new series, 58 (2005): 736–64.

Mihm, Steven. *A Nation of Counterfeiters: Capitalism, Con Men, and the Making of the United States.* Cambridge, MA: Harvard University Press, 2007.

Miller, William Lee. *Arguing about Slavery: The Great Battle in the United States Congress.* New York: Knopf, 1996.

"Mill Life in Lowell"; http://library.uml.edu/clh/mo.htm.

Myerson, Joel, ed. *The Brook Farm Book: A Collection of First-Hand Accounts of the Community.* New York: Garland, 1987.

Remini, Robert V. *Andrew Jackson and the Bank War.* New York: Norton, 1967.

Reynolds, David. *Waking Giant: America in the Age of Jackson.* New York: Harper Collins, 2008.

Rousseau, Peter L. "Jacksonian Monetary Policy, Specie Flow, and the Panic of 1837." *The Journal of Economic History* 62 (June 2002): 457–88.

Simon, Paul. *Freedom's Champion: Elijah Lovejoy.* Carbondale: Southern Illinois University Press, 1994.

Stevens, Kenneth R. *Border Diplomacy: The* Caroline *and McLeod Affairs in Anglo-American-Canadian Relations, 1837–1842.* Tuscaloosa: University of Alabama Press, 1989

Taylor, George Rogers. *The Transportation Revolution 1815–1860.* New York: Harper Torchbooks, 1968 (1951).

Panic of 1857

Brice, William R. *Myth, Legend, Reality: Edward Laurentine Drake and the Early Oil Industry.* Oil City, PA: Oil Region Alliance of Business, Industry, and Tourism, 2009.

Calomiris, Charles W., and Larry Schweikart. "The Panic of 1857: Origins, Transmission, and Containment." *Journal of Economic History* 51 (1991): 807–34.

Carr, Albert Z. *The World and William Walker*. Westport, CT: Greenwood Press, 1975 (1963).

Cutler, Carl C. *Greyhounds of the Sea: The Story of the American Clipper Ship*. 3rd ed. Annapolis, MD: Naval Institute Press, 1984 (1930).

Dando-Collins, Stephen. *Tycoon's War: How Cornelius Vanderbilt Invaded a Country to Overthrow America's Most Famous Military Adventurer*. Cambridge, MA: Da Capo Press, 2010.

Dawley, Alan. *Class and Community: The Industrial Revolution in Lynn*. 25th anniversary edition. Cambridge, MA: Harvard University Press, 2000 (1975).

DeBow's Review. Full text, 1846–1869. Making of America website. http://quod .lib.umich.edu/m/moajrnl/browse.journals/debo.hyml.

Earle, Jonathan H. *Jacksonian Antislavery and the Politics of Free Soil, 1824–1854*. Chapel Hill: University of North Carolina Press, 2003.

Etcheson, Nicola. *Bleeding Kansas: Contested Liberty in the Civil War Era*. Lawrence: University Press of Kansas, 2004.

Faler, Paul. *Mechanics and Manufacturers in the Early Industrial Revolution: Lynn, Massachusetts—1780–1860*. Albany: State University Press of New York, 1981.

Fehrenbacher, Don E. *Slavery, Law, & Politics: The Dred Scott Case in Historical Perspective*. New York: Oxford University Press, 1981.

Finkelman, Paul. Dred Scott v. Sandford: *A Brief History with Documents*. Boston: Bedford Books, 1997.

Foner, Eric. *Free Soil, Free Labor, Free Men: The Ideology of the Republican Party before the Civil War*. With a new introductory essay. New York: Oxford University Press, 1995 (1970).

Helper, Hinton Rowan. *The Impending Crisis*. 1857 version. http://docsouth .unc.edu/nc/helper/helper.html.

Huston, James L. *The Panic of 1857 and the Coming of the Civil War*. Baton Rouge: Louisiana State University Press, 1987.

Stampp, Kenneth M. *America in 1857: A Nation at the Brink*. New York: Oxford University Press, 1990.

Standard, Diffee W. "*De Bow's Review*, 1846–1880: A Magazine of Southern Opinion." Unpublished PhD dissertation, University of North Carolina, 1970.

Panic of 1873

Barreyre, Nicolas. "The Politics of Economic Crises: The Panic of 1873, the End of Reconstruction, and the Realignment of Politics." *Journal of the Gilded Age and Progressive Era* 10 (2011): 403–23.

Beth, Loren. "The Slaughter-House Cases Revisited." *Louisiana Law Review* 12 (1963): 587–605.

Brands, H. W. *American Colossus: The Triumph of Capitalism, 1865–1900.* New York: Doubleday, 2010.

Broehl, Wayne G. *The Molly Maguires.* Cambridge, MA: Harvard University Press, 1964.

Bruce, Robert. *1877: Year of Violence.* Indianapolis: Bobbs-Merrill, 1959.

Chernow, Ron. *Titan: The Life of John D. Rockefeller, Sr.* New York: Random House, 1998.

Foner, Philip S. *The Great Labor Uprising of 1877.* New York: Monad Press, 1977.

Friedman, Milton. "The Crime of 1873." *Journal of Political Economy* 98 (1990): 1159–94.

Gross, Linda P., and Theresa R. Snyder. *Philadelphia's 1876 Centennial Exhibition.* Charleston, SC: Acadia Publishing Company, 2005.

Kenny, Kevin. *Making Sense of the Molly Maguires.* New York: Oxford University Press, 1998.

Kirkland, Edward Chase. *Industry Comes of Age: Business, Labor, and Public Policy, 1860—1897.* New York: Harper Torchbooks, 1967 (1961).

Larson, Henrietta. *Jay Cooke: Private Banker.* New York: Greenwood Press, 1968 (1936).

Lubetkin, M. John. *Jay Cooke's Gamble: The Northern Pacific Railroad, the Sioux, and the Panic of 1873.* Norman: University of Oklahoma Press, 2006.

Polakoff, Keith Ian. *The Politics of Inertia: The Election of 1876 and the End of Reconstruction.* Baton Rouge: Louisiana State University Press, 1973.

Post, Robert C. Post, ed. *1876: A Centennial Exhibition.* Washington, D.C.: The National Museum of History and Technology, Smithsonian Institution, 1976.

Rives, Timothy. "Grant, Babcock, and the Whiskey Ring." *Prologue* 3 (Fall 2000): 143–53.

Robinson, Lloyd (Robert Silverberg). *The Stolen Election: Hayes vs. Tilden, 1876.* New York: Tom Doherty Associates, 2001 (1968).

Ross, Michael. "Justice Miller's Reconstruction: The Slaughter-House Cases, Health Codes, and Civil Rights in New Orleans, 1861–1873." *Journal of Southern History* 64 (1998): 649–76.

White, Richard. *Railroaded: The Transcontinentals and the Making of Modern America.* New York: Norton, 2011.

Woodward, C. Vann. *Reunion and Reaction: The Compromise of 1877 and the End of Reconstruction.* Boston: Little, Brown, 1966.

Depression of the 1890s

Bannister, Robert. *Social Darwinism: Science and Myth in Anglo-American Social Thought.* Philadelphia: Temple University Press, 1979.

Bensel, Richard Franklin. *Passion and Preferences: William Jennings Bryan and the 1896 Democratic National Convention.* Cambridge: Cambridge University Press, 2008.

Bensel, Richard Franklin. *The Political Economy of American Industrialization, 1877–1900.* Cambridge: Cambridge University Press, 2000.

Brook, Thomas. Plessy v. Ferguson: *A Brief History with Documents.* Boston: Bedford Press, 1997.

Bryan, William Jennings. *The First Battle: Story of the Campaign of 1896, Together with a Collection of His Speeches and a Biographical Sketch by His Wife.* Whitefish, MT: Kessinger Publishing Company, 2005 (1896).

Clanton, Gene. *Congressional Populism and the Crisis of the 1890s.* Lawrence: University Press of Kansas, 1998.

Clanton, Gene. *Populism: The Humane Preference in America, 1890–1900.* Boston: Twayne Publishers, 1991.

Degler, Carl. *In Search of Human Nature: The Decline and Revival of Darwinism in American Social Thought.* New York: Oxford University Press, 1991.

Digby-Junger, Richard. *The Journalist as Reformer: Henry Demarest Lloyd and Wealth against Commonwealth.* Westport, CT: Greenwood Press, 1996.

Eggert, Gerald G. *Richard Olney: Evolution of a Statesman.* University Park: Pennsylvania State University Press, 1974.

Goodwyn, Lawrence. *Democratic Promise: The Populist Movement in America.* New York: Oxford University Press, 1976.

Graff, Henry F. *Grover Cleveland.* New York: Times Books, 2002.

Hicks, John D. *The Populist Revolt: A History of the Farmers Alliances and the Populist Party.* Minneapolis: University of Minnesota Press, 1955 (1931).

Hofer, William James Hull. Plessy v. Ferguson: *Race and Inequality in Jim Crow America.* Lawrence: University Press of Kansas, 2012.

Hoffman, Charles. *The Depression of the Nineties: An Economic History.* Westport, CT: Greenwood Press, 1970.

Jernigan, E. Jay. *Henry Demarest Lloyd.* Boston: Twayne, 1976.

Kazin, Michael. *The Populist Persuasion: An American History.* New York: Basic Books, 1995.

Krause, Paul. *The Battle for Homestead, 1880–1892.* Pittsburgh: University of Pittsburgh Press, 1992.

McMurry, Donald L. *Coxey's Army: A Study of the Industrial Army Movement of 1894.* Seattle: University of Washington Press, 1968 (1929).

Medley, Keith Weldon. *We as Freemen:* Plessy v. Ferguson. Gretna, LA: Pelican Publishing Company, 2003.

Salvatore, Nick. *Eugene V. Debs: Citizen and Socialist.* 2nd ed. Urbana: University of Illinois Press, 2007 (1982).

Sanger, Martha Frick Symington. *Henry Clay Frick: An Intimate Portrait.* New York: Abbeville Press, 1996.

Schreiner, Samuel A., Jr. *Henry Clay Frick: The Gospel of Greed.* New York: St. Martin's Press, 1995.

Schwantes, Carlos A. *Coxey's Army: An American Odyssey.* Lincoln: University of Nebraska Press, 1985.

Standisford, Les. *Meet You in Hell: Andrew Carnegie, Henry Clay Frick, and the Bitter Partnership that Transformed America.* New York: Crown Publishers, 2005.

White, Richard. *Railroaded: The Transcontinentals and the Making of Modern America.* New York: Norton, 2011.

Wolff, Leon. *Lockout: The Story of the Homestead Strike of 1892—A Study of Violence, Unionism, and the Carnegie Steel Empire.* New York: Harper & Row, 1965.

Panic of 1907

Bruner, Robert F., and Sean D. Carr. *The Panic of 1907: Lessons Learned from the Market's Perfect Storm.* Hoboken, NJ: Wiley, 2007.

Chernow, Ron. *The House of Morgan: An American Banking Dynasty and the Rise of Modern Finance.* New York: Simon & Schuster, 1991.

Chernow, Ron. *Titan: The Life of John D. Rockefeller, Sr.* 2nd ed. New York: Vintage, 2004.

Daniels, Roger. *Asian America: Chinese and Japanese in America since 1850.* Seattle: University of Washington Press, 1988.

Dubofsky, Melvin. *"Big Bill" Haywood.* Manchester, UK: University of Manchester Press, 1987.

Ernst, Daniel R. *Lawyers against Labor: From Individual Rights to Corporate Liberalism.* Urbana: University of Illinois Press, 1995.

Friedman, Milton, and Anna Jacobson Schwartz. *A Monetary History of the United States, 1867–1960.* Princeton, NJ: Princeton University Press, 1971 (1963).

Garraty, John A. *Right-Hand Man: The Life of George W. Perkins.* Westport, CT: Greenwood Press, 1973 (1960).

Harbaugh, William H. *Power and Responsibility: The Life and Times of Theodore Roosevelt.* Newtown, CT: American Political Biography Press, 2002 (1961).

Lukas, J. Anthony. *Big Trouble: A Murder in a Small Western Town Sets Off a Struggle for the Soul of America.* New York: Simon & Schuster, 1997.

Merrit, Walter Gordo. "The Law of the Danbury Hatters' Case." *Annals of the American Academy of Political and Social Science* 36, no. 2 (September 1910); http://www.jstor.org./stable/1011702.

Minus, Paul. *Walter Rauschenbusch, American Reformer*. New York: Macmillan, 1988.

Moen, Jon, and Ellis W. Tallman. "The Bank Panic of 1907: The Role of Trust Companies." *Journal of Economic History* 52 (1992): 611–30.

Morris, Edmund. *Theodore Rex, 1901–1909*. New York: Harper Collins, 2002.

Reckner, James R. *Teddy Roosevelt's Great White Fleet*. Annapolis, MD: Naval Institute Press, 1988.

Rockoff, Hugh. "Banking and Finance, 1789–1914." In Stanley I. Engerman and Robert E. Gallman, eds. *The Long Nineteenth Century*. Cambridge: Cambridge University Press, 2000.

Strouse, Jean. *J. P. Morgan: American Financier*. New York: Random House, 1999.

Tarbell, Ida M. *History of the Standard Oil Company*. 2 vols. New York: Cosimo Classics, 2009 (1904).

Wicker, Elmus. *The Great Debate on Banking Reform: Nelson Aldrich and the Origins of the Fed*. Columbus: Ohio State University Press, 2005.

Wimmel, Kenneth. *Theodore Roosevelt and the Great White Fleet: American Sea Power*. Oxford: Brassey's Inc., 1998.

Woloch, Nancy. Muller v. Oregon: *A Brief History with Documents*. Boston: Bedford Books of St. Martin's Press, 1996.

Economic Downturn of 1913–1914

Brands, H. W. *Woodrow Wilson*. New York: Times Books, 2003.

Chace, James. *1912: Wilson, Roosevelt, Taft, and Debs—The Election that Changed the Country*. New York: Simon & Schuster, 2004.

Cooper, John Milton. *Woodrow Wilson: A Biography*. New York: Knopf, 2009.

Dubofsky, Melvin. *We Shall Be All*. 2nd ed. Urbana: University of Illinois Press, 1988.

Ekirch, Arthur A., Jr. "The Sixteenth Amendment: The Historical Background." *Cato Journal* (Spring, 1981); http://www.cato.org/cato-journal/spring-1981 [accessed August 8, 2013].

Faulkner, Harold U. *The Decline of Laissez Faire 1897–1917*. New York: Harper Torchbooks, 1968 (1951).

Glass, Carter. *An Adventure in Constructive Finance*. Garden City, NY: Arno Press, 1975 (1927).

Gongol, Brian. "The Clayton Anti-Trust Act." http://www.gongol.com/research/economics/claytonact/.

Gould, Lewis. *Four Hats in the Ring: The 1912 Election and the Birth of Modern Politics*. Lawrence: University Press of Kansas, 2008.

Hofstadter, Richard. *The Age of Reform: From Bryan to FDR*. New York: Vintage, 1955.

Hofstadter, Richard, ed. *The Progressive Movement, 1900–1915.* New York: Simon & Schuster, 1963.

Kolko, Gabriel. *The Triumph of Conservatism: A Re-interpretation of American History, 1900–1916.* New York: Free Press of Glencoe, 1963.

Kornbluh, Joyce, ed. *Rebel Voices: An IWW Anthology.* Expanded ed. Oakland, CA: PM Press, 2011.

Meltzer, Allan H. *A History of the Federal Reserve System. Vol. 1: 1913–1951.* Chicago: University of Chicago Press, 2003.

Milkis, Sidney M. *Theodore Roosevelt, the Progressive Party, and the Transformation of American Democracy.* Lawrence: University Press of Kansas, 2009.

Nevins, Allan, with the collaboration of Frank Ernest Hill. *Ford.* 3 vols. New York: Arno Press, 1976.

Silber, William. *When Washington Shut Down Wall Street: The Great Financial Crisis of 1914 and the Origins of America's Monetary Supremacy.* Princeton, NJ: Princeton University Press, 2007.

Watts, Steven. *The People's Tycoon: Henry Ford and the American Century.* New York: Knopf, 2005.

Weisman, Steven R. *The Great Tax Wars: Lincoln to Wilson—The Fierce Battles of Money and Power That Transformed the Nation.* New York: Simon & Schuster, 2002.

Winkler, John K. *Five and Ten: The Fabulous Life of F. W. Woolworth.* Freeport, NY: Books for Libraries Press, 1970 (1940).

Recession of 1920–1921

Baldwin, Neil. *Henry Ford and the Jews: The Mass Production of Hate.* New York: Public Affairs Press, 2002.

Cannadine, David. *Mellon: An American Life.* New York: Knopf, 2006.

Coben, Stanley. *A. Mitchell Palmer: Politician.* New York: Columbia University Press, 1963.

David, E. *Black Moses: The Story of Marcus Garvey and the Universal Negro Improvement Association.* Madison: University of Wisconsin Press, 1960.

Grin, Carolyn. "The Unemployment Conference of 1921: An Experiment in National Cooperative Planning." *Mid-America—A Historical Review* 55 (April 1973): 83–107.

Leuchtenburg, William. *The Perils of Prosperity, 1914–1932.* 2nd ed. Chicago: University of Chicago Press, 1993 (1958).

Murray, Robert K. *The Harding Era: Warren G. Harding and His Administration.* Minneapolis: University of Minnesota Press, 1969.

Murray, Robert K. *Red Scare: A Study in National Hysteria, 1919–1920.* New York: McGraw-Hill, 1964 (1955).

Neal, Steve. *McNary of Oregon: A Political Biography*. Portland: Oregon Historical Society, 1985.

Smith, Gene. *When The Cheering Stopped: The Last Years of Woodrow Wilson*. New York: Morrow, 1964.

Soule, George. *Prosperity Decade*. New York: Rinehart & Company, Inc., 1947.

Stein, Judith. *The World of Marcus Garvey: Race and Class in Modern Society*. Baton Rouge: Louisiana State University Press, 1986.

Woods, Thomas. "Warren Harding and the Forgotten Depression of 1920"; http://www.firstprinciplesjournal.com/articles.aspx?article=1322&theme =home&loc=b.

Great Depression, 1929–1933

Awalt, Francis G. "Recollections of the Banking Crisis of 1933." *Business History Review* LXIII (Autumn 1969): 347–71.

Badger, Anthony. *The New Deal: The Depression Years, 1933–1940*. Chicago: Ivan R. Dee, 1989.

Baskin, Alex. "The Ford Hunger March—1932." *Labor History* 13 (1972): 331–60.

Cannadine, David. *Mellon: An American Life*. New York: Knopf, 2006.

Cohen, Adam. *Nothing to Fear: FDR's Inner Circle and the Hundred Days That Changed America*. New York: Thorndike Press, 2009.

Daniels, Roger. *The Bonus March: An Episode of the Great Depression*. Westport, CT: Greenwood, 1971.

Dickson, Paul, and Thomas B. Allen. *The Bonus Army: An American Epic*. New York: Walker & Company, 2004.

Galbraith, John K. *The Great Crash: 1929*. Boston: Houghton Mifflin, 1961 (1955).

Heineman, Kenneth J. "Pilgrimage: Father James Cox and the Awakening of Catholic Social Activism." In *A Catholic New Deal: Religion and Reform in Depression Pittsburgh*, 11–33. University Park: Pennsylvania State University Press, 1999.

Irwin, Douglas. *Peddling Protectionism: Smoot-Hawley and the Great Depression*. Princeton, NJ: Princeton University Press, 2011.

Kennedy, David. *Freedom from Fear: The American People in Depression and War, 1929–1945*. Oxford: Oxford University Press, 1999.

Klehr, Harvey. *The Heyday of American Communism*. New York: Basic Books, 1985.

Leab, Daniel J. "United We Eat: The Creation of the Unemployed Councils." *Labor History* (Fall 1957): 300–316.

Leuchtenburg, William E. *Herbert Hoover*. New York: Times Books, 2009.

McElvaine, Robert S. *The Great Depression: America, 1929–1941.* New York: Times Books, 1984.

McJimsey, George. *Harry Hopkins: Ally of the Poor and Defender of Democracy.* Cambridge, MA: Harvard University Press, 1987.

Olson, James S. *Herbert Hoover and the Reconstruction Finance Corporation, 1931–1933.* Ames: Iowa State University Press, 1977.

Perino, Michael. *The Hellhound of Wall Street: How Ferdinand Pecora's Investigation of the Great Crash Forever Changed America's Finance.* New York: Penguin, 2010.

"Protectionism: The Battle of Smoot-Hawley." *The Economist,* December 18, 2008. http://www.economist.com/node/12798595/print.

Pusey, Merlo J. *Eugene Meyer.* New York: Knopf, 1974.

Schlesinger, Arthur M., Jr. *The Crisis of the Old Order.* Boston: Houghton Mifflin, 1960.

Shlaes, Amity. *The Forgotten Man: A New History of the Great Depression.* New York: HarperCollins, 2007.

White, Roland A. *Milo Reno, Farmers Union Pioneer.* New York: Arno Press, 1975 (1941).

Great Depression, 1933–1939

Aaron, Daniel, and Robert Bendiner, eds. *The Strenuous Decade: A Social and Intellectual Record of the Nineteen-Thirties.* Garden City, NY: Anchor Books, 1970.

Alinsky, Saul. *John L. Lewis: An Unauthorized Biography.* Urbana: University of Illinois Press, 1986 (1949).

Badger, Anthony. *The New Deal: The Depression Years, 1933–1940.* Chicago: Ivan R. Dee, 1989.

Black, Conrad. *Franklin Delano Roosevelt: Champion of Freedom.* London: Weidenfeld & Nicolson, 2003.

Burns, James McGregor. *Roosevelt: The Lion and the Fox.* New York: Harcourt, Brace & World, Inc., 1956.

Clarke, Jeanne N. *Roosevelt's Warrior: Harold L. Ickes and the New Deal.* Baltimore: Johns Hopkins University Press, 1996.

Davis, Kenneth S. *FDR: The New Deal Years, 1933–1937.* New York: Random House, 1979.

Dubofsky, Melvyn, and Warren Van Tine. *John L. Lewis: A Biography.* New York: Quadrangle Books, 1977.

Hiltzik, Michael. *The New Deal: A Modern History.* New York: Free Press, 2011.

Hyman, Sidney. *Marriner S. Eccles: Private Entrepreneur and Public Servant.* Chicago: University of Chicago Press, 1977.

Kennedy, David. *Freedom from Fear: The American People in Depression and War, 1929–1945*. Oxford: Oxford University Press, 1999.

Leuchtenburg, William E. *Franklin D. Roosevelt and the New Deal: 1932–1940*. New York: Harper Perennial, 2009.

Maher, Neil M. *Nature's New Deal: The Civilian Conservation Corps and the Roots of the American Environmental Movement*. New York: Oxford University Press, 2009.

Mayer, George H. *The Political Career of Floyd B. Olson*. With a new introduction by Russell W. Fridley. St. Paul: Minnesota Historical Society, 1987 (1951).

McJimsey, George. *Harry Hopkins: Ally of the Poor and Defender of Democracy*. Cambridge, MA: Harvard University Press, 1987.

Mitchell, Broadus. *Depression Decade: From New Era through New Deal, 1929–1945*. New York: Rinehart and Company, Inc., 1937.

Ohl, John Kennedy. *Hugh S. Johnson and the New Deal*. DeKalb: Northern Illinois Press, 1985.

Salmond, John. *The Civilian Conservation Corps, 1933–1942: A New Deal Case Study*. Durham, NC: Duke University Press, 1967.

Schlesinger, Arthur M., Jr. *The Coming of the New Deal, 1933–1935*. Boston: Houghton, Mifflin, 1959.

Schlesinger, Arthur M., Jr. *The Politics of Upheaval, 1935–1936*. Boston, Houghton Mifflin, 1960.

Taylor, Nick. *American-Made: The Enduring Legacy of the WPA—When FDR Put the Nation to Work*. New York: Bantam Books, 2008.

Watkins, T. H. *Righteous Pilgrim: The Life and Times of Harold L. Ickes, 1874–1952*. New York: Henry Holt, 1992.

Economic Downturns, 1974–1984

Ball, Howard. The Bakke Case: *Race, Education, and Affirmative Action*. Lawrence: University Press of Kansas, 2000.

Belz, Herman. "Affirmative Action." In *The Oxford Companion to the Supreme Court of the United States*, ed. Kermit L. Hall et al., 18–22. New York: Oxford University Press, 1992.

Berkowitz, Edward. *Something Happened: A Political and Cultural Overview of the Seventies*. New York: Columbia University Press, 2006.

Diggins, John Patrick. *Ronald Reagan: Fate, Freedom, and the Making of History*. New York: Norton, 2007.

Greene, John Robert. *The Presidency of Gerald R. Ford*. Lawrence: University Press of Kansas, 1995.

Isaacson, Walter. *Steve Jobs*. New York: Simon & Schuster, 2011.

Kaufman, Burton I. *The Presidency of James Earl Carter Jr.* Lawrence: University Press of Kansas, 1995.

McCartin, Joseph A. *Collision Course: Ronald Reagan, The Air Traffic Controllers, and the Strike That Changed America.* New York: Oxford University Press, 2011.

Morgan, Iwan. *The Age of Deficits: Presidents and Unbalanced Budgets from Jimmy Carter to George W. Bush.* Lawrence: University Press of Kansas, 2009.

O'Sullivan, Arthur, Terri A. Sexton, and Steven Sheffrin. *Property Taxes and Tax Revolts: The Legacy of Proposition 13.* Cambridge: Cambridge University Press, 1995.

Patterson, James. *Restless Giant: The United States from Watergate to* Bush v. Gore. New York: Oxford University Press, 2005.

Report of the President's Commission on the Accident at Three Mile Island; http://www.pddoc.com/tmi2/kemeny/index.htm.

Smith, D. A. "Howard Jarvis, Populist Entrepreneur: Re-evaluating the Causes of Proposition 13." *Social Science History* 23, 2 (1999): 173–219.

Spero, Joan Edelman. *The Failure of the Franklin National Bank: Challenge to the International Banking System.* Washington, D.C.: Beard Books, 1999 (1979).

Tosches, Nick. *Power on Earth.* New York: Arbor House, 1986.

Treaster, Joseph B. *Paul Volcker: The Making of a Financial Legend.* Hoboken, NJ: Wiley, 2004.

Walker, J. Samuel. *Three Mile Island: A Nuclear Crisis in Historical Perspective.* Berkeley: University of California Press, 2004.

Wilentz, Sean. *The Age of Reagan: A History, 1974–2008.* New York: Harper Collins, 2008.

Wooten, James A. *The Employment Retirement Income Security Act of 1974: A Political History.* Berkeley: University of California Press, 2004.

Wozniak, Steve, and Gina Smith. *iWon: From Company Geek to Cult Icon—How I Invented the Personal Computer, Co-Founded Apple, Had Fun Doing It.* New York: Norton, 2006.

Great Recession of 2008–2009

Acharya, Viral V., et al. *Guaranteed to Fail: Fannie Mae, Freddie Mac, and the Debacle of Mortgage Finance.* Princeton, NJ: Princeton University Press, 2011.

Blumenkraz, Carla, et al., eds. *Occupy: Scenes from Occupied America.* Brooklyn: Verso, 2011.

Byrne, Jane, ed. *The Occupy Handbook.* New York: Back Bay Books, 2012.

Cohan, William. *Money and Power: How Goldman Sachs Came to Rule the World*. New York: Doubleday, 2011.

Ellis, Charles. *The Partnership: The Making of Goldman Sachs*. New York: Penguin, 2008.

The Financial Inquiry Report: Final Report of the National Commission on the Causes of the Financial and Economic Crisis in the United States. New York: Public Affairs Press, 2011.

Flanders, Lara. "Obama Brags on Saving Detroit—But Auto Industry Bailout Came on the Backs of Working People." *The Nation*, February 5, 2012. http://www.alternet.org/tags/industry.

Gandel, Stephen. "How the Goldman Case Sheds Light on Hedge Funds." *Time Business*. http://www.time.com/time/business/article/0,8599,1982950,00.html#ixzz209lUiKCO.

Henriques, Diana B. *The Wizard of Lies: Bernard Madoff and the Death of Trust*. New York: Oxford University Press, 2011.

Lewis, Michael. *The Big Short: Inside the Doomsday Machine*. New York: Norton, 2010.

Lowenstein, Roger. *The End of Wall Street*. New York: Penguin, 2010.

Mallaby, Sebastian. *More Money Than God: Hedge Funds and the Making of a New Elite*. New York: Penguin, 2011.

McDonald, Lawrence G. *A Colossal Failure of Common Sense: The Inside Story of the Collapse of Lehman Brothers*. New York: Crown Business, 2009.

Morgenson, Gretchen, and Joshua Rosner. *Reckle$$ Endangerment: How Outsized Ambition, Greed, and Corruption Led to Economic Armageddon*. New York: Henry Holt, 2011.

Rubin, Robert. "Getting the Economy Back on Track." *Newsweek*, December 28, 2009. http://www.thedailybeast.com/newsweek/2009/12/28/getting-the-economy-back-on-track.html.

Rubin, Robert E., and Jacob Weisberg. *In An Uncertain World: Tough Choices from Wall Street to Washington*. New York: Random House, 2003.

Skocpol, Theda, and Vanessa Williamson. *The Tea Party and the Remaking of Republican Conservatism*. New York: Oxford University Press, 2012.

Slaughter, Jane. "Low Expectations Are Met in GM-UAW Deal." *Labor Notes*, September 19, 2011. http:///labornotes.org/blogs/jane?page=1.

Sorkin, Andrew Ross. *Too Big to Fail: The Inside Story of How Wall Street and Washington Fought to Save the Financial System—and Themselves*. New York: Penguin, 2009.

Tibman, Joseph. *The Murder of Lehman Brothers: An Insiders Look at the Global Meltdown*. New York: Brick Tower Press, 2009.

Turner, Giles. "The Darkest Dates from Hedge Fund History." *Financial News*, October 2011.

EDITOR AND CONTRIBUTORS

Editor

Daniel J. Leab is professor of history at Seton Hall University (South Orange, NJ), where he was director of American studies and the founding director of the university's multicultural program. He was editor of *Labor History* for 20 years and is currently editor of *American Communist History*. Among his books are *The Labor History Reader, "I Was a Communist for the FBI": The Life and Unhappy Times of Matt Cvetic*, and *Orwell Subverted: The CIA and the Filming of* Animal Farm.

Contributors

Brian Bixby received his PhD in American history from the University of Massachusetts, Amherst, in 2010. He has been a scholar in residence studying the papers of George S. Boutwell (President U.S. Grant's Secretary of the Treasury, 1869–1873), contributed a chapter on Shaker Villages to Philip Scranton and Janet Davidson, eds., *The Business of Tourism: Place, Faith, and History* (University of Pennsylvania Press, 2007), and taught courses in American and European history.

Robert H. Ferrell is professor emeritus of history, College of Arts and Sciences, Indiana University, Bloomington. He has written and coauthored numerous books on American diplomacy and on presidents of the United States. He served as editor of the papers and the diaries of presidents Harry S. Truman and Dwight D. Eisenhower, His Yale PhD dissertation won the John Addison Porter Prize. Among his notable visiting professorships are stints at Yale University and The War College.

Katherine Fleming earned an MA in history from Seton Hall University and a BA from Douglass College, Rutgers University. She is pursuing a career as a museum curator and has worked at the Ellis Island Immigration Museum, American Museum of Natural History, New Jersey State Archives, and Alexander Library at Rutgers University. She is additionally working on a historiography of mental illness and civil war soldiers.

Eric Gade earned graduate degrees in international and world history from Columbia University (MA) and the London School of Economics (MSc). He is currently a freelance writer and researcher splitting time between Virginia and London.

Kate Doyle Griffiths-Dingani is a doctoral candidate at the CUNY Graduate Center and earned a BA in history from New York University. She is an instructor in anthropology at Hunter College and Drew University.

Sean P. Harvey is assistant professor in the department of history at Seton Hall University. His research focuses on communication and ideas of language and race in Native American–white relations, and U.S. expansion and political economy. His work has appeared in *Journal of the Early Republic*. The National Endowment for the Humanities and numerous other organizations have supported his research (during the academic year 2009–2010 he was a fellow at the American Antiquarian Society).

Brigitte Koenig earned her MA and PhD degrees in U.S. history from the University of California, Berkeley, where she specialized in the politics of gender, culture, and labor in the Gilded Age and Progressive Era. Koenig's publications on American anarchism have appeared in *Labor History*, *The Encyclopedia of the American Left*, and Laurence Davis and Ruth Kinna, eds., *Anarchism and Utopianism*. She has also written the introduction to the centenary edition of Jack London's *The People of the Abyss*. Formerly associate professor of history and co-director of the Elizabeth Ann Seton Center for Women's Studies at Seton Hall University, she continues to instruct Seton Hall students in online U.S. history courses.

Alan Lucibello is adjunct professor of history at Seton Hall University, from which he earned a BA and an MA. He is an ABD from Catholic University. In 2010, he retired as supervisor of the social studies department at Montville High School. He and his programs have been the recipient of numerous grants and awards, including a $982,000 grant from the Teaching American History program sponsored by the U.S. Department of Education.

Denise Lynn is assistant professor of history at the University of Southern Indiana at Evansville, IN. She received her PhD in American history from

Binghamton University, SUNY, in 2006. Her dissertation dealt with gender and anti-Fascism in American Communism between 1935 and 1939. Her publications include "'United We Spend'—Communist Women and the 1936 Meat Boycott," *American Communist History* 10 (April 2011): 35–53.

A. E. L. Martin has degrees from Columbia University and the University of British Columbia. She has worked for CNN and various newspapers. She is the autographs and manuscripts editor for *American Book Prices Current*, the standard record of books, manuscripts, autographs, maps, and broadsides sold at auction.

Vanessa May earned graduate degrees (PhD and MA) in history from the University of Virginia and a BA from Vassar. She is assistant professor of history at Seton Hall University. Her articles have appeared in various journals, including the *Journal of Women's History*. She is the author of *Unprotected Labor: Household Workers, Politics, and Middle Class Reform in New York 1870–1940* (Chapel Hill: University of North Carolina Press, 2011).

Gerald W. McFarland received his BA from the University of California, Berkeley, and his MA and PhD from Columbia University. He was a member (1964–2008) of the department of history, University of Massachusetts, Amherst. He has published four scholarly books, numerous articles and reviews, and was a recipient of a John Simon Guggenheim Fellowship (1978–1979).

Victoria Phillips has earned MAs from both Columbia and New York Universities, as well as an MBA from Columbia. Her current work as a PhD candidate in history at Columbia focuses on the use of culture as diplomacy during the Cold War. Phillips has presented her work in Germany, England, France, and Denmark, as well as at numerous conferences and universities in the United States. She has curated exhibits at the Centre National de la Danse and the Library of Congress. Publications include the exhibition catalog *Dance Is a Weapon* (Pantin, France: CND, 2008), and articles in *American Communist History, Dance Research Journal, Dance Chronicle* (2010), and *Ballet Review*. Her articles on finance have appeared in *The New York Times* and *Grant's Interest Rate Observer*.

Andrew T. Presti is a research student (PhD) at the University of Cambridge. He earned his BA and MA in history from Seton Hall University. His current research project is entitled *The German Heraclitus: Spengler and the Revival of Mystical Thought in the 19th and 20th Centuries*. His research also includes the study of civilizational models, the philosophy and perception of world history, and mysticism's impact on historical awareness.

Jason Resnikoff is a graduate student and teaching fellow in the department of history at Columbia University.

Jason Roberts teaches history and government at Quincy College. He has received advanced degrees in 20th-century American political history from Northwest Missouri State University (MA) and George Washington University (PhD). His dissertation dealt with three New Left radicals from the 1960s onward. Roberts has worked as a research assistant at the National Security Archive. His articles and reviews have appeared inter alia in *American Communist History, Intelligence and National Security*, and *White House Studies*.

Michael Shapiro holds an MA in history from New York University and a PhD in history from the University of Massachusetts at Amherst. He was assistant editor on volume eight ("The Early Boston Years, 1882–1890") of the *Papers of Frederick Law Olmsted* (Johns Hopkins University Press, 2012) and has written several articles for *The New York Times* "Disunion" series on the Civil War. Shapiro is an independent scholar living in Atlanta, GA.

James R. Sofka is adjunct faculty, Federal Executive Institute, Charlottesville, VA. He received (1995) his PhD from the University of Virginia. Sofka has lectured on Jefferson's foreign policy at the Brookings Institution and the Monticello-based Robert H. Smith International Center for Jefferson Studies. Sofka helped commemorate the bicentennial of the Embargo Act (2007) at Monticello. He coedited (2010) with Silvia Marzagalli and John J. McCusker a volume of articles on the U.S. role in the Mediterranean during Jefferson's presidency. Sofka is the author of *Metternich, Jefferson, and the Enlightenment: Statecraft and Political Theory in the Early 19th Century* (PubliBlog del CSIC, 2011).

INDEX

unemployment and, 144
Waltham mill, 93–94, 113–114
mines and mining, 242–243, 264–266,
    362–365
    See also strikes; United Mine Workers
    (UMW)
minimum wage, 543–544
misery index, 588
Mississippi River, 10, 17, 30–31
Missouri
    Craig et al. v. Missouri, 718–724
    Dred Scott decision, xxviii, 184–185, 206–
        209, 744–746
    Missouri Compromise, xxvi
    stay law of, 105
Mitchell, Charles, 478
Model T, 408–411
Moley, Raymond, xlvii
Molly Maguires, 242–243, 264–266
money
    Aldrich-Vreeland Act, xxxvii, 347–349, 406
    Bland-Allison Act, 238–239, 260, 763–764
    Cleveland, Grover on financial soundness,
        769–774
    Coinage Act of 1873, 159–161
    "Cross of Gold" speech, 299–302, 774–777
    dollar value and, 1
    Emergency Banking Act, xlvi, 529–530
    Federal Reserve Act, 344, 392–393, 405–
        408, 788–791
    Glass-Owen Act, 344, 392–393, 405–408
    gold, xxxii–xxxiii, 1
    Independent Treasury, 163–165
    "Loco-focos", 148, 165–167
    paper money, 13, 14, 22, 37–38
    scaracity of, xxii, 12–13
    Sherman Anti-trust Act of 1890, 260
    silver, xxxii
    specie, 12–13
    Specie Circular, xxxvi–xxxvii, 139–140,
        173–176, 729–730
    SS *Central America*, 189–191
    Treasury Department and, xxxii–xxxiii
    world's gold supply and, xxxvi
    See also banks and banking; Federal
        Reserve system; gold; silver; specie
monopolies
    Rockefeller, John D., 245, 267–269

Slaughterhouse cases, 269–272
Standard Oil Company, 267–269, 374–377,
    425
*United States v. United States Steel
    Corporation*, 792–797
    See also Sherman Anti-trust Act of 1890;
    U.S. Steel
Monroe, James, 100
Moody, Paul, 113
Moore & Schley, 339, 340–341
Morgan, J. P.
    about, 365–368
    Panic of 1893 and, xxxiii
    Panic of 1907 and, xxxvi–xxxvii, 335–341,
        365–368
    Pujo Committee and, 388–389
Morris, Robert
    about, xxii
    Bank of North America and, 22
    at Continental Congress, 31–33
    national bank and, 2
    tobacco industry and, 40
Morse, Charles W., 332–334
mortgages, liv, 533
muckrakers, 311–314
Muller v. Oregon, 368–371
munitions, 88
Munn v. Illinois, 235–236

"nanny state", xlix
Napoleonic Wars, xxiii, 83–86
Napoleon's Berlin and Milan Decrees, 83–86,
    703–706
National Association of Securities Dealers
    (NASD), 640, 667–670
national bank
    about, 22–23
    Confederation Congress on, 2
    constitutionality of, 71–72
    Girard, Stephen on, 80
    National Monetary Commission on,
        xxxvii–xxxviii
national debt, 11–15, 77
National Farmers' Alliance of the Northwest,
    279–280
National Industrial Recovery Act (NIRA),
    xlvi, 818–823
National Labor Relations Act, 823–827

Baltimore & Ohio Railroad, 243–244, 262
credit for, xxix
establishment of, xxviii
McCabe, James Dabney on, 759–760
Olney, Richard, xxxiv, 309–310, 314–317
Panic of 1837 and, 145
Panic of 1857 and, 184
Panic of 1873 and, 228–229, 240–241,
    243–245, 261–263
Pennsylvania strikes, 244
Pullman walkout, xxxiii–xxxv, 287–290,
    308–311, 767–769
Reading Railroad, 243–244, 261–263
Tennessee Coal, Iron and Railroad
    Company (TC&I), 339, 340–341
transcontinental railroad, xxix, 278
working-class violence and, xxx
See also specific railroad companies
Randolph, John, 52, 69
Ratford, Jenkin, 65–66
Rauschenbusch, Walter, 350–353
Reading Railroad, 243–244, 261–263
Reagan, Ronald, lii–liii, 594–600, 853–855
recession of 1920–1921
    about, xxxix–xl, 438–446
    boom before, 431–438
    Dearborn Independent, 447–450
    Garvey, Marcus, 450–454
    Ledoux, Urbain, 454–457
    McNary, Charles L., 457–460
    Palmer, A. Mitchell, 460–464, 469–470,
        472
    President's Conference on Unemployment,
        xl, xliii, 464–467
    Red Scare, 460–464, 468–471, 472
    Sacco, Nicola, 471–475
    *United States v. United States Steel
        Corporation*, 792–797
    Vanzetti, Bartolomeo, 471–475
Reconstruction Finance Corporation (RFC),
    xliv–xlv, 489, 514–517
Red Scare, 460–464, 468–471, 472
*Regents of the University of California v.
    Bakke*, 617–620
Regulation Q, liii
religion and social reform, 350–353
Remedial Justice Act, 157
Reno, Milo, 517–520

Republican Party
    Compromise of 1877 and, 253–255
    formation of, 182
    Panic of 1857 and, 195–198
    Panic of 1873 and, 239–240
    Panic of 1893 and, 290–292
    Whiskey Ring, 272–275
Revenue Act of 1913, 391–392
reverse discrimination, 617–620
Revolutionary War, xxi–xxiii, 1–6, 8, 12–13
RFC (Reconstruction Finance Corporation),
    514–517
Rhode Island, 12, 13–14, 50
Ripley, George, 152–154
roads, 120–123, 127–129
robberies, 471–475
Rockefeller, John D., 245, 267–269
    See also Sherman Anti-trust Act of 1890;
        Standard Oil Company
Roosevelt, Franklin D.
    about, xlv–xlix
    bank stabilization by, 528–533
    Commonwealth Club Address of, 799–803
    fireside chats, xlvi, 499, 530–531
    Forbes Field Speech, 829–834
    Hoover, Herbert vs., 493–494
    inaugural address of, 809–813
    inauguration of, 527–528
    Social Security Act, 540, 828–829
Roosevelt, Theodore, xxxvi–xxxvii, 371–374
Roosevelt Recession, xlvii–xlix, 541–543
Rubin, Robert, 676–679
Rule of 1756, 54, 84
Rumsey, James, 29
Russia, 59
Rustbelt, 581–582

Sacco, Nicola, 471–475
Sandford, Dred Scott v., xxviii, 184–185,
    206–209, 744–746
San Francisco
    earthquakes in, 329, 330
    "Gentlemen's Agreement" and, 356–359,
        373–374
    protests in, xxx
Santa Anna, Antonio de, 177–178
Santelli, Rick, 680–681
Sapiro, Aaron, 449